Securing the Future

Securing the Future

Investing in Children
from Birth to College

Sheldon Danziger and Jane Waldfogel
Editors

THE FORD FOUNDATION SERIES ON ASSET BUILDING

Russell Sage Foundation ♦ New York

The Russell Sage Foundation

Library of Congress Cataloging-in-Publication Data

Securing the future : investing in children from birth to college / Sheldon Danziger and Jane Waldfogel, editors
     p. cm. — (The Ford Foundations series on asset building)
   Includes bibliographical references and index.
   ISBN 0-87154-899-2
    1. Child welfare—United States. 2. Children—United States—Social conditions. 3. Children—Government policy—United States. 4. Youth—United States—Social conditions. 5. Youth—Government policy—United States. I. Danziger, Sheldon. II. Waldfogel, Jane. III. Series.

HV741 .S385 2000
362.7'0973—dc21

00-028004

RUSSELL SAGE FOUNDATION
112 East 64th Street, New York, New York 10021
10 9 8 7 6 5 4 3 2 1

For our children,
Jacob and Anna, and Katie

Contents

Contents

Contributors

SHELDON DANZIGER is Henry J. Meyer Collegiate Professor of Social Work and Public Policy and director of the Center on Poverty Risk and Mental Health at the University of Michigan.

JANE WALDFOGEL is associate professor of social work and public affairs at the Columbia University School of Social Work and research associate at the Centre for Analysis of Social Exclusion at the London School of Economics.

DEBRA DONAHOE is senior analyst at Data Square, a marketing consulting firm in Rye, New York.

JACQUELYNNE S. ECCLES is the Wilbert McKeachie Collegiate Professor of Psychology, Education, and Women's Studies at the University of Michigan.

DAVID T. ELLWOOD is Lucius N. Littauer Professor of Political Economy at the John F. Kennedy School of Government, Harvard University.

JAMES J. HECKMAN is Henry Schultz Distinguished Service Professor of Economics in the Department of Economics at the University of Chicago and director of the Center for Social Program Evaluation at the Harris School, University of Chicago. He is also senior fellow of the American Bar Foundation.

ROBERT S. KAHN is assistant professor of pediatrics at the Cincinnati Children's Hospital Medical Center and at the University of Cincinnati College of Medicine.

THOMAS J. KANE is associate professor at the John F. Kennedy School of Government, Harvard University, and faculty research fellow at the National Bureau of Economic Research.

LANCE LOCHNER is assistant professor of economics at the University of Rochester.

LISA M. LYNCH is William L. Clayton Professor of International Affairs at the Fletcher School of Law and Diplomacy at Tufts University and research associate at the National Bureau of Economic Research and the Economic Policy Institute.

MELVIN L. OLIVER is vice president of the Ford Foundation. He is responsible for overseeing the Asset Building and Community Development Program.

Contributors

HILLARD POUNCY is adjunct faculty in urban studies at the University of Pennsylvania and visiting faculty at the Woodrow Wilson School of Public and International Affairs, Princeton University.

CRAIG T. RAMEY is University Professor of Psychology, Pediatrics, and Neurobiology and director of the Civitan International Research Center of the University of Alabama at Birmingham.

SHARON LANDESMAN RAMEY is professor of psychiatry, psychology, and neurobiology and director of the Civitan International Research Center of the University of Alabama at Birmingham.

ROBERT J. SAMPSON is Lucy Flower Professor of Sociology at the University of Chicago and senior research fellow of the American Bar Foundation.

MARGARET BEALE SPENCER is the Board of Overseers Professor of Education and director of the W. E. B. Du Bois Collective Research Institute at the University of Pennsylvania.

DENA PHILLIPS SWANSON is assistant professor of human development and family studies at The Pennsylvania State University and research affiliate at the Center for Health, Achievement, Neighborhood, Growth, and Ethnic Studies at the University of Pennsylvania.

MARTA TIENDA is Maurice P. During '22 Professor of Demographic Studies, Professor of Sociology and Public Affairs, and director of the Office of Population Research at Princeton University.

ALLAN WIGFIELD is professor of human development at the University of Maryland, College Park.

BARRY ZUCKERMAN, M.D. is professor and chairman of pediatrics at the Boston University School of Medicine and chief of pediatrics at Boston Medical Center.

Foreword

Melvin L. Oliver

The publication of this book edited by Sheldon Danziger and Jane Waldfogel constitutes the launch of a new series funded by the Ford Foundation and published by the Russell Sage Foundation. The new series will provocatively explore the strengths and policy relevance of the asset-building approach to poverty alleviation; it will also point to the areas in which any shortcomings of the approach indicate a need for further work. In this preface I would like to offer a personal introduction to the concepts embodied in this approach and to describe how it is being incorporated into the grant-making of the Ford Foundation.

In 1996 the Ford Foundation entered an era of new leadership. Susan Berresford succeeded Franklin Thomas as the foundation's president, and I became the vice president of a newly organized and expanded program to advance the foundation's goal of reducing poverty and injustice. I was given the task of uniting within a single program all of the foundation's work on urban and rural poverty, sexual and reproductive health, and program-related investments. After much consultation and discussion with the foundation's staff in New York and in our thirteen international offices, we organized our efforts around the theme of "asset building." Reflecting on the work that has engaged us worldwide, we feel strongly that the most successful work, and the work most needed, is that which empowers the poor to acquire key human, social, financial, and natural resource assets. Those so empowered, we believe, also acquire a stronger basis from which they can, in turn, reduce or prevent injustice.

This new focus is a departure from the conventional wisdom, both at the foundation and in the broader development community. Antipoverty policy in the United States and in international development programs worldwide has tended to emphasize increasing income to some predetermined minimum level as the "magic bullet" that "solves" poverty problems. But that notion builds on a common misconception that poverty is simply a matter of low income or low levels of consumption. Several important critiques of this notion of poverty have pointed out that its emphasis on income ignores key causes of inequity, overlooks the consequences of low asset accumulation, and fails to address long-term stability and security for individuals, families, and communities.

The Nobel laureate Amartya Sen foreshadowed this approach in his 1985 Hennipman Lectures in Economics (Sen 1999a) and discussed it again in *Development as Freedom* (1999b). For Sen, poverty is a function not simply of low income but of, among other things, "capability deprivation," where "capability" refers to the whole range of civil and financial abilities or entitlements, as well as to human development. Michael Sherraden appears to have reached similar conclusions quite independently in his pathbreaking 1991 work *Assets and the Poor*. Thomas Shapiro and I provide further support for the importance of the concepts of asset building for urban poverty alleviation in the United States in *Black Wealth/White Wealth* (Oliver and Shapiro 1995). And more recently, Anthony Bebbington has developed an application of the approach to rural areas in *Capitals and Capabilities* (1999).

An "asset" in this paradigm refers to a special kind of resource that an individual, organization, or entire community can use to reduce or prevent poverty and injustice. An asset is usually a "stock" that can be drawn on, built, or developed. It is a resource that can be shared or transferred across generations. Because assets are unevenly distributed in all societies, their distribution is highly related to both public policy decisions and cultural traditions and forces. These policies and traditions have affected how societies structure the ownership of assets and investments in assets. Women and members of racial and ethnic minorities, for instance, have often been excluded or prevented from developing assets. With assets at their disposal, the poor are more likely to control important aspects of their lives, to plan for their future, to deal with economic uncertainty, to support their children's educational achievement, and to ensure that the lives of the next generation will be better than their own.

Over the last three years, the staff of the Ford Foundation's Asset Building and Community Development Program have been reexamining its grant-making initiatives and asking hard-hitting questions about how they fit within an asset-building strategy. Not surprisingly, this assessment has required considerable analysis of the essential attributes of assets, the kinds of strategies needed to build them, and the methodology needed to help us measure progress in asset accumulation. We work primarily with nonprofit and governmental organizations, and we have tried to see how we can best support asset-building organizations and bring an assets perspective to the various fields of work we support, including those that generate and work on asset-building policy.

Our efforts to implement an assets approach have been enthusiastically received by our colleagues among practitioners and policymakers. The approach, they note, does not focus on the "deficits" or "deficiencies" of the poor and disempowered, nor does it treat them as impassive subjects of external forces, with no ability to affect their own future. It recognizes that injustice is as much a determinant of poverty as the vagaries of personal and community histories. The approach also builds on everyone's innate ability to develop skills and on the near-universal desire of all human beings to create better lives for themselves and their progeny. We have also found that some researchers are interested in advancing work on specific interventions to build assets. It is our hope that by presenting a broad and deliberate examination of concepts and strategies across a range of disciplines, this series will further advance the paradigm and practices of asset building.

Bernard Wasow of the Asset Building and Community Development Program's Community and Resource Development Unit developed a series of conferences that led to the edited volumes that explore these themes. He sought to bring together researchers who are concerned with various types of asset development, even though they may not have been accustomed to calling it such. He invited them to explore each of the following areas:

- The state of knowledge about the links between poverty and the various kinds of assets that might affect it
- The policy implications of an asset-building approach, particularly with respect to improving support for poor people and communities
- Further research questions to guide practitioners and policymakers in developing more effective strategies to alleviate poverty and reduce injustice

Sheldon Danziger and Jane Waldfogel took up that challenge and organized the first of what have now been four national conferences on asset-building strategies. This volume is a product of their conference on human asset development. Conferences have also been organized by Ed Wolfe and Thomas Shapiro on financial asset development and its relationship to poverty, by Mark Warren on social capital and the reduction of poverty, and by James Boyce on building natural capital assets as a mechanism for alleviating poverty and increasing environmental justice. Additional volumes will be published by the Russell Sage Foundation within the next few years, as part of this series. Support has also been provided to Michelle Miller-Adams to develop a volume for a less academic audience that will explore the application of these concepts by key asset-building organizations around the United States.

Each of these four conferences has brought some of the nation's best and most provocative academic thinkers in contact with leading practitioners from both government and civil society. Attendees have engaged in highly animated discussions of the topics at hand. Each conference identified further themes to explore, and the foundation is supporting additional research in those areas. Foundation staff gained important new insights from each conference into the links between asset building and the goals that we pursue, and we believe that these insights are beginning to be reflected in the work that we now support. We hope that the volumes in this series inspire other institutions worldwide to develop new approaches to alleviating poverty and injustice.

This series represents just one of many ways in which we at the Ford Foundation are both engaging our academic and practitioner colleagues and encouraging discussion of the most fundamental concepts that guide our grant-making in the Asset Building and Community Development Program. We congratulate Sheldon Danziger and Jane Waldfogel for the excellent volume they have produced, and we welcome further commentary on these themes.

REFERENCES

Bebbington, Anthony. 1999. *Capitals and Capabilities: A Framework for Analysing Peasant Viability, Rural Livelihoods, and Poverty in the Andes.* London: International Institute for Environment and Development.

Oliver, Melvin L., and Thomas M. Shapiro. 1995. *Black Wealth/White Wealth: A New Perspective on Racial Inequality.* New York: Routledge.

Sen, Amartya K. 1999a. *Commodities and Capabilities.* London: Oxford University Press. First published as *Commodities and Capabilities: Professor Dr. P. Hennipman Lectures in Economics,* vol. 7. London: Elsevier Science, 1985.

———. 1999b. *Development as Freedom.* New York: Alfred A. Knopf.

Sherraden, Michael. 1991. *Assets and the Poor: A New American Welfare Policy.* New York: M. E. Sharpe

Acknowledgments

Earlier versions of the papers in this volume were presented in October 1998 at a conference sponsored by the Ford Foundation's Program on Asset Building and Community Development. The editors thank Elizabeth C. Campbell, Ronald B. Mincy, Melvin L. Oliver, and Bernard Wasow of the Ford Foundation for their contributions to the planning of the conference, the discussants and conference participants for valuable comments on the conference drafts, and two anonymous referees for comments on the entire volume. We also thank Linda Chen for her contributions to organizing the conference, Ivye Allen for her help with the conference, and Sydney Van Nort for her help with this manuscript. Special thanks to Suzanne Nichols at the Russell Sage Foundation for excellent help in getting the book into print.

Sheldon Danziger
Jane Waldfogel

Introduction

Investing in Children: What Do We Know? What Should We Do?

Sheldon Danziger and Jane Waldfogel

When the National Science Foundation (1996, 1) announced the "Human Capital Initiative: Investing in Human Resources," it noted that

the human capital of a nation is a primary determinant of its strength. A productive and educated workforce is a necessity for long-term economic growth. Worker productivity depends on the effective use and development of the human capital of all citizens, which means that schools, families, and neighborhoods must function effectively. Unfortunately, there is substantial evidence that the United States is not developing or using the skills of its citizens as fully as possible. Only if the United States invests wisely in its human resources will it be able to maintain its place in a global economy where human creativity and human skill are increasingly more important than raw materials or physical infrastructure.

The chapters in this volume review what we know about the processes that affect child development and how we might wisely increase public and private investments in children to promote both their well-being and the productivity of the next generation. In October 1998, we convened scholars, policymakers, and practitioners to address this challenge. The conference, held at Columbia University and sponsored by the Ford Foundation's Program on Asset Building and Community Development, brought together psychologists, economists, sociologists, demographers, political scientists, social workers, and physicians. We began by examining current investments in children and how they affect the development of the skills and competencies children will need to succeed as adults in work, family, and society. Then we reviewed and synthesized what we have learned about childhood interventions from birth to college and what further investments in children are required, especially for disadvantaged children.

The chapters follow the life cycle, from early childhood through the school-age years, until the period when youth make the transition from high school to work and/or college. By focusing on childhood and adolescence, we emphasize those factors—families, neighborhoods, school systems, and government interventions—that affect the intergenerational transmission of well-being. If investing in children is as important to both individuals and the nation as the National Science Foundation report concludes, then equality of opportunity will not become a reality until all children are provided with enhanced opportunities to maximize their potential. The years we study are critical because they set the stage for adult success, or failure, in the labor market, family life, and so on.

Recent advances in brain research emphasize the importance of the earliest experiences in life. The brain grows very rapidly in the first three to five years, and what happens at this time shapes cognitive and socioemotional development (see, for example, Shore 1997). Recent social science research has documented the processes through which families, schools, neighborhoods, and government programs and policies interact to affect developmental outcomes (see, for example, Brooks-Gunn, Duncan, and Aber 1997; and Duncan and Brooks-Gunn 1997). The chapters in this volume summarize and extend research on these topics.

A major theme of the volume is how the high rate of child poverty and persistent racial residential segregation restrict access to investments in poor children and racial-ethnic minority children. These children face greater than average developmental obstacles, yet we tend to invest fewer than average resources in them. Another cross-cutting theme is the need to consider factors such as gender, race, and ethnicity in thinking about appropriate investments for children. The United States is becoming ever more diverse, and an increasing share of children are immigrants or have parents who are immigrants. If interventions are to be successful, they must be responsive to the diverse needs of children. In fact, several authors emphasize the need in some areas for programs that differentially target girls, African Americans, African American males, children living in neighborhoods of concentrated poverty, or Latinos, especially immigrants.

The authors review what we know about effective interventions throughout childhood and how to evaluate that knowledge and formulate effective strategies for expanding investments in children and adolescents from birth to college. In the concluding section of this introduction, we outline our views regarding a number of key investments.

A successful strategy for investing in children must incorporate American values and beliefs about government interventions. Americans have always been more favorably inclined to invest in children as a way to promote equal opportunity and reduce poverty in the next generation of adults than they have been to redistribute resources to reduce labor market disadvantages and poverty among adults. President Lyndon Johnson, in declaring the War on Poverty, promised "a hand up and not a hand out." It has been and remains the case that increasing or even maintaining public spending on cash transfers for the disadvantaged is more difficult than increasing spending on educational, nutrition, or medical care programs on their behalf.

Although service-oriented programs for disadvantaged children tend to be popular, federal budgetary rules, congressional politics, and public opinion now make it more difficult than in the past to garner support for any major initiatives. Thus, the authors' goal is to demonstrate that the policies discussed here represent sound investments in the productivity of the next generation.

A consensus has recently emerged among economists, developmentalists, and others that investments in early childhood are cost-effective. For example, a recent review (Karoly et al. 1998) found that a variety of early intervention programs have been successful in improving cognitive development and other outcomes for children. Several chapters in this volume provide further evidence on this point. In contrast, there is controversy about the cost-effectiveness of "second-chance" interventions to promote educational attainment among high school dropouts, welfare recipients, and other disadvantaged workers. For example, James Heckman (1996, 10), the author of chapter 2, has concluded that "adults past a certain age and below a certain skill level make poor investments." Lisa Lynch (1997, 16), the author of chapter 1, has challenged this conclusion: "However, this [discouraging evidence] does not mean that we should eliminate funding for all training programs. Instead we should be analyzing the most cost effective ways to improve the assistance to various 'at risk' groups so that they are successfully lifted out of poverty." Several chapters in this volume review the most recent evidence on promising second-chance programs and suggest how they can be further improved. The research evidence supporting early interventions is more favorable, and the political support is also greater. Investments in early childhood are seen as prudent because they come at an opportune time and because they can yield lasting benefits. The report of the Council of Economic Advisers (1997, 22) entitled "The First Three Years: Investments That Pay" reaffirmed the importance of early intervention:

> Scientists and educators have identified the first three years of life as a time when children have "fertile minds." Efforts to help children during these years are especially fruitful. Because of the long-lasting effects, early investments can have big payoffs. They avert the need for more costly interventions later in life, and so contribute to happier, healthier, and more productive children, adolescents, and adults.

The chapters that follow review what is known about investments in physical, social, and cognitive development from birth through young adulthood, based on research and "best program practices," and then derive implications for scholarly research and for programs and public policies.

OVERVIEW OF THE BOOK

The chapters are organized chronologically, according to the life cycle. After two introductory chapters, two chapters focus on early childhood development, three examine school-age outcomes, and three analyze the transition from high school to work and/or college. The authors emphasize how, depending on the stage of the life cycle, developmental, school, and labor market outcomes are affected by family, school, neighborhood, and public policy inputs and interventions.

Current Investments in Children

The two chapters in part I provide background on the extent of current investments in children and what they have both accomplished and failed to accomplish. They analyze aggregate trends in educational outcomes and the returns from various intervention programs.

Lisa Lynch documents the scope of investments in children and the extent to which outcomes for children and adolescents have declined in recent years. Because employers increasingly value skills and favor workers with education and training beyond high school, young people who leave school with a high school degree or less have found it harder to get jobs, especially ones that provide good wages and benefits. As the workplace continues to become more technologically advanced, employer demands for workers with literacy and numeracy skills have increased. Yet 20 percent of young workers lack even basic math skills. (The corresponding figure for most European countries is 5 percent.) The fault, according to Lynch, lies not just with the schools but also with the environments in which children are being raised. More children are living with single and/or working parents who have less time to spend with them than families did in the past. Fewer children are participating in extracurricular activities, and more are living in neighborhoods where violence threatens their safety.

Lynch notes, however, that several trends present opportunities as well as challenges. Consider the increased share of young children whose mothers are working in the labor market. Although this trend may reduce the amount of time that parents devote to their children, it poses an opportunity to provide young children with valuable experiences in early childhood education—that is, if access to child care and preschools of sufficiently high quality can be increased. The effects of maternal employment may be positive if working mothers are satisfied and challenged in their jobs and can thus provide a more stimulating environment for their children. However, these effects may be negative if mothers are stressed and fatigued by their jobs and devote less attention to their children.

Another challenge that embodies an opportunity is the growing share of children whose first language is not English. This trend challenges schools to devise programs to help these children succeed in school, but it also creates opportunities in that these children, because of their dual language skills, will be well positioned to compete in the globalized labor market.

Lynch emphasizes three main findings. First, education begets education, and education begets training. Those who complete more education initially are more likely to seek additional education and additional training. Second, education begins at home. The educational level of a child's parents is a primary determinant of how much education that child will get and how well she or he will do in school. Investments in parents' human capital not only raise their workplace productivity but also make them better teachers for their children. A government policy that focuses only on education and training for children will be ineffective if similar investments are not made in the parents. Third, individuals and employers, on their own, are likely to underinvest in children. Therefore, government policies that subsidize education and training are needed to offset private underinvestment.

James Heckman and Lance Lochner evaluate the issue of when in the life cycle investments in children's development are most effective and conclude, given our experience to date, that returns are highest in early childhood. As a result, their top priority is to expand investments during the preschool years. They reinforce the evidence presented in part II that the preschool years are very important for the development of cognitive skills, social skills, and motivation, and that early intervention programs can foster the development of these competencies.

Well-designed early intervention programs, according to Heckman and Lochner, are a more cost-effective investment than the ones that have garnered the largest share of public investment in education and training—"second-chance" programs for school-leavers and dropouts. For instance, investments that prepare children to enter school ready and motivated to learn have greater effects than additional investments in school resources, such as higher teacher salaries or reductions in class size. Heckman and Lochner also conclude that the returns to further subsidizing the costs of college are limited. They find that the lower college enrollment rates for youths from low-income families are due more to the youths' early educational experiences, which inhibited skills and motivation, than to financial constraints at the point of college entry. Investing in children at an early age has the advantage that the returns to those investments are cumulative over time—those who have higher levels of skills at kindergarten benefit more from later schooling and training.

Heckman and Lochner emphasize the higher returns of early investments relative to those at later ages, but they do find that some programs for school-age children and adolescents have been cost-effective. In particular, they report positive effects of some mentoring programs (such as the national Big Brothers/Big Sisters program and Philadelphia Futures' Sponsor-A-Scholar program) and some dropout prevention programs (such as the nationwide Quantum Opportunity Program). These programs raise young people's motivation and change their school attendance and other behaviors to a greater extent than they improve measured cognitive ability. Nor should investments stop after high school dropout or graduation— Heckman and Lochner conclude that additional private (as opposed to public) training for young adults who have completed their schooling would be beneficial.

Process of Early Childhood Development

The two chapters in part II focus on the processes of early childhood development and the impact of family and neighborhood resources and parenting practices on child well-being. They advocate expansion of the number of children served by programs that have been shown to be most effective.

Barry Zuckerman and Robert Kahn review the social and biological pathways that influence children's early health and development. Understanding these pathways, especially their effect on early brain development, is critical because the developmental foundation for the skills that children need to succeed in later years is laid during these years.

Zuckerman and Kahn emphasize the influences of maternal health and document how adverse social conditions, such as poverty, can be conveyed to children prenatally through maternal health-related behaviors or conditions such as smoking, substance use, folate deficiency, or bacterial vaginosis. The influence of maternal health continues into early childhood. Maternal depression has long been identified as a risk factor for children's cognitive development and behavioral adjustment. Children who witness domestic violence are at risk of emotional and behavioral problems; this may also be true of children who witness violence in their communities. The influence of fathers and paternal health has been less studied, but fathers' smoking, alcohol use, and obesity all affect child outcomes. Environmental factors, such as a shortage of dietary iron or exposure to lead, are also correlated with poverty and can place children at risk.

Zuckerman and Kahn call for expanded provision of comprehensive health services and new models of service delivery, including home visits to women of childbearing age, beginning before conception and continuing after birth. Particular attention should be given to providing services for low-income women whose children are at elevated risk of poor outcomes.

They also emphasize the connection between reading and early childhood development. Although reading was once thought to be a separate skill that children learned when they entered school, it is now understood that reading skills develop early in childhood and depend to a larger extent than previously thought on early environmental influences. Reading out loud to children, beginning as early as six months old, is probably the most effective intervention for developing literacy skills. Children from low-income families start out with disadvantages compared to those in higher-income families because they are less likely to be read to and because they grow up with fewer books in their homes. Zuckerman and Kahn call for increased investment in early childhood literacy promotion, especially programs such as Reach Out and Read that target both parents and children from low-income families.

Sharon Landesman Ramey and Craig Ramey examine the connections between early childhood experiences and developmental competencies. They emphasize two points: that experience matters and that providing the right experiences at the right developmental stages can enhance children's competencies. Both of these points apply with particular urgency to early childhood, given recent findings from brain research.

To grow and develop normally across a range of competencies, all children need what Ramey and Ramey call "psychosocial developmental priming mechanisms." These mechanisms include experiences that support development through activities such as encouraging exploration, rehearsing new skills, and guiding and limiting children's behavior. When children in low-resource environments do not have these experiences, their development suffers. As a result, early intervention programs that provide these experiences (through models such as Partners for Learning) can improve child development, particularly when they are well-designed, intensive, high-quality programs that target high-risk children. Gains seem to last longer when children receive follow-up services or enter schools that are at least reasonably supportive. Well-designed out-of-home programs, such as the Perry Preschool Project in Ypsilanti, Michigan, the Infant Health and Development Program (IHDP) in various states nation wide, and the Abecedarian Project in Chapel Hill, North Carolina, have demonstrated that they can compensate for experiences children do not receive at home.

However, poor-quality out-of-home programs can compromise children's development. This is a concern given that about 40 percent of young children are now in child care judged to be of poor quality. Thus, Ramey and Ramey call for more developmental programs, such as IHDP and the Abecedarian Project, that target the highest-risk children, as well as for broader strategies to improve the early childhood experiences of all children.

School-Age Interventions

The chapters in part III evaluate programs and policies that target children's development in the school-age years. Jacquelynne Eccles and Allan Wigfield examine the influence of elementary and middle schools on motivation and achievement; Margaret Beale Spencer and Dena Phillips Swanson consider the influence of families and communities on adolescent development; Robert Sampson evaluates the influence of neighborhoods and communities on youth outcomes.

Eccles and Wigfield review what is known about the development of motivation, an important determinant of performance in and out of school, and emphasize the influence of the classroom and the school on both motivation and learning outcomes. Programs to enhance motivation attempt to help students reduce test anxiety, overcome learned helplessness, maintain self-worth, and avoid apathy.

Eccles and Wigfield note that good teacher-student relationships provide the foundation for academic motivation and success. They review research on the kinds of teacher beliefs and classroom practices that facilitate motivation and achievement. For some disadvantaged children growing up in neighborhoods with few role models, effective teachers represent a stable source of nonparental role models. Eccles and Wigfield endorse programs that recognize the achievements of all students rather than those that reward only the best students, and they favor programs that evaluate students on their personal progress and mastery rather than ones that evaluate solely on the basis of outcomes. They conclude that ability tracking often perpetuates poor achievement and behavior among low-ability children, and they propose that, if used, grouping should be limited to certain classes, such as reading and math.

Because children make the transition from elementary to middle school or junior high school in the early stages of adolescent development, the environmental changes associated with this transition—from a smaller to a larger school, from teachers who have about thirty students for the whole day to ones who have five times as many and see each of them for only an hour a day—can negatively affect motivation and academic outcomes for some students. Eccles and Wigfield note that there is often a poor fit between the developmental needs of the early adolescent and the structure of the middle school environment. The creation of small schools, "schools within a school," and team teaching can foster, they argue, a sense of community to ease this transition. In addition, linkages between schools and the broader community, through initiatives such as Comer schools or Partnership 2000 schools, especially in high-risk neighborhoods, can facilitate adolescent development.

Spencer and Swanson focus on the barriers to development for adolescents, particularly African American youth, who grow up in poor families in poor neighborhoods. They point out that racial and economic inequalities compromise school adjustment and that perceptions of limited opportunities lead some disadvantaged youth, especially African American males, to react negatively to outcomes valued by the mainstream. Poor and minority parents thus need even greater school and neighborhood supports for socializing their children than do nonpoor and majority parents; however, they have less access to them.

Spencer and Swanson advocate the empowerment of families by informing them of available services and resources, promoting their skills in communication and assertiveness, and fostering their sense of "self-efficacy" so that they become more engaged with the schools and other institutions that play a role in the lives of their children. They suggest that teachers need training in cultural diversity so that they can better understand and work with the increasing numbers of students of color. They criticize school intervention programs that emphasize academic achievement and cognitive skills but neglect the overall sociocultural and emotional development of students.

Sampson reviews the literature on neighborhood contexts, which can either facilitate good outcomes or increase the risk for problem behaviors such as school dropout, teen childbearing, and low labor-force attachment. Racially isolated neighborhoods with high concentrations of poor people and high crime rates tend to have low social organization and lack the informal social controls that keep young people "on the right track." As a result, there are likely to be higher levels of troublesome child and adolescent behaviors in these neighborhoods.

Sampson conceptualizes community social organization as the ability to realize the common values of residents and to maintain social controls. Social control involves the realization of collective goals, such as the desire of community residents to live in safe environments, to have access to good schools and housing, and to experience high levels of economic activity and low levels of crime. He recognizes that community interventions are hard to implement, especially in the poor neighborhoods that need them the most.

Sampson emphasizes policy interventions that would restore safety, increase resources, and promote residential stability. These include community policing and collective strategies that organize residents to form patrols and pickets and to "take back" their neighborhoods, as well as initiatives that bring together the police and the community, such as Boston's Ten Point Coalition to reduce youth violence. Interventions that enhance social organization attempt to exert informal social control over adolescents and to supervise adolescent peer groups through such activities as organizing leisure-time activities, enforcing truancy laws, and promoting mentoring systems to build intergenerational ties between adults and youth. Interventions that would promote housing stabilization include policies such as resident management of public housing, rehabilitation of run-down housing, strict municipal code enforcement, and encouragement of community development corporations. He also sees promise in housing policies, such as Moving To Opportunity (MTO), that encourage (but do not require) increased neighborhood integration.

Sampson is optimistic that neighborhoods can be improved if residents join forces to build community and maintain social order. He cautions, however, that outcomes are ultimately shaped by forces broader than those that prevail in the neighborhood context, including, for instance, the national economy and the allocation of city services across neighborhoods.

Transitions to Work or College

Part IV turns to the transitions that adolescents and young adults make as they leave school and enter the world of work and/or continue on to college. Debra Donahoe and Marta Tienda focus on transitions from school to work; Hillard Pouncy reviews the evidence on "second-chance" workforce development programs for youth who have left school but have not yet settled in to work or college; and David Ellwood and Thomas Kane provide new evidence on how the transition from school to community college or college is affected by family background, student ability, public financing, and other factors.

Donahoe and Tienda document recent trends in educational attainment, labor-force participation, and unemployment for youth and examine the evidence on the timing of arrival to stable employment. Although basic and vocational skill levels among youth have not declined in absolute terms, they have not kept pace with the increasing employer demand for skills. This skills mismatch is a growing problem among poor urban youth and ethnic minorities, especially among Hispanics, who have the lowest rates of graduation from high school. Most youth find a stable job by their early twenties. However, youth who do not finish high school, and black youth in general, have difficulty finding stable work. Unemployment is particularly severe for black young men, and low wages are a problem for all youth with less than a high school degree.

Donahoe and Tienda analyze the potential benefits of early labor-market experience, which has been advocated as a way to improve labor-force outcomes. They conclude that because of the recent rise in the returns to education, youth employment is valuable only if it does not interfere with educational attainment, which is even more valuable in the long run. Programs designed to facilitate the school-to-work transition—such as vocational education, including co-op programs, career academies and career clusters, tech-prep programs, and youth apprenticeships, as well as second-chance programs for youths who have already left school—are likely to be beneficial only insofar as they also keep youth connected, or help reconnect them, to school.

Pouncy reviews the history of job training strategies for the disadvantaged and concludes that traditional programs, originally developed for unemployed or displaced workers, do not provide the broad range of services needed by most young, disadvantaged workers. He argues that the mismatch between the design of these job training programs and the needs and problems of the disadvantaged can be overcome by comprehensive "sectoral development" programs like the Center for Employment Training (CET) in San Jose, California. These programs focus on building trusting relationships with employers and trainees, teaching trainees the skills that employers want, and offering trainees a broad range of services. Other examples include Project STRIVE, which works with a broad range of young adults in New York City, and Project Match, which works with welfare recipients in Chicago. Few of these programs have been rigorously evaluated, but many of them can muster evidence that they help the most disadvantaged get jobs and move into the mainstream. Further research should be able to pinpoint the extent to which they have succeeded in helping clients and the extent to which successful programs such as CET, Project STRIVE, and Project Match can be replicated.

Ellwood and Kane analyze differences and recent trends in the extent of enrollment in two- and four-year colleges by youth according to their family income and parental education. Although differences in academic preparation account for many of the differences in college attendance by family background, very large gaps in college-going by students from high- and low-income and high- and low-education parents remain. Youth with similar academic preparation and test scores at the conclusion of high school enter college at very different rates, depending on parental income and education.

The influence of family background on enrollment has increased over time, with family income becoming a more important predictor. At the same time, parental education and income have become more highly correlated, owing to the increased payoff to education. Thus, students from high-income families are now doubly advantaged in that they tend to have parents with higher levels of education as well. This advantage leads to 5 to 10 percent higher earnings for these youth later in life.

Ellwood and Kane propose two types of policy responses to narrow the gap in college-going between low-income and high-income youth. In the long run, reducing the high school achievement gaps between low- and high-income youth would do the most to narrow this gap. However, this effort is likely to be difficult and to take a long time. In the meantime, Ellwood and Kane suggest expanding policies to address the barriers to college entry for low-income youth. Such policies include providing additional grants for low-income youth or helping youth make better use of available funding opportunities by, for instance, hiring more guidance counselors or simplifying eligibility procedures. They also suggest that states and schools consider providing a larger share of aid through income-contingent loan programs.

POLICY IMPLICATIONS

All of the authors discuss the implications of their findings for policymakers and program developers. Taken together, these chapters contain a wealth of detailed policy suggestions. We draw on these and offer our conclusions regarding the major components of a comprehensive investment strategy for maximizing opportunities for children and youth.

One key finding concerns the timing of investments and the advantages of investing early in the life cycle. Lynch, Heckman and Lochner, Zuckerman and Kahn, and Ramey and Ramey provide several reasons for emphasizing early investments. In addition to the evidence that early experience matters a great deal, especially for brain development, the evidence from early intervention programs shows that well-designed programs improve developmental outcomes. Early interventions come at a time when families are more open to interventions and lay the groundwork for later development and success.

This recommendation does not imply, however, that only investments in early childhood are warranted. Some children, especially the disadvantaged, may miss out on early investments and arrive at school not ready and motivated to learn. Other children may have thrived in early childhood but encounter problems in their school years if they experience new stresses, such as a move to a less supportive school or a more dangerous neighborhood, a family disruption, a decline in family economic status, or a health or learning problem. As Eccles and Wigfield note, many children need more support from teachers to cope successfully with school transitions (for example, the transition into primary school, or into secondary school). As Spencer and Swanson note, many students and their parents need more support during the transition from adolescence to adulthood. And as Donahoe and Tienda and Pouncy note, many adolescents and young adults need support during the transitions from school to work or school to training. Therefore, it is important to expand investments throughout childhood and adolescence in effective programs that build social competencies and vocational and academic skills.

A second implication concerns the providers of investments in children. At each stage of the life cycle, many adults can affect children's social and cognitive development. It is not the case that the only facilitators of development are the parents in the preschool years, schools in the school-age years, and then employers, trainers, or colleges in the postschool years. Most preschool-age children now spend substantial time in out-of-home care (whether child care or preschool), but that care is too often of less than adequate quality, as Ramey and Ramey point out. Although school-age children spend much of their time in school, families and communities continue to influence their development and their transitions from school to work or further education. As Spencer and Swanson emphasize, because parents are essential to guiding and monitoring their children's school success, additional efforts should be made to promote their involvement in schools. And as Sampson documents, community conditions and the interactions at that level between adults and youth can either facilitate or curtail children's development.

Investments in children are most successful when efforts are coordinated, when providers work in partnership, when their efforts are comprehensive, and when the child is treated as a whole person who is developing in the context of his or her family and community. Kahn and Zuckerman, for instance, conclude that pediatricians should broaden their focus beyond children's physical health to promote maternal health and child literacy and to advocate for families experiencing problems with inadequate income or housing. Programs such as Healthy Steps for Young Children and Reach Out and Read are promising examples.

A third implication concerns the benefits of investments in children. Because early investments lay the groundwork for later success, preschool interventions are particularly cost-effective: their benefits accumulate and are compounded over time. Some interventions for school-age children also yield benefits that exceed their costs. And these benefits can continue into later life: more education in the school-age years fosters additional education and training in adulthood. The benefits of these investments accrue not just to the children who participate in these programs. Other children benefit by having peers who are more focused and motivated in the classroom, and hence less involved in antisocial or harmful activities. Society benefits when the children in whom we invest today become the workers and taxpayers of tomorrow. Most important, the children of today are the parents of tomorrow. Effective investments in children today benefit the next generation of children because tomorrow's parents will be better positioned to support their development.

The benefits of investments are sometimes underestimated because program outcomes are defined too narrowly. As Heckman and Lochner note, programs that have little effect on cognitive ability may nevertheless raise children's motivation to learn, boost school attendance, and promote prosocial behavior. The Perry Preschool Project achieved its most lasting effects, not on test scores, but on outcomes such as higher employment and earnings and reduced crime. Benefits may sometimes be defined too narrowly in evaluations of second-chance programs for adults. As Lynch notes, such programs may enable parents to be better teachers for their children. As a result, a program that helps adults pass the high school equivalency exam may have benefits in addition to its impacts on adult earnings or employment.

There is no better way to break the intergenerational cycle of poverty and inequality than to invest in the current generation of children. Well-designed investments in children and adolescents today promote their future success in the labor market, family life, and social life. Yet we view these investments as more than a strategy for alleviating the problems of poverty and inequality. Although the poor, racial and ethnic minorities, and immigrants face greater challenges to successful child development and have fewer resources, an increasing share of children—well over half—are growing up in families with either only one parent or two parents who are each dividing their time between parenting and working.

Given the realities of today's labor market, many parents cannot provide all of the care, attention, and resources that children need to maximize their development. These challenges are particularly acute in the preschool years, when an increasing share of young children are spending time in child care that is often of dubious quality. Most school-age children could also benefit from programs that offer them a safer and more productive way to spend their time after school and on weekends. School-age children are often left unsupervised and, as a result, may be more likely to engage in a variety of risky behaviors.

Continuing changes in the labor market place further pressure on today's children as they become tomorrow's workers. As the workplace becomes increasingly technical, it is not just high school dropouts who face bleak prospects. Many high school graduates who do not receive further education or training may not have the skills needed to succeed in the labor market. In the late 1980s, the William T. Grant Foundation (1988) raised a warning flag about the situation of the "forgotten half"—youth who do not go on to college. Today, the prospects for these youth are even worse. Thus, the need to develop an investment strategy that prepares and motivates them to participate in further training or education, along the lines suggested in chapters 8, 9, and 10 by Donahoe and Tienda, Pouncy, and Ellwood and Kane, is even more critical. Chapters 8 and 9 show how schools and workforce development programs can better prepare high school graduates for the labor market, and chapter 10 demonstrates that college-going increases when financial subsidies and information about college access are improved.

Based on our reading of the chapters, we propose that parents, foundations, nonprofit organizations, and the government work together to expand investments in the following kinds of programs.

1. *Programs to improve the health of women of childbearing age:* Because maternal health has strong effects on child outcomes, because many of these effects begin before birth, and because many births (roughly 50 percent) are to first-time mothers, interventions that target only women who already have children fail to serve a substantial number of disadvantaged children. There is substantial evidence about a range of interventions that reduce the risks that can compromise outcomes for children prenatally. The challenge is to expand programs, such as school-based health clinics and public education programs, and convey that knowledge to young women before they have children. In addition, we need to expand programs, such as Healthy Steps for Young Children, the WIC program, and proven home visiting programs, to improve maternal health among women who are already pregnant or who already have children.

2. *Early childhood interventions that target the most disadvantaged children, who are at highest risk of school failure:* Much evidence documents the effectiveness of early childhood interventions in improving a range of developmental outcomes. We cannot afford to wait until children reach elementary school to undertake investments to improve their school achievement and other outcomes. Learning begins early in life, and our interventions must begin then too. The elements of successful programs are well established; the challenge is to expand them to reach larger numbers of children, whether through the expansion of model programs, such as IHDP or the Abecedarian Project, or larger-scale initiatives, such as Early Head Start.

3. *Measures to raise the quality of child care and early childhood education for preschool-age children:* The risks associated with poor-quality care in early childhood are not limited to disadvantaged children. Preschool-age children now spend a substantial portion of time in out-of-home care, much of which is of poor quality. Although there has been debate about what constitutes quality care, especially for very young children, the evidence reviewed in this volume, including new studies from the National Institute of Child Health and Development (NICHD Early

Child Care Research Network 1997, 1998), documents that children benefit when they are in settings that provide sensitive care and experiences that promote their development. We must increase access to preschools and improve the quality of child care, whether through universal preschool initiatives, such as Georgia's, or through more effective regulation and monitoring of child-care providers.

4. *After-school programs and mentoring programs for school-age children and adolescents:* Because parents need help in supervising their children after school, there is a need for expanded programs to serve children during these hours of the day. More generally, adolescents need more support than their schools and families can provide. Mentoring programs such as Big Brothers/Big Sisters and Sponsor-A-Scholar can help provide that support, and such programs should be expanded.

5. *Programs to raise the level of college attendance by high-ability youth from low-income families:* There is a substantial gap in college attendance between youth who have comparable levels of ability but differ in their level of family resources. Although some of this gap is explained by differences in school achievement prior to college entry, some of the gap is due to differences in family income. Expansion of programs to facilitate college enrollment by qualified low-income students is required if we are to achieve greater equality of opportunity in college attendance. These programs might entail expanded funding opportunities, different types of funding opportunities, or programs that help students make greater use of existing funding sources.

These program and policy enhancements do not exhaust the list of potentially beneficial investments. Given the current political environment, however, it would be difficult to persuade Congress to allocate the additional funds needed in just these five areas. Nonetheless, we are convinced that these investments would, in the long run, pay for themselves.

The chapters in this volume also provide evidence on other policies and programs that could be sources of investment in children. Readers will differ in what they believe to be the most promising programs and policies, but they should all conclude that the challenges documented here are substantial and that if we are willing to spend the requisite funds, we can invest prudently. Such investments can improve children's outcomes in later life, generating positive benefits that will accrue to other children and to society more generally and spill over to the next generation of children. We have pointed out what those investments should look like, when we should invest, and who the partners in investment should be. Although the effectiveness of some programs is still uncertain, the key elements of a strategy to secure our future by investing in children are clear. There is little time to lose: this generation of children cannot afford for us to wait any longer.

The authors thank Rachel Dunifon, Irwin Garfinkel, Lisa Lynch, Allan Wigfield, and two anonymous reviewers for helpful comments on a previous version.

REFERENCES

Brooks-Gunn, Jeanne, Greg J. Duncan, and J. Lawrence Aber, eds. 1997. *Neighborhood Poverty: Context and Consequences for Children.* New York: Russell Sage Foundation.

Council of Economic Advisers. 1997. *The First Three Years: Investments That Pay.* Washington, D.C.: Council of Economic Advisers.

Duncan, Greg J., and Jeanne Brooks-Gunn, eds. 1997. *Consequences of Growing Up Poor.* New York: Russell Sage Foundation.

Heckman, James J. 1996. "What Should Our Human Capital Investment Policy Be?" Milken Institute for Job and Capital Formation (Spring): 3–10.

Karoly, Lynn A., Peter W. Greenwood, Susan S. Everingham, Jill Hoube, M. Rebecca Kilburn, C. Peter Rydell, Matthew Sanders, and James Chiesa. 1998. *Investing in Our Children: What We Know and Don't Know About the Costs and Benefits of Early Childhood Interventions.* Santa Monica, Calif.: Rand.

Lynch, Lisa M. 1997. "What Can We Do?: Remedies for Reducing Inequality." Paper presented at the Council on Foreign Relations Study Group on Global Trade and Wages, New York (June 4, 1997).

National Science Foundation. 1996. *Investing in Human Resources: A Strategic Plan for the Human Capital Initiative.* Washington, D.C.: National Science Foundation.

National Institute of Child Health and Human Development (NICHD) Early Child Care Research Network. 1997. "The Effects of Infant Child Care on Infant-Mother Attachment Security: Results of the NICHD Study of Early Child Care." *Child Development* 68(5): 860–79.

———. 1998. "When Child Care Classrooms Meet Recommended Guidelines for Quality." Paper presented at the meeting "Child Care in the New Policy Context." U.S. Department of Health and Human Services, Bethesda, Md. (April 30, 1998).

Shore, Rima. 1997. *Rethinking the Brain: New Insights into Early Development.* New York: Families and Work Institute.

William T. Grant Foundation Commission on Work, Family, and Citizenship. 1988. *The Forgotten Half: Non-College Youth in America.* New York: William T. Grant Foundation.

Part I

Background

Chapter 1

Trends in and Consequences of Investments in Children

Lisa M. Lynch

The importance of investments in children, in particular in their human capital formation, has received considerable attention recently in the United
States from both scholars and public policy makers. Much of this attention
has been driven by the growth in income inequality over the past twenty years.
Many researchers have argued that this increase in inequality is due in large part
to technological shocks that have shifted the relative demand for skilled workers.
The United States is not alone in experiencing technology shocks, yet the growth of
income inequality is more pronounced here than in most of the other advanced, industrialized economies. One explanation of the variance in the degree of inequality across countries, in spite of similar technological shocks, is that the relative supply of skilled workers in some countries has kept up with the changes in the relative
demand for skilled workers better than in the United States. The relative supply of
skilled workers is determined by both the skill accumulation process of incumbent
workers and the skills that new entrants bring into the labor force. This chapter presents a background discussion on some of the trends in human assets embodied in
the inflow of new young workers into the labor force. The purpose of this overview
is not to discuss every possible trend but rather to highlight some of the key indicators and to lay out possible public policy issues. I leave it to the remaining chapters in this volume to develop in more detail the implications of the trends that I
discuss here.

TRENDS IN AND RETURNS TO INVESTMENTS
IN EDUCATION AND TRAINING

If economists can agree on anything, it is probably that investments in education and
training have a large and significant impact on the future labor-market outcomes of
workers. In addition, the benefits of staying in school, at least in the United States,
have increased dramatically over the past twenty years. As shown in figure 1.1, only
those heads of household with at least some years of college education have been

FIGURE 1.1 / Real Median Household Annual Earnings with Head Age Twenty-Five or Older, by Educational Attainment, 1979 to 1998 (1998 Dollars)

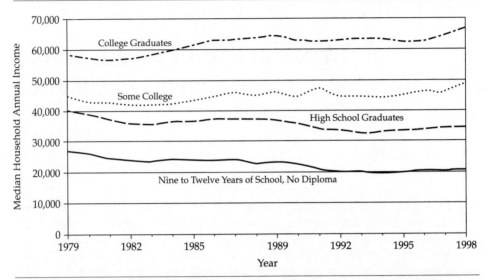

Source: U.S. Census Bureau, Current Population Survey, Historical Income Tables, H-13 and H14. Data from 1991 onward are not strictly comparable to previous years owing to a change in the definition of educational attainment. Data from 1993 onward are not strictly comparable with previous years owing to a change in earnings top-coding.

able to maintain or improve their standard of living since 1979. More educated workers earn more in the United States, and the gap is increasing. From 1979 to 1995, the ratio of median earnings of college to high school graduates rose for both full-time male and female workers, from 1.44 to 1.69 for men and from 1.29 to 1.67 for women. Finally, even as we continue to experience unemployment rates well below 5 percent, unemployment rates for those with less than a high school degree are four times higher than for those with a college degree.

Recent evidence indicates that the positive returns to schooling lie in the greater productivity of more educated employees, not in the screening out of low-ability individuals by higher education. Thomas Kane and Cecilia Rouse (1993) found that a year of post–high school education increased earnings by 5 to 10 percent after controlling for family background and test scores in high school. Work by Orley Ashenfelter and Alan Krueger (1994) on identical twins found that each year of additional schooling raised later earnings of the more educated twin by 13 percent.

It is important to note that not all years of college are the same. Evidence from a recent National Science Foundation (NSF) study found that annual median earnings for engineers who were college graduates and between the ages of thirty-five and forty-four in 1993 was $53,287, compared with $31,849 for those employed in philosophy, religion, or theology. For women aged thirty-five to forty-four, the median earnings of economics graduates, $49,175, are almost double the median earnings in philosophy, religion, and theology of $25,787 (U.S. Department of Labor 1997). More generally, Eric Eide (1994) has shown that changes in the distribution of college majors (more women have gone into technical and business fields over the past twenty years) contributed to a narrowing of the gender wage gap for college graduates during the 1980s.

Given these positive returns to remaining in school, it is not surprising that since 1960 more young people have chosen to enroll in college, especially women. In 1960, 54 percent of male high school graduates and 38 percent of female high school graduates enrolled in college. By 1997, college enrollment rates had risen dramatically for young women, to over 70 percent, and they had risen to 64 percent for young men. In terms of race and ethnicity, from 1980 to 1995 high school graduates' college enrollment rates rose for whites from 49.9 to 65.8 percent, for blacks from 41.8 to 51.4 percent, and for Hispanics from 49.9 to 51.1 percent. Although the rates rose for all racial and ethnic groups, they rose the most for whites but barely changed for Hispanics. At the same time, high school dropout rates declined across all demographic groups, especially for black non-Hispanic males (from 22.3 percent in 1972 to 13.2 percent in 1997).

Formal schooling is just one way in which young workers acquire skills for the workforce. Another source is participation in employer-provided training programs or apprenticeships. Although it may be difficult to tease out the impact of education and training on aggregate productivity, microlevel studies of establishments show significant gains in productivity associated with human capital investments. My colleague Sandra Black and I have recently found that increasing the average educational level of workers in a firm by one year raises productivity by as much as 8 percent in manufacturing, and 13 percent in nonmanufacturing (Black and Lynch 1996). Table 1.1 summarizes other evidence on the significant impact that private-sector training has had on wages and the productivity of firms. My own research found that a year of formal on-the-job training raises wages for non-college youths as much as a year of college (Lynch 1992). Work by Ann Bartel (1989, 1992) and John Bishop (1994) has also suggested that increased company-provided training can raise the company's productivity by 16 percent or more. These gains in productivity and wages are similar to what has been found in studies on the British, Danish, and Dutch labor markets.

Studies by Lynch (1992), Jacob Mincer (1991), James Brown (1989), Lee Lillard and Hong Tan (1986), John Bishop (1994), and John Barron and colleagues (1987) have shown that education begets training. Firm-provided training is much more likely to be obtained by more educated employees. This results in the creation of both a "virtuous" and a "vicious" circle of human capital accumulation. Individuals who acquire more schooling are also more likely to receive post-school, employer-provided training, while those with minimal education find it extremely difficult to make up this deficiency in human capital once they enter the labor market.

All of these studies suggest that the gains to workers and firms from investments in education and training are substantial. More specifically, more years of schooling

TABLE 1.1 / The Impact of Private-Sector Training on Wages and Productivity

Study	Impact
Outcome measure—wages	
Lynch (1992), United States, noncollege-bound	A year of formal on-the-job training raises wages as much as a year of college
Mincer (1991), United States	Rates of return associated with an additional year of training: 4.4 to 11 percent
Blanchflower and Lynch (1994), United Kingdom	Apprenticeship training increases earnings 9 to 12 percent
Tan et al. (1993), Australia	Apprenticeships increase earnings by 8 percent
Groot et al. (1994), the Netherlands	On-the-job training increases wages 4 to 16 percent
Westergard-Nielsen and Rasmussen (1997), Denmark	Apprenticeships raise earnings 10 percent
Outcome measure—productivity	
Bartel (1992), United States, all industries	Productivity increases 19 percent over three years in firms that train
Bartel (1989), United States, all industries	Training investment increases productivity by 16 percent
Bishop (1994), United States, all industries	Formal training increases an index of performance by 10 to 16 percent
Holzer et al. (1993), Michigan, manufacturing	When training investments are doubled, scrap rate decreases by 7 percent
Black and Lynch (1996), United States, nonmanufacturing	Computer training increases labor productivity by more than 20 percent
Black and Lynch (1996), United States, manufacturing	Providing a higher proportion of workers who train off the job increases productivity
Ichniowski, Shaw, and Prennushi (1995), steel	When training is linked with progressive human resources management practices, uptime is 7 percent higher
Groot (1993), the Netherlands	Company rates of return to training: 11 to 20 percent

Source: Author's compilation.

are associated with higher earnings, lower unemployment, and higher productivity. In addition, surveys of employee benefits show that those with more years of schooling are also more likely to receive employer-provided health insurance and pension benefits. But young people who enter the labor market with a high school degree or less are unlikely to find either much demand for their skills or employers who are willing to invest in their human-capital formation.

THE PROBLEM

Why do so many employers complain about the quality of young workers and the quality of schools? Almost one in five employers (see the *Educational Qualification of the Workforce 1996 National Employers Survey*) rate the quality of their local high school as unacceptable, while less than 5 percent of employers rate their local community or four-year college as unacceptable. Two-thirds of employers never use transcripts in hiring, and one in four sees no value in academic performance. What are they looking for in new young hires, and what has happened to the capacity of youths and schools to meet these employer skill needs over time? Figure 1.2 presents some data from a recent nationally representative survey of employers and their workplace practices in 1996. More employers expect nonmanagerial employees to work in teams

FIGURE 1.2 / Skill Requirements in a Changing U.S. Workplace, 1996 (Weighted Data)

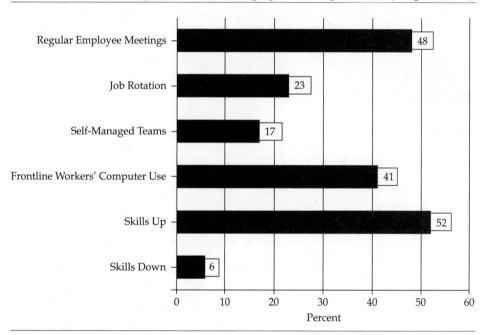

Source: National Employers Survey, second round.

Definitions: Regular employee meetings: the percentage of establishments reporting that 75 percent or more of workers meet regularly to discuss workplace issues; job rotation: the percentage of establishments reporting that 25 percent or more of workers rotate jobs; self-managed teams: the percentage of employers reporting that 25 percent or more of employees work in self-managed teams; frontline workers' computer use: the percentage of businesses reporting that 75 percent or more of their frontline workers use computers. Skills up is the percentage of establishments reporting that skill requirements in their business have risen over the past three years. Skills down are those businesses that report a fall.

or participate in problem-solving groups. Over 40 percent of employers report that three-quarters of their frontline workers use computers. As a result of these changes, most employers in the United States report that their skill requirements are rising and they are looking for workers with excellent communication skills and a positive attitude. As more employers adopt what are called "high-performance workplace practices," they say that they need more workers who not only can do specific tasks but can problem-solve and work in teams, are math- and computer-literate, and have learned how to learn—the so-called knowledge worker.

But when we look at trends in knowledge as measured by math and reading achievement by age in the United States (see figures 1.3 and 1.4), we see that for pre-college youth there has been no dramatic change in these scores since the early 1970s. This finding for math is especially surprising since Philip Levine and David Zimmerman (1995) have recently found that an additional half year of math in high school for young women increases their wages by 3 to 5.5 percent and raises their probability of attending and graduating from college. More generally, as discussed by Eric Hanushek (1996), inflation-adjusted per-pupil expenditures doubled between the late 1960s and the early 1990s, yet these achievement scores remained flat. Some in the academic and policy communities have concluded that money has no impact on schools' performance outcomes.

Yet when we look more closely at the average reading achievement for seventeen-year-olds over the past twenty-five years (see figure 1.5), we see very different trends in achievement by demographic group. More specifically, average reading skills have actually worsened for males, improved and then worsened for Hispanics, and

FIGURE 1.3 / Average Reading Achievement Scores, by Age, 1971 to 1996

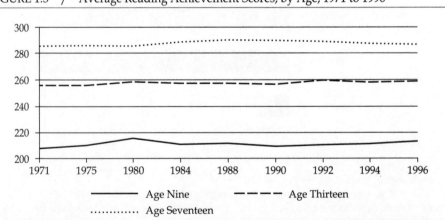

Source: U.S. Department of Education, National Assessment of Educational Progress Survey (NAEPS) 1996, Trends in Educational Progress. Level 150: simple arithmetic facts; level 200: beginning skills and understandings; level 250: numerical operations and beginning problem-solving; level 300: moderately complex procedures and reasoning; level 350: multi-step problem-solving and algebra.

FIGURE 1.4 / Average Math Achievement Scores, by Age, 1973 to 1996

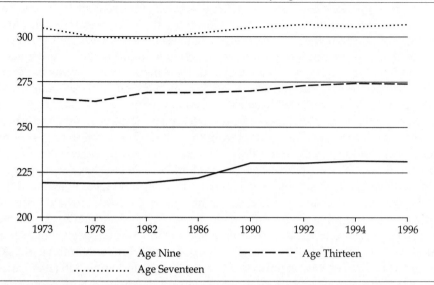

Source: U.S. Department of Education, NAEPS 1996, Trends in Educational Progress. Level 150: achieves simple discrete reading tasks; level 200: has partial skills and understanding; level 250: interrelates ideas and makes generalizations; level 300: understands complicated information; level 350: learns from specialized reading materials.

FIGURE 1.5 / Average Reading Achievement of Seventeen-Year-Olds, 1980 to 1996

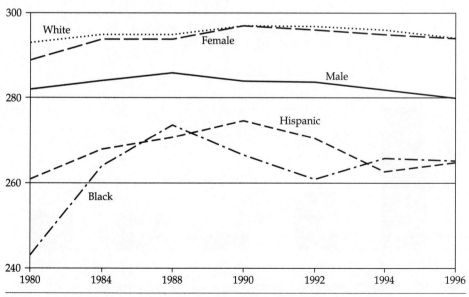

Source: U.S. Department of Education, NAEPS 1996, Trends in Educational Progress.

stagnated for whites. At the same time, there has been some slight improvement in average reading skills for females and a dramatic improvement for black non-Hispanics, especially during the 1980s. However, many of the gains achieved by non-Hispanic blacks in the 1980s were eroded in the late 1980s and early 1990s. Much of the increase in per-pupil spending was targeted at minority and disadvantaged students. What figure 1.5 suggests is that additional money may be quite important for minority students' performance but less important for advantaged students.

The picture, however, gets bleaker when we compare the basic skill competencies of young workers in the United States to their counterparts in other advanced, industrialized economies, using data from the recent Organization for Economic Cooperation and Development (OECD) International Adult Literacy Survey. As shown in figure 1.6, one in five *employed* workers between the ages of sixteen and twenty-four in the United States can barely add two numbers, compared with less than 10 percent in Canada and less than 5 percent in Germany, Sweden, and the Netherlands. In addition, those countries in the International Adult Literacy Survey that had higher variation in skills also experienced more inequality growth over the period from 1979 to 1990. Why are there such large differences in the basic skill levels of youth across these countries? Stephen Nickell and Brian Bell (1996) argue that an educational system like Germany's produces a much more compressed distribution of human capital than the U.S. system. In Germany, basic educational standards are set for all students to attain, and students know that their performance is a critical factor in the probability that they will attend university or obtain a good apprenticeship. In other words, the educational system sets high minimum

FIGURE 1.6 / Percentage of Employed Sixteen- to Twenty-Four-Year-Olds with Minimal Math Skills, by Country, 1994

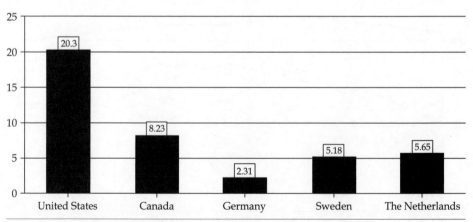

Source: OECD International Adult Literacy Survey, minimal quantitative score.

standards for all students and provides all of them with incentives to do well in school, not just those going on in higher education.

As many as three-quarters of German youth continue on in apprenticeship training after they complete their schooling. This school-to-work transition results in a very different level of skill attainment for new entrants in the labor market in Germany than in the United States, especially for those in the bottom half of the ability distribution. For example, Christoph Buechtemann, Juergen Schupp, and Dana Soloff (1993) followed two cohorts of youths leaving compulsory schooling in Germany and the United States in 1978 and 1979. They found that after twelve years, 80 percent of the German youths had attained a vocational training certificate or university degree after leaving school, while only 54 percent of their U.S. counterparts had obtained a certificate or degree. Nickell and Bell (1996) concluded that when a school system sets and achieves a high level of performance for those in the bottom half of the ability range and provides a comprehensive vocational training system for graduates, many of the negative consequences of a relative demand shift away from the unskilled can be minimized.

One solution to this problem of skill acquisition for new entrants into labor market is to get more students into higher education or to have more employers provide basic skills training if this is what they say they need. But Thomas Kane (1999) has recently argued that the rising costs of tuition in the face of imperfect capital markets have had an adverse effect on college completion. In addition, a recent study by the General Accounting Office (1996) showed that tuition at four-year public colleges and universities rose three times faster than the median household income between 1980 and 1995. Student aid has not kept pace with tuition levels, so students and their families are relying more heavily on loans, work while in school, and personal financial resources to go to college. Given these rising costs, some are unable to enter college at all; others are forced to delay entry, cannot concentrate as much on their studies because of the need to work, or must drop out of school in spite of the wage premium associated with acquiring more education.

Although employers say they need more educated workers and there appear to be large returns to employer-provided training, employers may not be able to provide skills training. A firm's decision to invest in training, especially more general training, may be influenced in part by the characteristics of the workers it employs. Employees who are perceived to have higher turnover rates are less likely to receive employer-provided training. In addition, training itself may contribute to employee turnover: if new skills are of value to other employers, firms risk having their trained employee hired away (the poaching or "cherry-picking" problem). Therefore, investments in nonportable, firm-specific training are more attractive to firms than investments in general training, unless employers can find some ways to "capture" their investment in general training. Firms that invest in the general skills of their employees only to have those workers leave for other employment may end up investing in a suboptimal level of training.

In addition, smaller firms may have higher training costs per employee than larger firms because they cannot spread fixed costs of training over a large group of employees. The loss in production from having one additional worker in off-site training is probably much higher for a small firm than for a larger one. Smaller firms are also less likely to have developed extensive internal labor markets that allow them to better retain and promote employees.

None of these issues would necessarily result in underinvestment in training if capital markets were perfect (so that workers could borrow to finance more general training), if the government subsidized general training, or if workers accepted lower wages during training spells. However, capital markets are far from perfect, and workers differ from employers in their attitudes toward risk and time horizons. As a result, there may be a market failure in the provision of general training and the proportion of workers trained in more general skills.

CHANGES IN THE ENVIRONMENT

Before we blame the education and training system for all our skill woes, let us also consider changes in the environment outside of school in which young people are acquiring both human and social capital. Given recent research on the importance of the environment in the early years of a child's life for subsequent cognitive and socio-emotional development (see Ramey and Ramey, this volume; and Zucherman and Kahn, this volume), I first look at the trends in family structure. As shown in figure 1.7, the percentage of children with two parents in the household has fallen for all demographic groups over the past twenty years. One-third of all children under eighteen live in single-headed households, and almost two-thirds of all black non-Hispanic children live in single-headed households. Only 13 percent of families fit the "traditional" model of husband as wage-earner and wife as full-time homemaker. Six out of ten mothers with children under the age of six are in the labor force. As a consequence of these changes, most preschool children are not cared for by a full-time, stay-at-home parent. Instead, families increasingly rely on child-care support from relatives, baby-sitting by nonrelatives, or organized child-care centers.

In fact, as shown in figure 1.8, the preschool enrollment rate of three- to five-year-olds in the United States jumped from slightly more than one-quarter of all children in this age group in 1965 to almost 65 percent by 1997. Therefore, preschool children are increasingly acquiring human capital from sources other than just the home. More children can take advantage of the additional learning opportunities provided in preschool programs, but, unfortunately, the quality of preschool programs is not the same across the country, nor is the degree of participation by economic status. In 1995, over 80 percent of children ages three to five in households with incomes over $75,000 participated in preschool programs, while only 48.8 percent of those in households with less than $10,000 (one-fifth of all children ages three to five who have not entered kindergarten) were in any type of preschool program. Programs attended by lower-income children typically have higher child-staff ratios, higher

FIGURE 1.7 / Percentage of Children Under Eighteen with Two Parents in the Household, 1980 to 1998

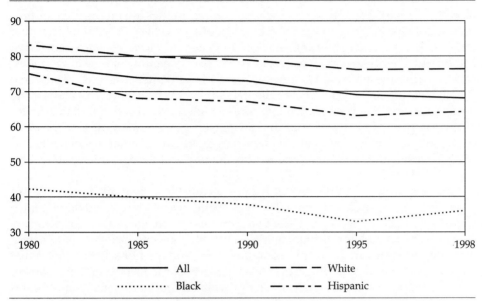

Source: Federal Interagency Forum on Child and Family Statistics, *America's Children: Key National Indicators of Well-being, 1999* (Washington, D.C.: U.S. Government Printing Office, 1999). Also available at http://www.childstats.gov/ac1999/AC99pt2.pdf.

FIGURE 1.8 / Preschool Enrollment of Three- to Five-Year-Olds, 1965 to 1997

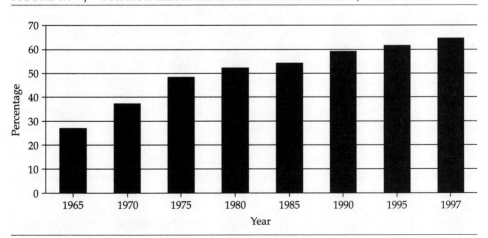

Source: U.S. Department of Education, *Digest of Education Statistics, 1998,* table 46. Data from 1990 onward are not strictly comparable to earlier years.

teacher turnover rates, and less formal curricula or guidelines for what students should learn (U.S. General Accounting Office 1995).

Head Start, first begun in 1965, is an attempt by the federal government to increase the participation of low-income children in high-quality preschool programs. In 1995, the program cost $3.5 billion and served over 750,000 children (just under 40 percent of eligible families) aged three to five. Head Start programs have been credited with raising IQ scores, lowering the probability of repeating grades, and lowering the probability of being placed in remedial education. The Perry Preschool program, which targets a clientele similar to Head Start's but at twice the level of funding, has been shown to improve high school completion rates, lower participation in criminal activities, and lower teenage pregnancy rates. (For a more comprehensive review of what we know and do not know about the benefits and costs of early childhood interventions, see Ramey and Ramey, this volume; and Karoly et al. 1998.)

However, in spite of the short-term gains seen in Head Start, the benefits of this program appear to fade with time. This is probably not an unexpected finding if we consider that many children in Head Start continue to face the same external factors (such as poverty, undernutrition, family instability, housing problems, and neighborhood infrastructure problems, including crime and inferior school quality) that made them eligible for the program in the first place. Consequently, the environment in which children are trying to learn and grow later undermines many of the gains they obtain while participating in the program. Janet Currie and Duncan Thomas (1998) have recently examined whether the short-term gains of Head Start disappear in the long term because Head Start children are subsequently more likely to be exposed to inferior schools. They found significant evidence that this is the case, and specifically that black students who participated in Head Start are systematically more likely than other black children to attend schools of poor quality.

But it is not just changes in family structure that have an impact on the environment in which children are learning and developing. As shown in figure 1.9, the percentage of five- to seventeen-year-olds who speak another language at home has risen over the past twenty years, especially but not solely in the West. Again, multilingualism presents both an opportunity and a challenge for the accumulation of human capital. For example, Joseph Altonji (1995) found that the high school academic subject that consistently has the most positive impact on future labor-market experience is foreign languages. Although estimation problems may bias this particular finding, the capacity to speak more than one language in an increasingly global economy must be an asset. Nevertheless, for those children who speak another language at home, slightly more than one-third report having difficulty in speaking English, and this share has been rising over time. By 1995, as a result, 2.4 million children who spoke another language at home reported having difficulty speaking English. A clear consensus on how best to address this problem within our K-12 educational system has yet to emerge.

Families play a critical role in the learning and development of children in many ways. One example is the amount of time children spend reading for fun or being read to at home. Table 1.2 shows the percentage of children ages three to five who

FIGURE 1.9 / Percentage of Five- to Seventeen-Year-Olds Speaking Another Language at Home, 1979 to 1995

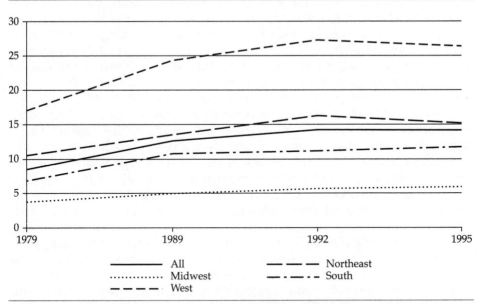

Source: Federal Interagency Forum on Child and Family Statistics, *America's Children: Key National Indicators of Well-being, 1999* (Washington, D.C.: U.S. Government Printing Office, 1999). Also available at http://www.childstats.gov/ac1999/AC99pt2.pdf.

TABLE 1.2 / Percentage of Children Ages Three to Five Who Were Read to Every Day in the Last Week by a Family Member

	1993	1995	1996
All	53	58	57
Race			
White	59	65	64
Black	39	43	44
Hispanic	37	38	39
Family type			
Two parents	55	61	61
One or no parent	46	49	46
Mother's education			
Less than high school	37	40	37
High school or GED	48	48	49
Vocational, technical, or some college	57	64	62
College graduate	71	76	77

Source: U.S. Department of Education, National Household Education Survey.

were read to by a family member every day in a survey week, over the 1990s. In general, the trend is upward except for single-headed households or those in which the mother has a high school education or less. Education begets education, and in those households with a mother who has a college degree, children are twice as likely to be read to as those in which the mother has less than a high school degree.

The number of parents reading to preschool children is up, but the percentage of children over the age of thirteen who "read for fun" at home is down. In 1996, more than 50 percent of nine-year-olds read for fun, approximately 30 percent of thirteen-year-olds read for fun, and only one in five seventeen-year-olds read for fun. In contrast, in 1984 more than 30 percent of seventeen-year-olds read for fun. Has reading for fun been replaced by television? As shown in table 1.3, the good news on television watching is that the percentage of nine- and thirteen-year-olds watching six or more hours a day is falling. The bad news is that the percentage of nine-, thirteen-, and seventeen-year-olds watching three to five hours of television a day has grown, and there has been a decline in the percentage of thirteen- and seventeen-year-olds who watch two hours of television or less per day. Unfortunately, this table does not tell us what young people are doing instead of television—participating in community service, studying, playing computer games? It is not likely to be studying, since the amount of time that thirteen- and seventeen-year-olds spend on studying did not change significantly between 1984 and 1996.

So what else is going on in young people's lives that may be affecting their learning and development? In particular, what have been the trends in their participation in "social capital" development, such as participation in extracurricular activities? Table 1.4 reports the percentage of high school seniors who participated in school-sponsored extracurricular activities in 1980 and 1992. Overall, participation rates have declined in academic clubs, athletics, music, drama, and debating clubs. For example, the black participation rate in academic clubs fell from 33 percent in 1980 to 20 percent in 1992. Only the percentage of seniors participating in a school newspaper or yearbook has remained unchanged, at around 20 percent. The only cate-

TABLE 1.3 / Daily Hours of Television Viewing by Youths, by Hours Watched per Day, 1996 to 1982

Age	Zero to Two Hours	Three to Five Hours	Six or More
Nine			
1996	47%	36%	18%
1982	44	29	26
Thirteen			
1996	39	48	13
1982	45	39	16
Seventeen			
1996	54	39	7
1978	69	26	5

Source: U.S. Department of Education, National Household Education Survey.

TABLE 1.4 / High School Seniors in School-Sponsored Extracurricular Activities, 1980 to 1992

| | Academic Clubs | | Athletics | | Music, Drama, Debate | |
	1980	1992	1980	1992	1980	1992
All	26%	25%	52%	43%	37%	27%
Male	20	23	64	55	28	23
Female	31	27	41	30	44	32
White	25	26	52	44	36	28
Black	33	21	54	41	43	32
Hispanic	24	23	49	35	31	22
Asian	27	32	49	45	37	25
Lowest income quartile	25	19	43	34	31	24
Middle two quartiles	24	25	52	42	36	27
Highest quartile	29	32	62	54	44	31

Source: U.S. Department of Education, *Digest of Education Statistics*, 1998, table 144.

gory that has seen participation go up is academic clubs for those from the highest socioeconomic quartile.

Unfortunately, there are no time-series data on the participation rates of young people in community service activities. However, a recent survey conducted by the U.S. Department of Education found that almost 50 percent of sixth- to twelfth-graders participated in some type of community service activity over the year. However, participation rates, as shown in table 1.5, vary by demographic group and school performance. In particular, the students doing best in school are twice as

TABLE 1.5 / Students in Grades Six Through Twelve Who Participated in Community Service

Male	45%
Female	53
Black	43
Hispanic	38
White	53
Other	50
A student	60
B student	48
C student	38
D student	30
All	49

Source: U.S. Department of Education, Student Participation in Community Service Activity, April 1997, NCES 97–331.

likely to be active in community service as those who are having the most difficulty. In other words, human capital and social capital are complementary.

FACTORS THAT UNDERMINE HUMAN CAPITAL ACCUMULATION

Poor families tend to be disproportionately concentrated in central cities, and this concentration of poverty has been rising over time. As Chris Mayer (1996) has documented, the share of the poor living in census tracts with a poverty rate of more than 40 percent increased from 16 to 28 percent between 1970 and 1990, while the percentage living in tracts with a poverty rate exceeding 20 percent rose from 55 to 69 percent. This increasing concentration of the poor in inner cities leads to social and economic isolation that may be having a profound impact on the quantity and quality of the human capital investments that some segments of our society experience. As mentioned earlier, Currie and Thomas (1998) showed that those from disadvantaged backgrounds get caught in a vicious cycle of inferior support that can undermine successful interventions such as Head Start. In addition, as the U.S. Department of Housing and Urban Development found in 1995, three-quarters of households with incomes at or below one-half the median income suffer from housing problems. One result of these housing problems, combined with worsening labor-market conditions for low-educated workers, may be that low-income families change both their home and their school district more often than do more affluent households.

More generally, the high degree of labor-market mobility in the United States, when paired with a highly decentralized school system, may be undermining the skill development of our children. As children move from school district to school district, they may miss important blocks of material simply because school districts are not coordinated to teach the same topics at the same time during the school year, or even in the same grade. This may explain in part why U.S. students perform relatively well in the fourth grade on international comparisons of math or science ability but their relative performance declines sharply as they age.

Other factors can also have a negative impact on the capacity of our children to learn and develop. For example, from the early 1970s to the end of the 1980s, arrest rates for sixteen- to twenty-four-year-old males rose from 44.6 to 52.6 per 1,000 population while real wages for males in this age range fell over 20 percent. The relationship between labor-market opportunities and the criminal behavior of youths has been examined in detail by Jeffrey Grogger (1997). Using unique data from the 1980 National Longitudinal Survey of Youth, he concluded that a 20 percent decline in wages would result in a 12 to 18 percent increase in youth participation in crime.

Not only are more youths engaging in criminal activity, especially those who have dropped out of school, but youths are quite often the victims of serious crimes and violence. As shown in table 1.6, the rates at which youths were victims of serious crime peaked in 1993 but fortunately have decreased sharply since then. The rates for black youths in particular have declined from 60 per 1,000 youth aged twelve to

TABLE 1.6 / Youth Victims of Serious Crimes, Age Twelve to Seventeen, 1980 to 1997 (Rates per 1,000)

	1980	1985	1990	1993	1995	1997
White	34.1	34.4	37.0	40.0	25.5	27.6
Black	60.2	35.2	77.0	71.5	44.5	30.4
Other	21.7	28.8	37.3	17.6	23.7	9.7
Male	54.8	49.8	60.5	53.9	39.0	33.1
Female	19.7	18.2	24.9	33.1	17.0	20.8
Total	37.6	34.3	43.2	43.8	28.3	27.1

Source: Federal Interagency Forum on Child and Family Statistics, *America's Children: Key National Indicators of Well-being* 1999 (Washington, D.C.: U.S. Government Printing Office, 1999). Also available at data: http://childstats.gov/ac1999/AC99pt2.pdf.

seventeen in 1980 to 30 per 1,000 in 1997. Unfortunately, as shown in table 1.7, the mortality rates due to firearms for fifteen- to nineteen-year-olds have risen over this same time period, especially for blacks. At the very minimum, a safe environment in which young people can learn and develop must be created before stagnation in reading and math achievement can be addressed.

At the same time, as shown in figure 1.10, the birth rate for unmarried fifteen- to seventeen-year-old women has risen from 20.6 per 1,000 in 1980 to 28.2 in 1997. The negative impact of teenage pregnancy on school completion rates and future labor-market outcomes has been well documented. The good news is that this rate, after rising sharply in the 1980s, started to fall in the later half of the 1990s. More generally, an increasing proportion of all new mothers are unmarried. As shown in figure 1.11, 18.4 percent of all births in 1980 were to unmarried women; by 1997 this percentage had risen to almost one-third of all births.

Finally, drug and alcohol use for twelfth-graders has declined since 1980, from 40 percent drinking heavily in 1980 to 30 percent in 1997. As shown in figure 1.12, illicit drug usage dropped from close to 40 percent of twelfth-graders in 1980 to slightly more than 15 percent in 1990. However, recently there has been a rise in drug abuse, so that by 1998 one in four twelfth-graders reported illicit drug use. Perhaps even more worrysome is the rise in heavy drinking and illicit drug use for

TABLE 1.7 / Mortality Rates Due to Firearms for Fifteen- to Nineteen-Year-Olds, 1980 to 1997 (per 100,000)

	1980	1985	1990	1993	1995	1997
White males	20.9	18.4	26.2	28.8	27.9	23.1
Black males	46.7	46.5	119.7	153.1	120.3	108.7
White females	4.1	3.5	4.6	4.9	4.2	3.8
Black females	7.5	6.1	12.1	15.8	14.2	11.7
All	14.7	13.3	23.3	27.8	24.5	21.2

Source: Federal Interagency Forum on Child and Family Statistics, *America's Children: Key National Indicators of Well-being* 1999 (Washington, D.C.: U.S. Government Printing Office, 1999). Also available at: http://www.childstats.gov/ac1999/AC99pt2.pdf.

FIGURE 1.10   /   Birth Rates for Unmarried Fifteen- to Seventeen-Year-Old Women,
1980 to 1997 (Births per 1,000 Unmarried Women)

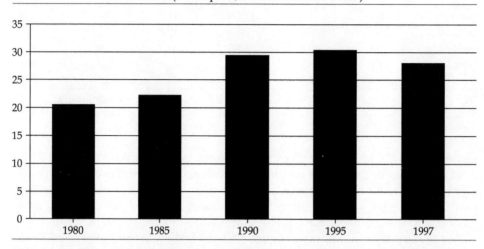

Source: Federal Interagency Forum on Child and Family Statistics, *America's Children: Key National Indicators of Well-being, 1999* (Washington, D.C.: U.S. Government Printing Office, 1999). Also available at: http://www.childstats.gov/ac1999/AC99pt2.pdf.

FIGURE 1.11   /   Percentage of All Births to Unmarried Women, 1980 to 1997
(All Ages of Mother)

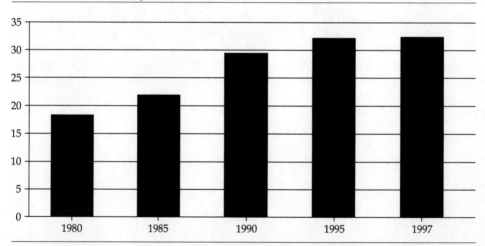

Source: Federal Interagency Forum on Child and Family Statistics, *America's Children: Key National Indicators of Well-being, 1999* (Washington, D.C.: U.S. Government Printing Office, 1999). Also available at: http://www.childstats.gov/ac1999/AC99pt2.pdf.

FIGURE 1.12 / Drug and Alcohol Use Among Youth, 1980 to 1998

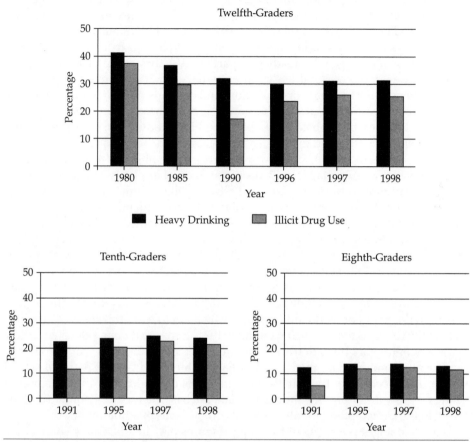

Source: Federal Interagency Forum on Child and Family Statistics, *America's Children: Key National Indicators of Well-being, 1999* (Washington, D.C.: U.S. Government Printing Office, 1999). Also available at http://childstats.gov/ac1999/AC99pt2.pdf. Note that "heavy drinking" is defined as having five or more alcoholic drinks in a row in the two weeks prior to the survey.

eighth- and tenth-graders. In 1998, more than one in five tenth-graders and slightly more than 10 percent of eighth-graders were either using illicit drugs or drinking heavily (five drinks or more in a row).

WHAT WE CAN DO

We could "fix" inequality by a variety of methods in the short term, but they might not be the policies we would want to keep in place in the long term to ensure that inequality did not reemerge. For example, we could use a combination of wage subsidies and tax credits to redistribute the gains of the haves to the have-nots. Lawrence Katz (1996) has done an interesting review of the impact of the wage subsidies programs in general and provided new evidence on young workers who were covered by the Targeted Jobs Tax Credit. He concluded that stand-alone programs targeted at very special socioeconomic groups appear to be less effective than more broadly targeted subsidies, in part because they stigmatize the targeted group. However, policies that use an intermediary (such as a public employment agency or a nonprofit training organization) and combine training with the subsidy appear to be more successful when targeting specific disadvantaged groups.

As discussed earlier, the costs of obtaining higher education have been rising much faster than household income, so expansion of financial assistance to encourage young adults to stay in school would be a worthwhile investment. (For more discussion of the advantages and disadvantages of broad-based subsidies for increasing enrollment rates, see Kane and Ellwood, this volume.) But we should not wait until our children are twelfth-graders before we identify and intervene to address skill deficiencies. As argued in this volume by James Heckman and Lance Lochner, early interventions such as Head Start and dropout prevention programs are more efficient ways to address the skills issues of our children and warrant further resources. But the skills problem in the United States is not confined to a small minority. We need to find ways to bring up the bottom half of the distribution. Possible ways to do this include school-to-work programs that educate and expose youths to the world of work and help motivate them to learn through real applications of the concepts they are being taught in the classroom. (For an extensive review of the school-to-work transition and examples of effective school-to-work programs, see Donahoe and Tienda, this volume.) Establishing and raising national school standards, especially for those in the bottom half of the ability distribution, may go a long way toward improving the high variance in basic literacy and numeracy skills found in the United States in international comparisons of adult literacy.

What role might government training programs play in addressing some of the skill deficiencies of young workers in particular? Some have argued that current expenditures for government training should be cut since those programs do not work and may even have a negative impact on the wages and earnings of displaced or disadvantaged youths and adults. However, a recent review of evidence on the effectiveness of government training programs (see U.S. Department of Labor 1995b) suggests that at least some types of government-funded training and employment programs have been successful for youths. Table 1.8 summarizes some of this evidence. Government training programs, such as residential programs for at-risk youths, the San Jose Center for Employment Training, some welfare-to-work programs, and job search assistance, have shown returns to society of $1.40 or more for each dollar invested. But, as noted by Heckman (1996), while conventional employment and training programs are often cost-effective, especially those for disadvantaged women, the amounts spent on these programs tend to be quite modest, and as a result they are unlikely to be sufficient to lift most participants out of poverty.

Recent experimental evaluations of the U.S. Job Training Partnership Act (JTPA) program for disadvantaged male youth found negative effects of training on their

TABLE 1.8 / Outcomes of Some U.S. Government Training Programs

Target Group	Program	Outcomes
In-school youth	Summer Youth Employment	This program represents a large share of summer employment in high-poverty, densely populated areas and includes many youth who have never worked before. The Inspector General's report on the 1992 summer program found that "with few exceptions the SDAs managed successful programs. . . . Participants were productive, interested, closely supervised, learned new skills they could apply to their schoolwork and took pride in their employment."
Out-of-school youth	Center for Employment Training (CET)—San Jose	This vocational training and job placement program resulted in 33 percent higher earnings. This highly successful program is being replicated in other U.S. cities.
Out-of-school youth	Job Corps	This residential program increased earnings by 15 percent, raised employment, reduced serious felony crime, and doubled college enrollment.
Disadvantaged youth	Job Training Partnership Act	About 50 percent of youth in JTPA Title II-C are still in high school but are at risk of dropping out. A number of dropout prevention programs have cut the dropout rate in half and increased college enrollment. Classroom training for female youth raised earnings 9 percent.

earnings and no effect on the earnings of disadvantaged female youth. This empirical analysis was given great weight by policymakers because of its more "scientific" basis: it was an experiment using controls and treatments rather than a statistical analysis that only a handful of economists could understand. It was cited as the justification for cutting funding of training programs for youth by 80 percent. However, as Heckman and Smith (1997) have argued, even these experimental impact estimates are quite sensitive to the construction of the experiment and as a result are quite fragile. Before abandoning these programs, I think it is incumbent on the research and public policy communities to get a better handle on why it is that some programs, such as California's Center for Employment Training program, do a much better job of assisting disadvantaged youths than other programs. (For a more exhaustive list of innovative programs, see Pouncy, this volume.) Does CET work because it does a better job of identifying specific skill needs for each client and then works with a variety of public and private vendors to address those needs? Do CET's close relationships with local employers ensure that counseling on job search and training programs helps youth get a better job match and that they are given more relevant training?

The Workforce Investment Act of 1998 will consolidate well over one hundred types of government training programs and establishes a training voucher system to be administered by the states to allow the unemployed (or even low-income workers in some cases) to purchase the training programs of their choice. Although in principle I think this is a good idea, workers will still need much assistance in matching training to job opportunities. In addition, given the precedent of rogue institutions emerging to take advantage of student loan and grant monies, states will need to establish a type of "consumer affairs" watchdog to ensure that workers' training vouchers are not wasted.

Finally, in a series of papers (including his chapter in this volume), James Heckman has argued that the costs of raising the educational levels of those at the bottom of the income distribution to get them back to the relative wages of the late 1970s would be prohibitively expensive. Assuming a 10 percent rate of return to investing in human capital, Heckman (1996) calculated that it would cost $426 billion in 1989 dollars to restore the earnings of male high school dropouts and graduates to their 1979 real earnings level. At first blush, this sum sounds like an extraordinarily large amount of money, but to put it in just one context, the government (federal, state, and local) currently spends well over $500 billion a year on education—$211 billion on higher education alone. New estimates by the American Society of Training and Development (1998) (and the author's own calculations), using data from the recent Bureau of Labor Statistics (BLS) 1995 survey of employer training practices suggest that U.S. employers are spending $55 billion to $80 billion a year on formal training. This figure more than doubles if we include informal training. Firms in 1995 spent $534 billion on durable equipment. The $426 billion that Heckman calculated would be required to restore the earnings of high school dropouts is a lot of money, but relative to the other investments in physical and human capital we make every year in the U.S. economy, it is not so extraordinary. Finally, why spend all this money in one year? As Gary Burtless (1990) and others have argued, something like a correctly targeted 10 percent increase in education and training investment per year for the next ten years could go quite a long way in bringing up the earnings of those with a high school education or less. Nevertheless, I agree very strongly with the broader point that Heckman makes in this volume: waiting until workers enter the workforce to address their skill deficiencies is inefficient at best and may be too late for some.

Figure 1.13 highlights a key issue in the federal financing of education and training programs. The percentage of the federal budget spent on education and training has fallen over the past twenty years from a peak of 5 percent to around 2.8 percent in 1997. This pattern holds even when we look at federal outlays in education and training as a percentage of gross domestic product (GDP). This ratio peaked in 1977 at just over 1 percent and has since fallen to just under 0.6 percent in 1997. At the

FIGURE 1.13 / Outlay Categories as a Percentage of the Federal Budget, 1970 to 1997

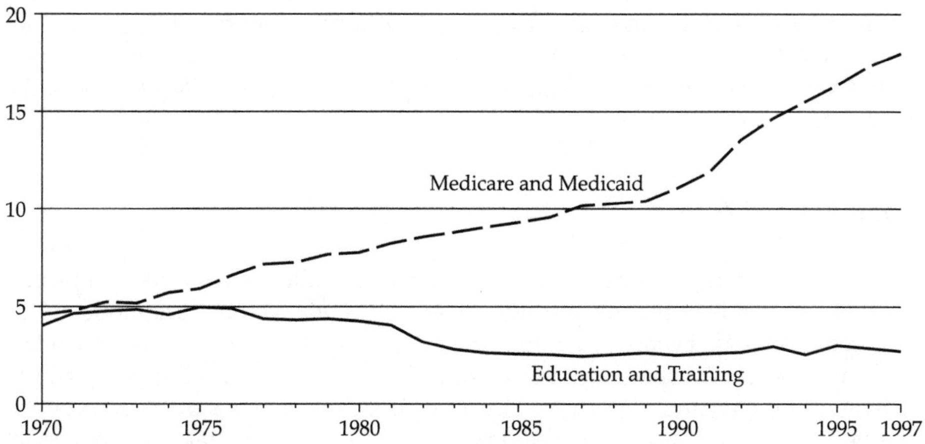

Source: Author's own calculations.

same time, expenditures on Medicare and Medicaid have accelerated rapidly, especially in the 1990s. It is increasingly difficult in the current budget atmosphere to allocate resources to education and training, and I believe we are seeing the consequences of this lack of investment in the labor market.

One solution would be to look to the private sector to help make up the skills gap. But as discussed earlier, employers are understandably reluctant to make general skills investments in their workers, who might then be poached away. In addition, small firms may face higher per-employee training costs than larger firms. As a result, we have a market failure in the provision of general training for incumbent workers.

A possible response to this problem is to give employers, especially small and medium-sized employers that hire many low-wage workers, additional tax credits for formal training expenditures. Another way is to reward suppliers of training to businesses (for example, community colleges) with additional resources for setting up training programs for employees with less education. A third strategy is to impose a training tax that sets a standard minimum (say, 1.5 to 2.5 percent) to be spent on training; employers would either spend that amount on training or pay a tax into a general training fund. This strategy, which is similar to the employer training tax in France, has the benefit of creating a level playing field across employers, and it also might solve the poaching problem. But the experience of Australia, which adopted and then abandoned such a tax, suggests that in practice the training levy can be relatively easy to avoid paying.

But whatever we do in education and training, it is important to recognize the importance of issues closer to home: family structure; who is caring for children; what children are doing in their nonschool hours; the degree of family support for learning; resources for nonclassroom community activities; and the safety of the neighborhoods in which children are growing up. Unfortunately, as this chapter tries to show, many of the trends indicating the health and safety of family, neighborhood, and school environments are going in a direction that does not favor the human capital investments of many children and youth, especially those with limited resources.

CONCLUSIONS

In sum, there is both good news and bad news, and challenges as well as opportunities, in the trends in the investments we are making in our children today. The good news is that in the face of significant increasing returns to remaining in school, enrollment rates in college have been rising sharply over the past forty years, especially for women and minorities. Mathematics achievement is up, especially for nine-year-olds, and black and Hispanic youth have made considerable progress in reading and math skills. If we look at factors that inhibit learning, such as drug and alcohol abuse, we see a sharp decline for high school seniors since 1980. The percentage of youths who are victims of serious crimes has also fallen since 1980, especially for blacks. Within families, we see that more parents are reading to their preschool children, and fewer older children are watching six hours or more of TV per day.

But the bad news is that the average scores in math and reading achievement of those about to leave high school have changed little since the early 1970s. In particular, average reading achievement has actually fallen in the 1990s for seventeen-year-olds in all demographic groups from where it was in the late 1980s and early 1990s. Perhaps more disturbingly, when we compare young employed workers in the United States with their counterparts in Europe, we find that one in five in the United States can barely add two numbers, compared to only 5 percent in Europe. We also know that if young people do not acquire skills in school, they are even less likely to acquire skills in the workplace.

There is even more bad news about the environment in which children and youths grow up and learn. Although drug and alcohol use is down for seniors in high school, it is up for eighth- and tenth-graders. More young people are dying from gunshots, especially young black males. The poor are increasingly concentrated in poor neighborhoods, and we know that poor local labor-market conditions are highly correlated with increases in crime. The percentage of thirteen- and seventeen-year-olds reading for fun at home has declined sharply over the past fifteen years, as has the proportion of high school seniors involved in extracurricular activities. The benefits from early intervention programs such as Head Start seem to be undermined because many students, especially blacks, end up in schools of poorer quality.

For those who do go on to college, tuition costs have risen three times faster than median income. In addition, more federal financing of higher education now comes in the form of loans rather than grants. In 1970, loans made up 40 percent of federal aid, but by 1990 they made up 65 percent of federal aid. As a result of the rising costs of tuition, more students find it necessary to work full-time while in school. In 1970, about one-third of college students worked full-time; at the end of the 1990s, almost half of all students work full-time. Students are taking on greater debt to attend school, and fewer can afford the luxury of being just a student and concentrating entirely on academics.

Finally, there are the trends that I put in the category of "challenges and opportunities" rather than good news or bad news. One such challenge and opportunity is the change in family structure. The challenge is that the percentage of children with two parents in the household has fallen for all demographic groups over the past twenty years. One-third of all children live in single-headed households, and two-thirds of all black children live in single-headed households. Six out of ten mothers with children under the age of six are working, and as a result, most preschool children are not cared for by a full-time, stay-at-home parent. The opportunity associated with this trend is that with two-thirds of all three- to five-year-olds enrolled in formal preschool programs, more school-age children will have benefited from these early learning opportunities, especially those from disadvantaged backgrounds. The challenge is to ensure that all preschool programs produce benefits similar to those obtained from programs such as the Abecedarian Project and the Perry Preschool program.

The second challenge lies in the increasing proportion of five- to seventeen-year-olds who speak a language at home other than English. One-third of these children report difficulty in speaking English. The opportunity afforded by this trend is that in a more global economy, the capacity to speak more than one language is an asset. But the challenge is to develop a clear consensus on how best to develop and nurture the positive aspects of bilingualism within our K-12 system.

To conclude, I think there are three main features of our investments in children.

1. *Education begets education and training:* It is the more educated who are more likely to receive additional training after they leave the formal school system, thus creating a virtuous circle of human capital investments. Unfortunately, those who drop out from formal education have difficulty making up any skill deficiencies in the workplace. Moreover, the debate on education and training is too often reduced to the questions of how to reallocate from one program to another and how to weigh the relative merits of funding Head Start against giving training vouchers to displaced workers. All of these programs are complementary, and when we do not recognize the synergies between education and training investments, we end up not taking advantage of all the possible returns these programs could give to individuals, firms, and society as a whole.

2. *Education begins at home:* As discussed by Heckman and Lochner (this volume) and Ellwood and Kane (this volume) and reviewed in Haveman and Wolfe (1995), one of the most important determinants of education is parental education. If we want to raise education levels in the United States, we need to consider invest-

ments in both youths and their parents, recognizing that parents are teachers too. Raising the skills and education of incumbent workers not only makes them more productive in the workplace but also contributes to the education of their children.

3. *No one can do it alone:* Employers report an increasing need for knowledge workers who are good communicators and can problem-solve, use computers, and work in teams. But employers cannot be expected to pick up all of the costs of raising the general skills of workers, and individuals find it increasingly difficult to afford the education and training they know they need. Whatever reforms are developed to improve our education and training system, we need to ensure that skills are certified, that all beneficiaries co-invest, that there is more cooperation between workers, employers, and government in designing effective training and education programs, and that these programs are cost-effective.

This chapter has documented some of the major trends in the environment in which our children learn. This changing environment presents both challenges and opportunities. It is our task as researchers, policymakers, educators, parents, and members of our communities to ensure that the challenges are met and the opportunities are not missed.

REFERENCES

Altonji, Joseph G. 1995. "The Effects of High School Curriculum on Education and Labor Market Outcomes." *Journal of Human Resources* (Summer): 409–38.

American Society for Training and Development (ASTD). 1998. "The 1998 ASTD State of the Industry Report." Alexandria, Va.: American Society for Training and Development.

Ashenfelter, Orley, and Alan Krueger. 1994. "Estimates of the Economic Returns to Schooling from a Sample of Twins." *American Economic Review* (December): 1157–73, .

Barron, John, Dan Black, and Mark Loewenstein. 1987. "Employer Size: The Implication for Search, Training, Capital Investment, Starting Wages, and Wage Growth." *Journal of Labor Economics* 5(January): 76–89.

Bartel, Ann. 1989. "Formal Employee Training Programs and Their Impact on Labor Productivity: Evidence from a Human Resource Survey." Working paper 3026. Cambridge, Mass.: National Bureau of Economic Research.

———. 1992. "Productivity Gains from the Implementation of Employee Training Programs." Working paper 3893. Cambridge, Mass.: National Bureau of Economic Research.

Bishop, John. 1994. "The Impact of Previous Training on Productivity and Wages." In *Training and the Private Sector: International Comparisons,* edited by Lisa Lynch. Chicago: University of Chicago Press.

Black, Sandra, and Lisa Lynch. 1996. "Human Capital Investments and Productivity." *American Economic Review* 86 (May): 263–68.

Blanchflower, David, and Lisa M. Lynch. 1994. "Training at Work: A Comparison of U.S. and British Youths." In *Training and the Private Sector: International Comparisons,* edited by Lisa M. Lynch. Chicago: University of Chicago Press.

Brown, James. 1989. "Why Do Wages Increase with Tenure?" *American Economic Review* 79 (December): 971–99.

Buechtemann, Christoph, Juerger Schupp, and Dana Soloff. 1993. "Roads to Work: School-to-Work Transition Patterns in Germany and the United States." *Industrial Relations Journal* 1 (June 24): 97–111.

Burtless, Gary. 1990. *A Future of Lousy Jobs?: The Changing Structure of U.S. Wages.* Washington, D.C.: Brookings Institution.

Currie, Janet, and Duncan Thomas. 1998. "School Quality and the Longer-Term Effects of Head Start." Working paper 6362. Cambridge, Mass.: National Bureau of Economic Research.

Educational Qualification of the Workforce 1996 National Employer Survey. Philadelphia: Institute for Research on Higher Education, University of Pennsylvania.

Eide, Eric. 1994. "College Major Choice and Changes in Gender Wage Gap." *Contemporary Economic Policy* 12(2, April): 55–64.

Grogger, Jeffrey. 1997. "Market Wages and Youth Crime." Working paper 5983. Cambridge, Mass.: National Bureau of Economic Research.

Groot, Wim. 1993. "Company Schooling and Productivity." Unpublished paper. Leiden University, The Netherlands.

Groot, Wim, Joop Hartog, and Hessel Oosterbeek. 1994. "Returns to Within-Company Schooling of Employees: The Case of the Netherlands." In *Training and the Private Sector: International Comparisons,* edited by Lisa Lynch. Chicago: University of Chicago Press.

Hanushek, Eric. 1996. "School Resources and Student Performance." In *Does Money Matter? The Effect of School Resources on Student Achievement and Adult Success,* edited by Gary Burtless. Washington, D.C.: Brookings Institution.

Haveman, Robert, and Barbara Wolfe. 1995. "The Determinants of Children's Attainments: A Review of Methods and Findings." *Journal of Economic Literature* 33(4, December): 1829–78.

Heckman, James J. 1996. "What Should Our Human Capital Investment Policy Be?" *Jobs and Capital.* Milken Institute for Job and Capital Formation (Spring): 3–10.

Heckman, James J., and Jeffrey A. Smith. 1997. "The Sensitivity of Experimental Impact Estimates: Evidence from the National JTPA Study." Working paper 6105. Cambridge, Mass.: National Bureau of Economic Research.

Holzer, Harry J., Richard N. Block, Marcus Cheatham, and Jack H. Knott. 1993. "Are Training Subsidies for Firms Effective?": The Michigan Experience." *Industrial and Labor Relations Review* 46(November): 625–36

Ichniowski, Casey, Kathryn Shaw, and Giovanna Prennushi. 1995. "The Effects of Human Resource Management Practices on Productivity." Working paper 5333. Cambridge, Mass.: National Bureau of Economic Research (November).

Kane, Thomas. 1999. *The Price of Admission: Rethinking How Americans Pay for College.* New York/Washington, D.C.: Russell Sage Foundation/Brookings Institution.

Kane, Thomas, and Cecilia Rouse. 1993. "Labor Market Returns to Two- and Four-Year College: Is a Credit a Credit and Do Degrees Matter?" Working paper 311. Princeton, N.J.: Industrial Relations Section, Princeton University (December).

Katz, Lawrence. 1996. "Wage Subsidies for the Disadvantaged." Working paper 5679. Cambridge, Mass.: National Bureau of Economic Research (July).

Karoly, Lynn, Susan S. Everingham, Jill Hoube, Rebecca Kilburn, C. Peter Rydell, Peter W. Greenwood, Matthew Sanders, and James Chiesa. 1998. *Investing in Our Children: What We Know and Don't Know About the Costs and Benefits of Early Childhood Intervention.* Santa Monica, Calif.: Rand.

Levine, Philip, and David Zimmerman. 1995. "The Benefits of Additional High-School Math and Science Courses for Young Men and Women." *Journal of Business and Economic Statistics* 13(2): 137–49.

Lillard, Lee, and Hong Tan. 1986. "Private Sector Training: Who Gets It and What Are Its Effects?" Rand monograph R-3331-D04RC. Santa Monica, Calif.: Rand.

Lynch, Lisa M. 1992. "Private-Sector Training and the Earnings of Young Workers." *American Economic Review* (March): 299–312.

Mayer, Chris. 1996. "Does Location Matter?" *New England Economic Review* (May/June).

Mincer, Jacob. 1991. "Job Training: Costs, Returns, and Wage Profiles." In *Market Failure in Job Training?*, edited by J. H. H. Ritzen and David Stern. Heidelberg, Germany: Springer-Verlag.

Nickell, Stephen, and Brian Bell. 1996. "Changes in the Distribution of Wages and Unemployment in OECD Countries." *American Economic Review* (May): 302–8.

Tan, Hong, Bruce Chapman, Chris Peterson, and Alison Booth. 1993. "Youth Training in the U.S., Great Britain, and Australia." *Research in Labor Economics* 13: 63–99.

U.S. Department of Housing and Urban Development. 1996. *American Housing Survey for the United States in 1995*. Washington: U.S. Government Printing Office.

U.S. Department of Labor, Bureau of Labor Statistics. 1995a. *1995 Survey of Employer Provided Training*. Washington: U.S. Government Printing Office.

U.S. Department of Labor, Office of the Chief Economist. 1995b. "What's Working (And What's Not): A Summary of Research on the Impacts of Employment and Training Programs." Washington: U.S. Government Printing Office.

———. 1997. "Report on the American Workforce." Washington: U.S. Government Printing Office.

U.S. General Accounting Office. 1995. "Early Childhood Centers: Services to Prepare Children for School Often Limited." Washington: U.S. Government Printing Office.

———. 1996. "Higher Education: Tuition Increasing Faster Than Household Income and Public Colleges Costs" (August).

Westergard-Nielsen, Niels, and Anders Rasmussen. 1997. "Apprenticeship Training in Denmark: The Impact of Subsidies." Working paper 97–07. Aarhus, Denmark: Center for Labour Market and Social Research.

Chapter 2

Rethinking Education and Training Policy: Understanding the Sources of Skill Formation in a Modern Economy

James J. Heckman and Lance Lochner

In response to the new labor market in which the real wages paid to high-skilled and highly educated workers have increased while the real wages paid to low-skilled and uneducated workers have decreased, there is renewed interest in policies designed to foster the formation of socially productive skills in the American economy. Politicians and social commentators routinely express concern about the political and social consequences of growing economic inequality. A consensus is emerging that increasing the skills of the unskilled will bring them into the modern economy and help to alleviate the problems of inequality.

Arguments for increasing college tuition subsidies rely heavily on the assumption that individuals from low-income families cannot borrow adequate funds to attend college. Support for additional spending on primary and secondary schools is based on the assumption that more teachers and greater spending per pupil can substantially improve student outcomes. The success of recent welfare reforms is premised, in part, on the assumption that adult job training programs and work experience can produce skills to make welfare recipients market-worthy job participants. In this chapter, we reexamine the widely accepted assumptions behind these proposals, drawing on a body of recent scholarship that challenges them.

In analyzing the evidence for these claims and their relevance for educational policy, it is important to distinguish between a world in which there is no education policy and the world in which we live. The relevant question is whether we should increase current subsidies—not whether there should be any subsidies at all. At a very low level of expenditure, increasing schooling quality definitely improves schooling outcomes. However, current expenditures on primary and secondary education are extremely high. With no subsidies or loan programs for college, credit constraints on lower-income students would no doubt be quite important. But the current subsidy of direct costs to students at major public universities is around 80 percent. Should that subsidy be increased?

Policy toward job training needs to be examined as well. Today's economy encompasses a large group of unskilled workers made obsolete by a rapid shift in demand toward more skilled workers. A dangerous myth that motivates welfare reform and training policy is that it is relatively cheap and easy to adapt adult unskilled workers to the modern economy. Nearly all the evidence points to the contrary: raising the skill levels and earnings of uneducated and unskilled workers is extremely costly, especially for older workers, who have only a short horizon over which they can use their new skills. Although many economists have begun to recognize this, many politicians have not. It is far from obvious that investments in low-skill workers who have been made obsolete by changes in technology are justified on any but political grounds. The major cost of such investment is the diversion of resources away from the young and the more trainable, for whom a human capital investment strategy is likely to be more effective and for whom it is likely to produce favorable outcomes in the long run. To the extent that public funds are spent on training the unskilled, we should begin shifting subsidies toward training in the private sector where firms (not government bureaucrats) can decide what skills should be learned.

Current policies regarding education and job training are also based on fundamental misconceptions about how the socially useful skills embodied in persons are produced. The conventional wisdom espoused by most politicians and educated laypersons, and even many academics, places formal educational institutions in a central role as the primary producers of the skills required by the modern economy. It often neglects important non-institutional sources of skill formation, such as families, neighborhoods, and firms, which are equally important—if not more important—producers of the social and cognitive skills needed in a modern economy.

The emphasis in policy discussions on formal schooling to the exclusion of informal, non-institutional sources of learning can be traced to a failure to recognize that learning is a lifetime affair. Learning starts in infancy, long before formal education begins, and continues throughout life. Recent research in psychology and cognition demonstrates the vital importance for skill formation of the early preschool years, when human ability and motivation are shaped by families and non-institutional environments (see Ramey and Ramey, this volume). Success or failure at this stage feeds into success or failure in school, which, in turn, leads to success or failure in postschool learning. Early learning begets later learning and early success breeds later success, just as early failure breeds later failure. Formal or institutional education is only one aspect of the learning process, and recent research indicates that it is not necessarily the most important one. Since the publication of the Coleman Report (Coleman et al. 1966), we have known that families and environments play a crucial role in motivating and producing educational success as measured by test scores. Failed families produce low-ability, poorly motivated students who do not succeed in school. Policies directed toward families and very young children may improve the performance of schools more effectively than direct expenditure on teacher salaries or new computer equipment.

At the same time, current thinking about human capital formation policies focuses on improving cognitive skills to the exclusion of noncognitive skills like motivation and social skills. A growing body of research indicates the importance of noncognitive skills for determining success in the economy and the society at large. (For a discussion of this issue, see Heckman, Hsee, and Rubinstein 1999.) These skills are more easily produced than cognitive skills. Thus, evidence that it is difficult to boost IQ in no way undermines programs that intervene to improve noncognitive skills.

On the other side of the educational process, work experience and skills acquired in the workplace in the form of job search, learning by doing, and workplace training are often neglected in popular discussions because they are not well measured. Postschool learning is an important source of skill formation that accounts for as much as one-third to one-half of all skill formation in a modern economy (see Heckman, Lochner, and Taber 1998a). Because much of this learning takes place in informal settings outside of educational institutions, it is often neglected by the educational technocrats and politicians, who commonly equate skill formation with classroom learning. Once we recognize the importance of informal sources of learning for skill formation, we can begin to think about policies to foster skills in a different way.

Consequently, we argue for a greater focus on young children, their families, and firm-provided training as more efficient means for increasing the earnings of the least-skilled. Available evidence suggests that programs that foster skills developed by the family and by private firms can produce a wide range of socially beneficial outcomes, including increases in schooling and in postschool earnings as well as reductions in delinquent and criminal behavior. We also suggest that new policies that target young children, families, and private firms be accompanied by rigorous evaluations to ensure successful implementation and cost-efficiency. We still have much to learn about these types of programs.

It is also important to recognize that it is not necessary to make everyone highly skilled. By increasing the supply of skilled workers, unskilled workers become more scarce, driving up their wage rates. James Heckman, Lance Lochner, and Christopher Taber (1998a) suggest that this change is already taking place, but that many older, unskilled workers are being left behind. It may not be cost-effective to train them all for the modern economy. We propose that efforts to train and educate younger workers be accompanied by subsidized employment for older workers harmed during the transition to a new, high-skilled economy.

Missing from discussions of education and training policy is any consideration of priorities, or even recognition of the need to prioritize. It is impractical to consider active investment programs for everyone. The real question is how to use available funds wisely. The best evidence supports the following simple policy prescription: for a fixed budget, the current returns to policies in place indicate that the best policy is to invest more in the very young to improve their basic learning and socialization skills, to invest less in mature adults and persons with low ability and motivation, and to subsidize work for the old and the severely disadvantaged in order to attach them to the economy and to society at large.

Figure 2.1 succinctly presents the argument in this chapter. At current levels of investment, the best available evidence suggests that marginal returns are highest at the youngest ages and for the most able people. A policy based on this insight

FIGURE 2.1 / Rate of Return to Human Capital as a Function of Age and Ability

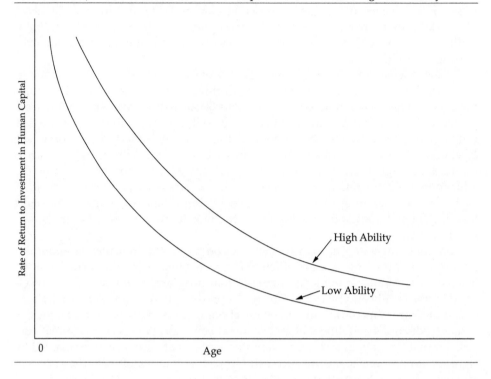

reallocates investment resources to the young so as to equalize the returns to investment across age groups. It also devotes fewer resources for human capital development to the less able. This does not mean that there should be no investment in the old and less able, just that there should be less than current levels provide. For these people, subsidized work is likely to be more efficient than subsidized training.

In the next section, we examine the well-documented negative correlation between family income and college attendance rates. We suggest that most of this correlation can be explained by differences in ability levels caused by long-term family and environmental deficits, not by short-term borrowing constraints experienced by families only during the college-going years. The following section presents the case for improving school quality in primary and secondary education. Even the most optimistic estimates suggest that spending more money on schools provides little return for students. We suggest in the next section that early childhood investments, mentoring programs for children and adolescents, and other alternative adolescent programs aimed at keeping teenagers enrolled and actively participating in school provide some of the best long-run solutions for improving the lot of the disadvantaged. We argue that efforts to train young unskilled adults should be guided away from large public training programs and toward firms and the private sector. The case for subsidizing the work (rather than education) of older unskilled workers is discussed in the section that follows. Finally, we offer concluding remarks about life-cycle skill formation.

THE EVIDENCE ON CREDIT CONSTRAINTS AND PARTICIPATION IN SCHOOLING AND TRAINING PROGRAMS

One of the most widely accepted arguments in policy and academic circles is that credit constraints prevent poor persons from participating in formal education. The empirical association between family income and college enrollment presented in figure 2.2 has attracted an enormous amount of attention in academic and policy circles. The most common interpretation of this evidence is that short-term family credit constraints prevent children from low-income families from attending school. (For examples of this argument, see Lynch, this volume; and Ellwood and Kane, this volume.) The Pell Grant program, the recently enacted HOPE fellowship program, and many government educational programs are premised on this interpretation. It is the most popular explanation for the time series of the ethnic and racial

FIGURE 2.2 / College Participation by Eighteen- to Twenty-Four-Year-Old High School Graduates and Equivalency Degree Holders

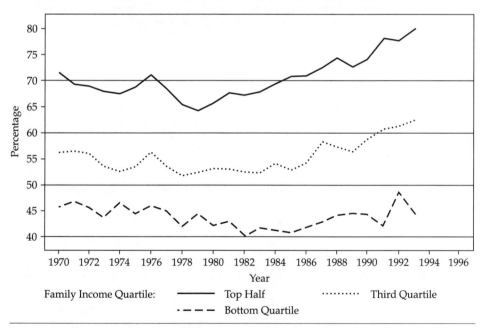

Family Income Quartile: ———— Top Half ·········· Third Quartile
· — — — Bottom Quartile

Source: Cameron and Heckman (1999b).
Note: These numbers were computed from 1971 to 1989 CPS P-20 School Reports and the 1990 to 1993 October CPS data files. Racial-ethnic categories are mutually exclusive.

gaps in college enrollment displayed in figure 2.3. Since minority families are concentrated in the lower end of the family income distribution, their failure to respond to the increase in the economic return to schooling is widely viewed as a manifestation of the more general phenomenon of a market failure due to borrowing constraints that prevent poor people from taking advantage of the increase in the return to skills.

The common interpretation of figure 2.2, and the one that guides many recent policy proposals for higher education, notes that real tuition costs have increased in percentage terms over the past sixteen years. At the same time, family incomes have declined among the bottom quartiles of the family income distribution. The real wages and employment of unskilled males have declined since the late 1970s. More families at the bottom of the family income distribution are headed by females with dependent children. Such families have lower earnings and income levels than families headed by males.

According to this interpretation, rising tuition costs and declining family resources have had a devastating impact on the college attendance decisions of children from low-income families. Based on this interpretation, policies that further subsidize the already substantial subsidies available to educate children from low-income families have been advocated (Hauser 1993; Orfield 1992).

FIGURE 2.3 / College Entry Proportions of Twenty-One- to Twenty-Four-Year-Old High School Graduates and Equivalency Degree Holders

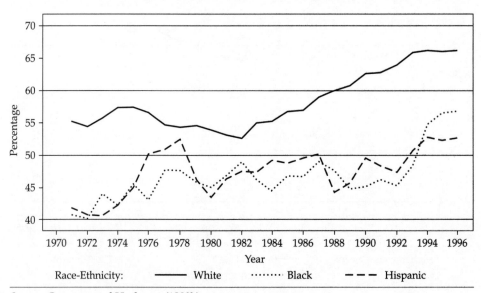

Source: Cameron and Heckman (1999b).
Note: The values represent three-year moving averages of March CPS data (two-year averages for 1971 and 1996). Racial-ethnic groups are mutually exclusive.

It is certainly true that real tuition costs have risen over the past sixteen years. Between 1980 and 1997, average public "sticker price" tuition levels rose by 100 percent at public four-year colleges and universities and by 77 percent at public two-year colleges (National Center for Educational Statistics 1997). At the same time, it is important to recognize that government subsidies to higher education are already large. All told, individuals attending public institutions of higher education pay, on average, less than 20 percent of the total direct cost of attending college. (Direct cost does not include forgone earnings.) Moreover, a substantial fraction of that 20 percent is actually paid by private foundations and charities that extend aid directly to students. (For more details on the extent of subsidy, see Cameron and Heckman 1999a, 1999b.)

It is easy to exaggerate the contribution of tuition costs in widening the gap in the college attendance of children from rich and poor families. Substantial loan and aid programs that target students from poorer families are already in place. At public two- and four-year institutions in the United States in 1996, average costs of tuition and fees were about $2,300. To offset these costs, both the Pell Grant and subsidized student loan programs are available to children of low-income families. In 1997, a first-year, dependent college student was eligible for a maximum of about $8,000 in federal grants and subsidized loans. The maximum rises to $11,000 for third- and fourth-year college students as subsidized loan limits rise. A host of other federal programs direct money to students in some form or another. In 1996 total institutional subsidies alone were approximately the size of the entire Pell Grant program (College Board 1997).

Two Explanations for the Positive Relationship Between Family Income and College Enrollment

The argument that family credit constraints are the most plausible explanation for the relationship depicted in figure 2.2 starts by correctly noting that human capital is different from physical capital. With the abolition of slavery and indentured servitude, there is no asset market for human capital. People cannot sell rights to their future labor earnings to lenders in order to secure financing for their human capital investments. Even if they could, there would be substantial problems in enforcing performance of contracts on future earnings given that persons control their own labor supply and the effort and quality of their work effort. The lack of collateral and the inability to monitor effort are widely cited reasons for current large-scale government interventions to finance education.

If people had to rely on their own resources to finance all of their schooling costs, there is no doubt that, in the long run, the level of educational attainment in American society would decline. To the extent that subsidies do not cover the full costs of tuition, students must raise tuition through private loans, through work while in college, or through forgone consumption. Children from families with higher income have access to resources unavailable to children from families with lower income, although children from higher-income families still depend on the goodwill of their parents to gain access to funds. Limited access to credit markets means that the costs of funds are higher for the children of the poor, and this limits their enrollment in college.

The purchase of education is governed by the same principles that govern the purchase of other goods. There is undoubtedly a consumption component to education. Families with higher incomes buy more of the good (in this case, education) for their children, as well as a higher-quality good. This factor partly explains the relationship between family income and college attendance presented in figure 2.2. Evidence presented in the chapter by Ellwood and Kane also suggests that this may be an important component of enrollment differences between high- and low-income families. After controlling for parental education, measured achievement, demographics, and tuition levels, they find a 9 percent difference in college enrollment rates (at four-year institutions) between children from families in the highest and lowest income quartiles. However, two-thirds of that gap is explained by differences between the two highest income quartiles—hardly the group we expect to be credit-constrained. Heterogeneity in the consumption value of schooling is a more likely explanation for differential responses at the high end of the income distribution.

An alternative and not necessarily mutually exclusive interpretation of the entire body of evidence is that long-run family and environmental factors play a decisive role in shaping the ability and expectations of children. Families with higher levels of resources produce children who are better able to perform in school and take advantage of the new market for skills.

Children whose parents have higher income have access to better-quality primary and secondary schools. Children's tastes for education and their expectations about their life chances are shaped by those of their parents. Educated parents are better able to develop scholastic aptitude in their children by assisting and directing their studies. The influences of family factors that are present from birth through adolescence accumulate over many years to produce ability, college readiness, and a taste for schooling.

This alternative interpretation stresses the role of family and the environment and does not necessarily rule out the importance of short-term borrowing constraints as a partial explanation for figures 2.2 and 2.3. However, if the finances of poor but motivated families hinder them from providing decent elementary and secondary schooling for their children, thereby producing insufficient college preparedness, government policy aimed at reducing the short-term borrowing constraints for college expenses is unlikely to be very effective. Policy that improves the environments that shape ability will be a more effective avenue for increasing college enrollment in the long run. The issue can be settled empirically.

The distinction between long-run family factors that promote college readiness and short-term borrowing constraints can be conceptualized by imagining an experiment in which poor families win the lottery. For lottery winners with young children, a much larger response to the lottery would be expected in terms of the college attendance of their children if parents invest in better schools and more academic opportunities for their children over a longer horizon. On the other hand, if short-term credit market constraints are the significant factor governing college attendance, then we expect a large response in college enrollments by children of poor families irrespective of the age of their children at the time the lottery is won.

Only to the extent that the family income and borrowing capacity of able high school graduates interested in attending college fall below the levels required to pay for college will short-term credit market constraints hinder college entry. Given the current college financial support arrangements available to low-income and minority children, the prospect that bright American students are being denied access to college because of credit constraints is highly suspect. We suggest that high tuition is not the main culprit explaining the relationship shown in figure 2.2.

Some Evidence on Ability and Short-Term Credit Constraints

We now pose and answer two questions:

1. Which factors have the most influence on schooling attainment?
2. Is the estimated influence of family income on college attendance a consequence of long-run family effects or short-term borrowing constraints?

To answer these questions, we compare the estimated effects of family background and family on college attendance when scholastic ability (Armed Forces Qualification Test [AFQT]) is included as an explanatory variable in a statistical analysis and when it is not. Measured scholastic ability is the outcome of long-term family and environmental factors produced in part from the long-term permanent income of families. To the extent that the influence of family income on college attendance is diminished by the inclusion of scholastic ability in an analysis of college-going, one would conclude that long-run family factors crystallized in AFQT scores are the driving force behind schooling attainment, not short-term credit constraints.

Table 2.1 presents a summary of a recent study by Stephen Cameron and James Heckman (1999a, 1999b), who examined what portion of the gap in college attendance between minority youth and whites is due to family income, to tuition costs, and to family background. Not controlling for ability measured at an early age, about half (five points) of the eleven-point gap between black and white college attendance rates is due to family income; about half (three points) of the seven-point difference between Hispanics and whites is due to family income. When scholastic ability is accounted for, less than one-half of one point of the eleven-point black-white gap is explained by family income. For Hispanics, the gap actually widens (increases by 2 and a half points) when family income is included, suggesting that income does not explain away differences in enrollment. Equalizing ability more than accounts for minority-majority college attendance gaps (see line 5). Similar differences show up in high school graduation rates and overall college attendance rates that are not conditional on high school graduation (see the evidence in Cameron and Heckman 1998, 1999a, 1999b). Ability produced by families and environments, not financial resources, accounts for pronounced minority-majority differences in

TABLE 2.1 / White-Minority Gap in College Entry Probabilities at Age Twenty-Four, Conditioned on High School Completion

Amount of Gap Explained By	Without AFQT Score		With AFQT Score	
	Blacks	Hispanics	Blacks	Hispanics
1. Equating all family background components individual components	.10	.11	.08	.05
1a. Number of siblings	.03	.03	.02	.01
1b. Highest grade of father	.08	.03	.06	.02
1c. Highest grade of mother	.003	.05	−.005	.02
1d. Broken home	−.01	.01	−.002	.01
2. Equating family income	.05	.03	.004	−.02
3. Equating local average wages	.004	.04	.002	.03
4. Equating tuition and college proximity	−.03	−.05	−.02	−.05
5. Equating AFQT scores	na	na	.15	.12
6. Equating lines 1 and 2	.14	.13	.08	.03
7. Equating lines 1, 2, 3, and 4	.12	.12	.06	.01
8. Equating lines 1, 2, 3, 4, and 5	na	na	.21	.13
9. Raw gap between whites and minorities	.11	.07	.11	.07

Source: Cameron and Heckman (1998).

schooling attainment. The disincentive effects of tuition on college attendance are dramatically weakened when ability is included in the analysis of college attendance.

Additional evidence in support of this point is provided by Jeanne Brooks-Gunn and Greg Duncan (1997). They establish that family income received at early ages determines completed schooling—not income received during high school or in the college-going years. This relationship holds up even when the same parental background factors are entered into an empirical analysis. Cameron and Heckman (1998, 1999a, 1999b) provide further empirical support of this relationship. Their estimates reveal large effects of family income on the probability that a student will complete the ninth grade by age fifteen (on track), but smaller effects on high school graduation by age twenty-four, and negligible effects on college enrollment conditional on high school completion. Whether they control for AFQT scores or not, the effects of family income on educational outcomes decline substantially with age. This evidence suggests that it is college readiness, not short-term credit constraints, that best explains the income-college-going relationship in figure 2.2. It is also consistent with the importance of early interventions in promoting skill formation, as we discuss later.

Our analysis suggests that it is long-run factors more than short-term borrowing constraints that explain the evidence in figures 2.2 and 2.3. Long-run factors affect both college preparedness and preferences for schooling. Evidence presented by

Cameron and Heckman (1998, 1999a, 1999b) and Brooks-Gunn and Duncan (1997) supports this assertion as it relates to college preparedness, and results in the Ellwood and Kane chapter suggest that preferences for schooling may also be important. None of these studies find strong evidence of substantial short-term credit constraints among college-age youth from low-income families. Credit constraints are more binding with respect to early investments in children. Early on in the family life cycle, parents may have more difficulties finding adequate funds to provide their children with the resources that foster lifetime skills. Programs that operate late in the life cycle, such as Hope scholarships, are likely to be ineffective in promoting college attendance and wasteful of public funds. We now consider just how ineffective and wasteful they are.

The Probable Impact of the HOPE Scholarship Program

Cameron and Heckman (1999a) present a simulation of the recently enacted HOPE scholarship program, using estimated enrollment responses to local college tuition rates. They raise two questions. First, holding other factors constant, what is the predicted enrollment response to the program? Second, how much of the cost of the program will go to families whose children would have gone to college without the program? The main feature of the program is a tax credit of up to $1,500 for two years of college (for details, see Cameron and Heckman 1999a).

Their estimated enrollment response to the HOPE program is an increase of 4.2 percentage points in two-year enrollments and a decrease of 0.9 percentage points in four-year enrollments. Thus, most of the response to the program will come in enrollment in two-year schools. At least 91 percent of the total expenditure of this program will be spent on people who would enter college in the absence of the program. Simulations by Heckman, Lochner, and Taber (1998b) suggested that once general equilibrium effects are accounted for, the effects on enrollment are likely to be one-tenth that size.[1] These findings offer little endorsement for additional college tuition subsidies. We now turn to an examination of other policy proposals to promote skill formation to see whether their empirical foundations are any better.

PRIMARY AND SECONDARY SCHOOLS

State and local governments heavily subsidize primary and secondary education. Virtually all direct operating costs are completely subsidized through high school; only the opportunity cost of the student's time remains unsubsidized. Many have questioned whether the amounts spent are adequate. Should teachers be paid more? Should class sizes be reduced? The latest pronouncements from Washington indicate that class size reductions promise big gains in test scores. Test scores are commonly used to judge the success or failure of educational reforms. Yet the connection between test scores, especially those measured in the early years of schooling, and later outcomes is weak at best (Cawley, Heckman, and Vytlecil 1999). Fortunately, in recent years a series of studies have appeared that link measures of schooling quality to measures of lifetime earnings and lifetime occupational achievement.

As a result of these studies, the consensus is growing that, within current ranges, measured inputs such as class size and spending per pupil have little, if any, effect on the future earnings of students (see Heckman, Layne-Farrar, and Todd 1996; Card and Krueger 1996). The most optimistic estimates show a mere 1 to 2 percent rise in future earnings for every 10 percent increase in per-pupil spending; however, even those estimates have been shown to depend crucially on ad hoc assumptions made by researchers. When those assumptions are relaxed, the effects of variation in per-pupil spending and class size around sample means are small and poorly determined (Heckman, Layne-Farrar, and Todd 1996).[2]

Even if we take the most favorable estimates from the literature and combine them with the best-case scenario for the costs of raising schooling quality at the secondary level, an across-the-board increase in per-pupil spending is not a wise investment. A few simple calculations make this clear. Consider the (gross) discounted returns to schooling quality for a 10 percent increase in per-pupil expenditure. A high estimate (relative to the literature) of a 2 percent increase in future earnings for a 10 percent rise in per-pupil spending yields a negative net return of such expenditure increases for all schooling levels. For high school graduates, the net loss is about $3,800, and for college graduates the net loss is over $4,400. Unless the same increase in spending raises future earnings by 5 percent or more per year—a number far higher than any study in the literature has produced—the financial costs of school quality far outweigh the returns. To justify additional spending on primary and secondary schools, we would need to appeal to other social benefits that are not captured by earnings.[3]

This evidence does not prove that school quality does not matter. Surely it does. We know that increasing school quality from very low levels has important effects. But there is little evidence that marginal improvements in current levels of schooling quality are likely to be effective. Pouring more funds into schools to lower class sizes by one or two pupils or to raise per-pupil spending by a few hundred dollars will not solve the problems of our primary and secondary school system. Although the effects of quality vary across environments and additional funding for some schools may be justified, more fundamental changes are required if we hope to see a significant improvement in our educational system.

NONTRADITIONAL EARLY CHILDHOOD, MIDDLE CHILDHOOD, AND ADOLESCENT INVESTMENTS

Recent studies of early childhood investments have shown remarkable success and indicate that the early years are important for learning and can be beneficially manipulated. This should not be surprising given the evidence presented earlier on the importance of family income at early ages. Early childhood interventions of high quality have lasting effects. Disadvantaged children of subnormal IQ were randomly assigned to the Perry Preschool program and treated intensively at ages four to five. Treatment was then discontinued, and the individuals were followed over their lives; they are now about thirty-five years old. The evidence indicates that those enrolled in the program had higher earnings and lower levels of criminal behavior in their late twenties than did comparable children randomized out of the program. Reported cost-benefit ratios for the program are substantial. Measured through age twenty-seven, the program returns $5.70 for every dollar spent. When returns are projected for the remainder of the program participants' lives, the return on the dollar rises to $8.70. As with the Job Corps (a residential adolescent training program we discuss further later in the chapter), a substantial fraction (65 percent) of the return to the program has been attributed to reductions in crime (Schweinhart, Barnes, and Weikart 1993).

The Syracuse University Family Development program provided family development support for disadvantaged children from prenatal care through age five. Reductions in problems with probation and criminal offenses ten years later were as large as 70 percent among children randomly assigned to the program. Girls who participated in the program also showed greater school achievement (Lally, Mangione, and Honig 1988). The Early Training program also targeted disadvantaged children between the ages of four and six, providing them and their families with home visits and part-day preschool services in the summer. It produced short-term gains in IQ and increases in high school graduation rates (Gray, Ramsey, and Klaus 1982). These and other studies of early intervention programs have found short-term increases in test scores, less grade retention, and higher secondary school graduation rates among enrolled children. Of those studies that examine predelinquent or criminal behavior, most have found lower rates of deviant behavior among program participants. See table 2.2 for a summary of the effects of selected early intervention programs on student test scores, schooling, earnings, and delinquency, and tables 2.3 and 2.4 for a summary of the Perry Preschool findings. (For a comprehensive survey of early intervention programs, see Karoly et al. 1998.)

Evidence on the more universal Head Start program is less clear, but the program is quite heterogeneous and not as well funded as the Perry Preschool program. Janet Currie and Duncan Thomas (1995) find short-term gains in test scores for all participating children; however, most of those gains decayed quickly for African American children. They conclude that differences either in local program administration or in subsequent schooling quality were at the root of the differences between the outcomes for black and white children. It is important to note, however, that similar declines in test scores were found for other programs, such as Perry Preschool, Syracuse University Family Development, and Early Training, but their long-term evaluations are quite favorable. The psychometric test score literature is not clear about the relationship between early test scores and success in school, graduation rates, socialization, and labor-market outcomes. The fade-out effects in test scores do not imply that there are no long-term beneficial effects of Head Start. Head Start may improve the lifetime prospects of its participants, despite yielding only short-term gains in test scores.

TABLE 2.2 / Effects of Early Intervention Programs

Program or Study	Costs[a]	Program Description	Test Scores	Schooling	Predelinquency Crime
Abecedarian Project[b] (Ramey et al. 1988)		Full-time, year-round classes for children from infancy through preschool	Higher scores at ages one to four	34 percent less grade retention by second grade; better reading and math proficiency	—
Early Training program[b] (Gray, Ramsey, and Klaus 1982)		Part-time classes for children in summer; weekly home visits during school year	Higher scores at ages five to ten	16 percent less grade retention; 21 percent higher high school graduation rates	—
Harlem Study (Palmer 1983)		Individual teacher-child sessions twice weekly for young males	Higher scores at ages three to five	21 percent less grade retention	—
Houston PCDC[b] (Johnson 1988)		Home visits for parents for two years; child nursery care four days a week in the second year (Mexican Americans)	Higher scores at age three	—	Rated less aggressive and hostile by mothers (ages eight to eleven)
Milwaukee Project[b] (Garber 1988)		Full-time, year-round classes for children through first grade; job training for mothers	Higher scores at ages two to ten	27 percent less grade retention	—

Program	Cost[a]	Services			
Mother-Child Home program (Levenstein, O'Hara, and Madden 1983)	—	Home visits with mothers and children twice weekly	Higher scores at ages three to four	6 percent less grade retention	—
Perry Preschool program[b] (Schweinhart, Barnes, and Weikart 1993)	$13,400	Weekly home visits with parents; intensive, high-quality preschool services for one to two years	Higher scores in all studied years (ages five to twenty-seven)	21 percent less grade retention or special services; 21 percent higher high school graduation rates	2.3 versus 4.6 lifetime arrests by age twenty-seven; 7 percent versus 35 percent arrested five or more times
Rome Head Start (Monroe and McDonald 1981)	$5,400 (2 yrs)	Part-time classes for children; parent involvement		12 percent less grade retention; 17 percent higher high school graduation rates	
Syracuse University Family Development (Lally, Mangione, and Honig 1988)	$38,100	Weekly home visits for family; day care year-round	Higher scores at ages three to four		6 percent versus 22 percent had probation files; offenses were less severe
Yale Experiment	$23,300	Family support; home visits and day care as needed for thirty months	Better language development at thirty months	Better school attendance and adjustment; fewer special school services (age twelve and a half)	Rated less aggressive and predelinquent by teachers and parents (age twelve and a half)

Sources: Donohue and Siegelman (1998), Schweinhart, Barnes, and Weikart (1993); Seitz (1990).

Notes: All comparisons are for program participants versus nonparticipants.

[a] Costs are valued in 1990 dollars.

[b] Studies used random assignment experimental design to determine program impacts.

TABLE 2.3 / Preschool Effects Related to Economic Benefits

Outcome Variable	Preschool	N	No Preschool	N
Education effects				
California Achievement Test at age nine	172.8	54	145.5	55
California Achievement Test at age fourteen	122.2	49	94.5	46
Classified mentally retarded[a]	15%	54	35%	58
Graduated from high school	67%	58	49%	63
Employment effects				
Employed at age nineteen	50%	58	32%	63
Monthly earnings at age twenty-eight	$1,129	54	$766	61
Crime effects				
Arrested by age nineteen	31%	58	51%	63
Five or more arrests by age twenty-eight	7%	58	35%	63
Welfare effects				
Received welfare at age nineteen	18%	58	32%	63
Received welfare at age twenty-eight	59%	58	80%	63

Source: Schweinkart, Barnes, and Weikart (1993).
Note: All group differences statistically significant at .05 level.
[a] At least one year in a classroom for "educably mentally impaired" children.

However, there is some evidence that Head Start may have smaller long-term effects than more intensive programs. Head Start's impact on special education placement and grade retention has been less dramatic than the results achieved from smaller demonstration projects like the Perry Preschool program (Haskins 1989). This is not surprising given the much lower spending per child and quality of service provided by the Head Start program. Unfortunately, there are no reliable long-term evaluations of the Head Start program that link interventions to conventional socioeconomic outcome measures like occupational attainment and earnings.

The weaknesses of Head Start can be attributed to the shorter period of intervention, lower intensity, and less-qualified staff than is typical of more ideal programs (Zigler 1994). With Head Start, as with most other things in life, you get what you pay for. For example, children enrolled in the Perry Preschool program received high-quality, full-time preschool services for one to two years (most received two years), and their parents benefited from weekly home visits by their children's teachers. There is substantial evidence that parents as well as children benefit from the family

TABLE 2.4 / Present Value of Costs and Benefits Per Child

Cost or Benefit	Recipients of Costs and Benefits		
	Whole Society	Preschool Participants	General Public
Preschool cost[a]	−$12,356	50	−$12,356
Measured benefits			
Child care	738	738	0
K-12 education	6,872	0	0
College[b]	−868	0	−868
Adult education	283	0	283
Employment[c]	14,498	10,269	4,229
Crime	49,044	0	49,044
Welfare	219	−2,193	2,412
Benefit subtotal	70,876	8,814	61,972
Projected benefits			
Earnings	15,833	11,215	4,618
Crime	21,337	0	21,337
Welfare	46	−460	506
Total benefits	108,002	19,569	88,433
Net present value	95,646	19,569	76,077

Source: Schweinhart, Barnes, and Weikart (1993).

[a] Costs and cost increases appear as negative numbers.

[b] Some small portion of college costs are likely to have been borne by the participants, but these could not be estimated from the available information.

[c] The benefits reported include all costs paid by the employer to hire a participant. Allocation to participants and the general public assume that (1) the marginal tax rate is 25 percent; (2) the value of fringe benefits received by the employee equals 10 percent of salary; and (3) the value of other fringes paid by the employer (for example, the employer's share of social security) equals 10 percent of salary.

interventions. The parents are more likely to work, improve their education, and reduce welfare participation. This produces a change in the home environment that lasts long after the initial intervention has ended. On the other hand, Head Start offers a much lower-quality (and lower-paid) staff, part-time classes for children, and limited parental involvement. The Head Start program has little effect on parental outcomes, in contrast to the Perry Preschool program or the Abecedarian Project (see Ramey and Ramey, this volume). In addition, the schools attended by participants in the Abecedarian and Perry Preschool programs after the intervention ended appear to be of higher quality than those attended by the typical Head Start child (Ramey and Ramey, this volume). Improvements in Head Start, proponents argue, are likely to produce effects closer to those observed in the more successful small-scale programs. Given the potential for success (as exhibited by the Perry

Preschool experiment), more studies of the long-term impacts of various types of small-scale and broad-based early intervention programs are certainly warranted. In particular, studies examining which interventions work best for children at different ages and with different backgrounds and deficiencies are in short supply; most studies are isolated and look only at the impacts of one program on a very homogeneous group of children.

Provocative calculations recently published by John Donohue and Peter Siegelman (1998) indicate that if programs like the Perry Preschool program were targeted at high-risk, disadvantaged, minority, male youth while they were in the preschool years, the substantial costs of these enriched programs (evident in table 2.2) would be more than repaid by the expected savings in incarceration costs alone.

A few recent studies of mentoring programs, such as the well-known Big Brothers/Big Sisters (BB/BS) and Philadelphia Futures' Sponsor-A-Scholar (SAS) programs, have shown broad positive social and academic impacts on participating school-age children and adolescents. BB/BS pairs unrelated adult volunteers with children from single-parent households for the purpose of providing each child with an adult friend who promotes positive youth development. No specific attempts are made to ameliorate particular deficiencies or to reach specific educational goals; a broad, supportive role is envisioned for the mentor. In a random assignment study, Joseph Tierney and Jean Grossman (1995) found that eighteen months after being matched with a mentor, Little Brothers and Sisters (ages ten to sixteen at the time of the match) were less likely to have initiated drug or alcohol use, to have hit someone, to have skipped class or a day of school, or to have lied to their parent; they had higher average grades and were more likely to feel competent in their schoolwork and to report a better relationship with their parent. (See table 2.5.)

The primary goal of SAS is to help students from Philadelphia public high schools make it to college. The program provides long-term mentoring (throughout high school and for one year beyond), substantial academic support, help with college application and financial aid procedures, and financial support for college-related expenses. In many ways, individually matched mentors serve as surrogate parents, providing a successful role model, monitoring student progress, and providing other social encouragement and support. SAS provides students with $6,000 in financial assistance throughout college for those choosing to enroll in an accredited two- or four-year postsecondary institution. The program also provides a coordinator for groups of about thirty students to ensure that a successful relationship is built between mentors and students. Using a matched sample of non-SAS students in Philadelphia high schools,[4] Amy Johnson (1998) estimated statistically significant increases in grade point average (GPA) for tenth and eleventh grades, as well as a 22 percent (16 percent) increase in college attendance one year (two years) after graduation from high school (see table 2.5). Because the primary goal of SAS was to increase college enrollment, other social and psychological measures were not studied.

Not all mentoring programs are effective (Sipe 1996). Programs that lack sufficient infrastructure to screen and monitor volunteer efforts or to match youth to appropriate mentors are unlikely to produce the strong positive relationships that are nec-

TABLE 2.5   /   Estimated Benefits of Mentoring Programs

Outcome Measure	Change
Big Brothers/Big Sisters	
Initiating drug use	−45.8**
Initiating alcohol use	−27.4*
Number of times hit someone	−31.7**
Number of times stole something	−19.2
Grade point average (1–4 scale)	3.0*
Skipped class	−36.7***
Skipped day of school	−52.2***
Trust in parent	2.7**
Lying to parent	−36.6**
Peer emotional support	2.3*
Sponsor-A-Scholar	
10th grade GPA (1–100 scale)	2.9*
11th grade GPA (1–100 scale)	2.5*
Attending college one year after high school	32.8*
Attending college two years after high school	28.1*

Source: Tierney and Grossman (1995); Grossman and Johnson (1998).

* Statistically significant at .10 level

** Statistically significant at .05 level

*** Statistically significant at .01 level

essary for success. Jean Grossman and Amy Johnson (1998) suggested a number of indicators for the success of mentor programs based on the BB/BS and SAS studies. By examining the impacts of those programs on different subgroups of program participants, they were able to isolate a number of features that can be linked to a successful mentoring relationship. SAS tends to focus more on academics and provides financial support for college (not a particular focus for BB/BS), but the effectiveness of both programs can nevertheless be linked to similar features. Both programs suggest that these quality measures of the relationship between mentor and child are useful indicators of program effectiveness: length of relationship, frequency of telephone contact, youth's perception of closeness, youth's sense of disappointment in the mentor, youth's perception of whether the relationship was youth-centered (activities centered on what the youth wanted to do), youth's emotional engagement in the relationship, and the case worker's assessment of whether the mentor took a negative approach (for instance, pushing the youth too hard or not setting appropriate limits). In addition, program impacts were typically larger for youth who were initially less successful academically (as measured by average grades), were having more school problems (as measured by days absent or classes skipped), and had less family support. This evidence suggests that mentors can play an important and positive role as a friend or surrogate parent for children who lack such a relationship.

For disadvantaged adolescents who are likely to drop out of school, a few other programs offer hope. Table 2.6 summarizes evidence on the effects of adolescent interventions on education, earnings, and crime rates. Both school-based and training-based programs are compared. We briefly discuss a few school-based interventions here, and youth training programs later in the chapter.

Much like SAS, the Quantum Opportunity Program (QOP) offered four years (the high school years) of social and emotional support as well as financial assistance for individuals interested in postsecondary training or education. There are a few significant differences, however, between SAS and QOP. First, QOP offered disadvantaged minority students financial incentives ($1.00 up front and $1.00 put in a college fund, plus occasional bonuses) for every hour spent in activities aimed at improving social and market skills (as compared to the $6,000 offered to all students in SAS who went to college). Students were randomly chosen to participate in the program and provided with a mentor-counselor at the beginning of ninth grade. (Approximately twenty-five students were assigned to each site mentor-counselor, compared to the one-to-one matches in SAS.) All participants were kept in the program for four years regardless of whether they dropped out of school or not. Over those four years, the average participant logged 1,286 hours of educational activities, such as studying with tutors or visiting museums. Two years after program completion, about one-third more QOP participants graduated from high school (or obtained their GED) than similar nonparticipants. Since many participants were enrolled in postsecondary schooling at the time of the follow-up study, it is difficult to determine the program's effect on earnings. However, arrest rates for program participants were one-half those for nonparticipants. These benefits did not come without cost, however: the average four-year cost per participant was $10,600. Nevertheless, a cost-benefit analysis estimated positive net social returns to QOP. (For a more detailed description of the program and its impacts, see Taggart 1995.) Table 2.7 presents a summary of the main findings from a randomized evaluation of QOP. The evaluation shows substantial reductions in crime and improvements in educational attainment.

Two other studies provide additional evidence that creative programs designed to keep adolescents in school can be effective. Ohio's Learning, Earning, and Parenting (LEAP) program and Teenage Parent Demonstration (TPD) provided financial incentives for teenage parents on welfare to stay in school or take GED classes. (Or, alternatively, they imposed financial penalties for non-enrollment.) Both programs have been evaluated by randomized trials. The evidence from these programs is presented in table 2.8. LEAP showed increases in high school graduation and GED rates among randomly assigned participants who were still enrolled in school when they entered the program. TPD showed mixed results on education depending on the program site. Moreover, there was cause for concern that young women who had already dropped out of school at the time of enrollment in the program (and, to a lesser extent, those who were still attending school when they entered the program) may have substituted GED training for high school graduation as an easier way to meet program requirements. (Cameron and Heckman [1993] have shown that a GED commands lower wages than a high school diploma in the labor market.) Both of these

TABLE 2.6 / Effects of Selected Adolescent Social Programs on Schooling, Earnings, and Crime

Program or Study	Costs	Program Description	Schooling	Earnings	Crime
Job Corps (Long Maller, and Thorton 1981)	$11,000	Seven months of educational and vocational training for sixteen- to twenty-one-years olds (mostly male)	No effect	Discounted present value of increased earnings of $10,000	Estimated reduction in crime valued at approximately $4,500
JTPA[a] (Bloom et al. 1993)	Males: $1,316 Females: $1,955	Job training and placement services for adolescents	No effect	No effect	—
STEP (Walker and Viella-Velez 1992)	—	Two summers of employment, academic remediation, and life skills for fourteen- and fifteen-year-olds	Short-run gains in test scores; no effect on school	—	—
Quantum Opportunity Program[a] (Taggart 1995)	$10,600	Counseling; educational, communication, and development services; financial incentives for participants (four years beginning in ninth grade)	34 percent higher high school graduation and GED rates (two years post-program)	—	4 percent versus 16 percent convicted; .28 versus .56 average number of arrests (two years post-program)

Source: Heckman, Lochner, Smith, and Taber (1997).
Note: All dollars in 1990 values.

[a] Studies used a random experimental design to determine program impacts.

TABLE 2.7 / The Quantum Opportunity Program: Second Postprogram-Year Impacts

	QOP Participants	Control Group	Difference
Completion			
Has high school diploma	63%	43%	+20%
Has GED certificate	25%	9%	+16%
Enrollment			
Currently in four-year college	23%	14%	+9%
Currently in a two-year college	34%	11%	+23%
Currently in training	18%	2%	+16%
Currently in GED	4%	11%	−7%
Currently in college, training, or GED	78%	38%	+40%
Employment			
Currently employed full-time	20%	7%	+13%
Currently employed part-time	16%	18%	−2%
Currently not in school, training, or work	14%	48%	−34%
Average yearly earnings (male and female)	$1,748	$1,591	+$157
Percentage with annual earnings greater than $0	56%	28%	+28%
Child-bearing			
Average children ever parented	.54	.75	−.21
Percentage with child ever parented	39%	41%	−2%
Dependency			
Self receiving food stamps	22%	43%	−21%
Self receiving welfare	20%	42%	−22%
Criminality			
Percentage ever arrested	19%	23%	−4%
Average number arrests (male and female)	.28	.56	−.28
Percentage males ever arrested	27%	39%	−12%
Average number arrests (males)	.46	1.05	−.59
Percentage ever incarcerated	13%	21%	−8%
Average number incarcerations (male and female)	.21	.49	−.28
Percentage males ever incarcerated	23%	50%	−27%
Average number incarcerations (males)	.38	.94	−.56

Source: Taggart (1995).

TABLE 2.8 / Estimated Impacts of New Chance, LEAP, and TPD on Program Participants (Percentage Changes)

Program	Ever Received High School Diploma or GED	Ever Received High School Diploma	Ever Employed in Previous Year	Average Monthly Earnings in Previous Year
LEAP				
Not enrolled	−3.4	−1.1	4.6*	8
Enrolled	7.0*	1.4	−2.6	−18
TPD				
Camden	2.0	4.4*	—	—
Newark	−2.0	−5.2**	—	—
Chicago	3.2	0.7	—	—
Full sample	—	—	−2.0	−18
Dropouts	—	—	−4.6	−56
Students	—	—	6.3**	79**
Graduates	—	—	−8.5**	−84**
New Chance	8.1***	−3.5***	2.8	−3

Source: Granger and Cytron (1998).

Notes: The follow-up periods for outcomes are approximately forty-two months for New Chance, thirty-six months for LEAP, and seventy-eight months for TPD.

* Statistically significant at .10 level

** Statistically significant at .05 level

*** Statistically significant at .01 level

programs showed positive postprogram effects on earnings and employment for students who were still in school when they entered the program. The effects were often negative, however, for participants who had already dropped out of school before entering the program. A key finding from both of these studies (for a summary, see Granger and Cytron 1998) was that the program's impact was more positive for individuals still enrolled in school (compared with dropouts). It is still unknown whether this finding is the result of higher ability, on average, in these participants compared to those who have already dropped out of school, or whether it signifies some advantage to intervening before adolescents leave school.

The evidence from QOP, LEAP, and TPD demonstrates that financial incentives to stay in school and participate in learning activities for disadvantaged students can increase schooling and improve employment outcomes. It should be noted, however, that these programs may positively influence employment and earnings (and, in the case of QOP, reduce crime), but they do not perform miracles. They affect motivation and social skills, but have little impact on cognitive skills. Combining mentors and tutoring with incentives, as QOP does, not only encourages students to remain in school but also provides them with the means and support to get the most from frequently inadequate schools and environments.

The New Chance program, operating in ten different states, provides less optimistic results for teenage mothers (see the last row of table 2.8). This program was voluntary for young single mothers, between the ages of sixteen and twenty-two, who were on welfare, had dropped out of high school, and had not yet received a high school diploma or GED. New Chance offered a comprehensive set of services to these mothers and their children, including instruction in basic skills and in subjects related to the GED, occupational training, work experience, and job placement services. The program increased the proportion of young mothers receiving a high school diploma or GED by 8.1 percent. However, that increase came entirely from an increase of 11.8 percent in GED recipients. In fact, program participants were less likely to receive a high school diploma than nonparticipants! There were no long-term impacts on earnings or employment (Quint, Bos, and Polit 1997; Granger and Cytron 1998). Two primary differences between this program and those just described are obvious. First, New Chance participants had already dropped out of school by the time they entered the program (the impacts for TPD and LEAP were much smaller [and mostly insignificant] for dropouts than for individuals still enrolled in school).[5] Second, New Chance was a strictly voluntary program that attempted to induce welfare teenage mothers to enroll based on program benefits, while QOP, TPD, and LEAP provided financial incentives to encourage academic activities.

Two other programs targeted at adolescents are widely discussed. The Summer Training and Employment Program (STEP) provided remedial academic education and summer jobs to disadvantaged youth ages fourteen and fifteen. Each summer participants enrolled in 110 hours of classes and 90 hours of part-time work. The program achieved modest short-term gains in reading and math skills, but those gains did not last. Two to three years after program completion, there were no effects on high school graduation rates, grades, or employment.

One criticism of the program was that it did not attempt to follow up on its summer program with a school-year curriculum. Maryland's Tomorrow program did just that. It combined an intensive summer program with a school-year follow-up, offering participants summer jobs and academic instruction, career guidance, and counseling through adult mentors, peer support, or tutoring. Although the program did not reduce final dropout rates, it delayed dropout. (Dropout rates were lower during the ninth grade but not by the end of twelfth grade.) The program also increased the pass rate for twelfth-grade students taking the Maryland Functional Tests (a basic skills test).

These program results suggest that sustained interventions targeted at adolescents still enrolled in school can have a positive impact on learning and subsequent employment and earnings. (For a more comprehensive survey of programs aimed at increasing the skills and earnings of disadvantaged youth, see U.S. Department of Labor 1995.) The outcomes of the QOP, LEAP, and TPD programs further suggest that simple incentives for schooling work. If successful, they can increase graduation rates, raise employment and earnings, and lower crime. However, we can expect only limited returns from merely preventing students from dropping out when they are already performing badly or their schools are failing them. The much larger and broader benefits of QOP suggest that combining incentives with the academic and social support of a caring and qualified mentor provides the greatest promise for troubled adolescents. These studies also suggest that interventions for dropouts are much less successful. Unfortunately, they do not tell us why. We do not know whether there is some advantage to intervening before the dropout decision is already made, or if those who choose to drop out have less motivation and lower ability, making programs less effective for them (regardless of when the intervention takes place). The analysis of Heckman, Hsee, and Rubinstein (1999) suggests that the latter explanation is more appropriate.

Programs that are successful in the long run do not achieve their success by boosting IQ. Evaluations of human capital programs have been preoccupied with achievement tests and measures of cognitive skill as indicators of the success of an educational intervention. Although it is certainly true that cognitive ability is important in life, and that the return to cognitive ability has increased over time, this narrow focus on cognition ignores the full array of socially and economically valuable noncognitive skills and motivation produced by schools, families, and other institutions. It critically affects the way certain early intervention programs have been evaluated. Enriched early intervention programs do not substantially alter IQ. However, they substantially raise the noncognitive skills and social attachment of participants and improve their home environment. An important lesson to draw from the Perry Preschool program and the entire literature on successful early interventions is that it is the social skills and motivation of the child that are most easily altered—not IQ. These social and emotional skills affect performance in school and in the workplace (Heckman, Hsee, and Rubinstein 1999). Because academics are biased toward believing that cognitive skills are of fundamental importance to success in life, the relatively low malleability of IQs after early ages has led many to proclaim a variety of interventions to be ineffective.

Yet the Perry Preschool program, the Abecedarian program, and the other programs we have surveyed have been shown to be highly effective in reducing criminal activity, promoting social skills, and integrating disadvantaged people into mainstream society. Similarly, the successful mentoring and other adolescent interventions operate more on motivation and socialization than on IQ. An abundance of evidence indicates that social skills and motivation have large payoffs in the labor market.

We next turn to the evidence on more traditional job training programs. Can they convert unskilled adults into skilled workers efficiently?

THE EFFECTIVENESS OF PRIVATE-SECTOR TRAINING AND THE INEFFECTIVENESS OF PUBLIC TRAINING PROGRAMS

Owing to a lack of data and a bias in favor of the funding of studies of government training, the returns to private-sector training are less well understood than the returns to public-sector training. Studies by Lisa Lynch (1992, 1993), Lee Lillard and Hong Tan (1986), John Bishop (1994), and Ann Bartel (1992) find sizable effects of private-sector training. In comparison with studies of public-sector training, most of these studies do not attempt to control for the fact that more able persons are more likely to take training, so the estimated rates of return would overstate the true returns to training by combining them with the return to ability. Thus, part of the measured return may be due to more motivated and able persons taking the training. Estimated initial returns range from 10 to 20 percent (Mincer 1993).

An important feature of private-sector training is that the more skilled do more investing even after they attain high skill levels. Different types of training and learning have strong complementarities. To the extent that effective training can be produced on the job, it is produced in the private sector and not in the public sector. Firms are also more sensitive to changing market demands for skills than are government bureaucracies. The best hope for getting a reasonable return from job training is to encourage private-sector investment.

It is important to note, however, that private-sector training typically excludes low-skilled persons. Firms can be exclusive in a way that government training programs for disadvantaged workers are designed not to be. The lack of interest of private firms in training disadvantaged workers indicates the difficulty of the task and the probable low return to this activity. In spite of this, the evidence presented next suggests that some of the more successful public training programs for disadvantaged workers are those programs that have close ties with private firms. This supports the hypothesis that efforts to train unskilled workers should be shifted to the private sector.

Evidence on Conventional Public Training and Work-Welfare Programs

How ineffective are current programs in moving people from welfare to work and in increasing their employment and earnings? Generally they are very ineffective. Consider the evidence for various groups.

ADULT WOMEN   Employment and training programs increase the earnings of adult female recipients of Aid to Families with Dependent Children (AFDC). Earnings gains are modest, persist over several years, arise from several different treatments, and are sometimes quite cost-effective. Table 2.9 displays evaluation results for a variety of programs. For example, participation in an Arkansas job search program was required for AFDC recipients with children over age three. Participants attended a group job search club for two weeks and then were asked to search as individuals for an additional two months. A program in San Diego required all AFDC participants to take job search assistance and mandated work experience. The gains were high for participants in both programs. The National Supported Work program provided intensive training and job search assistance at a cost of about $16,550 per recipient. The estimated rate of return to this program was only 3.5 percent.

The results from the recent experiment evaluating the Job Training Partnership Act, shown in table 2.10, corroborate these findings. The largest impacts are for adult women, many of whom were collecting AFDC during their participation in JTPA. The impacts were not sufficiently large, however, to move more than a tiny fraction of women out of poverty. As a general rule, conventional employment and training

TABLE 2.9 / Experimental Estimates of the Impact of Employment and Training
Programs on the Earnings of Female Welfare Applicants and Recipients

Services Tested or Demonstration	Net Cost Per Participant	Annual Earnings Gain (Loss) After	
		One Year	Three Years
Job search assistance			
Arkansas	140	220**	410**
Louisville, Kentucky (WIN-1)	170	350**	530**
Cook County, Illinois	190	10	NA
Louisville, Kentucky (WIN-2)	280	560**	NA
Job search assistance and training services			
West Virginia	320	20	NA
Virginia Employment Services	520	90	330*
San Diego I (EPP/EWEP)	770	600**	NA
San Diego II (SWIM)	1,120	430**	NA
Baltimore	1,160	190	630**
New Jersey	960	720*	—
Maine	2,450	140	1,140
Work experience and retraining			
AFDC Homemaker-Health Care	11,550	460**	NA
National Supported Work	16,550	460**	810**

Sources: Gueron and Pauly (1991, 15–20); Bell and Reesman (1987, tables 3 and 4);
Couch (1992, table 1).
Note: All figures in the table are expressed in 1990 dollars.

* Statistically significant at .10 level

** Statistically significant at .05 level

programs are often cost- effective for adult women (especially if the opportunity cost of trainee time is ignored or is sufficiently low) but do not produce dramatic changes in participant earnings or employment.

ADULT MEN The evidence for this group is consistent across programs. Returns are low but usually positive. Job search assistance is an effective strategy but produces only modest increases in mean earnings levels. For men, training programs do not make much of a difference in closing the wage gap between the skilled and the unskilled.

YOUTH Evidence from the recently concluded JTPA experiment indicates that this program produces only low or negative impacts on earnings. For male youth, the estimated negative effect is unbelievably low. If taken seriously, participation in JTPA has a more negative impact on the earnings of male youth than participation in the army, loss of work experience, or the cost of incarceration, as measured by many studies.

Securing the Future

TABLE 2.10 / Impacts on Total Eighteen-Month Earnings and Employment JTPA Assignees and Enrollees, Target Group

| | Adults | | Out-of-School Youths | |
Impact	Women	Men	Female	Male
Per assignee				
Earnings	$539**	$550	−$182	−$854**
As a percentage	7.2	4.5	−2.9	7.9
Percentage employed	2.1**	2.8**	2.8	1.5
Sample size (assignees and control group combined)	6,474	4,419	2,300	1,748
Per enrollee				
Earnings	$873[b]	$935[b]	−$295[b]	−$1,355[b]
As a percentage	12.2	6.8	−4.6	−11.6
Percentage employed[a]	3.5[b]	4.8[b]	4.5[b]	2.4[b]

Source: Bloom et al. (1993).
Note: Enrollee estimates obtained using the procedure in Bloom (1984).

[a] At any time during the follow-up period.

[b] Tests of statistical significance were not performed for impacts per enrollee

* Statistically significant at the .10 level

** Statistically significant at the .05 level

*** Statistically significant at the .01 level (two-tailed test)

Only a few training programs have demonstrated a positive impact on youth earnings. Probably the most well known is the Job Corps, an intensive program (around $20,000 per participant) that provides extremely disadvantaged youth with basic education, vocational skills, and a wide range of support services in a residential environment. A 1980 evaluation (Long, Mallar, and Thornton 1981) showed increases in education, employment, and earnings. Combining those gains with substantial reductions in crime, the estimated return from the program is roughly 8 to 9 percent. There is some basis for supporting expansion of this program, but even for this program the evidence is questionable. Part of the high return comes from a large estimate of the reduction in murder rates attributable to the program (see Donohue and Siegelman 1998).

Jobstart was designed to achieve impacts similar to those achieved from the Job Corps, without the associated costs. It offers less intensive services in a nonresidential setting, at a cost of about $6,000 per participant (substantially more than JTPA training, but less than half the cost of the Job Corps). Not surprisingly, the savings in costs are matched by a reduction in impacts. Although estimates suggest small increases in earnings and education and reductions in crime, those effects were typically not statistically significant for the overall sample of participants. Two particularly problematic subgroups showed large positive impacts on earnings: men arrested between age sixteen and program entry, and youth who had dropped out of school for educational reasons. Previous arrestees also showed some evidence of reduced crime and drug use as a result of the program. More surprising, however, are the sizable impacts reported by one program site—the Center for Employment Training (CET) in San Jose, California.

CET provides three to six months of vocational training for disadvantaged youth and adults, most of whom are high school dropouts. At a cost of only $4,200 per enrollee, the program shows sustained earnings gains of over $3,000 per year (a 40 percent increase!). The success of this program is not entirely understood, but it does have a few distinguishing features that are suggestive (U.S. Department of Labor 1995). First, the program has close ties to the local labor market. An industrial advisory board is set up to aid in skill selection; courses are taught by technicians from industry; and many area employers are on the advisory board. Second, CET emphasizes job skills training over learning basic skills. Basic skills are taught in the context of job training. Third, the CET curriculum is tailored specifically to the needs of each participant. Fourth, CET has been active in San Jose for over twenty-five years, and program staff have extensive local knowledge and contacts. The positive reputation it has earned among employers is likely to help the placement of new graduates.

A comparison of these programs suggests a few important lessons. First, you get what you pay for. The JTPA program cost very little and produced very little. The intensive residential nature of the Job Corps was not easily replaced by the less expensive Jobstart program (with the exception of CET). Second, the effects of treatment may vary substantially among subgroups. This is not only evidenced by the difference in effects for the JTPA across age and sex classifications, but it is also observed for subgroups in the Jobstart evaluation. Third, these types of programs have effects on behaviors beyond schooling and work that should also be considered. Both the Job Corps and Jobstart suggest that reductions in crime may be an important impact of programs targeted at male youth. (For additional evidence on the relationship between training, schooling, and crime, see Lochner 1999.) Consistent with the evidence from early intervention and adolescent interventions, improvements in motivation and socialization skills can substantially improve the social and economic outcomes of participants in these programs. Fourth, programs that are highly integrated with the local labor market and private sector are likely to be the most successful. This supports our claim that efforts should be made to shift training subsidies to the private sector.

Workfare and Learnfare

How effective are the recent "learnfare" and "workfare" programs? An evaluation of two programs conducted in Wisconsin is of interest (see Pawasarat and Quinn 1993). One program, the Community Work Experience Program (CWEP), required mandatory participation in unpaid community service jobs for nonexempt AFDC participants. A second program, Work Experience and Job Training, provided AFDC clients with assessment, job search activities, subsidized employment, job training, and community work experience. Participants who failed to find employment after completing their education and training were also required to participate in CWEP jobs.

Using randomized trials for one county and nonexperimental methods for the rest, researchers found no effect of these programs compared to existing program alternatives. The reduction in AFDC participation that is widely cited as a consequence of these programs is essentially due to the improvement in the Wisconsin economy during the time the programs were in place. These results are disappointing but consistent with previous studies of the efficacy of such programs by the Manpower Demonstration Research Corporation (MDRC) (Gueron and Pauly 1991). Mandatory work experience programs produce little long-term gain in employment or earnings. No cheap training solution has yet been found that can end the welfare problem. Lifting a welfare woman out of poverty by increasing her earnings by $5,000 per year ($100 per week) costs at least $50,000. This is the scale of required investment. No "quick fix," low-cost solution is in sight.

Training Programs for Displaced Workers

The displacement of older workers with substantial experience in the labor market has become an increasingly important phenomenon in recent years. In response to this trend, Congress passed Title III of the Job Training Partnership Act in 1982 and the Economic Dislocation and Worker Adjustment Assistance Act in 1988.

Duane Leigh (1990, 1995) summarized the evidence on a variety of these programs. Results from some of these evaluations suggest small to moderate wage gains lasting only about a year. A more recent evaluation by Mathematica Policy Research (see Corson et al. 1993; Decker and Corson 1995) of training provided under the Trade Adjustment Assistance Act to workers displaced as a result of foreign trade found no evidence of any effect of this long-term training program on the earnings and employment of recipients. Consistent with the other studies of government employment and training programs already discussed, the overall pattern for programs aimed at displaced workers is one of weak impacts for most groups. This is in sharp contrast to the high rates of return for private on-the-job training. We cannot rely on federal job training programs to convert adult unskilled workers into the skilled workers demanded by the modern economy.

The Impact of Training

Although these evaluations have shown little effect of public training programs, James Heckman, Neil Hohmann , and Jeffrey Smith (2000) have pointed out that they do not show that training itself has no effect. Social experiments like the JTPA estimate the effect of offering JTPA training to individuals. For classroom training, Heckman and his colleagues showed that the true effect of training is often three to five times as large as estimates from social experiments suggest, since nearly 30 to 40 percent of program participants receive no training and between

30 and 40 percent of individuals randomized out of the program receive some other form of comparable classroom training. Under reasonable assumptions about interest rates, the persistence of effects, and program costs (including the social costs of raising taxes to pay for training), they also report that classroom training in JTPA often provides positive net lifetime returns.

The fact that many nonparticipants were able to find comparable training elsewhere suggests that additional training programs are not necessary. In fact, that is precisely what estimates from social experiments tell us: the availability of these programs has small effects on earnings and employment. But training itself is not necessarily worthless, although even the corrected effects estimated by Heckman, Hohmann, and Smith (2000) do not suggest that small increases in training will pull the underprivileged out of poverty. Rather than spending more money on large-scale (and unnecessary) public training initiatives, we suggest that money is better spent by subsidizing private training, allowing firms to decide who to train and how to train them. If training particular groups is desirable for political reasons, then we would recommend subsidizing firms to train them however they see fit.

THE CONFLICT BETWEEN ECONOMIC EFFICIENCY AND THE WORK ETHIC

To the extent that there are strong complementarities between different types of skill investments, there is a conflict between policies that seek to alleviate poverty by investing in low-skill workers and policies that raise the wealth of society at large. Taking the available evidence at face value, the most *economically justified* strategy for improving the incomes of the poor, especially low-ability, low-skill adults, is to invest more in the highly skilled, tax them, and then redistribute the tax revenues to the poor.

However, many people view the work ethic as a basic value and would argue that cultivating a large class of transfer recipients breeds a culture of poverty and helplessness. If value is placed on work not only because it is an act of individual dignity but also because it has general benefits for families, communities, and society as a whole, then society may be prepared to subsidize inefficient jobs. Higher subsidies induce people to switch out of criminal activities (Lochner 1999). However, job subsidies are not the same as investment subsidies. Both theory and empirical evidence point strongly to the inefficiency of subsidizing the investment of unskilled older workers.

CONCLUSION: A LIFE-CYCLE PERSPECTIVE

In evaluating a human capital investment strategy, it is crucial to consider the entire policy portfolio of interventions together—training programs, school-based policies, school reform, and early interventions—rather than focusing on one type of policy in isolation from the others.

The best evidence suggests that learning begets learning. Early investments in learning are effective. Much of the recent emphasis on lower tuition costs for college students is misplaced when the value of early preschool interventions is carefully examined. In the long run, the skill levels of American workers, especially workers not attending college, are unlikely to improve significantly without substantial improvements in the arrangements that foster early learning. We cannot afford to postpone investing in children until they become adults, nor can we wait until they reach school age—a time when, for some, it may already be too late to intervene successfully. Learning is a dynamic process and is most effective when it begins at a young age and continues through adulthood. The role of the family is crucial to the formation of social and learning skills, and government interventions at an early age that mend the harm done by dysfunctional families have proven to be highly effective. The greatest success of these programs lies in improving the motivation and social skills of the participants, not in boosting IQ. An exclusive emphasis on cognitive skills misses the important point that noncognitive and social skills are equally important and more easily altered.

The returns to human capital investments are greatest for the young for two reasons: younger persons have a longer horizon over which to recoup the fruits of their investments, and skill begets skill. Skill remediation programs for adults with severe educational disadvantages are much less efficient compared to early intervention programs. So are training programs for more mature displaced workers. The available evidence clearly suggests that adults past a certain age and below a certain skill level obtain poor returns to skill investment. A reallocation of funds from investment in the old and least able to the young and more trainable, for whom a human capital strategy is more effective, is likely to produce more favorable outcomes in the long run.

Current training policies need to be reexamined. Private training programs have two advantages that public training programs do not: they can train workers who are likely to benefit most, and they can tailor their training programs to market needs. Although public training programs sometimes yield increases in participant earnings, those increases fall far short of those estimated for private training programs. More successful public training programs are already highly integrated with the private sector. Incentives to promote private-sector training should be expanded, and ineffective public-sector training programs should be reevaluated and eliminated. Firms are likely to choose younger and more able workers to train, rather than expending resources on those who will gain little from additional investments: older workers and those who are more difficult to train.

For older, low-skilled workers whose skills have been made obsolete by newer modes of production, wage subsidies offer a more efficient alternative for raising their incomes (see Phelps 1997). By encouraging work rather than unemployment and crime, wage subsidies may also provide social benefits that extend beyond individual increases in earnings.

All levels of government subsidize higher education, and those subsidies benefit both unskilled and skilled workers. The argument for increasing the current high level of subsidies, however, is not well documented. The evidence that borrowing constraints are important deterrents to college attendance is very weak. Students from low-income families tend to have much lower college attendance rates for reasons other than their inability to meet tuition and living expenses. Lower family income levels are associated with less productive family and neighborhood environments as well as lower motivation and ability by prospective students. These are factors not so easily remedied by student loans or fellowships. The available evidence does not suggest that additional loans or subsidies are necessary to alleviate credit constraints. There is also no evidence to suggest that massive direct externalities to education exist that require an expansion of existing levels of subsidy to education (Heckman and Klenow 1998). The strongest argument for social externalities of schooling is indirect. Lochner (1999) finds that, even after controlling for ability, high school graduation substantially reduces criminal participation. This does not, however, imply that *additional* education subsidies are justified—especially beyond high school.

Public primary and secondary schools are fully subsidized by taxes. The available evidence suggests that additional spending on public school quality would be inefficient. Instead, efforts should be made to ensure that adequate early childhood learning can take place. Additional funding for flexible early childhood programs that can respond to the specific needs of targeted children is warranted. But those programs need to be accompanied by rigorous new evaluations to ensure the success and promotion of efficient programs and to prevent the growth of wasteful ones. Some innovative programs for troubled adolescents have also shown promise and offer viable alternatives to the conventional policy response of simply throwing more public funds at current schools and curricula. These types of programs are the best way to get more out of our current schools. For those who still have difficulties acquiring the skills required by the modern economy, a policy that subsidizes private training for younger workers and employment for older workers is most efficient. It is important to recognize that different programs and policies are needed at different stages in the life cycle.

We are grateful for comments received from Sheldon Danziger, Jeanne Brooks-Gunn, Lynn Karoly, Larry Katz, Lindsay Chase- Lansdale, Craig Ramey, Jane Waldfogel, and two anonymous referees. Jean Grossman was especially helpful to our understanding of mentoring programs. This research was supported by NIH:R01-HD32058-03, NIH:R01-HD34958-01, NSF-SBR-93-21-048, NSF-97-09-873, and grants from the Mellon and Spencer Foundations.

NOTES

1. Increasing the relative supply of college graduates reduces their relative wages and causes fewer to enroll than would be predicted by the standard partial equilibrium analysis.

2. Alan Krueger (1997) carefully examined the evidence from the widely celebrated STAR program on the effect of reducing class size on test scores of primary school children and found little evidence for a strong effect except in the first year of small classes (especially

kindergarten). His evidence actually supports the case for intensive early interventions, not the case for a widescale expansion of class sizes at all ages.

3. These calculations were suggested to us by Sam Peltzman and first presented in Heckman et al. (1997). They assume that current expenditures are $6,500 per pupil and that individuals work two thousand hours per year until age sixty-five, and they discount future earnings at a 7 percent interest rate. All figures are in 1990 dollars.

4. Comparison students were matched with participants on the basis of race, gender, school attended, and ninth-grade academic performance.

5. The analysis of Heckman, Hsee, and Rubinstein (1999) suggested that dropouts have lower levels of motivation and noncognitive skills.

6. See the report entitled "What's Working (and What's Not)?" by the U.S. Department of Labor (1995) for a more comprehensive survey of programs aimed at increasing the skills and earnings of disadvantaged youth.

REFERENCES

Bartel, Ann. 1992. "Productivity Gains from the Implementation of Employee Training Programs." Working paper 3893. Cambridge, Mass.: National Bureau of Economic Research.

Bell, S., and C. Reesman. 1987. "AFDC Homemaker-Home Health Aide Demonstrations: Trainee Potential and Performance." Washington, D.C.: Abt Associates.

Bishop, John. 1994. "Formal Training and Its Impact on Productivity, Wages, and Innovation." In *Training and the Private Sector: International Comparisons*, edited by Lisa Lynch. Chicago: University of Chicago Press.

Bloom, Howard. 1984. "Accounting for No-shows in Experimental Evaluation Designs." *Evaluation Review* 8(2): 225–46.

Bloom, Howard, Larry L. Orr, George Cave, Stephen H. Bell, and Fred Doolittle. 1993. "The National JTPA Study: Title II-A Impacts on Earnings and Employment at Eighteen Months." Washington, D.C.: Abt Associates.

Brooks-Gunn, Jeanne, and Greg Duncan. 1997. "Consequences of Growing Up Poor." New York: Russell Sage Foundation.

Cameron, Stephen, and James J. Heckman. 1999a. "Should College Attendance Be Further Subsidized to Reduce Rising Wage Inequality? Does Family Income Foster Ability or Is It an Important Cash Constraint Limiting College Attendance?" In *Financing College Tuition: Government Policies Social Priorities*, edited by Marvin Kosters. Washington, D.C.: AEI Press.

———. 1999b. "Dynamics of Educational Attainment for Blacks, Whites, and Hispanics." Working paper W7249. Cambridge, Mass.: National Bureau of Economic Research.

———. 1998. "Life-Cycle Schooling and Educational Selectivity: Models and Choices." *Journal of Political Economy* 106(2): 262–333.

———. 1993. "The Nonequivalence of High School Equivalents." *Journal of Labor Economics* 11(1): 1–47.

Card, David, and Alan Krueger. 1996. "School Resources and Student Outcomes: An Overview of the Literature and New Evidence from North and South Carolina." *Journal of Economic Perspectives* 10(4): 31–50.

Cawley, John, James Heckman, and Edward Vytlecil. 1999. "A Note on Policies to Reward Value Added by Educators." *Review of Economics and Statistics* 81(November): 623–27.

Coleman, James, Ernst Campbell, Carol J. Hubson, James McPartland, Alexander Mood, Frederick Weinfeld, and Robert York. 1966. "Equality of Educational Opportunity." Washington, D.C.: U.S. Government Printing Office.

College Board. 1997. "Trends in Student Aid: 1986–1996." Washington, D.C.: College Board.

Corson, Walter, Paul Decker, Phillip Gleason, and Walter Nicholson. 1993. *International Trade and Worker Dislocation: Evaluation of the Trade Adjustment Assistance Program.* Princeton, N.J.: Mathematica Policy Research.

Couch, Kenneth. 1992. "New Evidence on the Long-term Effects of Employment Training Programs." *Journal of Labor Economics* 10(4): 380–88.

Currie, Janet, and Duncan Thomas. 1995. "Does Head Start Make a Difference?" *American Economic Review* 85(3): 341–64.

Decker, Paul, and Walter Corson. 1995. "International Trade and Worker Displacement: Evaluation of the Trade Adjustment Assistance Program." *Industrial and Labor Relations Review* 48(4): 758–74.

Donohue, John, and Peter Siegelman. 1998. "Allocating Resources Among Prisons and Social Programs in the Battle Against Crime." *Journal of Legal Studies* 27(1): 1–43.

Garber, Howard L. 1988. *The Milwaukee Project: Preventing Mental Retardation in Children at Risk.* Washington, D.C.: American Association on Mental Retardation.

Granger, Robert, and Rachel E. Cytron. 1998. "Teenage Parent Programs: A Synthesis of the Long-term Effects of the New Chance Demonstration, Ohio's Learning, Earning, and Parent (LEAP) Program, and the Teenage Parent Demonstration (TPD)." Working paper. New York: Manpower Demonstration Research Corporation.

Gray, Susan Walton, B. Ramsey, and R. Klaus. 1982. *From Three to Twenty: The Early Training Project.* Baltimore: University Park Press.

Grossman, Jean, and Amy Johnson. 1998. "Assessing the Effectiveness of Mentoring Programs." Working paper. Philadelphia: Public/Private Ventures.

Gueron Judith M., and Edward Pauly. 1991. *From Welfare to Work.* New York: Russell Sage Foundation.

Haskins, Ronald. 1989. "Beyond Metaphor: The Efficacy of Early Childhood Education." *American Psychologist* 44(2): 274–82.

Hauser, Robert. 1993. "Trends in College Attendance Among Blacks, Whites, and Hispanics." In *Studies of Supply and Demand in Higher Education,* edited by Charles T. Clotfelter and Michael Rothschild. Chicago: University of Chicago Press.

Heckman, James, Neil Hohmann, and Jeffrey Smith. 2000. "Substitution and Dropout Bias in Social Experiments: Evidence from an Influential Social Experiment." *Quarterly Journal of Economics.* (May).

Heckman, James, Jing Jing Hsee, and Yona Rubinstein. 1999. "The GED is a 'Mixed Signal': The Effect of Cognitive and Non-cognitive Skills on Human Capital and Labor Market Outcomes." Unpublished paper. University of Chicago.

Heckman, James, and Peter Klenow. 1998. "Human Capital Policy." In *Policies to Promote Capital Formation,* edited by Michael J. Boskin. Stanford, Calif.: Hoover Institution.

Heckman, James, Anne Layne-Farrar, and Petra Todd. 1996. "Human Capital Pricing Equations with an Application to Estimating the Effect of Schooling Quality on Earnings." *Review of Economics and Statistics* 78(6): 562–610.

Heckman, James, Lance Lochner, Jeffrey Smith, and Christopher Taber. 1997. "The Effects of Government Policy on Human Capital Investment and Wage Inequality." *Chicago Policy Review* 1(2): 1–40.

Heckman, James, Lance Lochner, and Christopher Taber. 1998a. "Explaining Rising Wage Inequality: Explorations with a Dynamic General Equilibrium Model of Earnings with Heterogeneous Agents." *Review of Economic Dynamics* 1(1): 1–58.

———. 1998b. "General Equilibrium Treatment Effects: A Study of Tuition Policy." *American Economic Review* 88(2): 381–86.

Johnson, Amy. 1998. *An Evaluation of the Long-term Impacts of the Sponsor-A-Scholar Program on Student Performance.* Princeton, N.J.: Mathematica Policy Research.

Johnson, D. 1988. "Primary Prevention of Behavior Problems in Young Children: The Houston Parent-Child Development Center." In *Fourteen Ounces of Prevention: A Casebook for Practitioners,* edited by Richard H. Price, Emory L. Cowen, Raymond P. Lorion, and M. Ramos-McKay. Washington, D.C.: American Psychological Association.

Karoly, Lynn A., Susan S. Everingham, Jill Hoube, Rebecca Kilburn, C. Peter Rydell, Peter W. Greenwood, Matthew Sanders, and James Chiesa. 1998. *Investing in Our Children: What We Know and Don't Know About the Costs and Benefits of Early Childhood Interventions.* Santa Monica, Calif.: Rand.

Krueger, Alan. 1997. "Experimental Estimates of Education Production Functions." Working paper 6051. Cambridge, Mass.: National Bureau of Economic Research.

Lally, J. Ronald, Peter L. Mangione, and Alice S. Honig. 1988. "The Syracuse University Family Development Research Program: Long-range Impact on an Early Intervention with Low-Income Children and Their Families." In *Parent Education as Early Childhood Intervention,* edited by Douglas R. Powell. Norwood, N.J.: Ablex.

Leigh, Duane. 1990. *Does Training Work for Displaced Workers?* Kalamazoo, Mich.: W.E. Upjohn Institute for Employment Research.

———. 1995. *Assisting Workers Displaced by Structural Change.* Kalamazoo, Mich.: W.E. Upjohn Institute for Employment Research.

Levenstein, Phyllis, John O'Hara, and John Madden. 1983. "The Mother-Child Program of the Verbal Interaction Project." In *As the Twig Is Bent: The Lasting Effects of Preschool Programs,* edited by the Consortium for Longitudinal Studies. Hillsdale, N.J.: Lawrence Erlbaum.

Lillard, Lee, and Hong Tan. 1986. *Private-Sector Training: Who Gets It and What Are Its Effects?* Santa Monica, Calif.: Rand.

Lochner, Lance. 1999. "Education, Work, and Crime: Theory and Evidence." Rochester Center for Economic Research working paper 465. University of Rochester, Rochester, N.Y.

Long, David A., Charles D. Mallar, and Craig V.D. Thornton. 1981. "Evaluating the Benefits and Costs of the Job Corps." *Journal of Policy Analysis and Management* 81(1): 55–76.

Lynch, Lisa. 1992. "Private-Sector Training and the Earnings of Young Workers." *American Economic Review* 82(1): 299–312.

———. 1993. *Training and the Private Sector: International Comparison.* Chicago: University of Chicago Press.

Mincer, Jacob. 1993. "Investment in U.S. Education and Training." Discussion paper 671. New York: Columbia University.

Monroe, E. A., and M. S. McDonald. 1981. "Follow-up Study of the 1996 Head Start Program." Rome, Ga: Rome City Schools.

National Center for Education Statistics (NCES). 1997. *The 1997 Digest of Education Statistics.* Washington: U.S. Government Printing Office.

Orfield, Gary. 1992. "Money, Equity, and College Access." *Harvard Educational Review* 62(3): 337–72.

Palmer, F. 1983. "The Harlem Study: Effects by Type of Training, Age of Training, and Social Class." In *As the Twig Is Bent: Lasting Effects of Preschool Programs,* edited by the Consortium for Longitudinal Studies. Hillsdale, N.J.: Lawrence Erlbaum.

Pawasarat, John, and Lois M. Quinn. 1993. "Evaluation of the Wisconsin WEJT/CWEP Welfare Employment Programs." Milwaukee: Employment and Training Institute, University of Wisconsin.

Phelps, Edmund. 1997. *Rewarding Work: How to Restore Participation and Self-Support to Free Enterprise.* Cambridge, Mass.: Harvard University Press.

Quint, Janet, Johannes Bos, and Denise Polit. 1997. *New Chance: Final Report on a Comprehensive Program for Young Mothers in Poverty and Their Children.* New York: Manpower Demonstration Research Corporation.

Ramey, Craig, Donna Bryant, Frances Campbell, Joseph Sparling, and Barbara H. Wasik. 1988. "Early Intervention for High-Risk Children: The Carolina Early Intervention Program." In *Fourteen Ounces of Prevention: A Casebook for Practitioners,* edited by Richard H. Price, Emory L. Cowen, Raymond P. Lorion, and M. Ramos-McKay. Washington, D.C.: American Psychological Association.

Schweinhart, Lawrence, Helen Barnes, and David Weikart. 1993. *Significant Benefits: The High/Score Perry Preschool Study Through Age Twenty-seven.* Ypsilanti, Mich.: High Scope Press.

Seitz, Victoria. 1990. "Intervention Programs for Impoverished Children: A Comparison of Educational and Family Support Models." *Annals of Child Development,* vol. 7. London: Jessica Kingsley Publishers.

Sipe, Cynthia. 1996. *Mentoring Adolescents: What Have We Learned?* Philadelphia: Public/Private Ventures.

Taggart, Robert. 1995. "Quantum Opportunity Program Opportunities." Philadelphia: Industrialization Center of America.

Tierney, Joseph, and Jean Grossman. 1995. *Making a Difference: An Impact Study of Big Brothers/Big Sisters.* Philadelphia: Public/Private Ventures.

U.S. Department of Labor, Office of the Chief Economist. 1995. "What's Working (and What's Not): A Summary of Research on the Economic Impacts of Employment and Training Programs." Washington, D.C.: U.S. Government Printing Office.

Walker, Gary, and Frances Viella-Velez. 1992. *Anatomy of a Demonstration.* Philadelphia: Public/Private Ventures.

Zigler, Edward. 1994. "Reshaping Early Childhood Intervention to Be a More Effective Weapon Against Poverty." *American Journal of Community Psychology* 22(1): 37–47.

Part II

Early Childhood

Chapter 3

Pathways to Early Child Health and Development

Barry Zuckerman and Robert Kahn

E arly child health and neurodevelopment provide a critical foundation for human asset development. The aim of this chapter is to describe the social and biologic pathways that both promote and undermine this foundation and offer the potential for new or refocused interventions. We examine selected childhood conditions that are prevalent and can convey long-term disadvantage. We focus on conditions that are subject to marked social disparities: the social patterning of disease often suggests the potential for interventions that would reduce health risks or increase health care access. In identifying upstream social determinants of early child outcomes, we focus on income poverty; because income data are not always available, however, we sometimes rely on data using correlates of income poverty, including race and education.

Existing models of child development emphasize the layered contexts that influence children: parents, neighborhoods, and broad social, economic, and political forces (Aber et al. 1997b; Bronfenbrenner 1979; Duncan and Brooks-Gunn 1997; Schor and Menaghan 1995). We propose a model for early child health and development that extends this work in three important regards (figure 3.1). First, we generalize existing models of child development to include child physical health outcomes. Empirical data link existing components of the models, such as parents and neighborhoods, to both developmental and physical health outcomes. A broadened approach to outcomes can then help further shape intervention strategies. Second, based on recent research findings, we include neurodevelopment, specifically brain development, as a major biologic endpoint of the pathway. Its inclusion in the model highlights the critical central nervous system "programming" and alterations that occur early in life as a result of the interaction between a child's developing brain and his environment. Third, the current emphasis on maternal mental health is expanded to include all aspects of maternal health. This broader view places maternal health and well-being in the role of a "final common pathway" for the social factors that influence early child outcomes. The transformation that allows social factors like poverty to "get under the skin" of very young children to cause disease is either directly mediated or indirectly modified in almost all cases by parents or caretakers (with most empirical work focusing on the role of mothers).

FIGURE 3.1   /   Pathways Leading to Early Child Health and Development

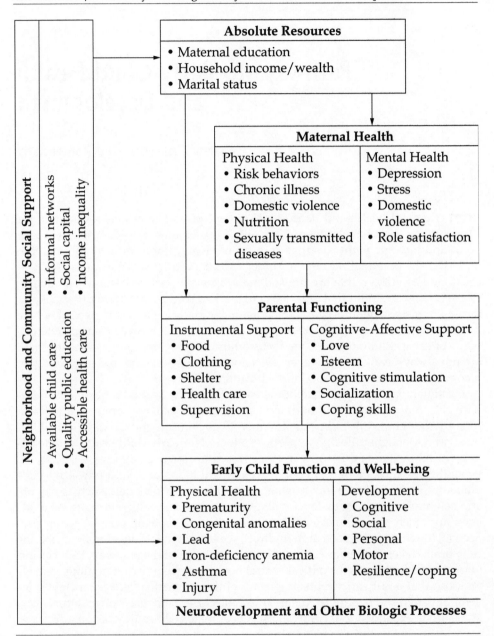

Source: Authors' compilation.

Adverse social conditions have a negative impact on the general health and well-being of women; socially distributed maternal risks are in turn conveyed to their children. Indeed, disparities in early child health closely reflect preexisting social disparities in the health of young women (Wise and Pursley 1992).

This chapter reviews current empirical support for the extended model outlined in figure 3.1. It starts with a description of recent research on neurodevelopment and early learning, then reviews a range of child outcomes, highlighting existing social disparities and elaborating on the role of maternal health. We then summarize current knowledge on the upstream roles of social context, including the influence of neighborhoods and income inequality. We conclude with a policy discussion of the interventions focused on early child learning and women's health that could uncouple adverse social forces from children's health and human asset development.

THE DEVELOPING BRAIN AND EARLY LEARNING
Brain Development

From an economic perspective, recent research on brain development underscores not only the tremendous potential of human asset development but also the biologic sensitivity of children to various deprivations and stresses. Early child health and neurodevelopment remain the core of human asset development because what is formed in the brain is the basis for later functioning. This includes cognition (problem-solving), language and literacy skills, emotional regulation, curiosity, caring for others, creativity, and fine and gross motor skills. These important attributes, which derive from the critical early interaction between a child's experience and the developing brain, form the basis not only for child well-being (an important end in itself) but also for later adult productivity at work and social relations within the family and community. If a time has to be chosen to increase economic investments in learning skills, the current evidence supports choosing the time when learning starts, at birth, not at age three or age six. We agree with James Heckman and Lance Lochner (this volume) that learning builds on itself, and that gaps can be hard to fill. Support and opportunities for learning vary by age, but the key is starting early and continuing throughout childhood. It is important to note, however, that while the biological evidence is clear that the earliest years may *set the stage*—or in some cases, *limit the stage*—much less work has been done to understand critical windows of opportunity in later childhood (Kupfer 1998).

The new understanding of brain development in children has emphasized the importance in these first years of the role of the brain in linking early experiences to later development and behavior (see also Ramey and Ramey, this volume). The architecture of the adult brain is shaped by very early experiences. Positron emission tomography (PET) scans, magnetic resonance imaging (MRI), and pathologic specimens have shown that in humans (unlike all other mammals) the full complement of approximately 100 billion neurons is formed before the third trimester of gestation.

However, the connections between these neurons take place in substantial part after birth. For example, at birth the human brain has about 50 trillion synapses. This number reaches a peak by three years of age with one quadrillion synapses. These appear to be more than are needed to function in any sociocultural environment, since half of these synapses are lost by age fifteen (Cowan 1979). It is believed that these excess synapses allow the organism to adapt to any evolutionary niche—from a solitary, primitive hunter-gatherer eons ago to a sophisticated, online member of modern society who may speak any one of hundreds of human languages. This exuberant synaptogenesis at birth is largely under genetic control (Shore 1997). Synapses are lost through the "pruning" of unused neural connections and the selective strengthening of those that are used to foster environmental adaptation (Huttenlocher 1984). Recent evidence suggests that this pruning is directed, in large part, by the child's experience. In a sort of "neural Darwinism," the synapses that are not utilized through the child's experience tend to wither.

Thus, the child's experience, like a sculptor carving a complex statue from a large block of stone, shapes the child's brain. But such "plasticity" of the neural networks does not last forever. As an example, language development is a key milestone of the first years. The infant's innate neural circuitry allows her brain to be able to recognize any phoneme. However, after a few years of experience in a certain linguistic environment, the child becomes able to differentiate only those phonemes she typically hears in her language and loses the ability to perceive other phonemes. For example, individuals who have spent their first decade in an Asian culture, where the phonemes r and l are interchangeable, are unable to differentiate those sounds (Werker and Tees 1984). PET scans have demonstrated that the r and l sounds are decoded in separate parts of the brain of an English-speaking person, but these sounds are processed in the exact same part of the brain of someone in a culture where differentiation of these phonemes has no semantic meaning (Chugani, Phelps, and Mazziotta 1987). In other words, the young brain is the ultimate "use it or lose it" system.

Another example is the difference in the ease of acquiring a second language in the early years compared to adolescence. If a child learns two languages in early childhood, he will speak both languages with sophisticated grammatical construction and accent. If a second language is learned in high school or college, even proficient speakers do not have as complete a mastery of grammatical construction or accent as early speakers or native speakers (MacLaughlin 1978). Furthermore, PET scans have shown that when a child grows up learning two languages, all language activity is found in the same place in the brain (Kim et al. 1997). Children who learn a second language at a later age show two foci of language activity. One interpretation is that learning a second language later in life is more difficult than when language is learned at its developmentally optimal time because it is processed and wired in a different place. This processing may rely much more heavily on memorization of words and rules of grammar.

The importance of early experience for brain development has also emerged from research on the hormone cortisol, a central mediator of the body's adaptive response to stress that, in normal circumstances, is released in the presence of an environmental challenge. Receptors for cortisol in the brain function like a thermostat to monitor and maintain control of the cortisol-based stress response.

The early postnatal environment, in particular early exposure to nurturance and stimulation, appears to modify the brain's ability to control the stress response (Carlson and Earls 1997; Meaney et al. 1996; Shore 1997). For example, in a population of extremely deprived children in a Romanian orphanage, cortisol levels failed to turn off after a mild stress and were highly correlated with the children's poor mental and motor performance and poor physical growth (Carlson and Earls 1997). In a study of U.S. preschool children, patterns of cortisol release in response to mild stress were significantly correlated with whether the child received sensitive, responsive caretaking and had a secure attachment to her mother (Gunnar et al. 1997). Laboratory work with animals appears to be consistent with the notion that the early environment "programs" the nervous system's response to stressors. Increased maternal grooming and licking of rat pups was found to augment gene expression of the cortisol receptors necessary for control of the stress response (Liu et al. 1997). This difference persisted into adulthood.

Poorly controlled cortisol release in response to stress has particularly adverse effects on the hippocampus, an area of the brain that is central to memory and learning. Excess cortisol is thought to result in hippocampal neuron damage and loss by altering vulnerability to other potential neurotoxins—namely, calcium and glutamate (McEwen 1998). MRI scans have shown actual atrophy of the hippocampus in persons with stress-related conditions, including recurrent depression and post-traumatic stress disorder (PTSD) from severe childhood physical and sexual abuse (Sapolsky 1996). These patients also appeared to be at increased risk of associated short-term memory deficits (Bremner et al. 1995b). Recent animal research also links cortisol to memory and learning capacity. Rats taught to swim to a platform lost that ability when subjected to stress-induced cortisol release. The stress did not interfere with their ability when cortisol release was chemically blocked. Conversely, when cortisol was directly injected, it was again impaired (de Quervain, Roozendaal, and McGaugh 1998). Although findings in animal models can be extended to human beings only with great caution, the sum of this early work on cortisol helps to highlight one of the complex mechanisms by which early experience shapes the brain's role in learning, memory, and behavior.

Early Learning

The gap between our understanding of neurodevelopment and child behavior and learning continues to narrow (Nelson and Bloom 1997), and this progress has provided a focus for much of the recent attention (Shore 1997). All infants are born learners, and learning occurs within relationships primarily with their parents and other caregivers. Learning in the early years focuses on basic building blocks, such as cause and effect, confidence, curiosity, self-control, the capacity to communicate, and relatedness. In this manner, early child health and development in general, and the developing brain in particular, can be viewed as a most critical economic asset.

With good caregiver experiences, young children learn to feel trusting, to experience intimacy with others, to communicate well before words are possible, and to grasp the beginnings of logic and reason.

The following vignettes of a feeding experience represent an example of infant learning (a type of learning that differs from what most adults think of as learning) (Zero to Three 1992).

A mother hears her two-month-old infant John crying at 3:00 A.M. She gets out of bed anticipating seeing and feeding her baby. When she reaches him, she picks him up and cradles him next to her body, then talks to him about being hungry. John nurses for about a half-hour, pausing occasionally to gaze up into the eyes of his mother, who responds by speaking softly to her son. Following burping, the mother puts John in the crib, kisses him, and covers him as he slowly begins to drift off to sleep.

John is learning many important things as a result of this interaction, which is repeated throughout the day. He is learning about cause and effect. His experience of hunger leads to crying, which brings his mother, who helps end his distress. He learns that the adults in his life are trustworthy and can be counted on to help him if he is frustrated or in need. Early learning occurs not only through books and flashcards but through everyday interactions such as this one.

Another mother hears her two-month-old baby Sean crying in the crib, also at 3:00 A.M. She has just fallen asleep after a fight with her husband. She has difficulty getting out of bed and shouts, "Just a minute, just a minute, I'm coming." When she reaches her baby, she lifts him up abruptly and puts him to her breast. She stares fixedly ahead, going over the recent fight with her husband. She grows more agitated as she recalls the details. Sean responds to his mother's tension by squirming restlessly, stiffening, and finally arching and drawing back from her nipple to cry. The mother responds, "You don't want to eat, fine, don't eat." She puts her somewhat hungry baby back into the crib and goes back to bed yelling, "Shut up, just shut up," in response to Sean's crying.

Baby Sean is also learning—that to be handled and held can be uncomfortable and distressing, and that being hungry and crying only leads to a harsh tone, rough handling, and partially met needs. He is learning to be wary and distrustful of others. Even learning about cause and effect is tainted for Sean because of the negative affect. John, by contrast, may develop a love of learning because the brain circuitry connects cause and effect to pleasure.

Although parent-child relationships are important during all stages of development, parent-child interactions in the first year have a special and lifelong influence on children's development. The influence on a child's emotional development extends not only to his readiness to succeed in school but also to his ability as an adolescent and young adult to succeed in other areas of life. Research shows that children who received sensitive, responsive care in the first few years of life were more likely to have the following positive developmental outcomes (Sroufe 1988):

- Ability to form relationships more easily with peers in preschool and early adolescence
- Higher levels of school achievement, especially in adolescence
- Lower likelihood of requiring special education
- Fewer behavioral problems
- Lower likelihood of using drugs and alcohol during adolescence

This research suggests that children who had an early history of responsive caretaking and secure relationships were less vulnerable to environmental threats than those who had poorer early relationships.

The new understanding of how children learn reading and writing (early literacy), called emergent literacy, emphasizes the importance of the skills children acquire while still very young (Whitehurst and Lonigan 1998). Previously, reading and writing were felt to be separate cognitive processes that required a specific form of tutoring in order to develop. As a result, formal reading and writing instruction began at school age (when children were seen as ready) and was considered far more important in the development of literacy than exposure to books in the home and reading aloud by parents. However, it is now understood that the development of literacy is a continuous process that begins early in life and is extremely dependent on environmental influences (Whitehurst et al. 1988). Literacy is a developmental process that occurs naturally when optimal conditions are present in the child's environment.

A 1985 National Commission on Reading study reported that reading aloud to children is the single most important intervention for developing their literacy skills. This can start by six months of age, when infants respond enthusiastically to pictures in books, especially pictures of faces. Sharing books with children at this age does not involve teaching the alphabet or words. Rather, books are used to point out pictures, tell stories, and make sounds. More generally, books provide an opportunity for focused, pleasurable interaction between parent and child that not only supports a child's literacy development but supports her social and emotional development, memory, curiosity, and fine motor skills (for example, turning pages). Even parents with minimal literacy skills can point to pictures to tell stories and have an enjoyable interaction with their child.

Early failure in learning to read affects 20 to 35 percent of American children. Children who grow up in poverty are at especially high risk (Fitzgerald, Spiegal, and Cunningham 1991). As a group, children from low-income families grow up with fewer books in the home and are exposed to relatively little reading aloud. These deficits could be due to lack of discretionary income to purchase books, lack of an understanding of the importance of reading to young children, lack of children's bookstores in most urban and rural settings, or parental illiteracy or difficulty in school that precludes parental enjoyment of reading.

EARLY CHILD OUTCOMES: EMERGING COMPONENTS OF THE CAUSAL PATHWAY

The Income–Child Outcome Link

If we conceptualize optimal health and development in young children—and in particular its biologic basis in the developing brain—as a critical goal of human asset development, then the pathways that promote or undermine that potential need to be better understood to identify strategies for intervention. We begin with evidence concerning income's impact on early child outcomes. We then consider the conceptual and empirical basis for understanding *how* income affects child outcomes, extending previous work with a new focus on the role of maternal health as a central mediator.

Poverty has a strong and consistently negative effect on child intelligence and achievement (Duncan and Brooks-Gunn 1997; Parker, Greer, and Zuckerman 1988). Poverty's effects have recently been better delineated with the use of prospective data sets and longitudinal income information. Greg Duncan and his colleagues, using data from the Infant Health and Development Program, found that a doubling of family income (averaged over time), from the poverty line to twice the poverty line, was associated with an increase of 3.6 points in child IQ at age five (Duncan, Brooks-Gunn, and Klebanov 1994). The duration of a child's poverty experience was also critical. Compared to never-poor children, children in persistent poverty (four years of poverty) averaged 9.1 IQ points less; children in transient poverty (one to three years of poverty) averaged 4.0 points less. Examining cumulative poverty exposure in relation to known covariates such as race-ethnicity, maternal education, and family structure provides important additional insights. After adjustment for the duration of poverty, the effect on child IQ of household structure disappeared and the effect of race was substantially diminished.

A recent book by Greg Duncan and Jeanne Brooks-Gunn (1997) detailed the effects of income on child achievement and behavior. In analyzing longitudinal data from a variety of sources, they found large negative effects of poverty on verbal, reading, and math test scores among children under six years; the impact on early child behavior was more mixed. Beyond the poverty threshold, increasing income in middle-class and affluent families had much more limited impact on child outcomes.

Beyond cognitive and developmental effects, research has also linked socioeconomic status to child mortality (including effects on infant mortality, mortality related to fire and injuries, and homicide) and morbidity (including both acute and chronic conditions) (Parker, Greer, and Zuckerman 1988; Starfield 1992; Starfield et al. 1991; Wise et al. 1985; Wise and Meyers 1988). The precise contribution of income, however, independent of parental education and other covariates, has not been studied as well because of the lack of adequate income data to capture the longitudinal poverty experience of children. Only two studies have examined the long-term poverty experience of families and its implications for child health.

Starfield and his colleagues (1991) found that persistent poverty among whites was associated with a 3.3-fold greater risk of a low-birthweight infant compared to non-poor whites, controlling for potential confounders. Black women had an elevated risk of giving birth to a low-birthweight infant regardless of income. Low height-for-age (stunting) and low weight-for-height (wasting) is also much more common among families living in long-term poverty (Miller and Korenman 1994).

Whether income causes or is simply associated with negative child outcomes has come under greater scrutiny recently (Mayer 1997). Observational studies may fail to account for omitted variables such as parental traits or values that might jointly determine income and child outcomes. Indeed, recent analyses seeking to account for such unmeasured parental characteristics found consistently smaller income effects than conventionally obtained (Mayer 1997). Nevertheless, these analyses had their own set of limitations. Several studies of outcomes in children have addressed this issue with a variety of strategies, including incorporating an expanded set of potentially confounding variables, examining change in outcome over time, comparing income effects on siblings, and using structural models. In most of these studies, income's effects are reduced but still significant, particularly for younger children and for those in deeper and more persistent poverty (Duncan and Brooks-Gunn 1997).

Model of Pathways Linking Income to Early Child Outcomes

The link between poverty and child outcomes has been well documented; attention has now turned to determining the specific intervening variables that lie in the pathway between them. As noted earlier, poverty must in some way "get under the skin" of a child to influence health and development. Recently the mediating roles of the home environment and maternal-child interactions with respect to developmental outcomes have been extensively documented (Duncan and Brooks-Gunn 1997). However, the general health and well-being of young women plays a central but often neglected role in the process as well. We posit that one important causal pathway starts with persistent adverse social conditions generating social disparities in the health and health-related knowledge of women. These social disparities may then be directly conveyed to their children; for example, maternal smoking or failure to take folate during pregnancy can undermine birth outcomes. Alternatively, these social disparities may more indirectly influence child outcomes; for example, a mother with no outside resources may be unable to shield her child from domestic violence, or an addicted mother on a treatment waiting list may be unable to obtain routine checkups for her infant.

The nature of this pathway varies with time. During pregnancy, social factors by definition operate entirely through maternal health to affect the fetus. After pregnancy, the linkage remains close, since a young child remains highly dependent on parental support (see figure 3.1). Only with time does the child have significant direct exposure to adverse social conditions in the community. Recognition of the maternal role, particularly in the early child years, elevates the importance of strategies that address the health of both women and their children.

Following the model outlined in figure 3.1, we now review child health and development conditions that are prevalent, subject to social stratification, and may have a long-term impact on human asset development. We focus on the mediating role of maternal health and well-being. The conditions are divided into birth outcomes and those rooted in early child health.

The Effect of Social Disparities in Maternal Health on Child Outcomes

BIRTH OUTCOMES   Adverse birth outcomes are related primarily to low birthweight and congenital anomalies. Approximately 7.4 percent of children are born at a low birthweight (less than 2,500 grams), and 1.4 percent are born at a very low birthweight (less than 1,500 grams) (Guyer et al. 1997). In 1996, 64 percent of infant deaths occurred among this 7.4 percent (Guyer et al. 1997). The morbidity associated with low birthweight includes such neurological sequelae as cerebral palsy, hydrocephalus, blindness, deafness, and seizures (Hack, Klein, and Taylor 1995), with the incidence ranging up to 20 percent in babies born under 1,000 grams (McCormick et al. 1992). Significant cognitive impairment can also result. The prevalence of mental retardation (IQ less than 70) in a population of children born in the mid-1980s varied from 21 percent in those born at less then 750 grams to 8 percent in those born at 750 to 1,500 grams (Hack et al. 1994; McCormick et al. 1992). Infants born at very low birthweight appear to account for approximately one-third of children with cerebral palsy and 10 percent of those with mental retardation (McCormick 1997).

Infant mortality and low birthweight are excellent examples of the degree to which disparities in child outcomes reflect social disparities in the general health status of women. Infant mortality in a population is determined by two components: the birthweight distribution and birthweight-specific mortality. In 1996 the black-to-white infant mortality rate ratio was 2.4 to 1 (Guyer et al. 1997). This disparity was almost entirely due to the higher incidence of black low-birthweight babies rather than to black mortality at any given birthweight. Racial disparities in infant low-birthweight rates in turn are a function of disparities in maternal health prior to delivery. This is mirrored in a rate of maternal mortality (death related to the pregnancy within six weeks of delivery) that is four times higher for black women compared to white women (Centers for Disease Control 1998a).

The substantial racial disparity in low-birthweight rates has been poorly understood, but recent research has begun to clarify pieces of the pathway. Robert Goldenberg and his colleagues (1996) found that black women of reproductive age are significantly more likely than white women to have bacterial vaginosis (a vaginal tract infection) during pregnancy (23 percent versus 9 percent). Bacterial vaginosis, in turn, increases by 40 percent the risk of prematurity and consequent low birthweight (Hillier et al. 1995). The higher prevalence of this infection in black women is estimated to explain 30 to 40 percent of the racial gap in prematurity rates (Fiscella 1996; Goldenberg et al. 1998). Of note, a recent intervention trial in which women with bacterial vaginosis received antibiotics in the second trimester of pregnancy reduced preterm delivery by 18 percent (Hauth et al. 1995). Thus, the social determinants of disparities in infant mortality act in part through a treatable infection in women of reproductive age. The challenge is that the infection must be identified before or at least early in pregnancy.

Spina bifida, one of the neural tube defects, is another condition that can confer lifelong disability on affected children and whose incidence demonstrates a socio-economic gradient (Wasserman et al. 1998). This pathway operates largely through maternal nutritional status prior to conception. Studies in the 1980s and early 1990s clearly demonstrated that inadequate folate intake can cause a malformation of the developing neural tube. Simple supplementation of folate reduced the incidence of the disease by 72 percent (*Lancet* 1991; Laurence et al. 1981). However, knowledge about folate, and about prenatal multivitamin use in general, remains significantly stratified by socioeconomic status (March of Dimes 1997; Yu et al. 1996). Despite recent folate enrichment of grain products, additional folate supplementation must start prior to or very early in the first trimester of pregnancy. This continues to leave low-income women, who have higher rates of unplanned pregnancy and delayed prenatal care (Brown and Eisenberg 1995), at increased risk. Again, a socially strat-ified, disabling, and largely preventable child health condition has its origins in the general health of women prior to pregnancy.

The impact of tobacco on birth outcomes and child morbidity is well documented. Cigarette smoking, the single largest modifiable risk factor for low birthweight and infant mortality (Shiono and Behrman 1995), is responsible for roughly 1,700 infant deaths per year (Centers for Disease Control 1993). Its consequences for children in-clude higher rates of asthma, ear infections, pneumonia, and sudden infant death (SIDS) (DiFranza and Lew 1996). The social stratification in smoking cessation among pregnant women remains substantial; women with a high school education or above are almost 50 percent more likely to quit than women with less than a high school education (National Center for Health Statistics 1997). Even though national policy concerning federal regulation of tobacco products has stalled, clinical innovation has produced nicotine patches and other pharmacological agents that assist in smoking cessation. Whether low-income populations with the greatest need will have full access to them remains in doubt. Nicotine patches are not usually covered by health insurance, and the recommended six-week course of therapy can cost over $150.

Finally, the negative impact of maternal substance abuse on birth outcomes is now amply documented (Zuckerman et al. 1989; Frank, Bresnahan, and Zuckerman 1993). Though socioeconomic disparities in maternal substance abuse may be over-estimated (Chasnoff, Landress, and Barrett 1990), maternal substance abuse with an onset well before pregnancy is yet another example of the mechanisms by which poverty's cumulative influence on women's health is ultimately translated into disparate birth outcomes.

EARLY CHILD OUTCOMES   The impact of women's health on the health of their chil-dren is not limited to birth outcomes; maternal health conditions and behaviors continue to mediate the link between social factors and child outcomes well after delivery. Significant progress has been made in understanding its contributions to social disparities in child development. The effects of persistent poverty found by Duncan, Brooks-Gunn, and Klebanov (1994) are explained in substantial measure by parental mental health, social support, and the home environment (learning stimulation, parent-child interaction). The mediating effects of parental mental health and the home environment have been demonstrated now in several studies (Korenman, Miller, and Sjaastad 1994; Miller 1998).

The vulnerability of child behavioral and developmental outcomes to maternal depression has been increasingly recognized. Cognitive outcomes for young children have been clearly linked to early maternal depression. These effects appear to persist through ages four to five (Cooper and Murray 1998). Another study found that three-year-old children whose mothers were depressed had worse reading skills at age eight (Richman, Stevenson, and Graham 1982). Depressive symptoms in a mother appear to lead to diminished maternal-infant attachment and less spontaneous interaction with the child (Zuckerman and Beardslee 1987). Recent work suggests that these children exhibit significantly reduced activity in a region of the brain specialized for expression of positive emotions (Dawson et al. 1997). The prevalence of maternal depression shows a strong social gradient, correlating with educational attainment, housing, marital relationship, work role, and stressful life events (Weissman and Olfson 1995; Zuckerman and Beardslee 1987). The documented links between social disadvantage and maternal mental health, and, in turn, between maternal mental health and child outcomes, again highlight the role of maternal health as a mediator in the causal pathway.

Child abuse and neglect have been the focus of considerable public attention, but less well recognized is the impact of witnessing violence on child health and development (Taylor et al. 1994; Zuckerman et al. 1995). An estimated 1.8 million women a year are physically assaulted by their husbands or partners (Stets and Straus 1990). A 1985 survey reported that more than 3.3 million children per year witnessed physical abuse between their parents (Strauss and Gelles 1986). Children who witness domestic violence are at risk for a range of sequelae, from mild behavioral and emotional problems to post-traumatic stress disorder (Kilpatrick, Litt, and Williams 1997). Of note, a recent study found atrophy in the hippocampal region of the brain in adults with PTSD associated with childhood abuse (Bremner et al. 1997); other studies have identified similar findings in Vietnam veterans with PTSD (Bremner et al. 1995a; Gurvits et al. 1996). Domestic violence is reported to be more prevalent among women who are younger and less educated (Centers for Disease Control 1994); this social stratification, however, may reflect substantial underreporting in other groups. Children who are poor are more likely to witness violence in their community; thus, it is likely that cumulative violence exposure is socially stratified. Much work remains to be done to delineate the long-term consequences for children; nevertheless, early evidence suggests that violence against women has substantial ripple effects on the health of children.

More traditional threats to child health still exist, though their impact has been increasingly marginalized to low-income children. Iron deficiency remains the most common nutrient deficiency in children. An estimated 9 percent of children ages twelve to thirty-six months are iron-deficient, and 3 percent have iron-deficiency anemia (IDA). Rates are approximately double in poor children and black children. The social patterns of IDA closely mirror those found in women of reproductive age (Centers for Disease Control 1998b; Looker et al. 1997). The sequelae of early iron-deficiency anemia include persistent developmental delays and behavior problems such as decreased attention to tasks and poor social interaction (Booth and Aukett 1997; Lozoff, Jimenez, and Wolf 1991). Furthermore, IDA predisposes children to greater gastrointestinal absorption of lead. Lead toxicity (defined as a lead level above ten micrograms/deciliter) itself now affects 4.4 percent of U.S. children between the ages of one and five, a significant improvement since 1976 (Pirkle et al. 1994). The current rates, however, are substantially higher in lower-income children than in higher-income children (8 percent versus 1 percent), and higher in black children than in white children (11 percent versus 2 percent) (Centers for Disease Control 1997). Even mildly elevated lead levels have been associated with lower IQ, reading disability, impaired coordination, and school dropout (Bellinger et al. 1991; Bellinger, Stiles, and Needleman 1992; Needleman et al. 1990). The improved iron and lead status of middle- and upper-income children threatens to distract public attention away from the continued importance of these problems. The dependence of children on their parents for supervision of their nutrition and their home environment makes it unlikely that these conditions will be alleviated without targeted efforts to address the disparities in the health-related knowledge of parents.

THE IMPACT OF PATERNAL HEALTH   The historical emphasis on a maternal and child health agenda has left a large empirical gap with respect to paternal health. There are limited data on the direct paternal health contribution to child outcomes outside of genetic inheritance. Most studies focus on the effects of paternal health behaviors. Paternal smoking has been linked to increased prevalence of childhood respiratory symptoms and asthma (Cook and Strachan 1997; Ehrlich et al. 1996), low birthweight (Martinez, Wright, and Taussig 1994), birth defects (Zhang et al. 1992), SIDS (Alm et al. 1998; Blair et al. 1996), cancer (Ji et al. 1997), and health risk behaviors (Burke et al. 1998; DiLorenzo et al. 1998). Among the most significant effects of paternal smoking is its negative influence on pregnant women's capacity to quit smoking and to sustain cessation (Wakefield et al. 1998). Paternal alcohol use is associated with behavior problems in children (Carbonneau et al. 1998). There is a strong link between paternal obesity and child obesity, though the appropriate apportioning of risk to shared genetic factors versus common behavioral and nutritional patterns is still unclear (Lake, Power, and Cole 1997; Whitaker et al. 1997).

Fathers are known to influence behavior patterns in their children (Moss et al. 1995), and positive parental involvement with low-birthweight infants is associated with improved cognitive outcomes (Yogman, Kindlon, and Earls 1995). Children benefit from the presence of fathers in the household. Children in continuously intact two-parent families have relatively fewer academic, behavioral, and psychological problems compared to children in divorced families (Amato

1994). Yet the degree to which positive paternal effects are mediated by added time and affection or by increased household income remains unclear (Smith, Brooks-Gunn, and Klebanov 1997). Among single-mother households, continued paternal involvement was associated with better academic achievement and fewer behavior problems (Coley 1998).

THE IMPACT OF CUMULATIVE STRESSES   Each of these threats to child health probably has an independent effect on brain development, but many of them occur at the same time. Multiple social and family risk factors combine to increase the risk for poor child outcomes (Parker, Greer, and Zuckerman 1988; Sameroff et al. 1993; Sameroff et al. 1987; Zuckerman et al. 1989). For example, consider a child born at thirty-four weeks' gestation to a single mother living in poverty who received minimal prenatal care. Following a three-week hospitalization, the infant is mildly hypotonic and has difficulty maintaining an alert state. The mother feels overwhelmed and depressed. The child's passivity exacerbates the mother's feelings of inadequacy, resulting in a worsening of her depression. Positive interactions with her child are rare. The child does not look to the environment for his stimulation, nor does he vocalize much. This further heightens the mother's feelings of inadequacy and depression. The child's neurological development is further challenged by mild iron-deficiency anemia and a modest lead burden. By two years the child will be clearly delayed in language and cognitive development. What is the cause of his developmental delay? It is the biologic vulnerability secondary to prematurity and anemia, exacerbated by maternal depression, inadequate environmental stimulation, and insufficient social support. In fact, all these factors operate together to shape the child's outcome. Each factor modifies and potentiates the other. Together, they weave a complex pattern that cannot be fully understood by examining the thread of only a single risk.

LATENT HEALTH OUTCOMES: CHILDHOOD ANTECEDENTS TO ADULT DISEASE   The significance of exposure to early childhood risks is likely to be underestimated if health outcomes are measured only in the short term. Increasingly, socioeconomic status in childhood appears to be an important predictor of adult health outcomes. In a prospective observational study, George Davey Smith and his colleagues found that social class in childhood, independent of social class in adulthood, influenced adult mortality from stroke, stomach cancer, and coronary heart disease (Davey Smith et al. 1997; Davey Smith et al. 1998). A study of more than thirteen thousand adults in a large health maintenance organization found a strong graded association between childhood exposure to abuse (psychological, physical, or sexual) or household dysfunction (parental violence, substance abuse, mental illness, or imprisonment) and multiple risk factors for several leading causes of death in adults (Felitti et al. 1998). In addition, fetal undernutrition and low birthweight appear to increase the likelihood of several risk factors for cardiovascular disease. These may operate by programming the body for altered responses to insulin and growth hormone as one in utero adaptation to decreased nutrients (Barker 1995, 1997). It remains controversial whether fetal nutrition and birthweight independently predict adult mortality and are not simply correlates of socioeconomic status in childhood (Kramer and Joseph 1996).

Both child outcomes (such as prematurity, iron deficiency, asthma, and developmental delay) and women's health status (for example, bacterial vaginosis, poor nutrition, smoking, and depression) are strongly linked to each other and to upstream social factors. Not surprisingly, the few studies that focus on women's health (usually depression) in their models as a potential mediator of social factors have found sizable effects (Duncan, Brooks-Gunn, and Klebanov 1994; Korenman, Miller, and Sjaastad 1994; Miller 1998). Yet analytically, women's health has been approached as a series of distinct risk factors posing threats to specific child outcomes. Lost has been the breadth and depth of the influence of women's physical and mental health on child health, both as a mediator of social forces and as an independent determinant of child health. Many intervention and policy opportunities have been missed as a result of the failure to recognize that many child health disparities have their origins further upstream in the general health of women. A more integrative model of these relationships can inform both conceptual and practical approaches to future investments in children (figure 3.2).

FIGURE 3.2 / The Mediating Role of Women's Health in Child Health Outcomes

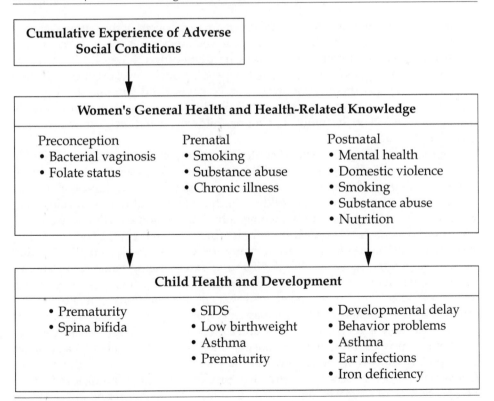

Source: Authors' compilation.

The close relationship between women's health and well-being and child outcomes can also be framed in the context of broader discussions of the investments that adults make in their children. Economists have sought to explain variations in the success of children by examining the availability of parental resources and time, and the choices made regarding the distributions of these assets to their children. Yet it seems clear that women's health—perhaps usefully conceptualized as "health capital" (Cutler and Richardson 1999)—represents a human asset that has a powerful and persisting influence on early child well-being. The clinical twist on the economic theory is the degree to which women are able to make real choices about their health even when framed as an important "investment" on behalf of their children. The fundamental constraints on choice that define, for example, domestic violence, depression, addiction, and unwanted pregnancy, as well as the profound social patterning of these conditions, suggest that parental "investment" models built on individual preferences and rational choice assumptions cannot adequately explain child outcomes. A model that can better account for the health component of women's assets may substantially increase its capacity to explain child outcomes.

The Effect of Social Context on Child Outcomes

NEIGHBORHOOD INFLUENCES A more upstream component of the pathways influencing child outcomes that has received renewed attention is the social context of neighborhoods and communities (Brooks-Gunn, Duncan, and Aber 1997). Lawrence Aber and his colleagues (1997a) posit that, depending on the level of contact between a child and a neighborhood's resources (schools, parks, child care, and so on), neighborhood effects may have a direct impact on the child or may operate more indirectly through their effect on the family. For young children, the indirect, family-mediated effect has been postulated.

The influence of neighborhood context on young children has been less well explored than its effects on older children; nevertheless, several studies merit attention. A series of analyses have examined neighborhood effects on child outcomes among low-birthweight children in the Infant Health and Development Program. Controlling for family income, a higher fraction of affluent neighbors appeared to increase child IQ at three years (Brooks-Gunn et al. 1993) and at five years (Duncan, Brooks-Gunn, and Klebanov 1994). Conversely, a higher fraction of poor neighbors increased the likelihood of externalizing behavior problems, again independent of family income. Explanations of these findings are tentative, since the studies were not designed to answer specific questions on neighborhood effects. However, one possible explanation is that the presence of affluent neighbors leads to a stronger economic base and a greater availability of private services and community resources (Chase-Lansdale et al. 1997). Alternatively, a stronger set of positive norms or social networks may be in place in these neighborhoods. Conversely, in neighborhoods with a large proportion of poor families, there may be a perception of increased danger, and a child's aggressive, acting-out behavior may be seen as adaptive (Duncan, Brooks-Gunn, and Klebanov 1994).

SOCIAL CAPITAL   These preliminary findings suggest that "social capital" plays an important role in explaining neighborhood effects on child outcomes. Social capital may be thought of as the resources that inhere in the relationships between and among people, such as within families, communities, or other social organizations, and that result in networks, norms, and social trust (Coleman 1990). Measurement of social capital in a neighborhood may include attempts to capture family or individual membership in community groups, shared information networks, informal mechanisms to monitor each other's children, and trust between neighbors (Brooks-Gunn, Duncan, and Aber 1997).

Few studies have examined the association between social capital and outcomes for young children. Ichino Kawachi and colleagues (1997) found that state-to-state variation in infant mortality rates was related to several indicators of social capital, including the average number of groups or associations to which state residents belonged and the average level of mutual trust among residents (measured in response to the question "Do you think most people would try to take advantage of you if they got a chance, or would they try to be fair?"). A second study of "high-risk" preschool children used a different measure of the parents' social capital (church affiliation, perception of social support, and neighborhood support) and found a strong association with two measures of child development and behavior (Runyan et al. 1998). The generalizability of the findings, however, should be viewed cautiously, since the sample was a unique mix of biologic and foster parents caring for children both "at risk" for maltreatment and already subject to maltreatment. Finally, Jason Fields and Kristin Smith (1998) examined the relationship between neighborhood social capital and grade retention among children aged six to seventeen years, using data from the Survey of Income and Program Participation (SIPP). Although strong bivariate associations were found, effects attributable to social capital disappeared once other individual household characteristics were accounted for in a multivariate model.

INCOME INEQUALITY   There has been a perceived erosion of social capital in the United States (Putnam 1995). An unprecedented increase in income inequality has been proposed as one explanation for this erosion (Kawachi and Kennedy 1997; Wilkinson 1997). Rising income and wealth disparities between the rich and the poor are the subject of increased public attention. Between 1977 and 1994, families in the highest income quintile saw their average after-tax income rise 25 percent, compared to a 16 percent drop among those in the bottom quintile (Shapiro and Greenstein 1997). Wealth disparities have increased even faster: between 1983 and 1989, the top 1 percent of income recipients garnered 62 percent of the new wealth that was generated (Wolff 1995).

Recent medical literature suggests that relative income inequality may have effects on adult mortality that are independent of a household's absolute income. Across developed countries and among the fifty states, greater income disparity between the rich and the poor is associated with shorter life expectancy and higher rates of mortality from coronary heart disease, suicide, and homicide (Wilkinson 1996). In studies of the fifty states, absolute income, measured as either state median income or percentage in poverty, was only weakly associated with state rates of various health outcomes (Kaplan et al. 1996; Kennedy, Kawachi, and Prothrow-Stith 1996). Bruce Kennedy and his colleagues (1996) found that state income disparity explained 20 percent of the variance in state-to-state infant mortality rates. Kaplan and his colleagues (1996) reported an even stronger relationship between income inequality and infant mortality and low-birthweight rates.

Disagreement remains over the nature of the association between income inequality and poor health. Some argue that the inequality-health findings should be viewed tentatively at best. The majority of studies have relied on ecological data and omitted key variables, such as individual absolute income (Gravelle 1998). The three studies that included both ecological- and individual-level data showed more mixed results (Daly et al. 1998; Fiscella and Franks 1997; Kennedy et al. 1998). Others suggested that the ecological effect is real, but that societies that tolerate high levels of income inequality also tolerate underinvestment in community structural resources. It is through this structural underinvestment that income inequality leads to poor health (Davey Smith 1996; Kaplan et al. 1996). For example, among the fifty states, high income disparity is strongly associated with reduced investment in education and higher rates of unemployment, incarceration, and lack of medical insurance (Kaplan et al. 1996). Lastly, Wilkinson (1996) and others suggested that in countries with a high per capita income, absolute income indeed has little impact. Income inequality acts to reduce social cohesion, which, in turn, operates through psychosocial mechanisms to create stress, depression, social isolation, and ultimately poor health. One potential danger of this social cohesion argument is that it may undermine calls for greater material support and resources for young families (Skocpol 1996).

Much work remains to be done to understand the effects of social context on young children. Conceptual models need to delineate more fully how the relevant neighborhood social and structural resources ultimately relate to young children. Different pathways are probably important depending on the child outcome examined. What does a lack of social capital or a high level of income inequality mean to an infant, toddler, or preschool-age child? Little is known about how parents, siblings, extended family, and out-of-home caretakers might mediate these effects on children. Clearly, more nuanced approaches combining aggregate and individual data, along with a wider range of child health outcomes, are needed to understand fully the impact of income inequality on child health.

POLICY APPROACHES TO IMPROVING EARLY CHILD OUTCOMES
Providing the Basics for Child Well-being

There is a large literature on programs to meet children's basic needs (Devaney, Ellwood, and Love 1997; Lewit, Terman, and Behrman 1997; Plotnick 1997). We focus here on initiatives that offer the opportunity to uncouple adverse social factors from their effects on the health of women and their children.

Women's Health: Access to Effective Health Services

If major advances in child health and development are to be made over the next decade, much greater attention must be paid to women's health and health services. The full extent of women's health and health behaviors that bear on child outcomes remains significantly underappreciated. As discussed earlier, these wide-ranging conditions usually exist prior to conception, and their impact often begins well before any effective prenatal care intervention can be put in place or be effective. Many of these problems continue to have a negative impact long after delivery. Effective treatments for such problems as domestic violence, depression, poor nutrition, cigarette smoking, drug and alcohol use, and infections require timely and prolonged therapies that are not well served by prenatal care that starts long after conception and often ends with a single postpartum visit. Maternal and child health has a long and illustrious history, but traditional strategies that emphasize reproductive health, and specifically prenatal care, are unlikely to address adequately the women's and children's conditions outlined here.

New, effective clinical interventions for such problems as depression (Katon et al. 1995), smoking (Hurt et al. 1997), drug addiction (National Consensus Development Panel on Effective Medical Treatment of Opiate Addiction 1998), and emergency and nonemergency contraception (Glasier 1997) increase the need to reevaluate existing systems of care for women. The goal must be improving the capacity to engage women in comprehensive health care before, during, and after pregnancy so that they have timely access to these treatments. Substantial barriers, however, continue to limit access for women of reproductive age. Between 10 and 16 percent of women report no regular source of health care (Bindman et al. 1996; Cornelius, Beauregard, and Cohen 1991). In 1997, 19.6 percent of women between eighteen and forty-four were uninsured; the rate for eighteen- to twenty-four-year-old women, 26.4 percent, was particularly high (U.S. Bureau of the Census 1999). Among those women receiving public health insurance, there is often significant discontinuity. More than one-quarter of Medicaid recipients under age sixty-five disenroll within two years (Farley Short 1996); among sixteen- to thirty-four-year-old recipients, the rate appears to be far higher (Carrasquillo et al. 1998). Approximately 15 percent of disenrollees are women who qualified only because of a pregnancy and lost coverage soon after delivery (Farley Short 1996). Uninsured women are more likely to report themselves to be in fair or poor health and less likely to have had a Pap smear, breast examination, or cholesterol screen (Centers for Disease Control 1995). Indeed, children have better access to care than their mothers: almost 40 percent of women with a young child reported at least one barrier to comprehensive health care (Kahn et al. 1999).

Even those women who enter the health care system face substantial fragmentation of their health services (Weisman 1996). Obstetrician-gynecologists tend to be more thorough in the provision of Pap smears, breast examinations, and mammography, while other adult care providers are more likely to offer cholesterol screening, smoking cessation aids, and screening and initial treatment for depression. The likelihood that a woman sees both a gynecologist and an internist increases with higher income and more years of education. A second contributing factor has been the splintering of reproductive health care services, such as family planning and abortion, from mainstream medicine (Gottlieb 1995).

One way to improve the health of women of reproductive age and their children might be to eliminate the financial barriers to health care faced by many adults. Given the focus on the expansion of Medicaid and State Children's Health Insurance Program (SCHIP), a recent analysis examined the possibility of enrolling the parents of these children as well (Thorpe and Florence 1998). In the families of uninsured children who are likely to be eligible for Medicaid or SCHIP, there are 5.1 million uninsured parents. There are another 1.5 million uninsured parents of children already enrolled in Medicaid. Program expansion to uninsured parents of SCHIP-eligible children might cover approximately 1.8 million adults at a combined federal and state cost of $4.2 billion; expansion of Medicaid to parents of Medicaid-eligible children would cover an estimated 5.2 million adults at a cost of $12.8 billion. Such an effort would probably have positive ripple effects, with increased participation rates for children and the opportunity for continuous, family-centered health care. State variations in implementation offer an opportunity to investigate the outcomes and costs of such expansions (Guyer and Mann 1999).

Finally, initiatives that jointly address the health needs of women and children might alleviate some policy conflicts. The intense focus on the health of infants and children with relatively little regard for the general health of young women is reflected in the current proliferation of infant mortality initiatives. Almost every state has a program to provide prenatal care and infant health care services, yet only five states have a component that addresses women's health more broadly (Chavkin, Breitbart, and Wise 1995). Beyond the programmatic implications, this child-first approach has generated conflicts in which specific maternal health behaviors are viewed merely as threats to the fetus rather than as harmful to the mother as well. The result has been prosecution of pregnant women around a variety of health issues, including drug use and medical compliance (Annas 1987; Chavkin et al. 1998).

Public Health: Reaching All Women of Reproductive Age

Because roughly 50 percent of births are first births, an approach that is limited to women who already have children does not ultimately address those health behaviors and conditions that affect first pregnancies. The need for more universal approaches to health insurance remains imperative to improve the general health status of young women. Moreover, medical insurance to cover traditional health services is only part of the access problem. The social patterns around inadequate use of folate, incorrect positioning of infants for sleep, limited access to over-the-counter smoking cessation aids, barriers to the marketing of emergency contraception, and inadequate provisions for women subject to domestic violence need to be confronted. Public health strategies must be developed to target messages for selected groups of mothers at high risk because of low literacy, limited English proficiency, and social or cultural marginalization.

Such an effort must not only provide women with basic health-related information but also seek to change social norms regarding both the long-term implications of health during the reproductive years and its relationship to children's health. General health promotion efforts have gone a long way toward reducing cigarette smoking, drinking, and driving, but targeted messages for young women have primarily focused on pregnancy (for example, early prenatal care enrollment). Campaigns that highlight the mutual benefits for women and their children of breastfeeding, folic acid supplementation, protection against domestic violence, treatment of depression, and particularly, smoking cessation should be explored. Particular attention must be paid to linguistic and cultural barriers to ensure that messages reach all women at risk.

Much has been learned about the process of behavior change among adults. Not only does this information need to be disseminated among professionals, but the information should also be part of a public health campaign to give individuals information to understand better the context of their behaviors and the potential barriers to or support for achieving behavior change.

Other public health agents can alter health outcomes for women and their children through systems such as home visiting. Home visiting by nurses during the prenatal period and early years of a child's life has shown a number of positive influences. In one large randomized trial, home visiting decreased the rate of repeat pregnancies, the prevalence of high-risk health behaviors (Olds and Kitzman 1990), the length of AFDC receipt, arrests, and perpetration of child abuse (Olds et al. 1997). Nurse-visited children had fewer injuries and demonstrated greater intellectual achievement, owing in part to the intervention's effects on maternal health behaviors (Olds, Henderson, and Tatelbaum 1994). At a fifteen-year follow-up, these children showed significantly lower rates of antisocial behaviors and emergent substance abuse (Olds et al. 1998).

These particularly impressive outcomes for women and children should be viewed with some caution because there is considerable variation in the conceptualization, content, and implementation of home visiting programs (Gomby, Culross, and Behrman 1999; Gomby et al. 1993). A review of seventeen parent-focused, home-based early intervention programs found that relatively few examined maternal outcomes, and that among programs that did, the strongest maternal effects remain those found in the Olds project (Brooks-Gunn, Berlin, and Sidle Fuligni 1998). Moreover, many targeted outcomes, such as reduction in the rate of low-birthweight births, have not been achieved. Despite these limitations, research to date provides evidence to support the use of home visiting services as one component of a system of care for women and children.

The potential of center-based early intervention programs should also be noted. The Infant Health and Development Program, a center-based program for low-birthweight children, has documented significant improvements in maternal status, including reduced depressive symptoms (Brooks-Gunn, Berlin, and Sidle Fuligni 1998) and increased access to health insurance (Brooks-Gunn et al. 1994). In addition, there is an extensive literature that examines the positive influence of both home visiting and center-based care on other maternal behaviors that are not specifically related to their health per se—namely, those maternal behaviors relevant to maternal-child interactions. Research has demonstrated that these interventions can enhance maternal capacity to provide enriched, supportive environments at home for children, with positive benefits for child development.

The literature suggests that child intervention programs that include components to address maternal outcomes can make a difference for both women and their children. The common paradigm is one that recognizes the parent as a key component of the pathway through which child outcomes can be improved. Important questions remain. Would there be additional (or even synergistic) positive effects on women's and children's outcomes if central issues like parental mental health were addressed? What should the content, timing, and duration of these new components be? Could effects demonstrated in model programs be sustained once they were implemented more broadly? The full potential of child-intervention programs with respect to improved maternal health and child outcomes should remain an area of active investigation.

Innovative Programs to Improve Early Child Outcomes

DEVELOPING INTEGRATED MODELS OF PEDIATRIC CARE   Despite the range of home visitation models, most have remained largely unconnected to clinical care for children. One early programmatic effort, Pediatric Pathways to Success, recently demonstrated the potential of integrating home visiting into traditional pediatric primary care. Compared to historical controls, children who received the integrated model had reduced rates of both hospitalization and emergency room use (Kaplan-Sanoff, Brown, and Zuckerman 1997).

Drawing on this success, a new national initiative entitled Healthy Steps for Young Children is being evaluated (Zuckerman et al. 1997). Healthy Steps seeks to restructure the way pediatric care is delivered to promote child development and women's health more fully. Expanded services include home visitors originating from the pediatric practice, parent groups, enhanced information for parents, and increased linkages with community resources. Pediatric practices have been randomized in over twenty sites in an effort to evaluate the program's health impact and costs. A family's ability to benefit fully from these new resources may depend on the extent to which its basic needs have been met (food, safety, and housing), but the program seeks to close one of the many gaps that undermine services for young children and their parents.

PROMOTING EARLY LITERACY   Data from a random national sample of parents show that lack of reading to young children is not confined to those families with a low income; 16 percent of all parents did not read to their child during the past week, and 23 percent read to their child only one or two times (Taaffe Young et al. 1998). Although low-income families in particular may face such hurdles as lack of books, poor access to bookstores, and language barriers, there are additional barriers that parents of all income strata may face. Single parents and dual-career parents may not have time and energy when they come home from work or may not understand the importance of reading to their children. Efforts to promote early literacy need to address these and other barriers.

From a policy standpoint, books should be made available to young children. Reopening closed neighborhood libraries and instituting mobile library vans are two strategies. Child settings, such as child care, family support programs, and pediatric practices are other potential sites to accomplish such a goal. For example, an intervention designed and offered by pediatricians called Reach Out and Read provides age-appropriate books at each well-child visit for low-income children between six months and five years, as well as advice to parents about age-appropriate literacy-promoting activities. An initial evaluation of this effort demonstrated that mothers were four times more likely—and mothers on welfare were eight times more likely—to read to their children compared to mothers not in the program (Needlman et al. 1991). Subsequent studies have replicated these findings and extended the documented benefits to include more books in the home and enhanced language development (Golova et al. 1999; High et al. 1998). Parallel efforts to ensure that age-appropriate books and literacy activities are available in all child-care settings should be evaluated in terms of outcomes and costs.

Until recently, little public policy attention or funding for reading programs has been directed at the early child years. For example, only 5 percent of books in the federally funded Reading Is Fundamental program go to children five years and younger. Legislation is pending in the U.S. Senate that would provide funds for books for children under five years in amounts similar to those being spent for school-age children. A number of states have also included funds in their budgets to make books available to low-income children.

Another strategy to promote child literacy is to promote parental literacy and literacy-related activities. Messages about the importance of reading to children can be disseminated through posters on the walls of child-care centers, pediatrician offices, and supermarkets or through print and television media. Messages should be tailored to meet the specific cultural and linguistic needs of minorities. More fundamentally, these efforts should promote parental literacy and English as a second language (ESL). Presently, most adult literacy and ESL programs have long waiting lists because they are underfunded. Parents who are themselves proficient are in a better position to promote child literacy activities. Policies that support adult literacy offer an opportunity to improve family health outcomes as well. When parents have difficulty understanding information on prescription bottles, patient education materials, discharge instructions, and appointment slips, there are well-documented health consequences (Ad Hoc Committee on Health Literacy for the Council on Scientific Affairs 1999).

COMMITTING CHILD-FOCUSED PROFESSIONALS TO THE HEALTH OF WOMEN Since attention to the well-being of her child is often the best way to engage a mother concerning her own health needs, professionals and programs involved with young children are important gateways to comprehensive health care for women, especially those with unmet needs. Although the fragmentation of health and social services makes it difficult to link the health of women and their children, there are several strategies that might effectively move us toward a comprehensive, two-generational approach to child health.

Practitioners and programs that serve children from conception through the earliest years of life can no longer afford to miss opportunities to improve children's health by enhancing the health, safety, and well-being of their mothers. Using child health, early care and education, and early intervention settings as the gateway to comprehensive women's health care holds promise as a sustainable, generalizable approach to a two-generational health care strategy.

Community-based program staff in a wide range of settings can help to reintegrate fragmented health and social services, beginning with the mothers and children they serve in their own settings. They can identify clinicians in their community who are interested in addressing the health needs of women comprehensively, including nutrition, gynecological care, and behavioral health. Special attributes, such as consultation in languages other than English, should be noted. Practitioners can then make a list of adult health care providers in the community who are available to program participants. In addition, they can help mothers make appointments with adult health practitioners and monitor referrals to ensure that they "take."

In the effort to enhance and expand pediatric care to a two-generational approach, pediatricians can help to address the unmet health needs of women by emphasizing to the mother the importance of her own health care, both for her own sake and for that of her child's well-being. The provider should stress the importance of a regular source of health care in which a trusting relationship can be developed. A study in four pediatric primary care settings recently found that two-thirds of mothers bringing their infants for health supervision visits reported health problems of their own, including asthma, smoking, depression, and physical abuse; almost 40 percent reported at least one barrier to getting health care for themselves (Kahn et al. 1999). Unfortunately, traditional child health, early child care and education, and early intervention services have no regular mechanisms in place to reach out to women, assess their health care needs, and connect them to appropriate care.

Assuming that confidentiality in a setting is ensured, nurses, family advocates, social workers, and others who have developed a relationship with a mother can help her assess her health care needs and suggest appropriate services. A "women's wellness record" that could be used by women to collect and record their health history, including illnesses and hospitalizations, prenatal history, medications, allergies, and preventive screening results is one approach under investigation. The record would contain self-help information and information on health promotion and disease prevention, especially in connection with domestic violence, depression, and other mental health problems, diet, family planning, exercise, cigarette smoking, alcohol use, and other issues. Like a child health and development record, the women's wellness record would belong to the woman. Its purpose would be to help her take ownership of her health problems and to serve as a complete record of health information that she could share with different health providers. Although a woman could fill out the record herself, a staff member who already has a relationship with her might spend time with her completing the initial information to identify potential health issues and suggest needed services.

CONCLUSION

Early child health and development provide a basic foundation for human asset development. In this chapter, we have sought to characterize more fully the pathways that influence this foundation and to identify additional opportunities for intervention. First, we believe that work on early child outcomes can now be anchored in basic neurobiology and brain development. Basic research has begun to outline the neural wiring involved in the processes critical for early learning and future success, including language development, memory, and emotional regulation. The advantage of anchoring child outcomes in such a way is evident in the recent attention to early nurturance and children's brain development. Second, we have reemphasized the importance of maternal health as a part of the causal pathway between social disadvantage and child health. The contribution of family and neighborhood poverty to disparities in child outcomes has recently been highlighted. Not as well recognized is the critical role of women's health (broadly defined) in mediating these influences. Examination of both developmental and physical health outcomes for children makes this role clearer.

The linkage of child outcomes to brain development and to women's health has several important policy and programmatic implications. Specifically, though all aspects of child development need to be supported, promoting early literacy in infancy and early childhood increases the likelihood of later school success. A program that offers books to families and supports their use is a simple, effective, and relatively inexpensive strategy to accomplish this objective. Second, to further improve children's health, women need access to comprehensive health care that can address their own unmet health needs before, during, and after pregnancy. This needs to be accompanied by public health strategies that engage and support women around such difficult issues as domestic violence, depression, and substance abuse.

REFERENCES

Aber, J. Lawrence, Neil G. Bennett, Dalton C. Conley, and Jai Li. 1997. "The Effects of Poverty on Child Health and Development." *Annual Review of Public Health* 18: 463–83.

Aber, J. Lawrence, Martha A. Gephart, Jeanne Brooks-Gunn, and James P. Connell, eds. 1997. *Development in Context: Implications for Studying Neighborhood Effects.* New York: Russell Sage Foundation.

Ad Hoc Committee on Health Literacy for the Council on Scientific Affairs. 1999. "Health Literacy: Report of the Council on Scientific Affairs." *Journal of the American Medical Association* 281: 552–57.

Alm, B., J. Milerad, G. Wennergren, R. Skjaerven, J. Oyen, G. Norvenius, A. K. Daltveit, K. Helweg-Larsen, T. Markestad, and L. M. Jrgens. 1998. "A Case-Control Study of

Smoking and Sudden Death Syndrom in Scandinavian Countries, 1992 to 1995. The Nordic Epidemiological SIDS Study." *Archives of Disease in Childhood* 78: 329–34.

Amato, P. R. 1994. "Life-Span Adjustment of Children to Their Parents' Divorce." *Future of Children* 78: 329–34.

Annas, George J. 1987. "Protecting the Liberty of Pregnant Patients." *New England Journal of Medicine* 316: 1213–14.

Barker, David J. 1995. "Fetal Origins of Coronary Heart Disease." *British Medical Journal* 311: 171–74.

———. 1997. "Intrauterine Programming of Coronary Heart Disease and Stroke." *Acta Paediatrica: Supplement* 423: 178–82.

Bellinger, David, Jone Sloman, Alan Leviton, Michael Rabinowitz, Herbert L. Needleman, and Christine Waternaux. 1991. "Low-level Lead Exposure and Children's Cognitive Function in the Preschool Years." *Pediatrics* 87(2): 219–27.

Bellinger, David C., Karen M. Stiles, and Herbert L. Needleman. 1992. "Low-level Lead Exposure, Intelligence, and Academic Achievement: A Long-term Follow-up Study." *Pediatrics* 90(3): 855–61.

Bindman, Andrew B., Kevin Grumbach, Dennis Osmond, Karen Vranizan, and Anita L. Stewart. 1996. "Primary Care and Receipt of Preventive Services." *Journal of General Internal Medicine* 11: 269–76.

Blair, Peter S., Peter J. Fleming, David Bensley, Iain Smith, Chris Bacon, Elizabeth Taylor, Jem Berry, Joan Golding, and John Tripp. 1996. "Smoking and the Sudden Infant Death." *British Medical Journal* 313(7051): 195–98.

Booth, I. W., and M. A. Aukett. 1997. "Iron Deficiency Anemia in Infancy and Early Childhood." *Archives of Disease in Childhood* 76(6): 549–54.

Bremner, J. Douglas, Penny Randall, Tammy M. Scott, Richard A. Bronen, John P. Seibyl, Steven M. Southwick, Richard C. Delaney, Gregory McCarthy, Dennis S. Charney, and Robert B. Innis. 1995a. "MRI-Based Measurement of Hippocampal Volume in Patients with Combat-Related Post-Traumatic Stress Disorder." *American Journal of Psychiatry* 152(7): 973–81.

Bremner, J. Douglas, Penny Randall, Tammy M. Scott, Sandi Capelli, Richard Delaney, Gregory McCarthy, and Dennis S. Charney. 1995b. "Deficits in Short-term Memory in Adult Survivors of Childhood Abuse." *Psychiatry Research* 59(7): 97–107.

Bremner, J. Douglas, Penny Randall, Eric Vermetten, Laurence Staib, Richard A. Bronen, Carolyn Mazure, Sandi Capelli, Gregory McCarthy, Robert B. Innis, and Dennis S. Charney. 1997. "Magnetic Resonance Imaging–Based Measurement of Hippocampal Volume in Post-Traumatic Stress Disorder Related to Childhood Physical and Sexual Abuse: A Preliminary Report." *Biological Psychiatry* 41(1): 23–32.

Bronfenbrenner, Urie. 1979. *The Ecology of Human Development.* Cambridge, Mass.: Harvard University Press.

Brooks-Gunn, Jeanne, Lisa J. Berlin, and Allison Sidle Fuligni. 1998. "Early Childhood Intervention Programs: What About the Family?" In *Handbook of Early Childhood Intervention,* edited by Jack P. Shonkoff and Samuel J. Meisels. New York: Cambridge University Press.

Brooks-Gunn, Jeanne, Greg J. Duncan, and J. Lawrence Aber. 1997. *Neighborhood Poverty: Context and Consequences for Children.* New York: Russell Sage Foundation.

Brooks-Gunn, Jeanne, Greg J. Duncan, Pamela K. Klebanov, and Naomi Sealand. 1993. "Do Neighborhoods Influence Child and Adolescent Development?" *American Journal of Sociology* 99(2): 353–95.

Brooks-Gunn, Jeanne, Marie C. McCormick, B. Sam Shapiro, April A. Benasich, and George W. Black. 1994. "The Effects of Early Education Intervention on Maternal Employment, Public Assistance, and Health Insurance: The Infant Health and Development Program." *American Journal of Public Health* 84(3): 924–31.

Brown, Sarah S., and Leon Eisenberg. 1995. *The Best Intentions: Unintended Pregnancy and the Well-being of Children and Families.* Washington, D.C.: National Academy Press.

Burke, Valerie, Mark P. Gracey, R. A. K. Milligan, Claire Thompson, Andrew C. Taggart, and Lawrie J. Beilin. 1998. "Parental Smoking and Risk Factors for Cardiovascular Disease in Ten- to Twelve-Year-Old Children." *Journal of Pediatrics* 133(2): 206–13.

Carbonneau, René, Richard E. Tremblay, Frank Vitaro, Patricia L. Dobkin, Jean-Francoise Saucier, and Robert O. Pihl. 1998. "Paternal Alcoholism, Paternal Absence, and the Development of Problem Behaviors in Boys from Age Six to Twelve Years." *Journal of Studies on Alcohol* 59: 387–98.

Carlson, Mary, and Felton Earls. 1997. "Psychological and Neuroendocrinological Sequelae of Early Social Deprivation in Institutionalized Children in Romania." *Annals of the New York Academy of Science* 807: 409–28.

Carrasquillo, Olveen, David U. Himmelstein, Steffie Woolhandler, and David H. Bor. 1998. "Can Medicaid-Managed Care Provide Continuity of Care to New Medicaid Enrollees?: An Analysis of Tenure on Medicaid." *American Journal of Public Health* 88: 464–66.

Centers for Disease Control and Prevention. 1993. "Cigarette Smoking–Attributable Mortality and Years of Potential Life Lost: United States, 1990." *Morbidity and Mortality Weekly Report* 42: 645–47.

———. 1994. "Physical Violence During the Twelve Months Preceding Childbirth: Alaska, Maine, Oklahoma, and West Virginia, 1990–1991." *Morbidity and Mortality Weekly Report* 43: 132–37.

———. 1995. "Health Insurance Coverage and Receipt of Preventive Health Services: United States, 1993." *Morbidity and Mortality Weekly Report* 44: 219–23.

———. 1997. "Update: Blood Lead Levels: United States, 1991–1994." *Morbidity and Mortality Weekly Report* 46: 141–46.

———. 1998a. "Maternal Mortality: United States, 1982–1996." *Morbidity and Mortality Weekly Report* 47: 705–7.

———. 1998b. "Recommendations to Prevent and Control Iron Deficiency in the United States." *Morbidity and Mortality Weekly Report* 47(RR-3): 1–30.

Chase-Lansdale, P. Lindsay, Rachel A. Gordon, Jeanne Brooks-Gunn, and Pamela K. Klebanov, eds. 1997. *Neighborhood and Family Influences on the Intellectual and Behavioral Competence of Preschool and Early School-Age Children.* New York: Russell Sage Foundation.

Chasnoff, Ira J., Harvey J. Landress, and Mark E. Barrett. 1990. "The Prevalence of Illicit Drug or Alcohol Use During Pregnancy and Discrepancies in Mandatory Reporting in Pinellas County, Florida." *New England Journal of Medicine* 322: 1202–6.

Chavkin, Wendy, Vicki Breitbart, Deborah Elman, and Paul H. Wise. 1998. "National Survey of the States: Policies and Practices Regarding Drug-Using Pregnant Women." *American Journal of Public Health* 88: 117–19.

Chavkin, Wendy, Vicki Breitbart, and Paul Wise. 1995. "Efforts to Reduce Perinatal Mortality, HIV, and Drug Addiction: Surveys of the States." *Journal of the American Medical Women's Association* 50: 164–66.

Chugani, Harry T., Michael E. Phelps, and John C. Mazziotta. 1987. "PET Study of Human Brain Functional Development." *Annals of Neurology* 22: 487–97.

Coleman, James S. 1990. *Foundations of Social Theory.* Cambridge, Mass.: Harvard University Press.

Coley, Rebekah L. 1998. "Children's Socialization Experiences and Functioning in Single-Mother Households: The Importance of Fathers and Other Men." *Child Development* 69(1): 219–30.

Cook, Derek G., and David P. Strachan. 1997. "Health Effects of Passive Smoking: 3. Parental Smoking and Prevalence of Respiratory Symptoms and Asthma in School-Age Children." *Thorax* 52(1): 1081–94.

Cooper, Peter J., and Lynne Murray. 1998. "Postnatal Depression." *British Medical Journal* 316(7148): 1884–86.

Cornelius, L., K. Beauregard, and J. Cohen. 1991. *Usual Sources of Medical Care and Their Characteristics (AHCPR 91–0042)*. National Medical Expenditure Survey Research Findings 11. Rockville, Md.: U.S. Public Health Service.

Cowan, William M. 1979. *The Development of the Brain*. San Francisco: Freeman.

Cutler, David M., and Elizabeth Richardson. 1999. *Your Money and Your Life: The Value of Health and What Affects It*. Cambridge, Mass.: National Bureau of Economic Research.

Daly, Mary C., Greg J. Duncan, George A. Kaplan, and John W. Lynch. 1998. "Macro-to-Micro Links in the Relation Between Income Inequality and Mortality." *Milbank Quarterly* 76(3): 315–39.

Davey Smith, George. 1996. "Income Inequality and Mortality: Why Are They Related?: Income Inequality Goes Hand in Hand with Underinvestment in Human Resources." *British Medical Journal* 312(7037): 987–98.

Davey Smith, George, Carole Hart, David Blane, Charles Gillis, and Victor Hawthorne. 1997. "Lifetime Socioeconomic Position and Mortality: Prospective Observational Study." *British Medical Journal* 314(7095): 547–52.

Davey Smith, George, Charles Hart, David Blane, and David Hole. 1998. "Adverse Socio-economic Conditions in Childhood and Cause-Specific Adult Mortality: Prospective Observational Study." *British Medical Journal* 316(7148): 1631–35.

Dawson, Geraldine, Karin Frey, Herocles Panagiotides, Julie Osterling, and David Hessl. 1997. "Infants of Depressed Mothers Exhibit Atypical Frontal Brain Activity: A Replication and Extension of Previous Findings." *Journal of Child Psychology and Psychiatry and Allied Disciplines* 38(4): 179–86.

De Quervain, Dominique J. F., Benno Roozendaal, and James L. McGaugh. 1998. "Stress and Glucocorticoids Impair Retrieval of Long-term Spatial Memory." *Nature* 394: 787–90.

Devaney, Barbara L., Marilyn R. Ellwood, and John M. Love. 1997. "Programs That Mitigate the Effects of Poverty on Children." *Future of Children* 7(2): 88–112.

DiFranza, Joseph R., and Robert A. Lew. 1996. "Morbidity and Mortality in Children Associated with the Use of Tobacco Products by Other People." *Pediatrics* 97(4): 560–68.

DiLorenzo, Thomas M., Renee C. Stucky-Rupp, Jillian S. Vander Wal, and Heather J. Gotham. 1998. "Determinants of Exercise Among Children: 2. A Longitudinal Analysis." *Preventive Medicine* 27(3): 470–77.

Duncan, Greg J., and Jeanne Brooks-Gunn. 1997. *Consequences of Growing Up Poor*. New York: Russell Sage Foundation.

Duncan, Greg J., Jeanne Brooks-Gunn, and Pamela K. Klebanov. 1994. "Economic Deprivation and Early Childhood Development." *Child Development* 65(2): 296–318.

Ehrlich, Rodney I., Diane DuToit, Esme Jordaan, Merrick Zwarenstein, Paul Potter, James A. Volmink, and Eugene Weinberg. 1996. "Risk Factors for Childhood Asthma and Wheezing: Importance of Maternal and Household Smoking." *American Journal of Respiratory and Critical Care Medicine* 154(3): 681–88.

Farley Short, Pamela. 1996. "Medicaid's Role in Insuring Low-Income Women." New York: Rand.

Felitti, Vincent J., Robert F. Anda, Dale Nordenberg, David F. Williamson, Alison M. Spitz, Valerie Edwards, Mary P. Koss, and James S. Marks. 1998. "Relationship of Childhood Abuse and Household Dysfunction to Many of the Leading Causes of Death in Adults: The Adverse Childhood Experiences (ACE) Study." *American Journal of Preventive Medicine* 14(4): 245–58.

Fields, Jason M., and Kristin E. Smith. 1998. "Poverty, Family Structure, and Child Well-being: Indicators from the SIPP." Washington, D.C.: Population Division, U.S. Bureau of the Census.

Fiscella, Kevin. 1996. "Racial Disparities in Preterm Births: The Role of Urogenital." *Public Health Reports* 111: 104–13.

Fiscella, Kevin, and Peter Franks. 1997. "Poverty or Income Inequality as Predictor of Mortality: Longitudinal Cohort Study." *British Medical Journal* 314(7096): 1724–28.

Fitzgerald, Jennifer, David L. Spiegal, and Jane W. Cunningham. 1991. "The Relationship Between Parental Literacy Level and Perceptions of Emergent Literacy." *Journal of Reading Behavior* 23: 191.

Frank, Deborah, K. Bresnahan, and Barry Zuckerman. 1993. "Maternal Cocaine Use and Child Health and Development." In *Advances in Pediatrics*, edited by James T. Cassidy. Chicago: Yearbook Medical Publishers.

Glasier, Anna. 1997. "Emergency Postcoital Contraception." *New England Journal of Medicine* 337(2): 1058–64.

Goldenberg, Robert L., Jay D. Iams, Brian M. Mercer, Paul J. Meis, Atef H. Moawad, Rachel L. Copper, Anita Das, Elizabeth Thom, Francae Johnson, Donald McNellis, Menachom Miodovnik, J. Peter Van Dorsten, Steve N. Caritis, Gary R. Thurnau, and Sidney F. Bottoms. 1998. "The Preterm Prediction Study: The Value of New Versus Standard Risk Factors in Predicting Early and All Spontaneous Preterm Births: NICHD MFMU Network." *American Journal of Public Health* 88(4): 233–38.

Goldenberg, Robert L., Mark A. Klebanoff, Robert Nugent, Marijane A. Krohn, Sharon Hillier, and William W. Andrews. 1996. "Bacterial Colonization of the Vagina During Pregnancy in Four Ethnic Groups: Vaginal Infections and Prematurity Study Group." *American Journal of Obstetrics and Gynecology* 174(5): 1618–21.

Golova, Natalia, Anothny J. Alario, Patrick M. Vivier, Margarita Rodriguez, and Pamela High. 1999. "Literacy Promotion for Hispanic Families in a Primary Care Setting: A Randomized, Controlled Trial." *Pediatrics* 103(5): 993–97.

Gomby, Denise S., Patti L. Culross, and Richard E. Behrman. 1999. "Home Visiting: Recent Program Evaluations: Analysis and Recommendations." *Future of Children* 9(7): 4–26.

Gomby, Denis S., Carol S. Larson, Eugene M. Lewit, and Richard E. Behrman. 1993. "Home Visiting: Analysis and Recommendations." *Future of Children* 3(3): 6–22.

Gottlieb, Barbara R. 1995. "Abortion—1995." *New England Journal of Medicine* 332: 532–33.

Gravelle, Hugh. 1998. "How Much of the Relation Between Population Mortality and Unequal Distribution of Income Is a Statistical Artefact?" *British Medical Journal* 316(7128): 382–85.

Gunnar, Megan R., Katherine Tout, Michelle de Haan, Susan Pierce, and Kathy Stansbury. 1997. "Temperament, Social Competence, and Adrenocortical Activity in Preschoolers." *Developmental Psychobiology* 31(1): 65–85.

Gurvits, Tamara V., Martha E. Shenton, Hiroto Hokama, Hinokaau Ohta, Natasha B. Lasko, Mark W. Gilbertson, Scott P. Orr, Ron Kikinis, Ferenc A. Jolesz, Robert W. McCarley, and Roger K. Pitman. 1996. "Magnetic Resonance Imaging Study of Hippocampal Volume in Chronic, Combat-Related Post-Traumatic Stress Disorder." *Biological Psychiatry* 40(11): 1091–99.

Guyer, Bernard, Joyce A. Martin, Marian F. MacDorman, Robert N. Anderson, and Donna M. Strobino. 1997. "Annual Summary of Vital Statistics: 1996." *Pediatrics* 100(6): 905–18.

Guyer, Joycelyn, and Cindy Mann. 1999. "Employed but Not Insured: A State-by-State Analysis of the Number of Low-Income Working Parents Who Lack Health Insurance." Washington, D.C.: Center on Budget and Policy Priorities.

Hack, Maureen, Nancy K. Klein, and H. Gerry Taylor. 1995. "Long-term Developmental Outcomes of Low-Birthweight Infants." *Future of Children* 5(1): 176–96.

Hack, Maureen, H. Gerry Taylor, Nancy Klein, Robert Eiben, Christopher Schatschneider, and Nori Mercuri-Minich. 1994. "School-Age Outcomes in Children with Birthweights Under 750 Grams." *New England Journal of Medicine* 331: 753–59.

Hauth, John C., Robert L. Goldenberg, William W. Andrews, Mary B. DuBard, and Rachel L. Copper. 1995. "Reduced Incidence of Preterm Delivery with Metronidazole and Erythromycin in Women with Bacterial Vaginosis." *New England Journal of Medicine* 333: 1732–36.

High, Pamela, Marita Hopmann, Linda LaGasse, and Holly Linn. 1998. "Evaluation of a Clinic-Based Program to Promote Book Sharing and Bedtime Routines Among Low-Income Urban Families with Young Children." *Archives of Pediatric Adolescent Medicine* 152(5): 459–65.

Hillier, Sharon L., Robert P. Nugent, David A. Eschenbach, Marijane A. Krohn, Ronald S. Gibbs, David H. Martin, Mary F. Cotch, Robert Edelman, Joseph G. Pastorek II, A. Vijaya Rao, et al. 1995. "Association Between Bacterial Vaginosis and Preterm Delivery of a Low-Birthweight Infant: The Vaginal Infections and Prematurity Study." *New England Journal of Medicine* 333: 1737–42.

Hurt, Richard D., David P. L. Sachs, Elbert D. Glover, Kenneth P. Offord, J. Andrew Johnston, Lowell C. Dale, Moise A. Khayrallal, Darrell R. Schroeder, Penny N. Glover, C. Rollynn Sullivan, Ivana T. Croghan, and Pamela M. Sullivan. 1997. "Comparison of Sustained-Release Buproprion and Placebo for Smoking Cessation." *New England Journal of Medicine* 337: 1195–202.

Huttenlocher, Peter R. 1984. "Synapse Elimination and Plasticity in Developing Human Cerebral Cortex." *American Journal of Mental Deficiency* 88: 488–96.

Irgens, L. M. 1998. "A Case-Control Study of Smoking and Sudden Death Syndrom in Scandinavian Countries, 1992 to 1995. The Nordic Epidemiological SIDS Study." *Archives of A Serge in Childhood* 78: 329–34.

Ji, Bu-Tien, Xiao-Ou Shu, Martha S. Linet, Wei Zheng, Sholom Wacholder, Yu-Tang Gao, Da-Ming Ying, and Fan Jin. 1997. "Paternal Cigarette Smoking and the Risk of Childhood Cancer Among Offspring of Nonsmoking Mothers." *Journal of the National Cancer Institute* 89: 238–44.

Kahn, Robert S., Paul H. Wise, Jonathan A. Finkelstein, Henry Bernstein, Janice A. Lowe, and Charles H. Homer. 1999. "The Scope of Unmet Maternal Health Needs in Pediatric Settings." *Pediatrics* 103(3): 576–81.

Kaplan, George A., Elsie R. Pamuk, John W. Lynch, Richard D. Cohen, and Jennifer L. Balfour. 1996. "Inequality in Income and Mortality in the United States: Analysis of Mortality and Potential Pathways." *British Medical Journal* 312(7037): 999–1003.

Kaplan-Sanoff, Margot, Tom Brown, and Barry Zuckerman. 1997. "Enhancing Pediatric Care for Low-Income Families: Cost Lessons Learned from Pediatric Pathways to Success." *Zero to Three* (June-July): 34–36.

Katon, Wayne, Michael Von Korff, Elizabeth Lin, Edward Walker, Gorg E. Simon, Terry Bush, Patricia Robinson, and Joan Russo. 1995. "Collaborative Management to Achieve

Treatment Guidelines: Impact on Depression in Primary Care." *Journal of the American Medical Association* 273: 1026–31.

Kawachi, Ichiro, and Bruce P. Kennedy. 1997. "Health and Social Cohesion: Why Care About Income Inequality?" *British Medical Journal* 314(7096): 1037–40.

Kawachi, Ichiro, Bruce P. Kennedy, Kim Lochner, and Deborah Prothrow-Stith. 1997. "Social Capital, Income Inequality, and Mortality." *American Journal of Public Health* 87: 1491–98.

Kennedy, Bruce P., Ichiro Kawachi, Roberta Glass, and Deborah Prothrow-Stith. 1998. "Income Distribution, Socioeconomic Status, and Self-Rated Health: A U.S. Multi-level Analysis." *British Medical Journal* 317(7163): 917–21.

Kennedy, Bruce P., Ichiro Kawachi, and Deborah Prothrow-Stith. 1996. "Income Distribution and Mortality: Cross-sectional Ecological Study of the Robin Hood Index in the United States." *British Medical Journal* 312(7037): 1004–7.

Kilpatrick, Kym, M. Litt, and Leanne M. Williams. 1997. "Post Traumatic Stress Disorder in Child Witnesses to Violence." *American Journal of Orthopsychiatry* 67(4): 639–44.

Kim, Karl H. S., Norman R. Relkin, Kyoong-Min Lee, and Joy Hirsch. 1997. "Distinct Cortical Areas Associated with Native and Second Languages." *Nature* 388: 171–74.

Korenman, Sanders, Jane Miller, and John E. Sjaastad. 1994. "Long-term Poverty and Child Development in the United States: Results from the NLSY: DP 1044–94." Madison, Wisc.: Institute for Research on Poverty.

Kramer, Michael S., and K. S. Joseph. 1996. "Enigma of Fetal/Infant-Origins Hypothesis." *Lancet* 348: 1254–55.

Kupfer, David J. 1998. "Developmental Plasticity: Is It the 'Plastics' of the 1990s?" In *Advancing Research on Developmental Plasticity: Integrating the Behavioral Science and Neuroscience of Mental Health*, edited by D. M. Hann, L. C. Huffman, I. I. Lederhendler, and D. Meinecke. Washington, D.C.: NIH Publications.

Lake, Julie K., Chris Power, and Tim J. Cole. 1997. "Child to Adult Body Mass Index in the 1958 British Birth Cohort: Associations with Parental Obesity." *Archives of Disease in Childhood* 77(5): 376–81.

Lancet. 1991. "Prevention of Neural Tube Defects: Results of the Medical Research Council Vitamin Study: MRC Vitamin Study Research Group." Vol. 338: 131–37.

Laurence, K. M., Nansi James, Mary H. Miller, G. B. Tennant, and H. Campbell. 1981. "Double-blind Randomised Controlled Trial of Folate Treatment Before Conception to Prevent Recurrence of Neural Tube Defects." *British Medical Journal—Clinical Research Edition* 282: 1509–11.

Lewit, Eugene M., Donna L. Terman, and Richard E. Behrman. 1997. "Children and Poverty: Analysis and Recommendations." *Future of Children* 7(3): 4–24.

Liu, Dong, Josie Diorio, Beth Tannenbaum, Christian Caldji, Darlene Francis, Alison Freedman, Shakti Sharma, Deborah Pearson, Paul M. Plotsky, and Michael J. Meaney. 1997. "Maternal Care, Hippocampal Glucocorticoid Receptors, and Hypothalamic-Pituitary-Adrenal Responses to Stress." *Science* 277: 1659–62.

Looker, Anne C., Peter R. Dallman, Margaret D. Carroll, Elaine W. Gunter, and Cliford L. Johnson. 1997. "Prevalence of Iron Deficiency in the United States." *Journal of the American Medical Association* 277: 973–76.

Lozoff, Betsy, Elias Jimenez, and Abraham W. Wolf. 1991. "Long-term Developmental Outcome of Infants with Iron Deficiency." *New England Journal of Medicine* 325: 687–94.

MacLaughlin, Barry. 1978. *Second Language Acquisition in Childhood*. Hillsdale, N.J.: Lawrence Erlbaum.

March of Dimes. 1997. "Preparing for Pregnancy II: Second National Survey of Women's Behavior and Knowledge Relative to Consumption of Folic Acid and Other Vitamins and Pre-Pregnancy Care." White Plains, N.Y.: March of Dimes.

Martinez, Fernando D., Anne L. Wright, and Lynn M. Taussig. 1994. "The Effect of Paternal Smoking on the Birthweight of Newborns Whose Mothers Did Not Smoke." *American Journal of Public Health* 84(1): 1489–91.

Mayer, Susan E. 1997. *What Money Can't Buy: Family Income and Children's Life Chances.* Cambridge, Mass.: Harvard University Press.

McCormick, Marie C. 1997. "The Outcomes of Very Low-Birthweight Infants: Are We Asking the Right Questions?" *Pediatrics* 99(6): 869–76.

McCormick, Marie C., Jeanne Brooks-Gunn, Kathryn Workman-Daniels, JoAnna Turner, and George J. Peckham. 1992. "The Health and Developmental Status of Very Low-Birthweight Children at School Age." *Journal of the American Medical Association* 267: 2204–8.

McEwen, Bruce S. 1998. "Protective and Damaging Effects of Stress Mediators." *New England Journal of Medicine* 338(3): 171–79.

Meaney, M. J., J. Diorio, D. Francis, J. Widdowson, P. LaPlante, C. Caldji, S. Sharma, J. R. Seckl, and P. M. Plotsky. 1996. "Early Environmental Regulation of Forebrain Glucocorticoid Receptor Gene Expression: Implications for Adrenocortical Responses to Stress." *Developmental Neuroscience* 18: 49–72.

Miller, Jane E. 1998. "Developmental Screening Scores Among Preschool-Aged Children: The Roles of Poverty and Child Health." *Journal of Urban Health* 75: 135–52.

Miller, Jane E., and Sanders Korenman. 1994. "Poverty and Children's Nutritional Status in the United States." *American Journal of Epidemiology* 140(3): 233–43.

Moss, Howard B., Ada Mezzich, Jeffrey K. Yao, Judith Gavaler, and Christopher S. Martin. 1995. "Aggressivity Among Sons of Substance-Abusing Fathers: Association with Psychiatric Disorder in the Father and Son, Paternal Personality, Pubertal Development, and Socioeconomic Status." *American Journal of Drug and Alcohol Abuse* 21(3): 195–208.

National Center for Health Statistics. 1997. *Healthy People 2000 Review: 1997.* Hyattsville, Md.: U.S. Public Health Service.

National Consensus Development Panel on Effective Medical Treatment of Opiate Addiction. 1998. "Effective Medical Treatment of Opiate Addiction." *Journal of the American Medical Association* 280: 1936–43.

Needleman, Herbert L., Alan Schell, David Bellinger, Alan Leviton, and Elizabeth N. Allred. 1990. "The Long-term Effects of Exposure to Low Doses of Lead in Childhood: An Eleven-Year Follow-up Report." *New England Journal of Medicine* 322(21): 83–88.

Needlman, Robert, Lise E. Fried, Debra S. Morley, Sunday Taylor, and Barry Zuckerman. 1991. "Clinic-Based Interventions to Promote Literacy." *American Journal of Diseases of Children* 145(8): 881–84.

Nelson, Charles A., and Floyd E. Bloom. 1997. "Child Development and Neuroscience." *Child Development* 68(5): 970–87.

Olds, David L., John Eckenrode, Charles R. Henderson Jr., Harriet Kitzman, Jane Powers, Robert Cole, Kimberly Sidora, Pamela Morris, Lisa M. Pettit, and Dennis Luckey. 1997. "Long-term Effects of Home Visitation on Maternal Life Course and Child Abuse and Neglect: Fifteen-Year Follow-up of a Randomized Trial." *Journal of the American Medical Association* 278: 637–43.

Olds, David, Charles R. Henderson, Robert Cole, John Eckenrode, Harriet Kitzman, Dennis Luckey, Lisa Pettit, Kimberly Sidora, Pamela Morris, and Jane Powers. 1998. "Long-term Effects of Nurse Home Visitation on Children's Criminal and Antisocial Behavior: Fifteen-

Year Follow-up of a Randomized Controlled Trial." *Journal of the American Medical Association* 280(2): 1238–44.

Olds, David L., Charles R. Henderson Jr., and Robert Tatelbaum. 1994. "Intellectual Impairment in Children of Women Who Smoke Cigarettes During Pregnancy." *Pediatrics* 93(2): 221–27.

Olds, David L., and Harriet Kitzman. 1990. "Can Home Visitation Improve the Health of Women and Children at Environmental Risk?" *Pediatrics* 86(1): 108–16.

Parker, Steven, Steven Greer, and Barry Zuckerman. 1988. "Double Jeopardy: The Impact of Poverty on Early Child Development." *Pediatric Clinics of North America* 35: 1227–40.

Pirkle, James L., Debra J. Brody, Elaine W. Gunter, Rachel A. Kramer, Daniel C. Paschal, Katherine M. Flegal, and Thomas D. Matte. 1994. "The Decline in Blood Lead Levels in the United States: The National Health and Nutrition Examination Surveys (NHANES)." *Journal of the American Medical Association* 272: 284–91.

Plotnick, Robert D. 1997. "Child Poverty Can Be Reduced." *Future of Children* 7(1): 72–87.

Putnam, Robert D. 1995. "Bowling Alone: America's Declining Social Capital." *Journal of Democracy* 6(11): 65–78.

Richman, Niomi, Jim Stevenson, and Phillip J. Graham. 1982. *Preschool to School: A Behavioral Study.* New York: Academic Press.

Runyan, Desmond K., Wanda M. Hunter, Rebecca S. Socolar, Lisa Amaya-Jackson, Diana English, John Landsverk, et al. 1998. "Children Who Prosper in Unfavorable Environments: The Relationship to Social Capital." *Pediatrics* 101(1): 12–18.

Sameroff, Arnold J., Ronald Seifer, Alfred Baldwin, and Clara Baldwin. 1993. "Stability of Intelligence from Preschool to Adolescence: The Influence of Social and Family Risk Factors." *Child Development* 64(1): 80–97.

Sameroff, Arnold J., Ronald Seifer, Ralph Barocas, Melvin Zax, and Stanley Greenspan. 1987. "Intelligence Quotient Scores of Four-Year-Old Children: Social-Environmental Risk Factors." *Pediatrics* 79: 343–50.

Sapolsky, Robert M. 1996. "Why Stress Is Bad for Your Brain." *Science* 273: 749–50.

Schor, Edward L., and Elizabeth G. Menaghan. 1995. *Family Pathways to Child Health.* New York: Oxford University Press.

Shapiro, Isaac, and Robert Greenstein. 1997. "Trends in the Distribution of After-Tax Income: An Analysis of Congressional Budget Office Data." Washington, D.C.: Center on Budget and Policy Priorities.

Shiono, Patricia H., and Richard E. Behrman. 1995. "Low Birthweight: Analysis and Recommendations." *Future of Children* 5(2): 4–18.

Shore, Rima. 1997. *Rethinking the Brain: New Insights into Early Development.* New York: Families and Work Institute.

Skocpol, Theda. 1996. "Unraveling from Above." *The American Prospect* 25: 20–25.

Smith, Judith R., Jeanne Brooks-Gunn, and Pamela K. Klebanov. 1997. "Consequences of Living in Poverty for Young Children's Cognitive and Verbal Ability and Early School Achievement." In *Consequences of Growing Up Poor,* edited by Greg J. Duncan and Jeanne Brooks-Gunn. New York: Russell Sage Foundation.

Sroufe, L. Alan. 1988. "The Role of the Infant-Caregiver Attachment in Development." In *Clinical Implications of Attachment,* edited by Jay Belsky and Teresa Nezworski. New York: Lawrence Erlbaum.

Starfield, Barbara. 1992. "Effects of Poverty on Health Status." *Bulletin of the New York Academy of Medicine* 68(1): 17–24.

Starfield, Barbara, Sam Shapiro, Judith Weiss, Kung-Yee Liang, Knut Ra, David Paige, and Xiaobin Wang. 1991. "Race, Family Income, and Low Birthweight." *American Journal of Epidemiology* 134(10): 1167–74.

Stets, Jim E., and Murray A. Strauss. 1990. *Gender Differences in Reporting Marital Violence and Its Medical and Psychological Consequences*. New Brunswick, N.J.: Transaction Publishers.

Strauss, Murray A., and K. Richard J. Gelles. 1986. "Societal Change and Change in Family Violence from 1975 to 1985 as Revealed by Two National Surveys." *Journal of Marriage and the Family* 48: 465–79.

Taaffe Young, Kathryn, Karen Davis, Cathy Schoen, and Steven Parker. 1998. "Listening to Parents: A National Survey of Parents with Young Children." *Archives of Pediatric Adolescent Medicine* 152(3): 255–62.

Taylor, Laura, Barry Zuckerman, Vaira Harik, and Betsy M. Groves. 1994. "Witnessing Violence by Young Children and Their Mothers." *Journal of Developmental and Behavioral Pediatrics* 15(2): 120–23.

Thorpe, Kenneth E., and Curtis S. Florence. 1998. *Covering Uninsured Children and Their Parents: Estimated Costs and Number of Newly Insured*. New York: Commonwealth Fund.

U.S. Bureau of the Census. 1999. Washington, D.C.: U.S. Government Printing Office.

Wakefield, Melanie, Yolande Reid, Lyn Roberts, Robyn Mullins, and Pamela Gillies. 1998. "Smoking and Smoking Cessation Among Men Whose Partners Are Pregnant: A Qualitative Study." *Social Science and Medicine* 47(5): 657–64.

Wasserman, Cathy R., Gary M. Shaw, Steve Selvin, Jeffrey B. Gould, and S. Leonard Syme. 1998. "Socioeconomic Status, Neighborhood Social Conditions, and Neural Tube Defects." *American Journal of Public Health* 88: 1674–80.

Weisman, Carol S. 1996. "Women's Use of Health Care." In *Womens's Health: The Commonwealth Fund Survey*, edited by Marilyn M. Falik and Karen S. Collins. Baltimore: Johns Hopkins University Press.

Weissman, Myrna M., and Mark Olfson. 1995. "Depression in Women: Implication for Health Care Research." *Science* 269: 799–801.

Werker, James F., and R. C. Tees. 1984. "Cross-Language Speech Perception: Evidence for Perceptual Reorganization During the First Year of Life." *Infant Behavior and Development* 7: 49–63.

Whitaker, Robert C., Jeffrey A. Wright, Margaret S. Pepe, Kristy D. Seidel, and William H. Dietz. 1997. "Predicting Obesity in Young Adulthood from Childhood and Parental Obesity." *New England Journal of Medicine* 337(13): 869–73.

Whitehurst, Grover J., Fred L. Falco, Christopher J. Lonigan, et al. 1988. "Accelerating Language Development Through Picture Book Reading." *Developmental Psychology* 24: 552–59.

Whitehurst, Grover J., and Christopher J. Lonigan. 1998. "Child Development and Emergent Literacy." *Child Development* 69(3): 848–72.

Wilkinson, Richard G. 1996. *Unhealthy Societies: The Afflictions of Inequality*. New York: Routledge.

———. 1997. "Socioeconomic Determinants of Health: Health Inequalities: Relative or Absolute Material Standards?" *British Medical Journal* 314(7080): 591–85.

Wise, Paul H., Milton Kotelchuck, Mark L. Wilson, and Mark Mills. 1985. "Racial and Socioeconomic Disparities in Childhood Mortality in Boston." *New England Journal of Medicine* 313: 360–66.

Wise, Paul H., and Alan Meyers. 1988. "Poverty and Child Health." *Pediatric Clinics of North America* 35: 1169–86.

Wise, Paul H., and DeWayne M. Pursley. 1992. "Infant Mortality as a Social Mirror." *New England Journal of Medicine* 326(23): 1558–60.

Wolff, Edward N. 1995. "How the Pie Is Sliced: America's Growing Concentration of Wealth." *The American Prospect* 22: 58–64.

Yogman, Michael W., Daniel Kindlon, and Felton Earls. 1995. "Father Involvement and Cognitive-Behavioral Outcomes of Preterm Infants." *Journal of the American Academy of Child and Adolescent Psychiatry* 34(1): 58–66.

Yu, Stella M., Kenneth G. Keppel, Gopal K. Singh, and Woodie Kessel. 1996. "Preconceptional and Prenatal Multivitamin-Mineral Supplement Use in the 1988 National Maternal and Infant Health Survey." *American Journal of Public Health* 86: 240–42.

Zero to Three. 1992. *Heart Start: The Emotional Foundations of School Readiness.* Arlington, Va.: National Center for Clinical Infant Programs.

Zhang, Jun, David A. Savitz, Pamela J. Schwingl, and Wen-Wei Cai. 1992. "A Case-Control Study of Paternal Smoking and Birth Defects." *International Journal of Epidemiology* 21(2): 273–78.

Zuckerman, Barry, Marilyn Augustyn, Bestsy M. Groves, and Steven Parker. 1995. "Silent Victims Revisited: The Special Case of Domestic Violence." *Pediatrics* 96(3): 511–13.

Zuckerman, Barry S., and William R. Beardslee. 1987. "Maternal Depression: A Concern for Pediatricians." *Pediatrics* 79: 110–17.

Zuckerman, Barry, Deborah A. Frank, Rolph Hingson, Hortensia Amaro, Suzette M. Levenson, Herbert Kayne, Steven Parker, Robert Vinci, Kwabena Aboagye, Lise E. Fried, et al. 1989. "Effects of Maternal Marijuana and Cocaine Use on Fetal Growth." *New England Journal of Medicine* 320(12): 762–68.

Zuckerman, Barry, Margot Kaplan-Sanoff, Steven Parker, and Kathryn Taaffe-Young. 1997. "The Healthy Steps for Young Children Program." *Zero to Three* (June-July), 20–25.

Chapter 4

Early Childhood Experiences and Developmental Competence

Sharon Landesman Ramey and Craig T. Ramey

This chapter is guided by two themes, each strongly supported by carefully conducted studies on children. The first is simply that experience matters—*a lot*. The second is that a child's developmental competence can be increased by providing *the right experiences at the right time*. Collectively, the scientific evidence is impressive that children's well-being depends on the opportunities they have.

At one level, these themes appear self-evident. Why, then, devote a chapter to presenting supportive research findings and considering their social policy implications? The answer is that there is strong controversy about whether systematic interventions can truly improve children's outcomes. Further, the most recent findings are not necessarily well known. Even more important, certain deeply held beliefs about whether success in life is largely determined by genetic and individual factors or by environmental conditions are all too often not discussed. These beliefs, in turn, influence society's investment in children. To achieve consensus about effective strategies to improve the future of children, such differences in beliefs need to be reevaluated in the context of what is known from scientific inquiry.

BELIEFS ABOUT CHILDREN'S EMERGING COMPETENCIES

Many prevailing beliefs about the competence of individual children have relied heavily on an *individual* or *fixed traits model*. Such a model is based on three assumptions about how children come to be more or less competent. The first assumption is that, from early on, children display individual differences that indicate whether they have more or less of what contributes to being competent in a given area, such as "school smarts." The second assumption is that these individual differences to a large extent reflect biological factors present at birth, often influenced by strong genetic predispositions. Finally, the third assumption is that the early expression of a child's competence is a reliable indicator of later competence, because the trait itself is stable and "belongs" to the individual.

It is important to recognize that the individual trait model is not unique to the area of developmental competence but is found in almost all areas related to personality and individual differences. Although the origins of individual trait models are largely philosophical, until recently these views dominated much of the research in human development and yielded an impressive amount of data that, practically speaking, seem to support the three assumptions cited here.

We have proposed an alternative conceptual framework for understanding human development. This view, known as *biosocial developmental contextualism* (Ramey and Ramey 1998a), interprets development as occurring within a complex and dynamic system. As figure 4.1 shows, biology and experience are not pitted against each other but rather are conceptualized as reciprocal and interdependent processes that influence development.

FIGURE 4.1 / Schematic Portrayal of Biosocial Developmental Contextualism

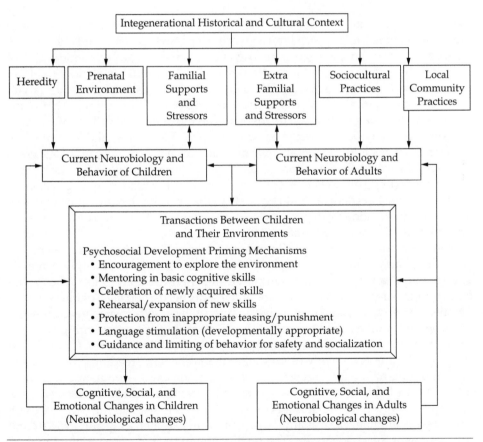

Note: Adapted from Ramey and Ramey (1998a). The principles of general systems theory are hypothesized to be operative throughout this model (Ramey, MacPhee, and Yeates 1982). The meaning and consequences of different patterns of child and caregiver behavior, however, are further influenced by contextual factors, including historical, cultural, and community-level factors.

Without both biology and experience, there can be no development. Besides elaborating this conceptual framework, we provide key findings that underscore the centrality of experiences for children's intellectual and social-emotional competence. These findings strongly refute earlier, more simplistic notions that children's developmental fates are essentially predetermined at or shortly after birth. These findings suggest that specific brain mechanisms and pathways are affected by early experience. In turn, these neurobiological changes increase or decrease the chances for children to succeed at specific tasks at later stages of development. These findings have clear implications for shaping public policy so that children who start life with many odds against them will not be permanently damaged and socially marginalized, thus fulfilling the pessimistic prophecies that derive from a fixed traits model.

CHILDHOOD EXPERIENCES

Experience is the interplay between the environment and the child. Registered in brain and other neural tissue, it is an active, not a passive, process, and one not necessarily equated with mere exposure to events or activities. The dynamic nature of experience is readily apparent when thinking about how differently individuals respond to exactly the same event, at the same time, in the same place. In the jargon of social ecology, this is known as "person × environment interaction." That is, the impact and meaning of what occurs depends on the person as well as the event.

Experience may be thought of as what happens inside the child's brain when there are changes in the external environment. For instance, we know that how a baby sees the world changes dramatically over the first year of life. Similarly, how a child hears subtle differences in the sounds of his or her native language changes. And how a child recognizes and responds to the emotional expressions of others also differs tremendously depending on both age (maturation) and environmental opportunities (Ramey and Ramey 1999).

Without a doubt, a child contributes a great deal to his or her environment. For more than four decades, investigators have demonstrated convincingly that even young infants can alter the caregiving environment by their behavior. When an infant provides cues about his or her emotional state, needs, and level of interest, then parents are able to be more responsive. Infants who provide easy-to-read cues and are generally good natured typically bring forth more positive parenting behavior than do infants whose behavior is negative or difficult to interpret. On the other hand, some parents are truly more skilled than others in "reading" their infant's cues, and some have a larger repertoire of skills in consoling, stimulating, and playing with their babies. Accordingly, the most central figures in an infant's early environment have a powerful influence over early experiences. In turn, these experiences result in changes in many biological systems, including the growth and functioning of the child's brain. The quality, quantity, and appropriate timing of these experiences all contribute to a child's developmental competence (Shore 1997; Zuckerman and Kahn, this volume). These experiences also are frequently linked to a child's family and community circumstances.

What Can Be Learned from Adopting a Child's Perspective on the World?

In the 1960s, Dr. Bettye Caldwell of the University of Arkansas at Little Rock suggested that the child's home environment should be assessed *from the perspective of the child*. This was a revolutionary notion that led to a new measurement strategy (Caldwell and Bradley 1984). Rather than count, for example, the number of books or records (before the age of tapes and compact discs) in the home, Caldwell proposed counting only those that the child could see, reach, and use; rather than just noting the mother's marital status, she proposed finding out how often the father joined the family for mealtimes. Thus, the child's home was seen in terms of its experiential potential for the child, rather than as a mere inventory of social and physical resources. This strategy resulted in greater understanding of the important variations among children's homes, especially for children with similar socioeconomic circumstances. Within poor families, for example, there is a tremendous range of differences in the quality, quantity, and timing of positive experiences—and these cannot be explained simply by marker variables such as the family's income, maternal age, marital status, or housing conditions.

Adopting the child's perspective has also led to refinement in teaching strategies for very young children. In early childhood education circles, this is referred to as developmentally appropriate practices, which provide activities matched to each child's level of development (Bredekamp and Copple 1997). This has its origins in Dr. J. McVicker Hunt's (1961) classic book *Intelligence and Experience.* He proposed "the problem of the match" as fundamental to effective stimulation of a child's continuous intellectual curiosity and growth. For the environment to support the development of a child's intelligence, it must be neither too boring (understimulating) nor too advanced. This idea of "matching" the environment to the child's stage of development and individuality has been extremely important in developmental science (Landesman and Ramey 1989).

Another powerful element in very young children's emerging competency is a class of experiences described as response-contingent experiences. Response-contingent learning involves the opportunity for a child to observe the impact of his or her behavior on the world. Several examples of response-contingent experiences illustrate the dynamic interplay between the child and the environment and why such experiences are so important to subsequent learning.

When a baby plays with a busy-box mounted in the crib, thus producing interesting sounds and sights by moving dials or pressing buttons, the baby is engaged in response-contingent stimulation. His or her behavior makes things happen. When a parent smiles in response to a baby's new sounds or mimics a child's utterances, the baby is experiencing a social form of response contingency. The baby is eliciting a desirable parent behavior.

In marked contrast, a baby watching television, even so-called educational television, is not actively engaged, and what happens on the screen does *not* depend on what the child does. Similarly, if an alert infant is in the presence of adults but is not included in any of the ongoing exchanges, there is little or no meaningful stimulation. Random hugs, kisses, and exclamations are far less meaningful than are these same behaviors in response to the child's behavior.

At an extreme, when infants seek to explore and manipulate objects in their environment and are repeatedly restrained from doing so, they are being taught to be disengaged, not curious, and noninteractive. Sometimes parents think they are teaching their baby good manners, respect for property, or how to be well behaved, but in fact they are inadvertently preventing their infant from having valuable, growth-promoting experiences. (We note, however, that there are times when safety issues are paramount and lead to temporary restriction or efforts to engage the baby in alternative activities.)

Children learn from response-contingent experiences that their own actions *matter*. That is, a child's self-initiated interactions with people and with objects can create interesting, enjoyable, and informative experiences. It is through such interactions that the child learns a great deal about natural consequences and their variation. Similarly, when a child actively tunes in to the surrounding environment and responds in appropriate ways, he or she increases the opportunities for learning and for becoming socially and intellectually connected to the environment. In essence, children who are engaged in frequent, positive transactions with their environment are helping to solve "the problem of the match."

Right from birth, infants are remarkably aware and actively seeking appropriate and beneficial forms of stimulation—that is, stimulation that provides immediate rewards as well as lasting benefits in terms of "wiring" their brains well (Ramey and Ramey 1999). When infants and young children spend lots of time in environments that support and encourage such behavior, they flourish. When children experience unresponsive environments, or environments that lack sufficient stimulation to engage them, they show delays in mental, social, and language development.

A FRAMEWORK FOR UNDERSTANDING DEVELOPMENT

Biosocial developmental contextualism emphasizes that the developing child is part of multiple, dynamic, and interrelated systems. Development is not a simple linear process but represents the cumulative effects and correlates of multiple biological, social, and behavioral systems, including the child's proximal (or immediate) environment and more distal events (such as stressors or supports that affect the family and the community at large). Figure 4.1 illustrates these systems.

In the center of figure 4.1 is a box labeled "Transactions Between Children and Their Environments." Many influences on a child's development operate through this provision of direct transactional experiences. The model emphasizes the *biosocial* nature of development by indicating that each child starts life with a distinctive neurobiological and behavioral profile. This profile is influenced by factors such as heredity and the integrity of the prenatal environment. The consequences of such biological and behavioral individuality (often referred to as individual temperament or personality) depend, however, to a considerable degree on how the very young child is treated by others. For example, some babies are more fussy, some sleep less, and some prefer much more touch and cuddling than do others. These differences are not known to be inherently good or bad. Rather, it is how parents and others perceive these differences, and how they respond to them, that contribute to a child's overall adjustment and sense of well-being. Certainly some of these early individual differences may be predictive of later patterns of development, such as being more or less curious about certain dimensions of the environment, but remarkably little is known about the continuity of early temperamental differences that have received different responses.[1]

The social aspect of this framework is apparent in the identification of supports and stressors that impinge on the family. The term "social" denotes the people side of early development, an undeniably important aspect of the quality and quantity of a child's early experiences. Social influences extend beyond the family, including neighborhood and community influences as well as broader cultural and societal beliefs, practices, and norms. These social influences can affect both the child and the caregivers, although for infants and young children these influences appear to be largely mediated through their *effects on* parents. As children become older and more independent, peers and other adults have increasingly more direct influence on them.

A central concept is that of development itself, an ongoing process that is apparent through changes in the biobehavioral competency of the child. Development represents the acquisition of a greater array of skills and strategies to adapt to one's environment, including problem-solving skills, general and specialized knowledge, and the ability to identify and enact effective decisionmaking in diverse situations. Thus, development is not simply change or getting older; rather, it encompasses those changes that increase a child's overall competency and effectiveness in the world. For purposes of study and education, children's competencies often are dimensionalized into different domains—such as cognitive, language, social, and emotional. However, the evidence indicates that there are strong interdependencies between these domains and that the distinctions between them are often arbitrary or academic (Ramey and Ramey 1997).

Children who have vastly different experiences in terms of their transactions with their environments achieve different levels of development. Certain assessment strategies thus detect children who appear to show "delayed" or "accelerated" development when using age norms as the marker for expected development. Alternatively, development can be thought of in terms of how well a child's level of development allows him or her to function successfully in his or her environment at a given age. This takes into account changing societal expectations and the opportunities for children to acquire the skills they need.

The term "contextualism" captures this latter point quite well. All development occurs within a context that has time and place parameters as well as psychological and cultural dimensions. A child's biobehavioral development is influenced by the contexts in which he or she spends time. Further, the adequacy of a child's behavior—or the standards by which it is judged—is heavily dependent on context: what is considered well-mannered behavior, the skills a child needs to succeed later in life (for example, does the society require industrial or agrarian skills?), and how individuals are expected to be at different ages or stages in life. In addition, the nature and severity of the consequences associated with certain risk-taking behavior vary tremendously in *different* contexts. Several examples illustrate the importance of contextualism.

In some societies, boys were expected to be able to hunt independently and bring home food by the age of ten or so. In American society today, many consider it extremely dangerous and potentially immoral to teach such a young child to operate firearms. In this time and place, universal literacy is considered a highly desirable and achievable goal. When our country was founded, however, only a minority of individuals were literate. Adolescents who become parents today are considered "deviant" and judged to be less competent than older parents in their twenties, thirties, or forties. For centuries, however, the normative age for becoming a parent was in the adolescent years. The family context and extended supports undoubtedly made adolescent pregnancy in the past different from the experience in today's world.

Unlike the fixed traits models, this framework does not assume that a child's earlier biosocial profile is merely a younger version of what will appear later. Instead, a child's competencies at one age influence the transactions with the people and objects in his or her environment; these transactions are then encoded in the form of memories and neurobiological changes that influence subsequent experiences. A central assumption is that a child's development is conjointly determined by biological and environmental forces, which contribute to his or her cumulative set of experiences. Another important assumption is that the effort to separate biology from behavior in any absolute or precise sense is futile and impossible. These factors are inextricably linked as part of the total child. Although scientists can measure aspects of development that, on the surface, appear to represent basic biology (for example, from functional imaging of the brain while actively processing information about the environment) or pure behavior (for example, performance on a standardized test of intelligence), these distinctions are fundamentally arbitrary. One very important fact of life has been overlooked in the fixed traits models of children's competency: namely, that children are born into favorable or unfavorable life circumstances and usually continue to spend most of their lives in similar contexts. It is only relatively recently that systematic efforts have been made to test the extent to which the competency of children in nonoptimal or low-resource environments, as well as those with disabilities, can be raised significantly through the provision of higher-quality, more frequent, and appropriately timed experiences (for example, positive transactions that fulfill Hunt's notion of "the match") (Guralnick 1997). Even the so-called natural experiments involving adoption and twins, used as the primary paradigm in behavioral genetics, are constrained by their reliance on relatively crude and infrequent indices of parenting and the environment and their use of outcome measures (notably, personality and intelligence tests) that systematically eliminated items that showed variation across measurement periods!

Theoretically, a child's history of experiences may be measured in terms of the following dimensions:

- *Content:* The extent to which a child has experiences relevant to supporting (or harming) development in specific domains, including sensory, motor, intellectual, language, social-emotional, and self-worth

- *Timing:* When particular kinds of experiences begin (onset) and end (offset), and how long they last

- *Amount:* The number and density of particular experiences or classes of experiences

- *Continuity and predictability:* The degree to which positive experiences occur consistently and predictably rather than intermittently or unpredictably

- *Emotional tone:* Whether the child's experiences occur within a positive emotional context or in a context with a negative or neutral tone; emotional tone is particularly important for a young child's engagement in new learning activities

- *Control by child:* The extent to which particular types of experiences can be controlled or directly influenced by the child (for example, started, encouraged, modified, withdrawn from, or ended)

Based on an extensive review of the infant and early child development literature about the conditions and activities that foster positive intellectual growth in children (Ramey and Ramey 1992; Ramey and Ramey 1999), we identify specific kinds of activities as essential for normal cognitive and social growth and development. In figure 4.1, these are identified as "psychosocial developmental priming mechanisms" to indicate their central role in preparing a child for subsequent developmental progress. More specifically, we conclude, based on strong empirical evidence, that seven such mechanisms are essential for supporting young's children behavioral development:

1. *Encourage* exploration with all the senses, in familiar and new places, with others and alone, safely and with joy

2. *Mentor* in basic skills, showing the whats and whens, the ins and outs of how things and people work

3. *Celebrate* developmental advances—learning new skills, little and big, and becoming a unique individual

4. *Rehearse* and extend new skills, showing the baby how to practice again and again, in the same and different ways, with new people and new things

5. *Protect* from inappropriate disapproval, teasing, neglect, or punishment, and *comfort* responsively

6. *Communicate* richly and responsively with sounds, songs, gestures, words; bring the baby into the wonderful world of language and its many uses

7. *Guide* and limit behavior to keep a child safe and to teach what is acceptable and what is not—in other words, the rules of being a cooperative, responsive, and caring person

WHY EARLY LIFE CONDITIONS MATTER

This conceptual framework explains why poverty and other challenging life circumstances all too often are associated with decreased developmental competence in children. The multiple forces impinging on the caregivers and the child can alter the child's biological integrity at birth (for example, inadequate prenatal nutrition, exposure to teratogens), the health status of the primary caregivers (including mental health), and daily transactions between the child and the environment. Specifically, a subset of children in extremely low-resource environments receive woefully inadequate levels of the psychosocial developmental priming mechanisms—that is, the types of experiences critical to support normative development. The reasons for these inadequate levels of environmental stimulation are both many and diverse, and correcting these inadequacies represents a major challenge for social policy. One of the most popular and tried strategies is a multipronged, two-generational intervention (Smith 1995) that seeks to provide a comprehensive needs assessment and a broad array of services and supports to the entire family. All too often such programs do not yield immediate benefits to infants and very young children, as measured by the quality, quantity, and appropriate timing of positive transactions with their environment (Ramey et al. 1995a), because many of them concentrate their efforts and resources on improving the mother's life situation, such as housing, education, and training to increase subsequent employability, and on providing mental health and substance abuse counseling services for affected family members. Supports such as these are undoubtedly needed but often only *indirectly* change the child's everyday experiences.

As the national "I Am Your Child" campaign states, "Babies can't wait!" As described by Barry Zuckerman and Robert Kahn (this volume), without the adequate provision of appropriate daily experiences, infant brain development reflects environmental inadequacies (Shore 1997). Most programs that seek to improve the family's overall life situation have failed to recognize the urgency of an infant's developmental needs for positive daily experiences. *Even programs that provide home visiting and parenting classes to teach mothers more about their child's development and effective parenting practices have yet to prove effective in improving the child's actual daily experiences.* This may be because the initial levels of appropriate stimulation are so drastically low for some children and families that relying on one primary caregiver to alter the situation may simply be unrealistic to achieve in the short term. For some infants, the levels of appropriate transactions with their environments may be drastically below the minimal levels needed to support normal development and may be dramatically different from the levels received by infants in high-resource homes (Landesman and Ramey 1989; Ramey and Ramey 1998a).[2]

How Early Experience Affects Brain Development and Later Learning

The new synthesis about the relationship between brain development and behavioral development (Shore 1997) is that *experiences—the right experiences—enable the central nervous system to become properly wired and to function optimally.* Further, all behavioral development depends on the functioning of the brain. Here we provide a brief synopsis of some of the key findings that are relevant to designing effective strategies to optimize developmental outcomes for young children.[3] (For further discussion of early brain development, see Zuckerman and Kahn, this volume.)

A baby's brain at birth is one-fourth the size of an adult's and has approximately 100 billion nerve cells (neurons). Most neurons have one axon that transmits signals to other neurons. They also have many dendrites that receive impulses from other cells.

Brain cells at birth are plentiful in number and may change little over the individual's life. A newborn's brain nonetheless is incomplete in many ways. For example, the cells are not yet well connected. One of the brain's main tasks in infancy is connection. Axons and dendrites become linked and form trillions of synaptic connections.

The result is a highly complex, exquisitely efficient circuitry that carries all of the brain's impulses. These impulses control how our bodies function as well as everything from thinking and feeling to memory, learning, and creativity. Impulses are facilitated in their travel by neurotransmitters, such as serotonin and dopamine, chemicals that can enhance or inhibit certain other brain activities as well as behavior.

Peter Huttenlocher's research (Huttenlocher et al. 1991; Huttenlocher and Dabholkar 1997) shows that a young child's brain forms nearly twice as many connections (synapses) as will ever be used. Those that are used most often will become strengthened and survive; the unused ones will be replaced by other pathways or they will disappear—they will be "pruned," to use neurobiology jargon.

Two figures illustrate the dramatic changes that occur within the early years of life. The first, from Huttenlocher's laboratory (Huttenlocher and Dabholkar 1997), documents the tremendous growth and later pruning of synapses. Note that the time course is somewhat different for different areas of the cortex—visual, auditory, and prefrontal. All these areas are vital for higher-order mental processes such as learning, memory, and reasoning.

The next figure, from Harry Chugani's laboratory (1997), presents impressive images from PET scans of young infants and provides an opportunity to compare their brain activity to that of adults. The darker areas represent higher levels of brain activity associated with glucose utilization during brain activity.

The dramatic changes over the first year of life seen in figure 4.3 reflect what is graphically illustrated in Huttenlocher's data. We might add that a behavioral description of a typically developing infant's competency would be every bit as impressive—from an essentially passive, reflexive organism to an individual who is actively playing, walking, beginning to talk, thinking, and showing evidence of early awareness of self. Figures 4.2 and 4.3 underscore that *experience matters.* Chugani has observed the brain activity of children reared in extremely depriving environmental conditions—namely, Romanian orphanages. The PET scan images from their brains indicate delays and immaturity of a significant magnitude.

Our behavioral work in comparable Romanian orphanages (Ramey et al. 1995a) confirms equally dramatic delays in behavioral, cognitive, social, and language

FIGURE 4.2 / Mean Synaptic Density of the Human Brain from Conception to Adulthood

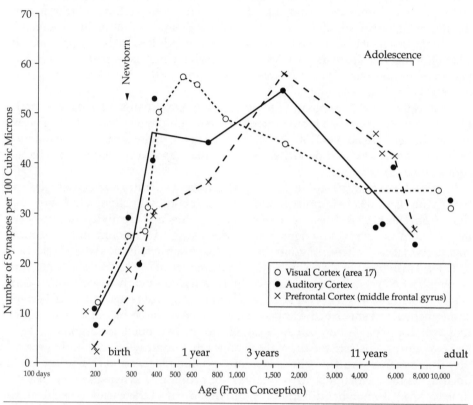

Source: Adapted from Huttenlocher and Dabholkar (1997). Reprinted with permission of Peter Huttenlocher and Goddard Press.

FIGURE 4.3 / Growth of the Brain in the First Year of Life Compared to an Adult Brain

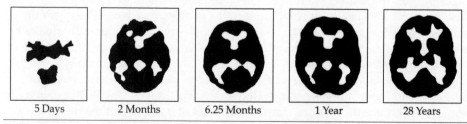

Source: Harry T. Chugani, M.D., Children's Hospital of Michigan/Wayne State University. Reprinted with permission from Harry Chugani and Goddard Press.

development. After a year of intensive environmental enrichment—specifically, providing the psychosocial developmental priming mechanisms cited earlier—these children showed steady developmental gains, as shown in figure 4.4. Despite this progress, however, there was no evidence that the intensive enrichment provided after the age of two or three could correct for the earlier deficiencies. That is, these children did not show true "catch-up" in their development, although they showed a capacity for developing at a normal rate *when they received large increases in the daily quality, quantity, and appropriateness of transactions with the people and objects in their environment.* These experiences were provided through a systematic program of early childhood education, known as Partners for Learning (Sparling, Lewis, and Ramey 1997), that proved effective in preventing developmental delay and mental retardation among high-risk infants in ten separate randomized trials in the United States, involving more than 1,100 children (Ramey and Ramey 1998b). The Romanian orphans received this enrichment from trained and supervised caregivers for six hours per day, five days a week, for at least eleven months. Figure 4.4 illustrates these findings. Children's development is displayed in terms of developmental age equivalents, such that a typically developing fifteen-month-old, for example, would be shown as having a developmental age of fifteen months in the areas of personal-social, fine motor, adaptive language, and gross motor development. On average, the infants in this Romanian orphanage showed developmental delays of almost eight months when they were fifteen months, and this increased to a delay of fourteen months by the time they were twenty-seven months old. Thus, they appeared to be developing at about half the expected normal rate (relying on U.S. norms).

In summary, the most active period of brain growth and development is during the first three years of life (Shore 1997). Although this development is remarkably flexible, there is at the same time a general order to the way the brain develops and a logical sequence to that order. At first, the most active parts of the brain are those that govern vital functions and are essential for survival, such as breathing, heart functioning, and reflexes. Right alongside these functions are the sensory activities—sights, smells, sounds, touch, movement, and taste—through which the newborn is actively processing information. These are combined into perceptual patterns and experiences that can be interpreted and remembered. The pattern of development, at both the biological and behavioral levels, is to add new skills as well as to make connections between skills. In general, brain growth is from the interior to the exterior, the latter being more closely associated with higher cognitive, language, and memory activity. The brain never stops changing and continues to develop throughout life. *How an infant's brain develops is unquestionably a complex blend of inheritance and experience.* Each brain is decidedly individual and has the potential to develop in many different ways. These ways depend on many forces, including genetics, experiences in the social and physical worlds, and health and nutrition. The quality of the relationships a child has in the first three years has a deep and lasting impact on how the brain develops, although much remains to be documented about the details of individual variations. The early formation of the brain sets the biological foundation for development in almost every aspect of life. Finally, brain development and behavior are reciprocally bound together. They dynamically and continually influence each other.

FIGURE 4.4 / Changes in Developmental Competence as a Function of Education Intervention for Romanian Orphanage Children

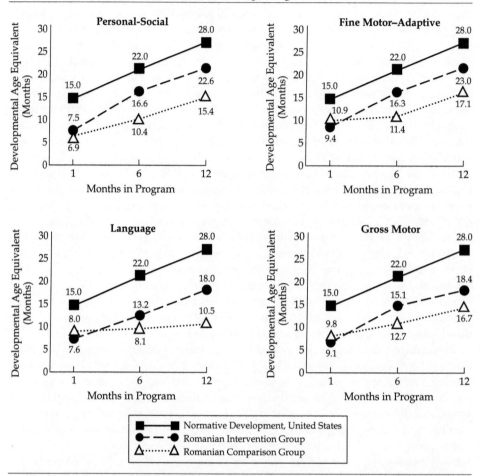

Note: The mean chronological age of children was fifteen months when intervention began. Scores reflect development age equivalents—that is, the age at which 50 percent of the norming sample showed comparable performance. The assessments were administered by examiners unfamiliar with the children's treatment condition.

CHILD CARE AND EARLY CHILDHOOD EDUCATION

A child's experience of the world is not compartmentalized the way it is for adults. For a child, the caregiving environment and the world of interesting things to experience is a continuous and dynamic one. Although very young babies can recognize from quite early on who their parents are, what counts for the overall biobehavioral development of infants is the quality of their everyday transactions with all others. Thus, the importance of the quality of child care is highly salient. To the extent that children spend time in nonparental care, the quality of this care is a marker for what a child actually experiences. Poor-quality child care takes a toll that is real and may be as profound and lasting as that associated with neglectful or abusive parenting. *It is the totality of a child's experience that lays the foundation for a lifetime of greater or lesser competency.*

The basic facts about child care in the United States today are alarming and warrant mention here (Galinsky 1992; Hofferth 1992, 1996). More than 60 percent of mothers enter the workforce when their children are young. More infants under twelve months of age are in child care than at any other time in history. There also is a national shortage of spaces for infant care—and the majority of infant out-of-home care providers are not licensed and come nowhere near to meeting the minimal standards recommended by the National Association for the Education of Young Children (NAEYC). Further, it is estimated that approximately 40 percent of infants and children under the age of three receive nonparental care that is judged to be of poor quality and potentially harmful to them. This poor-quality care is by no means limited to children of poverty but extends to private care paid for by many working middle-class and even upper-class families. This national crisis is predicted to increase, perhaps to acute stages, in the coming few years as changes in welfare programs are fully implemented in the fifty states. Somewhat remarkably, most public policies have tended to view the provision of child care as simply a necessity to help mothers enter and remain in the workforce, rather than as an important means for protecting and even improving the future development of children themselves.

The most up-to-date information about the consequences of different types, amounts, and quality of child care comes from a ten-site, longitudinal, interdisciplinary study of early child care sponsored by Congress and enacted by the National Institute of Child Health and Development (NICHD). Since 1991, this study has followed some thirteen hundred children from diverse ethnic, cultural, and economic groups. The study has documented the complexity and unpredictability of child care for many children; for example, many mothers anticipated returning to the workforce but changed their minds, and vice versa. Moreover, stability in young children's caregiving environments often was lacking. The types of care that children experienced included: full-time care by the mother, part-time care by other family members, part-time care in another's home, part-time care in their own homes supervised by a nonrelative, or part-time care in a child center or preschool. Note that "part-time" refers to the child's perspective, although many policymakers think of forty hours a week in a child care facility as "full-time." In fact, the typical child in this study who received nonparental care did so for an average of thirty-three hours per week.

There are some sweeping and very important conclusions to be made thus far from this study. One is that the quality of child care during the first three years of life is consistently, although modestly, associated with children's cognitive and language development. The higher the quality of child care, *as indicated through direct measurement of language stimulation and the transactions between the children and their adult caregivers,* the higher the children's language competencies were at fifteen, twenty-four, and thirty-six months of age. Further, the children's overall cognitive development was also higher at age two, as was school readiness at age three (NICHD Early Child Care Research Network 1997).

One mechanism that probably accounts for the findings about individual differences in the children's competencies in the early years of life is the quantity of specific growth-promoting experiences. One example is seen in the results from a separate study (Huttenlocher et al. 1991) that carefully documented the level of maternal speech to infants. As figure 4.5 shows, mothers who regularly used a higher level of language in their transactions with their babies had children whose language development, as indexed by size of vocabulary, was markedly higher. By twenty-six months of age, the differences in children's vocabulary competency are quite large. Specifically, the vocabulary of infants experiencing a richer maternal language environment is almost eight times larger than that of infants who experience much lower levels of language stimulation. Although genetics and a child's experience are inextricably linked in the family context, the findings from both the Romanian orphanage study and the NICHD study of child care corroborate the importance of the child's *total* language experience, not just the correlation between levels of maternal and child vocabulary.

FIGURE 4.5   /   Effects of Mothers' Speech on Infant Vocabulary

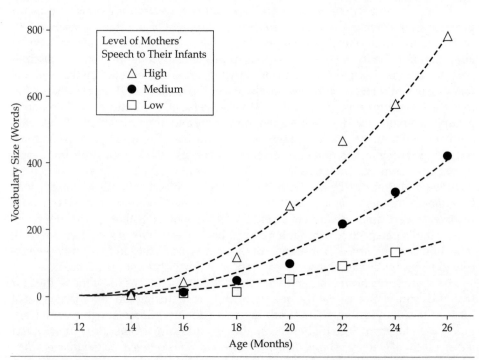

Source: Huttenlocher et al. (1991). Reprinted by permission of Janellen Huttenlocher and Goddard Press.

Naturalistic studies provide evidence of correlations and probable causal pathways but can never adequately answer the question of whether and to what extent developmental outcomes can be improved through systematic increases in the quality, quantity, and timing of experiences. Thus, a skeptic might claim that statistical control in naturalistic studies can never rule out the fact that parents who provide low levels of environmental stimulation may themselves be below average in their competencies, and therefore the observed child outcomes may be mostly attributable to "inferior genes." Fortunately, there have been well-controlled experimental studies that directly focused on the potential benefits of environmental enrichment for "at-risk" infants and young children. These are reviewed in the following section (see also the recent review by Heckman and Lochner, this volume).

EARLY INTERVENTION STRATEGIES

"Early intervention" is a generic term that refers to systematic activities planned to benefit a child. Typically early intervention is provided to children who already have a known disability or are judged at risk for nonoptimal development, based on biological, psychosocial, or other life factors. In contrast, "child care" is a much broader term that encompasses all forms of nonparental care for children. The emphasis in child care is on providing care when parents cannot be there. In fact, many forms of early intervention involve child care. Yet what distinguishes early intervention from child care is the specification of goals or outcomes for the child and a means for achieving them. For at-risk children, the most frequent outcomes specified include improved intellectual or cognitive functioning (ideally within the normal range) and positive social-emotional behavior.

Head Start is our country's best-known form of early intervention; begun in the mid-1960s, it continues to expand in terms of the numbers of children and families served (Zigler and Valentine 1979). Originally, Head Start was a summer program to help children from poor families get ready for school—to have a "head start" on kindergarten. Today, Head Start typically is a half-day program provided four days a week, seven months of the year. Mothers are encouraged to become actively involved in their children's education, and Head Start is described as a "two-generation" program with an emphasis on the adult development of the parent as well as the child's development. As remarkable as it seems, this very large program has never been subjected to rigorous evaluation, although numerous descriptive studies have provided information that is consistent with the conclusion that it is beneficial (see, for example, McKey et al. 1985). It also is true that the quality of Head Start, like that of child care in general, varies tremendously, from excellent programs to programs that are woefully lacking by any professional standards (Zigler and Muenchow 1992).

Another type of early intervention for poor children—a form that is far more intensive, begins earlier, and lasts longer than Head Start—has been subjected to rigorous and long-term evaluation. This type of intervention may be characterized as highly educational and child-oriented, although such programs often provide parent education and social support to families as well. The two best-known and most widely cited are the High/Scope Perry Preschool Project conducted in Ypsilanti, Michigan (Schweinhart, Barnes, and Weikart 1993) and the Abecedarian Project in Chapel Hill, North Carolina (Campbell and Ramey 1995; Ramey and Ramey 1998b). Both of these early intervention projects focused on raising the intellectual, academic, and social development of children from very economically impoverished, multi-risk families. The Perry Preschool Project included 123 children who were recruited because they showed intellectual delays by the age of three or four, the age when they were enrolled in the program. Half of the children were randomly selected to receive the educational intervention. This included a daily, half-day preschool program in a special center, using a specially developed curriculum known as High/Scope. The Abecedarian Project began when children were very young infants, prior to any developmental delays. In fact, all participating children were full-term, normal birthweight, and healthy at birth. The Abecedarian Project enrolled 111 families, half of whom were randomly assigned to receive free nutritional supplements for their infants along with social services and free or low-cost pediatric follow-up services (referred to as the control group, although they were not "untreated controls"); the other half received these same nutrition, social, and pediatric services and were also enrolled by four months of age in a full-day, five-day-a-week program that operated fifty weeks per year at the University of North Carolina. The curriculum, known as LearningGames (Sparling and Lewis 1979, 1984), emphasized different aspects of development: cognitive-fine motor, social-self, motor, and language. Children were enrolled in this program for five full years, at which time they entered public kindergarten.[4]

What were the results? In both studies, the treated children showed clear benefits in terms of their intellectual development during the preschool years. For example, in the Abecedarian Project, starting at eighteen months of age and continuing at every measurement period thereafter, the children who received the educational intervention showed significant IQ benefits. The IQ benefits averaged between ten and fifteen points higher than the scores of the children in the comparison group during the preschool years. Figure 4.6 summarizes these results.

Just as important, detailed studies of the ways in which the treated children in the Abecedarian Project learned and interacted with their mothers revealed benefits as well. For example, children participating in the educational enrichment elicited more frequent, positive, and growth-promoting responses from their mothers (Farran and Ramey 1980). As infants, they also showed the ability to learn new tasks faster than did the children who received only nutrition, social, and pediatric services (Ramey and Smith 1977). In terms of language development, there were multiple indicators of benefits for those in the educational intervention, including increased mean length utterances, larger vocabularies, better comprehension, and overall better pragmatic use of language (Gordon and Bernard 1981). Another impressive difference was that children in the educational intervention group were rated by trained examiners as more task-oriented and more socially responsive; moreover, their mothers rated them as having better temperaments compared to the ratings made

FIGURE 4.6 / Intellectual Performance of Children in the Abecedarian Project
During the Preschool Years

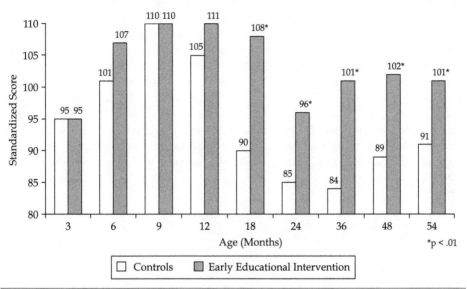

Source: Data are based on Ramey and Campbell (1984) and Ramey et al. (2000).
Note: From three to eighteen months, the scores reflect the Mental Development Index from
administration of the Bayley Scales of Infant Development ($M = 100$, $SD = 15$); from eighteen to
forty-eight months, scores represent Stanford-Binet IQ scores ($M = 100$, $SD = 15$); at fifty-four
months, the scores are a composite summary from the McCarthy Scales of Children's Abilities.
All group differences from eighteen months and later are significant at $p < .01$.

by mothers of children who did not receive the educational intervention (Ramey,
MacPhee, and Yeates 1982; Burchinal et al. 1997). Mothers of the treated children,
particularly teenage mothers, were more likely to continue their education beyond
high school and to be employed (Ramey et al. 2000). We think these real-world findings, indicative of increased developmental competence in many areas, are the most
important—far more so than the early and impressive IQ benefits alone. These findings reflect the cumulative impact of positive early experiences as indexed by children having high-quality, frequent, and well-timed positive transactions with their
environments.

Lasting Benefits of Early Intervention: Confirmation or Controversy?

One question is asked about any early intervention program more frequently than
any other: Did the benefits last? This question is important and understandable,
but it reflects an assumption that providing an infant or young child with a good

start in life is sufficient to yield long-term yields. In some ways, the hope is that early intervention, if successful, will function like an inoculation. However, the environments where children spend a great deal of time have powerful effects on their behavioral development and everyday performance, building directly on any earlier foundation. Although early enrichment may enhance performance, in order to sustain such benefits children must continue to experience highly supportive environments (Ramey and Ramey 1998a).

The news from both the Perry Preschool Project and the Abecedarian Project, however, is positive about long-term benefits. Specifically, children in both projects who received the educational preschool interventions showed long-term gains in their academic achievement, as indexed by standardized test performance and by decreased rates of grade retention. They also had lower rates of placement in special education (see figure 4.7). Why did these programs produce lasting benefits?

FIGURE 4.7 / Rates of Special Education Placement and Grade Retention in the Abecedarian Project

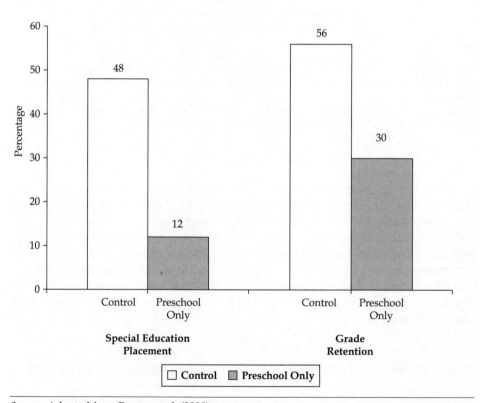

Source: Adapted from Ramey et al. (2000).
Note: Data reflect cumulative rates at age fifteen for both groups. Differences are significant at p < .01.

We think the explanation is related to several important issues. First, both programs provided very high-quality interventions that were carefully controlled and monitored. Second, both programs targeted children at very high risk for poor school performance if they did not receive additional enrichment early in life. Indeed, measures of the Abecedarian children's home environments confirmed that the majority were seriously lacking in the positive dimensions associated with normative intellectual development (Ramey et al. 1975). Third, in both places the children entered school systems that were considered at least reasonably supportive to excellent. That is, these children did not enter schools that were challenged by the serious conditions now present in our country's worst inner-city schools, including crime, drugs, and general demoralization. Remember, these projects were launched in the early 1960s and 1970s, when the conditions impinging on families and schools were different in many ways from those of the 1990s.

Another point we would like to underscore is that these long-lasting benefits, as promising as they are, still leave room for questioning what the upper limits of the benefits of providing positive experiences could be. A few numbers are illustrative. Even though the children who received preschool educational enrichment performed significantly better than controls did, their test scores are lower than the national average. In the Perry Preschool Project, for example, at age fifteen the treated children scored on average at about the sixteenth percentile on the California Achievement Test, while the controls scored below the tenth percentile; for those in the Abecedarian Project, treated children averaged around the fortieth percentile, and those in the control group scored just below the thirtieth percentile on reading and mathematics tests (Ramey, Campbell, and Blair 1998). By age fifteen, the IQ differences between the two groups in the Perry Preschool Project were nonexistent, with both groups scoring about 80. In the Abecedarian Project, the treated children continued to have significantly higher IQ scores than the controls did, although the magnitude of this difference was much less than during the preschool years. The treated children at age fifteen had IQ scores that averaged 95—very close to the national average of 100—and the controls had average scores of 90.

Even longer-term benefits through the young adult period have been reported for participants in the Perry Preschool Project, including higher rates of high school graduation and adult employment and lower rates of criminal activity and teen pregnancy. The results from the follow-up of the Abecedarian Project participants, at age twenty-one, will be published soon.

Although these two projects are the most well known, they are not the only early intervention studies that confirm the benefits of improving children's early experiences. In recent reviews, we have summarized the results from nine other randomized trials that delivered essentially the same type of educational enrichment as that provided to children participating in the Abecedarian Project (Ramey and Ramey 1998b; Ramey and Ramey 1999). One study, Project CARE, was designed as a replication of the Abecedarian Project and yielded almost identical benefits. A noteworthy aside is that Project CARE sought to provide the same stimulation to a third group of infants by teaching their mothers to provide their children with more frequent, high-quality experiences. An adaptation of the preschool curriculum was used in the home, and families were scheduled to receive weekly home visits for five years. Despite the fact that parents were quite positive about this home-based educational intervention, no measurable benefits were ever detected in the children's actual performance—a truly disappointing, and unexpected, finding (Wasik et al. 1990). Another intervention that confirmed preschool benefits appeared in an eight-site, randomized, control trial of educational intervention for low-birth-weight, premature infants. In this project, the Infant Health and Development Program, all eight sites showed benefits overall for children by age three (Infant Health and Development Program 1990; Ramey and Ramey 1998b).

Figure 4.8 summarizes an important finding from the Infant Health and Development Program that consistently appears in the Abecedarian and CARE Projects as well: namely, that the children who demonstrate the greatest benefits are those from families with the lowest educational resources, as indexed by the mother's educational attainment.

In summary, early educational interventions have proven effective when they are sufficiently intensive, sustained, and high-quality and when they are targeted at known high-risk children. The benefits are greatest during and just after the educational interventions, although some long-term benefits have been documented in at least two major studies.

FIGURE 4.8 / Children's IQ at Thirty-Six Months as a Function of Maternal Education Level and Early Intervention of Control Group Status from the Infant Health and Development Program

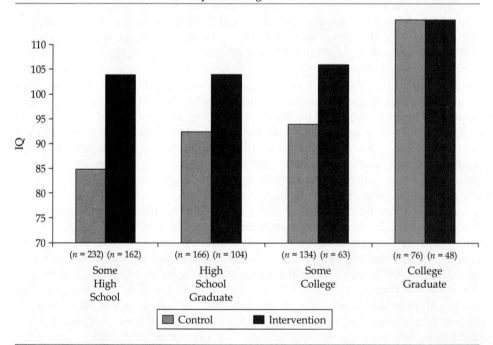

Source: Authors' tabulations.

The Controversies and Uncertainties About Early Intervention

Even though there is evidence that high-risk children's competence can be significantly improved, many controversies and unresolved dilemmas remain in the social policy arena and warrant review. These include concerns about the ethics of intervening with infants and very young children and their families; issues of responsibility; the adequacy of the evidence about cost-effectiveness; and the accumulating evidence that big government programs intended to improve child and family outcomes apparently do not work.

The concern about whether it is ethical to intervene with certain families comes, somewhat surprisingly, from two very distinct political positions. One represents a conservative view that the family is a private matter, and that society should not be interfering with what parents do with their children. The expressed and deeply held fears are that the government would extend such programs to include all families and that standards would be set for what parents should or should not do to their children. Related fears are that the use of corporal punishment will be forbidden and monitored; that certain practices associated with religious beliefs will not be supported; and that parents will fundamentally lose control over their own children. The other group that is ambivalent about early intervention believes that most of the programs imply a "deficit model" for poverty and minority families. They oppose the idea that such families are inadequate in some of their child-rearing practices and claim that a dominant culture perspective (namely, Anglo and middle-class) permeates the interventions. Examples of this so-called dominant culture emphasis include encouraging parents to read to very young children and to provide clear verbal guidance to children rather than negative and judgmental remarks; using positive rewards for desirable behavior rather than restrictive and physically punitive techniques that have been found ineffective in the systematic research conducted on parenting practices; and providing group care in high-quality child-care centers, often a preschool experience with children from diverse socioeconomic and cultural groups.

A second concern is about responsibility. Many citizens believe that parents must be held responsible for taking care of their children. Accordingly, spending large sums of public monies to "fix" the problems observed in high-risk families is viewed as undermining parental responsibility. In the worst-case scenario, parents essentially have no reason to become responsible and simply permit others to take over and rear their children. This view is consistent with the criticism that the welfare programs of the past three decades have failed because they have undermined the incentives for individuals to become economically self-sufficient. This viewpoint sometimes includes a lack of concern for the negative outcomes for some children, based on an attitude that if some parents do not care enough about their own children, why should others (that is, society at large) care? This view is grounded in an individualistic philosophy that one reaps the rewards or punishments of one's actions. The sometimes negative impact on communities and society, however, is ignored and indeed regarded as inevitable.

Concerning whether early intervention is cost-effective, we conclude that the data are only sketchy. The most widely cited study (Barnett 1985) sought to estimate the cost of the social and educational failures in the Perry Preschool Project for the control children. It then took the cost of the preschool program and provided a cost-benefit ratio. The conclusion was that for every dollar invested, there was an estimated savings of three dollars. More recent analyses have extended this ratio to seven dollars, based on subsequent performance. The limitations of extrapolating from this single economic analysis are readily apparent. Further, there are relatively few studies available for which careful cost-effectiveness studies can be conducted. Above all, some of the costs associated with inadequate early experiences may not be measurable in dollars. Children with even low standardized achievement scores can complete school and become employed. Whether their lifelong level of competence has been compromised may or may not translate directly into dollar savings for society. Increasingly, aspects of human capital include recognition of worldwide competitiveness based on the efficiency and skills of our workforce and the decrease in our nation's well-being attributable to family violence, neglect of children, substance abuse, family disruptions, and pervasive mental health problems. Clearly, much more evidence needs to be gathered about the potential and actual cost-effectiveness of early intervention, in both monetary and human capital terms.

Finally, several very large-scale interventions have been implemented for pregnant women or families with young infants to improve the overall family outcomes and the developmental competence of children. These include New Chance, the JOBS Program, and the Comprehensive Child Development Program. Each involved a treated group and a comparison group that were randomly assigned and initially equivalent. Another feature was that local programs had a great deal of control over project activities. Furthermore, none of these projects contained systematic early educational intervention that approached the quality and amounts provided by the Perry Preschool Project and the Abecedarian Project. In each project, a large number of families participated in multiple sites and a large-scale evaluation was conducted. The evaluations concluded that there were essentially no significant benefits *for children*, who typically scored well below the national average on measures of intellectual development, thus confirming their original risk status. Somewhat surprisingly, detailed analyses of the probable reasons for these failures were rarely included in the final reports of the evaluation projects. In general, we conclude that these large-scale government programs were not effective primarily because they did not directly provide the needed types of experiences to the young, at-risk children. Instead, at the level of implementation, these so-called two-generation interventions concentrated their efforts mostly on the parent generation. This was not sufficient to translate into positive changes in young children's everyday experiences (Hamilton and Brock 1994; Quint, Bos, and Polit 1997; St. Pierre et al. 1997).

RECOMMENDATIONS FOR FUTURE DIRECTIONS

We conclude that significant numbers of high-risk children today do not have the opportunities and resources that were available to most of their parents and grandparents one and two generations ago. Just as alarming is the fact that many children from middle-class families who generally have been considered *not* at risk are now exposed to potential risks in the form of poor-quality infant and child care. Many societal changes have contributed to this new profile of vulnerabilities for our nation's youngest citizens, including a general loss or fragmentation of the sense of community and shared social purpose, increased disruptions to family life, and marked increases in domestic and public violence as well as substance abuse in certain sectors of the population. Two of the most important societal institutions that historically have supported the positive socialization and education of children—schools and organized religion—have declined in their ability to do so effectively, particularly in places where the risk conditions have escalated dramatically and resources are woefully inadequate to provide corrective actions. Collectively, these changes have a particularly detrimental effect on the youngest members of society. The urgency of this situation is underscored by the impressive amount of evidence about the importance of high-quality early experiences for the normal development of the brain. The magnitude of the danger is indexed only superficially by the estimate that at least one-third of our country's children are judged "not ready to learn" by their teachers (Carnegie Task Force on Meeting the Needs of Young Children 1994).

Our recommendations for future directions are grounded in the research evidence from the past three decades about how to better prepare children for school and success in society. There is little encouraging evidence that this knowledge is being appropriately, systematically, or vigorously applied to the full benefit of children and families. There is presently an extraordinary opportunity to improve the ways in which our country invests in young children. Specifically, we propose that the following activities or strategies be enacted:

1. Conduct comprehensive reanalyses of carefully collected longitudinal data sets that are likely to contain highly informative clues about why some programs have succeeded and others have failed; explore whether certain subgroups of participants have benefited differentially.

2. Establish powerful coalitions on behalf of very young children, building on the many statewide "Zero to Three" initiatives and the national "I Am Your Child" campaign. These coalitions could work in a more coordinated, efficient way to share information in a timely manner and to minimize the delays associated with strategies that are unlikely to yield positive outcomes. Such coalitions could expand and develop plans that are feasible, both politically and financially, including identification of future resources and administrative supports to make these plans a reality. These coalitions also would help to increase public awareness about the importance of learning experiences in the first three years of life.

3. Expand the provision of high-quality programs for preschool-age children, recognizing that there is no one "best" program or strategy. An important consideration in launching and maintaining high-quality family and child supports is that the responsible individuals must be active contributors, empowered to make changes in a timely way. No copied program will succeed everywhere.

Just as important, actively engaging key stakeholders at the local level, including parents, business and spiritual leaders, educators, and health care providers, increases the willingness of families to participate and increases the availability of resources for this effort. Ideally, quality early child care and early intervention for high-risk children are combined, so that there are no separate, segregated programs based solely on indicators such as poverty income or a diagnosed disability.

4. Seek legislative backing for an expanded, broad-based, and coordinated early childhood initiative. The national support for programs such as Early Head Start has been strong and bipartisan. What is often missing from such efforts, unfortunately, is a serious commitment to providing the quality and intensity of early childhood experiences *known to produce positive results.*

5. Provide higher levels of supports and services to those children in greatest need. In a democracy, offering more supports and services to some is often considered problematic. But the evidence suggests that targeted programs are more effective. An analogy we often use is the apparent moral dilemma of whether to administer a less than full dose of antibiotics to everyone in need—to avoid denying medication to some—yet knowing scientifically that no one will benefit if less than a full dose is administered.

6. Create a strong, adequately funded technical assistance and continuous quality assurance program that is responsive to the needs of providers and programs, especially those serving young children and families in greatest need. There is considerable expertise in colleges and universities regarding elements of effective early childhood programs. This expertise, however, has not been adequately coordinated and made available to service providers and families. Many programs spend a great deal of time and money seeking expert advice, often with only limited benefit or without the needed long-term efforts to support these programs as they encounter new difficulties and challenges. A number of training and technical assistance efforts already are in place and funded, but no systematic effort has been made to combine this expertise into a highly efficient and readily available system of supports. Training and technical assistance, like the service delivery system itself, is currently fragmented and inadequately funded.

7. Develop and sustain ongoing model programs and supports throughout the country that can serve as local training and technical assistance centers. There are outstanding programs throughout the country, although they often are small and limited in their capacity to be "mentors" to other providers or to provide them with technical assistance. These programs need to continue and others need to be created to serve as resource and training centers for staff and parents. Some areas in the country lack such model or exemplary programs, and the possibility of strengthening existing programs to meet these standards is worth pursuing. The principles of effective early intervention (Ramey and Ramey 1992) can be used to distinguish what qualifies as a "successful" program.

CONCLUSION

During the last four decades, there have been dramatic changes in American family life and in how early childhood is conceptualized. Public policy changes are being stimulated by a robust and rapidly evolving scientific literature about early development and about the many forces that contribute to the wide range of individual differences that are readily observed. The emerging general understanding is that the quality and quantity of developmentally appropriate early childhood experiences are strongly linked to later performance in school and in society. Healthy lifestyles, good mental health, and civility have their roots in early childhood experiences. It is in our society's most basic interest to support young children and those who care for them as well as we can. It is the smart thing to do. It is the right thing to do.

NOTES

1. An interesting point rarely made about the measurement of infant temperament over time is that those individual differences in behavior that do *not* show high stability or test-retest reliability are deleted from these tools. Thus, the available tools for measuring individual differences tap only a select subset of a wide array of behavioral predispositions that differentiate children from one another. In essence, the behavioral characteristics that may be most strongly influenced by the environment, especially parenting strategies, have been discounted as not representing "true temperament."

2. We use the term "low-resource" home not simply as a synonym for economic poverty; similarly, a "high-resource" home is not indexed simply by a high family income. There is tremendous, documented diversity within families participating in government programs targeted for poverty families (Ramey, Ramey, and Gaines-Lanzi 1998). Fortunately, the majority of children from poor families develop normally, fare reasonably well in school, and show no clinical pathology (see, for example, Huston 1991). Nonetheless, it is also true that significantly higher proportions of children from poor families do not fare well, as demonstrated by markedly higher rates of school failure and dropout, mental retardation and learning disabilities, deviant social behavior, and poor health status (see, for example, Huston, McLloyd, and Garcia-Coll 1994).

3. This description is adapted from a parenting book we have recently written (Ramey and Ramey 1999).

4. The Abecedarian Project also provided a three-year, school-age treatment for half of the children in each group. This involved an intensive home-school liaison program, summer enrichment, and special supports for parents and classroom teachers. A recent summary of the results including this additional treatment is provided in Ramey et al. (2000).

REFERENCES

Barnett, W. Steven. 1985. "Benefit-Cost Analysis of the Perry Preschool program and Its Long-term Effects." *Educational Evaluation and Policy Analysis* 7: 387–414.

Bredekamp, Sue, and Carol Copple, eds. 1997. *Developmentally Appropriate Practice in Early Childhood Programs*, rev. ed. Washington, D.C.: National Association for the Education of Young Children.

Burchinal, Margaret R., Frances A. Campbell, Donna M. Bryant, Barbara H. Wasik, and Craig T. Ramey. 1997. "Early Intervention and Mediating Processes in Cognitive Performance of Children of Low-Income African American Families." *Child Development* 68(5): 935–54.

Caldwell, Bettye M., and R. H. Bradley. 1984. "Home Observation for Measurement of the Environment (HOME)." Unpublished paper. Little Rock: University of Arkansas at Little Rock.

Campbell, Frances A., and Craig T. Ramey. 1995. "Cognitive and School Outcomes for High-Risk African American Students at Middle Adolescence: Positive Effects of Early Intervention." *American Educational Research Journal* 32(4): 743–72.

Carnegie Task Force on Meeting the Needs of Young Children. 1994. *Starting Points: Meeting the Needs of Our Youngest Children*. New York: Carnegie Corporation.

Chugani, Harry T. 1997. "Neuroimaging of Developmental Non-Linearity and Developmental Pathologies." In *Developmental Neuroimaging: Mapping the Development of Brain and Behavior*, edited by Robert W. Thatcher, G. Reid Lyon, J. Rumsey, and N. Krasnegor. San Diego: Academic Press.

Farran, Dale Clark, and Craig T. Ramey. 1980. "Social Class Differences in Dyadic Involvement During Infancy." *Child Development* 51(1): 254–57.

Galinsky, Ellen. 1992. "The Impact of Child Care on Parents." In *Child Care in the 1990s: Trends and Consequences*, edited by Alan Booth. Hillsdale, N.J.: Lawrence Erlbaum.

Gordon, A. H., and J. A. Bernard. 1981. "Effect of Day-Care Intervention on the Language Performance of High-Risk Children." Paper presented at the biennial meeting of the Society for Research in Child Development, Boston (1981).

Guralnick, Michael J., ed. 1997. *The Effectiveness of Early Intervention*. Baltimore: Brookes Publishing.

Hamilton, G., and T. Brock. 1994. *The JOBS Evaluation: Early Lessons from Seven Sites*. Washington, D.C.: U.S. Department of Health and Human Services.

Hofferth, Sandra. 1992. "The Demand for and Supply of Child Care in the 1990s." In *Child Care in the 1990s: Trends and Consequences*, edited by Alan Booth. Hillsdale, N.J.: Lawrence Erlbaum.

———. 1996. "Child Care in the United States Today." *Future of Children* 6(2): 41–61.

Hunt, J. McVicker. 1961. *Intelligence and Experience*. New York: Ronald Press.

Huston, Aletha C. 1991. "Antecedents, Consequences, and Possible Solutions for Poverty Among Children." In *Children in Poverty: Child Development and Public Policy*, edited by Aletha C. Huston. New York: Cambridge University Press.

Huston, Aletha C., Vonnie C. McLloyd, and Cynthia Garcia-Coll. eds. 1994. *Child Development* 65 (special issue on poverty and children). Chicago: University of Chicago Press.

Huttenlocher, Janellen, W. Haight, A. Bruk, Michael Seltzer, and T. Lyons. 1991. "Early Vocabulary Growth: Relation to Language Input and Gender." *Developmental Psychology* 27(2): 236–48.

Huttenlocher, Peter R., and Arun S. Dabholkar. 1997. "Regional Differences in Synaptogenesis in Human Cerebral Cortex." *Journal of Comparative Neurology* 387(2): 167–78.

Infant Health and Development Program. 1990. "Enhancing the Outcomes of Low-Birthweight, Premature Infants." *Journal of the American Medical Association* 263(22): 3035–42.

Landesman, Sharon, and Craig T. Ramey. 1989. "Developmental Psychology and Mental Retardation: Integrating Scientific Principles with Treatment Practices." *American Psychologist* 44(2): 409–15.

McKey, R. H., L. Condelli, H. Ganson, B. J. Barrett, C. McConkey, and M. C. Plantz. 1985. "The Impact of Head Start on Children, Families, and Communities." Department of Health and Human Services Publication 8531193. Washington, D.C.: U.S. Government Printing Office.

NICHD Early Child Care Research Network. 1997. "Results of the NICHD Study of Early Child Care." *Child Development* 68(5): 860–79.

Quint, Janet C., Johannes M. Bos, and Denise F. Polit. 1997. *New Chance: Final Report on a Comprehensive Program for Young Mothers in Poverty and Their Children.* New York: Manpower Demonstration Research Corporation.

Ramey, Craig T., and Frances A. Campbell. 1984. Preventative Education for High Risk Children: Cognitive Consequences of the Carolina Abecedarian Project. *American Journal of Mental Deficiency* 88(5): 515–23.

Ramey, Craig T., Frances A. Campbell, and Clancy Blair. 1998. "Enhancing the Life-Course for High-Risk Children: Results from the Abecedarian Project." In *Social Programs That Really Work,* edited by Jonathan Crane. New York: Russell Sage Foundation.

Ramey, Craig T., Frances A. Campbell, Margaret Burchinal, M. L. Skinner, D. M. Gardner, and Sharon Landesman Ramey. 2000. "Persistent Effects of Early Childhood on High-Risk Children and Their Mothers." *Applied Developmental Science Education* 4: 2–14.

Ramey, Craig T., D. MacPhee, and K. O. Yeates. 1982. "Preventing Developmental Retardation: A General Systems Model." In *Facilitating Infant and Early Childhood Development,* edited by J. M. Joffee and Lynne A. Bond. Hanover, N.H.: University Press of New England.

Ramey, Craig T., P. Mills, Frances Campbell, and C. O'Brien. 1975. "Infants' Home Environment: A Comparison of High-Risk Families and Families from the General Population." *American Journal of Mental Deficiency* 80: 40–42.

Ramey, Craig T., and Sharon Landesman Ramey. 1997. "The Development of Universities and Children." Paper commissioned for the Harvard Project on Schooling and Children. Cambridge, Mass.: Harvard University Press.

———. 1998a. "Early Intervention and Early Experience." *American Psychologist* 53(2): 109–20.

———. 1998b. "Prevention of Intellectual Disabilities: Early Intervention to Improve Cognitive Development." *Preventive Medicine* 27(2): 224–32.

———. 1999. *Right from Birth: Building Your Child's Foundation for Life.* New York: Goddard Press.

Ramey, Craig T., Ramey, Sharon Landesman, and Robin Gaines-Lanzi. 1998. "Differentiating Developmental Risk Levels for Families in Poverty: Creating a Family Typology." In *Families, Risk, and Competence,* edited by Michael Lewis and Candice Feiring. Hillsdale, N.J.: Lawrence Erlbaum.

Ramey, Craig T., Sharon Landesman Ramey, Robin Gaines-Lanzi, and C. Blair. 1995a. "Two-Generation Early Intervention Programs: A Child Development Perspective." In *Two-Generation Programs for Families in Poverty: A New Intervention Strategy, vol. 9: Advances in Applied Developmental Psychology,* edited by Sheila Smith. Norwood, N.J.: Ablex.

Ramey, Craig T., and B. J. Smith. 1977. "Assessing the Intellectual Consequences of Early Intervention with High-Risk Infants." *American Journal of Mental Deficiency* 8: 318–24.

Ramey, Sharon Landesman, and Craig T. Ramey. 1992. "Early Educational Intervention with Disadvantaged Children: To What Effect?" *Applied and Preventive Psychology* 1: 131–40.

Ramey, Sharon Landesman, Joseph Sparling, C. Dragomir, Craig Ramey, K. Echols, and L. Soroceanu. 1995b. "Recovery by Children Under Three Years Old from Depriving Orphanage Experiences." Symposium presentation at the meeting of the Society for Research in Child Development, Indianapolis, Ind. (March 31, 1995).

Schweinhart, Lawrence J., Helen V. Barnes, and David P. Weikart. 1993. "Significant Benefits: The High/Scope Perry Preschool Study Through Age Twenty-seven." Monographs of the High/Scope Educational Research Foundation 10. Ypsilanti, Mich.: High/Scope Press.

Shore, Rima. 1997. *Rethinking the Brain: New Insights into Early Development.* New York: Families and Work Institute.

Smith, Sheila, ed. 1995. *Two-Generation Programs for Families in Poverty: A New Intervention Strategy,* vol. 9, *Advances in Applied Developmental Psychology.* Norwood, N.J.: Ablex.

Sparling, Joseph, and Isabelle Lewis. 1979. *Learning Games for the First Three Years: A Guide to Parent-Child Play.* New York: Walker.

———. 1984. *Learning Games for Threes and Fours: A Guide to Adult and Child Play.* New York: Walker.

Sparling, Joseph, Isabelle Lewis, and Craig T. Ramey. 1997. *Partners for Learning.* Lewisville, N.C.: Kaplan Companies.

St. Pierre, Robert G., Jeanne I. Layzer, Barbara D. Goodson, and Lawrence S. Bernstein. 1997. *The Effectiveness of Comprehensive Case Management Interventions: Findings from the National Evaluation of the Comprehensive Child Development Program.* Research in Child Development and Family Studies. Cambridge, Mass.: Abt Associates.

Wasik, Barbara H., Craig T. Ramey, Donna M. Bryant, and Joseph J. Sparling. 1990. "A Longitudinal Study of Two Early Intervention Strategies: Project CARE." *Child Development* 61(6): 1682–96.

Zigler, Edward, and Susan Muenchow. 1992. *Head Start: The Inside Story of America's Most Successful Educational Experiment.* New York: Basic Books.

Zigler, Edward F., and Jeanette Valentine, eds. 1979. *Project Head Start: Legacy of the War on Poverty.* New York: Free Press.

Part III

School-Age Children

Chapter 5

Schooling's Influences on Motivation and Achievement

Jacquelynne S. Eccles and Allan Wigfield

In this chapter, we review two bodies of research relevant to investing in children. First, we review what we know about the development of motivation, focusing on the middle childhood and early adolescent years. As motivational psychologists, we believe that children's performance in and out of school is greatly influenced by their motivation to learn and their willingness to engage in productive learning activities. If we are to design effective programs to help children acquire the soft skills and the knowledge needed for a successful transition to adulthood, we need to understand the motivational bases underlying their willingness to participate and engage in such programs. Second, we review what we know about classroom-level and school-level influences on motivation and learning. We focus on instructional practices in elementary and middle schools. In each section, we discuss policy implications and describe programs that have been effective in improving children's motivation and achievement.

We focus on the early adolescent years because that is a time of great change in many different aspects of children's lives. Sustaining children's motivation through this transitional period can be crucial to their future success. A number of the authors in this volume—for example, James Heckman and Lance Lochner; Craig Ramey and Sharon Landesman Ramey; and Barry Zuckerman and Robert Kahn—emphasize the importance of early investments in children to their later developmental outcomes. We agree that early intervention is important, but like Margaret Beale Spencer and Dena Phillips Swanson in this volume, we believe that the early adolescent years are another crucial time period in which investments in children's development can have important benefits to them.

MOTIVATIONAL BASES OF COMPETENCE DEVELOPMENT

Psychologists have proposed many different components of academic motivation. We ourselves have attempted to capture these components (Eccles, Wigfield, and Schiefele 1998) in four basic motivation questions that children can ask themselves: Can I succeed at this task? Do I want to do this task? Why am I doing this task?

What do I have to do to succeed at this task? The answers to these questions determine children's engagement with academic tasks as well as their general commitment to the educational goals of their parents and teachers. Children and adolescents who develop positive, productive answers to these questions are likely to engage in their schoolwork and to thrive in school settings. Those who develop less positive or less effective answers are likely to experience school failure and to withdraw their psychological attachments from school, increasing the likelihood that they will turn to riskier and less productive settings for psychological nurturance. In the first part of this chapter, we focus on the first three questions.

"Can I Succeed at This Task?": Children's Competency Beliefs and Expectations

In this section, we focus on constructs related to ability self-perceptions and expectations of success. The empirical evidence linking these beliefs to task engagement and learning is not reviewed here (see Eccles et al. 1998). We discuss instead the general decline in these beliefs as children pass through elementary and secondary school. For some, this decline begins as soon as they enter school; for others, it begins later and then accelerates as they pass through secondary school. The implications of these declines for engagement in school are a major concern for educational policymakers.

EXPECTANCY-VALUE THEORY   Jacquelynne Eccles and her colleagues have tested an *expectancy-value model* of achievement-related choices and engagement (see, for example, Eccles et al. 1983; Eccles et al. 1998; Wigfield and Eccles 1992). In this model, expectancies and values are assumed to influence performance, persistence, and task choice directly. Expectancies and values are assumed to be influenced by task-specific beliefs such individuals' perceptions of their own competence, perceptions of the difficulty of different tasks, and their individual goals and self-schema. These social-cognitive variables, in turn, are influenced by the individuals' perceptions of other peoples' attitudes and expectations for them, by their own interpretations of their previous achievement outcomes, and by their affective memories of, or affective expectations about, similar tasks. Individuals' task perceptions and interpretations of their past outcomes are assumed to be influenced by the behaviors and beliefs of socializers, by their own histories of success and failure, and by the broader cultural milieu and unique historical events.

Eccles and her colleagues (1983) defined "expectancies for success" as a children's beliefs about how well they would do on either immediate or future tasks, and "beliefs about ability" as the children's evaluations of their more general level of competence in different areas. However, empirical work has shown that children and adolescents do not distinguish between these two different levels of beliefs (Eccles and Wigfield 1995). Apparently, even though these constructs are theoretically distinguishable from each other, in real-world achievement situations they are highly related and empirically indistinguishable.

CHANGE IN THE MEAN LEVEL OF CHILDREN'S COMPETENCE-RELATED BELIEFS   Children's competence-related beliefs for different tasks decline across the elementary school years and into the middle school years (see Eccles et al. 1998; Stipek and Mac Iver 1989). John Nicholls (1979) showed, for instance, that most first-graders ranked themselves near the top of the class in reading ability and that there was essentially no correlation between their ability ratings and their performance level. In contrast, the twelve-year-olds' ratings were more dispersed, and their correlation with school grades was .70 or higher. Similar declines occur in other subject areas (particularly math), often continuing into and through secondary school (Eccles et al. 1983; Eccles et al. 1989; Wigfield et al. 1991; Wigfield et al. 1997).

Allan Wigfield and his colleagues (1997) reported the results of a three-year longitudinal study of three cohorts of elementary school-age children. Children's music and reading ability self-concepts declined the most, especially across grades one through four. Math and sports ability self-concepts also declined. The Michigan Study in Adolescent Life Transitions (MSALT) (see Eccles et al. 1989; Wigfield et al. 1991) examined how students' self-concepts of ability changed across the transition to junior high school. Students were interviewed two times in sixth grade and two times in seventh grade. Their confidence in their math and English abilities showed a marked decline over this school transition and during the first year of junior high school. Self-esteem also dropped over the school transition, followed by a partial rebound during the seventh grade (Wigfield et al. 1991).

Entrance into elementary school and then the transition from kindergarten to first grade introduce several systematic changes in children's social worlds. First, classes are age-stratified, making social comparisons of within-age ability much easier. Second, formal evaluations of competence by "experts" begin. Third, formal ability grouping begins, usually with reading group assignments. Fourth, peers have the opportunity to play a much more constant and salient role in children's lives. Each change has an impact on children's motivational development. Parents' expectations for, and perceptions of, their children's academic competence are also influenced by report card marks and the standardized tests given during the early elementary school years, particularly for mathematics (Alexander and Entwisle 1988; Arbreton and Eccles 1994).

There are long-term consequences of first-grade experiences, particularly those associated with ability grouping and differential teacher treatment. For example, teachers assign first-graders to reading groups based on characteristics like interest and persistence, race, gender, and social class (see, for example, Alexander, Dauber, and Entwisle 1993; Brophy and Good 1974). These assignments and the associated patterns of teacher-student interactions affect motivation and achievement several years later.

In conclusion, children's competence beliefs and expectancies for success become more negative as they get older, at least through early adolescence. The negative changes in children's achievement beliefs have been explained in two ways. First, because children become better at understanding, interpreting, and integrating evaluative feedback, and because they engage in more social comparison with their peers, many of them should become more accurate or realistic in their self-assessments, leading some to become relatively more negative. Second, because school environments change in ways that make evaluation more salient and competition between students more likely, some children's self-assessments decline as they get older (see, for example, Eccles, Midgley, and Adler 1984; Eccles and Midgley 1989). We return later to the ways in which instructional practices can alleviate these declines.

"Do I Want to Do This Task?": Subjective Task Values and Intrinsic Motivation

Eccles and her colleagues (1983) outlined four motivational components of task value: attainment value, intrinsic value, utility value, and cost. They defined "attainment value" in terms of the personal importance of doing well on the task and the relevance for an individual of engaging in a task for confirming or disconfirming salient aspects of his or her self-schema; "intrinsic value" in terms of the enjoyment the individual receives from performing the activity, or the subjective interest he or she has in the subject; and "utility value" in terms of how well a task relates to the individual's current and future goals, such as career goals. A task can have positive value because it facilitates important future goals, even if the individual is not interested in the task for its own sake. For instance, students often take classes that they do not enjoy but that they need to take to pursue other interests, to please their parents, or to be with their friends. Finally, Eccles and her colleagues conceptualized cost in terms of the negative aspects of engaging in the task, such as performance anxiety and fear of both failure and success, as well as the amount of effort needed to succeed and the lost opportunities resulting from making one choice rather than another.

Ability self-concepts and performance expectancies predict performance in mathematics and English, whereas task values predict course plans and enrollment decisions in mathematics, physics, and English and involvement in sports activities even after controlling for prior performance levels (Eccles 1984; Eccles et al. 1983; Eccles and Harold 1991). Both expectancies and values predict career choices (see Eccles et al. 1998).

Even during the early elementary grades, children appear to have distinct beliefs about what they are *good* at and what they *value*. As with competence-related beliefs, there are age-related declines in children's valuing of certain academic tasks (see, for example, Eccles et al. 1983, 1993; Eccles and Midgley 1989; Wigfield and Eccles 1992). For instance, among elementary school children, *beliefs* about the usefulness and importance of math, reading, instrumental music, and sports activities decreased over time (Wigfield et al. 1997). In contrast, their *interest* decreased only for reading and instrumental music—not for either math or sports.

The decline in the valuing of math continues through high school (Eccles 1984). Eccles and her colleagues (1989) and Wigfield and his colleagues (1991) also found that children's ratings of both the importance of math and English and their liking of these school subjects decreased across the transition to junior high school. In math, students' importance ratings continued to decline across seventh grade, whereas their importance ratings of English increased somewhat during seventh grade.

Over time, particularly in the achievement domain, children may begin to attach more value to activities in which they do well, for several reasons. First, the positive affect they experience when they do well should become attached to activities that yield success (see Eccles 1984). Second, lowering the value attached to activities with which they are having difficulty can be an effective way to maintain a positive global sense of efficacy and self-esteem (see Eccles 1984; Eccles, Wigfield, and Blumenfeld 1984; Harter 1990). Thus, at some point the two kinds of beliefs should become positively correlated.

INTRINSIC MOTIVATION   When individuals are *intrinsically* motivated, they do activities for their own sake and out of interest in the activity. When *extrinsically* motivated, individuals do activities for instrumental reasons, such as receiving a reward.

DEVELOPMENTAL CHANGES IN INTRINSIC MOTIVATION   Intrinsic motivation in general, and for different subjects in particular, declines over the elementary school years (Harter 1981; Wigfield et al. 1997). The transition from elementary to middle school also results in a decrease in intrinsic motivation and interest in different school subjects (see Eccles et al. 1993). Such changes are likely to lead to decreased school engagement. The origins of these changes are probably similar to the causes of declines in expectations and ability-related self-confidence, namely, shifts in the nature of instruction across grade levels, cumulative experiences of failure, and increasing cognitive sophistication.

"Why Am I Doing This?": Achievement Goal Orientations

Goal theory focuses on why children think they are engaging in particular achievement-related activities and what they hope to accomplish (see, for example, Ames 1992b; Maehr and Midgley 1996; Thorkildsen and Nicholls 1998). Questions like "Will I look smart?" and "Can I outperform others?" reflect ego-involved goals. In contrast, with task-involved goals, individuals focus on mastering tasks and increasing their competence. Questions such as "How can I do this task?" and "What will I learn?" reflect task-involved goals. With ego-involved (or performance) goals, children try to outperform others and are more likely to do tasks they know they can do. Task-involved (or mastery-oriented) children choose challenging tasks and are more concerned with their own progress than with outperforming others.

The little available developmental work reveals a pattern of change not unlike the patterns discussed earlier for expectancy-related beliefs and values. At the population level, there appears to be an increase in ego-focused goals and competitive motivation. Given what we know about individual differences in goal orientation, such a shift is likely to lead at least some children (particularly those doing poorly in school) to disengage from school as they get older.

The Nature and Development of Motivation: Policy Implications

Children's competence-related beliefs, task values, intrinsic motivation, and goal orientations are thought to be among the most crucial aspects of motivation. Unfortunately, for many children these aspects of motivation become less positive over the school years. Moreover, less desirable aspects of motivation (extrinsic motivation, performance goals, anxiety) often increase during these years. What can be done to alleviate these declines so that more children will be able to maintain positive motivation? Some policy-oriented researchers have developed programs that focus on changing the individual. Others have worked on changing classroom and school environments to facilitate motivation.

DEVELOPMENT AND REMEDIATION OF TEST ANXIETY Kennedy Hill and Seymour Sarason (1966) found that anxiety both increases across the elementary and junior high school years and becomes more negatively related to subsequent grades and test scores. Highly anxious children's achievement test scores were up to two years behind those of their low-anxiety peers, and girls' anxiety scores were higher than boys'. Hill and Wigfield (1984) estimated that as many as 10 million children and adolescents in the United States experience significant evaluation anxiety.

High anxiety is hypothesized to emerge when parents have overly high expectations and put too much pressure on their children; to date few studies have tested this proposition. Anxiety continues to develop in school as children face more frequent evaluation, social comparison, and (for some) experiences of failure; to the extent that schools emphasize these characteristics, anxiety becomes a problem for more children as they get older (Hill and Wigfield 1984). Successful anxiety intervention focuses on changing the negative, self-deprecating thoughts of anxious individuals and replacing them with more positive, task-focused thoughts (Wigfield and Eccles 1989).

DEVELOPMENT AND REMEDIATION OF LEARNED HELPLESSNESS Helpless individuals are more likely to attribute their failures to uncontrollable factors, such as lack of ability, and their successes to unstable factors (see Dweck and Goetz 1978). When encountering difficult tasks, helpless children begin to perform badly, ruminate about their difficulties, and focus on their inadequacies. By contrast, when confronted by difficulty (or failure), mastery-oriented children persist, stay focused on the task, and sometimes even use more sophisticated strategies. Further, helpless children view their intelligence as fixed, whereas mastery-oriented children believe they can improve their intelligence.

The development of learned helplessness depends on the kinds of feedback children receive from parents and teachers about their achievement outcomes, particularly feedback that their failures are due to lack of ability. Audrey Hokoda and Frank Fincham (1995) found that mothers of helpless third-grade children (in comparison to mothers of mastery-oriented children) gave fewer positive affective comments to their children, were more likely to respond to their children's lack of confidence in their ability by telling them to quit, were less responsive to bids for help, and did not focus them on mastery goals. Girls may be more likely than boys to receive negative ability feedback in elementary school classrooms, although the research is not completely consistent (see Dweck et al. 1978; Eccles et al. 1983).

Various training techniques (including operant conditioning and specific attributional feedback) can improve children's task persistence and performance by changing their failure attributions from lack of ability to lack of effort (see, for example, Dweck 1975). However, two problems have been noted. First, what if the child is already trying very hard? Then the attribution retraining may be counterproductive. Second, telling children to "try harder" without providing specific strategies to improve performance is likely to backfire: children may put in massive amounts of effort and still not succeed if they don't know how to apply that effort. Therefore, some researchers (such as Borkowski and Muthukrisna 1995) have advocated using strategy retraining in combination with attribution retraining to provide specific ways to remedy achievement problems.

Self-efficacy training can alleviate learned helplessness. First, the training increases both children's performance and their sense of self-efficacy (Schunk 1991). Second, training children to attribute their success to ability has a strong impact on self-efficacy. Third, training children to set proximal, specific, and challenging goals enhances self-efficacy and performance. Fourth, training that emphasizes process goals (analogous to task goals) increases self-efficacy and skills in writing more than an emphasis on product (ego) goals (Schunk 1991). Combining strategy training, goal emphases, and feedback to show children how various strategies relate to their performance has a strong effect on subsequent self-efficacy and skill development.

SELF-WORTH MAINTENANCE   Because children spend so much time in classrooms and are evaluated so frequently there, Martin Covington (1992) argued, they must protect their sense of academic competence in order to maintain their sense of self-worth. One way to accomplish this goal is to attribute success to both ability and effort and to attribute failure to insufficient effort (Covington and Omelich 1979; Parsons, Kaczala, and Meece 1982). Attributing failure to lack of ability is a particularly problematic attribution that students wish to avoid.

However, school evaluation, competition, and social comparison make it difficult for many children to maintain the belief that they are academically competent. Thus, many children develop strategies to avoid appearing to lack ability, including procrastination, making excuses, avoiding challenging tasks, and, most important, not trying. Although trying is critical for success, if children try and fail, it is difficult to escape the conclusion that they lack ability. Therefore, if failure seems likely, some children will not try, precisely because trying and failing threatens their ability self-concepts. Covington (1992) suggested that reducing the frequency and salience of competitive, social-comparative, and evaluative practices and focusing instead on effort, mastery, and improvement would allow more children to maintain their self-worth without having to resort to the failure-avoiding strategies just described.

STUDENT APATHY   Perhaps the most difficult motivation problem is student apathy. As Jere Brophy (1998) noted, anxious and helpless students have problems dealing with difficult material and are at risk for failing, but they continue to value learning. Because apathetic students see little value in learning, it is difficult for teachers to engage them in learning and to see its purposes. Teachers can work with apathetic students by developing contracts to get them involved in work, trying to build close relationships with them, capitalizing on the things they are interested in, and helping them to appreciate what learning can do for them. Brophy notes, however, that this often is a difficult process and may not be successful. Along with these efforts focused on the individual student, broader changes in classroom instructional methods may be needed.

SCHOOLING AND HUMAN DEVELOPMENT

Children spend many of their waking hours in either schools or various community-based settings (such as churches, playgrounds, and neighborhood streets). Schools hold a central place in children's development. From the time they enter school until they complete formal schooling, children spend more time in schools than any other place outside their homes. Consequently, educational institutions play a central role in both promoting children's acquisition of knowledge and shaping the ways in which they learn to regulate their attention, emotions, and behavior. Schools can either promote or undermine children's developmental competence. First we focus on some general ways in which schools and classrooms influence motivation to learn; then we discuss the transition from elementary school into either junior high or middle school.

School resources and structure are an important issue in their own right (see Lynch, this volume; and Heckman and Lochner, this volume). Two aspects of structure are worth noting. One is school size: children of all ages (and their teachers) scored better on a wide variety of indicators of successful development if they were in small rather than large schools (see Wigfield, Eccles, and Pintrich 1996). A second structural issue is how schools are organized; we focus on middle school structure in this chapter. Beyond resources and structure, the organizational, social, and instructional *processes* that occur in schools also affect development.

School effects operate at different levels: at the level of the school as a whole, in the classroom, and at the interpersonal level. School's effects on children's behavior are mediated through various psychological processes at the individual level. These mediating processes include both children's achievement-related beliefs and their perceptions of the school context.

Classroom-Level Influences: Teachers' Roles and Beliefs

TEACHER'S GENERAL BELIEFS ABOUT THEIR ROLE   The teacher's beliefs about his or her role as a teacher affect children's functioning by influencing the nature of the interactions between children and the teacher. Consider the distinction between the role of "academic instructor" (oriented toward teaching academic content and getting children to master academic material; fostering the "good student") and the role of "socializer" (oriented toward addressing children's social-emotional and behavioral needs and problems; fostering the "good citizen"). Brophy (1985) found that teachers who saw themselves primarily as instructors responded more negatively to underachieving, academically unmotivated, or disruptive students during learning activities than to other students. In contrast, teachers attuned to their role as a socializer responded most negatively to hostile, aggressive, and defiant students or to those who thwarted the teachers' efforts to form close personal relationships. The most effective elementary school teachers blended these two aspects of the teacher role, although emphasis on academics was critical to ensuring academic achievement.

Some teachers think of themselves as responsible for weeding out students who are less capable; others think of themselves as cultivators of all students. "Weeders" endorse the view that intelligence cannot be increased with practice, tend to hold performance goals for their students, and are more likely to use competitive motivational strategies. These culturally rooted beliefs about the nature of intelligence and the role of teachers influence the teacher practices in ways that either facilitate all children's performance or create disparities in performance and motivation.

GENERAL SENSE OF EFFICACY   When teachers hold high generalized expectations for student achievement and students perceive these expectations, students achieve more, experience a greater sense of esteem and competence as learners, and resist involvement in problem behaviors (Eccles and Wigfield 1985, 1995; Roeser, Eccles, and Sameroff 1998; Rutter 1983; Weinstein 1989). Such expectations, when communicated to the child, become internalized in positive self-appraisals that enhance feelings of worth and achievement. Similarly, teachers who feel they can reach even difficult students, who believe they can affect students' lives and influence developmental outcomes above and beyond other social influences, tend to communicate such positive expectations and beliefs to their students. Thus, a high sense of teacher efficacy can enhance children's own beliefs about their ability to master academic material, thereby promoting effort investment and achievement (Ashton 1985; Midgley, Feldlaufer, and Eccles 1989). On the other hand, low feelings of teacher efficacy often lead to behaviors that are likely to reinforce feelings of incompetence in the child, potentiating both helpless responses to the classroom and the development of depressive symptoms (see Cole 1991; Roeser, Eccles, and Sameroff 1998).

DIFFERENTIAL TEACHER EXPECTATIONS   Teachers form differential expectations about students, and students believe that teachers treat them differently based on these expectations. High achievers are seen by all students as receiving higher expectations, more opportunities to participate in class, and more choice about work, whereas low achievers are seen as receiving more negative feedback, more control, and more feedback on completing work and following rules. The greater the perceived differential treatment in a classroom, the greater the impact of teacher expectations on achievement and children's self-perceptions of competence (Weinstein 1989).

Research on teacher expectancy effects has focused on differential treatment related to gender, racial-ethnic group, and social class, investigating the potential undermining effects of low teacher expectations on girls (for math and science), on minority children (for all subject areas), and on children from families of lower socioeconomic class (SES) (for all subject areas) (for reviews, see Brophy and Good 1974; Eccles and Wigfield 1985; Jussim, Eccles, and Madon 1996). Although teacher expectancies by and large are accurate (Jussim, Eccles, and Madon 1996), biased teacher expectancies are more apt to affect girls, low-SES students, and minority students. Claude Steele (1992) linked this differential treatment, particularly for African American students, to school disengagement and disidentification (the separation of the child's self-esteem from all forms of school-related feedback). Steele argued that African American students become aware of the fact that teachers and other adults have negative stereotypes of their academic abilities. This awareness increases their anxieties, which, in turn, lead them to protect their self-esteem by disidentifying with the school context.

Bernard Weiner (1986) hypothesized that teachers' emotional reactions convey their expectations to students; that is, they are likely to display pity in providing negative feedback to those students for whom they have low expectations, and anger toward those students for whom they have high expectations. Such a difference in affect could underlie teacher expectancy effects. Sandra Graham (1991) manipulated bogus instructors' emotional reactions to experimental subjects' (learners') performance on a laboratory task: "instructors" who showed pity and offered excessive help, for example, produced "learners" who either attributed their "failures" to lack of ability and lowered their expectations for success (Graham and Barker 1990) or engaged in a variety of behaviors (for example, making excuses for their poor performance) designed to maintain their sense of self-worth (Covington 1992). Similarly, Jacquelynne Parsons, Carol Kaczala, and Judith Meece (1982) demonstrated that, when praise conveys low teacher expectations (patronizing praise, for instance, for low-level successes), it undermines junior high school students' confidence in their abilities as well as their expectations for success. When overt criticism conveys high teacher expectations (that is, when the teacher uses public criticism only with the high-performing students because the teacher wants to protect the low-performing students' egos), high rates of criticism are associated with higher student confidence in their academic ability.

TEACHERS' BELIEFS REGARDING THE NATURE OF ABILITY   Some individuals conceive of intellectual abilities as stable, largely inherited potentials; others see them as acquired skills. Carol Dweck and Elaine Elliott (1983) refer to this distinction as the difference between an entity view of intelligence and an incremental view. When the entity view of intelligence is emphasized in schools, grouping by ability, differential rewards for high achievers, public evaluative feedback, and academic competitions are more common. Such practices can promote the notion that academic success is the outperforming of others and the proving of ability (Ames 1992a). Unfortunately, most youth, by definition, are not "the best" and thus may not receive rewards and recognition in classrooms that emphasize relative ability. In ability-oriented classrooms, children are more likely to use low-level strategies to learn, to experience more anxiety and negative affect, and to devote attentional resources to strategies intended to make themselves look smarter or to avoid looking dumber than others (Ames 1992b; Covington 1992). Responding to academic failure with learned helplessness, avoiding engagement in work, and having a negative emotional experience are reactions that low-ability students are more likely to have in ability-focused environments (Dweck and Elliott 1983; Nicholls 1984).

In contrast, teachers who hold an incremental view of intelligence tend to adopt a "task goal" orientation that stresses self-improvement and effort as the major hallmarks of academic success. These teachers acknowledge individual effort and improvement regardless of a child's current ability level, provide choice and collaborative work, and emphasize that mastering new content, learning from mistakes, and continuing to try are all crucial hallmarks of success. Such practices reduce children's concerns about their ability relative to peers and their feelings of self-consciousness, anxiety, or disenfranchisement. In mastery-focused environments, children use deeper processing strategies to learn, report more positive and less negative affective states, and seem less concerned with their current ability and more concerned with task mastery, understanding, and self improvement (Ames 1992b).

TEACHER ROLES AND BELIEFS: POLICY IMPLICATIONS   Teacher beliefs and expectancies have a strong impact on children's motivation and performance. These effects may be stronger for minority students and for girls. There are several policy implications. First, teachers must be convinced that all students can learn—that is, that ability is incremental and not entity-based. Second, teachers must believe in their ability to reach different students and increase achievement for all. Teachers should expect the most from each of their students, not just from some. Third, teachers must be aware that their expectancies for students sometimes can undermine students' motivation and performance, especially for minority students and for girls in subject areas like math and science.

How can these goals be accomplished? First, teacher training programs should teach about the effects of beliefs and expectancies. Second, teacher training programs and subsequent professional training should emphasize how to monitor expectancies for different students and how to change them as appropriate. Third, principals and others should observe teachers in the classroom and document how they behave toward different students. Because the pace of classroom instruction is so quick, teachers often find it difficult to monitor how they treat different students, and so observers can provide this information.

Classroom-Level Influences: Instructional Practices

ORDERLINESS AND PREDICTABILITY   In rooms where teachers have established efficient procedures for monitoring student progress, providing feedback, enforcing accountability for work completion, and organizing group activities, student achievement and conduct are enhanced. The quality of classroom management also contributes to differences in children's motivation. For example, Phyllis Blumenfeld and her colleagues (1983) found that classroom academic orientation has benefits for children's perceptions of the importance of adherence to classroom work norms. Where children are held accountable, they may exert more effort, value success more, see themselves as more able, and consequently do better.

CONTROL AND AUTONOMY   Classroom authority structure is important for the development of children's regulation of their achievement behavior (Deci and Ryan 1985). Some researchers (Boggiano et al. 1992; Deci and Ryan 1985) have argued that intrinsic motivation is good for learning and that classroom environments that are overly controlling undermine intrinsic motivation, mastery orientation, ability self-concepts and expectations, and self-direction. In classroom settings where children are given opportunities to make choices, pursue their interests, and contribute to classroom discussions and decisions, a sense of autonomous, self-determined behavior in relation to schoolwork is inculcated. By contrast, in classrooms where few provisions for self-determined behavior are granted and where external rewards, punishments, and praise are frequently used to induce achievement behavior, children often believe their behavior is being controlled by factors outside themselves. In such a controlling environment, children may begin to work toward some goal extrinsic to learning, often with the least possible effort to attain a reward, rather than approaching learning for its intrinsic qualities of knowledge building and enjoyment.

Highly controlling practices in classrooms with troubled children can lead to escalating behavior problems and plummeting motivation (Cooper and Upton 1990). Teachers often respond to children who show poor achievement histories or underregulated behaviors, such as inattention, impulsivity, and aggression, with controlling methods (sanctions, public feedback) to get them to learn or behave. Excessive use of extrinsic rewards and behavioral sanctions undermines low achievers' intrinsic motivation (Skinner and Belmont 1993) and leads to an escalation of negative behavior and feelings of defiance in emotionally troubled children (Cooper and Upton 1990). Unfortunately, classrooms with many low-ability or difficult children are often characterized by more teacher control and less innovative instructional practices (Oakes, Gamoran, and Page 1992). Such an emphasis on control is no doubt a response to characteristics of the students, though such practices are not likely to enhance behavioral or emotional engagement.

Despite these findings, adults have a strong preference for controlling teachers. Researchers videotaped teachers teaching children a set of tasks using either a controlling strategy or a less controlling strategy (Flink, Boggiano, and Barrett 1990). Observers of the tapes rated the more controlling teachers as better teachers despite the fact that the children had actually learned more under the less controlling teachers.

GENERAL TEACHING PRACTICES LINKED TO SELF-EVALUATION AND MOTIVATION
Susan Rosenholtz and Carol Simpson (1984) suggested a cluster of teaching practices (for example, individualized versus whole group instruction; ability grouping practices; and public feedback) that should affect motivation because they make ability differences in the classroom especially salient to students (see also Mac Iver 1988). They assumed that these practices affect motivation by increasing the salience of extrinsic motivators and ego-focused learning goals, leading to a greater incidence of social comparison behaviors and increased perception of ability as an entity state rather than an incremental condition. These changes should reduce the quality of children's motivation and learning, but the negative consequences should be greater for low-performing children: as these students become more aware of

their relatively low standing, they are likely to adopt a variety of ego-protective strategies that undermine learning and mastery (Covington 1992; Rosenholtz and Rosenholtz 1981).

Evaluation practices also influence students' self-evaluation. Although students primarily use feedback and grades to judge their ability, how teachers report on and recognize performance affects the degree to which ability-related information is accessible, comparable, and salient (Rosenholtz and Rosenholtz 1981). Public methods for charting progress, such as wall posters, provide information that is readily available to students. In addition, teachers who frequently contrast students' performances, grant privileges to "smart" children, or award prizes for the "best" performances may increase the importance of ability and heighten the negative affect associated with failure (see Ames 1992a, 1992b). When there are few winners and many losers, relative performance may be more salient to children (Nicholls 1989). In contrast, in more cooperative or mastery-oriented classrooms, everyone who performs adequately can experience success. Youngsters in mastery-oriented rooms are more likely to focus on self-improvement than on social comparison, to perceive themselves as able, and to have high expectations for success (Covington 1992; Nicholls 1989). Finally, when variations in evaluations are either attributed to entity-based differences in competence or used as a controlling strategy rather than primarily for information on progress, intrinsic motivation is reduced. Thus, mastery evaluation practices are better at fostering and maintaining motivation than social-normative, competitive, or controlling evaluation practices (see also Maehr and Midgley 1996).

GIRLS AND MATH: GIRL-FRIENDLY CLASSROOMS   Sex differences in children's preference for different types of learning contexts are likely to interact with subject area to produce sex differences in interest in different subject areas (Casserly 1980; Eccles 1989; Hoffmann and Haeussler 1995). Girls appear to respond more positively to math and science instruction if the teacher avoids sexism and if the subject is taught in a cooperative or individualized manner rather than a competitive manner, from an applied and person-centered perspective rather than from a theoretical-abstract perspective, and with a hands-on approach rather than a "book learning" approach. The reason given for these effects is the fit between the former teaching style and instructional focus, on the one hand, and girls' values, goals, motivational orientation, and learning, on the other. When more girl-friendly instructional approaches are used in math and science classes, girls as well as boys are more likely to continue taking courses in these fields and to consider working in them when they become adults.

TEACHER-STUDENT RELATIONSHIPS   Quality teacher-student relationships provide the affective underpinnings of academic motivation and success (Moos 1979). Teachers who are trusting, caring, and respectful of students provide the social-emotional support that students need to persist on academic learning tasks and to develop positive, achievement-related self-perceptions and values (Goodenow 1993; Midgley, Feldlaufer, and Eccles 1989; Wentzel 1999). Students' perceptions of caring teachers enhance their feelings of self-esteem, school belonging, and positive affect in school (Roeser, Eccles, and Sameroff 1998). Teachers represent one stable source of nonparental role models for adolescents. They teach but also can provide guidance and assistance when social-emotional or academic problems arise, and they may be particularly important in promoting developmental competence when conditions in the family and neighborhood do not (Simmons and Blyth 1987).

TEACHING PRACTICES LINKED TO SELF-EVALUATION AND MOTIVATION: POLICY IMPLICATIONS Programs designed to facilitate student motivation and achievement emphasize teaching practices that facilitate competence beliefs, intrinsic motivation, and mastery goals. These programs have been implemented in elementary and middle school classrooms and have been successful in enhancing student motivation and achievement. We highlight some of these programs in this section (for further discussion, see Blumenfeld et al. 1991; Brophy 1998; Maehr and Midgley 1996; Stipek 1996).

There also are some school-based programs that use extrinsic rewards to foster student motivation and engagement. Many of these programs focus on reading during the early elementary school years (for a review, see Gambrell and Marniak 1997). These programs have been shown to increase the time and effort that students spend on activities such as reading, at least over the short term. However, such programs may not foster long-term engagement in learning (Anderman, Maehr, and Midgley, forthcoming; Brophy 1998). We therefore focus on programs designed to stimulate intrinsic motivation to learn and mastery goals.

Carole Ames (1992a) used the acronym TARGET to discuss the crucial characteristics of instructional practices that influence student motivation. TARGET stands for tasks, authority, recognition, grouping, evaluation, and time. Ames worked with elementary school teachers to structure each of these aspects of instruction in ways to maximize student motivation. To facilitate positive motivation in the classroom, tasks should be reasonably challenging and of interest to students. Authority in the classroom should be shared so that students have opportunities to participate in decisionmaking and to take responsibility for their own achievement. All students should receive recognition for their learning and effort. Grouping in class should be heterogeneous, and all students should work with a diverse mixture of their classmates. Students should be evaluated on progress and mastery rather than solely on outcomes, and comparative forms of evaluation should not be used. Finally, students need different amounts of time to master various classroom tasks. Ames (1992a) reported that the implementation of an elementary school curriculum based on the TARGET principles increased children's interest in learning, use of effective cognitive learning strategies, and attitudes toward learning.

Katheryn Au and her colleagues (Au 1997; Au et al. 1990) developed curricula to foster the development of literacy skills in native Hawaiians, a group that traditionally has done poorly in school. Their program, called the Kamehameha Elementary Education Program (KEEP), promotes students' sense of ownership over what they are learning by making the materials used culturally relevant to the children. Evaluations have shown that students are strongly engaged in the literacy activities and have a strong sense of ownership over them. In addition, over 67 percent of the students in the program were at or above grade level in writing, whereas far less than half of the students in traditional classrooms were at or above grade level. The results of this program are especially encouraging because it has been implemented with students who traditionally do not do well in school and see little value in learning.

The Concept Oriented Reading Instruction (CORI) program, which is designed to foster engagement and achievement in reading (see Guthrie and Alao 1997; Guthrie et al. 1996), integrates science and reading, with a special emphasis on hands-on activities, collaborative projects, the use of interesting texts, and strategy instruction. The program was implemented in several elementary schools serving diverse student populations. Students in CORI achieve better and have stronger intrinsic motivation than do students in the same schools in traditional reading programs.

Maehr and Midgley (1996) argued that even when classroom-level programs are successful, there often are barriers at the school level that impede their full implementation. They therefore focused on changing the entire motivational culture of one elementary school and one middle school to enhance students' motivation and achievement. The basis for the intervention was Ames's (1992a) TARGET approach, which they expanded to the school level. They worked closely with staff at the schools to bring about the changes in school culture. Anderman, Maehr, and Midgley (forthcoming) assessed the effects of the program on student motivation, focusing on the elementary school students. They found no differences in student motivation during elementary school. However, students in the TARGET elementary school had more positive motivation in middle school than did students in a comparison school.

Academic Tracking and Curricular Differentiation

Tracking refers to regularities in the ways in which schools structure learning experiences for different students (Oakes, Gamoran, and Page 1992). Providing different educational experiences for students of different ability levels is a widespread, yet controversial, practice. Grouping takes different forms at different grades. It includes within-class ability grouping for different subjects, or between-class ability grouping in which different types of children are assigned to different teachers; the latter type often is referred to as tracking. Within-classroom ability grouping for reading and math is common in elementary school. During middle and high school, tracking becomes more widespread; students bound for different postsecondary school trajectories (college preparation, general, vocational) take sequences of specific courses. Tracking determines not only the quality and kinds of opportunities to learn the child receives (Oakes, Gamoran, and Page 1992) but also the child's exposure to different peers and thus, to a certain degree, the nature of social relationships formed in school (Fuligni, Eccles, and Barber 1995).

The best justification for tracking derives from a person-environment fit perspective. Children are more motivated to learn if the material can be adapted to their competence level. There is some evidence consistent with this perspective for children placed in high-ability classrooms, high-within-class ability groups, and college tracks (Dreeban and Barr 1988; Fuligni, Eccles, and Barber 1995; Gamoran and Mare 1989; Pallas et al. 1994).

The results for children placed in low-ability and noncollege tracks differ. The use of either whole class instruction or within-class ability groups often creates situations that highlight ability differences and leads to both social comparison and differential teacher treatment of high and low achievers in the classroom (Eccles, Midgley, and Adler 1984). When this happens, low-ability children come to feel less competent, worthy, or valued precisely because their relatively lower ability is made salient (Covington 1992; Rosenholtz and Simpson 1984). These low-ability children also come to be perceived by their peers as less desirable than their high-achieving classmates—a perception that, in turn, is likely to increase their social isolation.

Low track placements have been related to poor attitudes toward school, feelings of incompetence, and problem behaviors both within school (nonattendance, crime, misconduct) and in the broader community (drug use, arrests), as well as to educational attainments (Oakes, Gamoran, and Page 1992). But whether academic tracks promote such outcomes or reflect preexisting differences remains a matter of considerable debate. These negative effects result from the stereotypically biased implementation of ability-grouping programs. A different result might emerge for the low-competence students if their teachers provided high-quality instruction and motivational practices tailored to the competence level of the students.

Another way to think about the impact of ability grouping on development is in terms of its impact on peer groups: between-classroom ability grouping and curricular differentiation promotes continuity of contact among children and adolescents with similar levels of achievement and engagement with school. For those doing poorly in school, such practices can structure and promote friendships among students who are similarly alienated and are more likely to engage in risky or delinquent behaviors (Dryfoos 1990). The "collecting" of children with poor achievement or adjustment histories also places additional burdens on their teachers, who often are new to the system when they are given these difficult assignments (Oakes, Gamoran, and Page 1992).

Tracking and ability grouping can also concentrate children with similar behavioral vulnerabilities. For instance, Kellam and his colleagues (1994) found that rates of moderate to severe aggression ranged between 7 to 8 percent and 63 percent among children in two different first-grade classrooms in the same school. This was due to between-class ability grouping policies. As a result, children in these two classrooms were exposed to different environments: one in which aggression was deviant (only 7 to 8 percent of students were aggressive) and one in which it was the norm (63 percent of students were aggressive). In classrooms with high rates of aggression, aggressive behavior may not lead to peer rejection, as it often does in other classrooms (Coie and Dodge 1998). In such an environment, aggression may confer status and social rewards among peers and thus be reinforced. By placing children with similar vulnerabilities in the same environment, the reinforcement of negative behavior and the promotion of friendships among similarly troubled children are more probable outcomes.

In summary, tracking provides an example of how school policy, teacher beliefs and instruction, and student characteristics can interact to create maladaptive transactions that perpetuate poor achievement and behavior among low-ability children. The placement of many low-ability children in a low-track classroom may cause some teachers to feel overwhelmed and ineffective. This response may translate into poor instruction, low expectations, and use of controlling strategies. These responses can fuel student disengagement, which then feeds back into the teachers' beliefs and practices. Eventually, the academic failure of certain low-ability children results from these reciprocal processes.

TRACKING AND ABILITY GROUPING: POLICY IMPLICATIONS What can be done to alleviate the problems associated with ability grouping and tracking? One suggestion is to eliminate them altogether. Many parents, teachers, and school administrators resist this suggestion. Another practice already occurs in many schools: using grouping in only certain classes (such as reading and math) and not using it for other subjects.

The use of collaborative or cooperative groups is an increasingly popular alternative to whole-group, ability-grouped, or individualized instruction at the elementary level. Robert Slavin (1990) concluded that cooperative learning techniques in which small groups of students receive recognition based on group performance lead to increases in achievement, self-esteem, and social acceptance among students of different social statuses and racial-ethnic backgrounds. Cooperative groups can provide numerous "niches" for students with different strengths to participate in the learning process, increase the amount of social support and reinforcement available for learning complex material, and increase contact among students of different abilities. Such consequences foster broader friendship networks and lessen social isolation (Slavin 1990).

Another controversial aspect of tracking is how students are placed in different classes and how they are moved between class levels as their academic needs and competencies change after initial placements are made. These issues are important both early (see, for example, Entwisle and Alexander 1993) and later in adolescence, when course placement affects post–high school options. Sanford Dornbusch (1994) found that 85 percent of his high school sample stayed in the same track; there was little mobility. Also, many average students were misassigned to lower track courses. Misassignment put these students on a path that would not lead them into the higher educational system. Of particular concern was the fact that these youth were more likely to be of color and poor. Neither the students nor their parents were informed of this tracking.

THE TRANSITION FROM ELEMENTARY SCHOOL TO MIDDLE SCHOOL

School transitions are a demonstration of how the multiple levels of school interact to affect development. All school districts must decide when they allow children to begin school and how they will group the grade levels within various buildings. One common arrangement is to group kindergarten through sixth grade in elementary school, grades seven through nine in junior high school, and grades ten through twelve in senior high school. The other most common arrangement places the transitions after grade fives and eight—creating elementary, middle, and senior high schools. Children typically move to a new and often larger building at each of the major school transition points. These moves usually involve increased busing and exposure to a diverse student body. Such transitions influence children's development (see Eccles, Midgley, and Adler 1984; Higgins and Eccles-Parsons 1983). We focus on the transition from elementary school to middle school because it has been most widely researched.

There is substantial evidence of declines in academic motivation and achievement across the early adolescence years (approximately ages eleven to fourteen; see Anderman and Maehr 1994; Eccles and Midgley 1989; Eccles et al. 1993; Wigfield, Eccles, and Pintrich 1996). In many cases, the declines in motivation and achievement coincide with school transitions. For example, school grades decline as students move into junior high school (Simmons and Blyth 1987), as does their interest in school (Epstein and McPartland 1976), intrinsic motivation (Harter 1981), self-concepts and self-perceptions (Eccles et al. 1989; Wigfield et al. 1991), and confidence in their intellectual abilities, especially following failure (Parsons and Ruble 1977). There are also increases in test anxiety (Wigfield and Eccles 1989), learned-helplessness responses to failure (Rholes et al. 1980), focus on self-evaluation rather than task mastery (Nicholls 1990), and truancy and school dropout (Rosenbaum 1976). Academic failure and dropout are especially problematic among some ethnic groups and among youth from low-SES communities and families (Finn 1989). These groups are particularly likely to show these declines in academic motivation and self-perception as they move into and through the secondary school years.

Eccles and Midgley (1989) proposed that these negative developmental changes result from the fact that traditional junior high schools do not provide developmentally appropriate educational environments for early adolescents. They suggested that different types of educational environments may be needed for different age groups to meet individual developmental needs and foster continued developmental growth. Exposure to a developmentally appropriate environment would facilitate both motivation and continued growth; in contrast, exposure to a developmentally inappropriate environment, especially a developmentally regressive environment, should create a particularly poor person-environment fit, leading to declines in motivation as well as to detachment from the goals of the institution.

Factors Influencing Students' Adjustment to Junior High or Middle School

SCHOOL SIZE AND DEPARTMENTALIZATION   Roberta Simmons and Dale Blyth (1987) pointed out that most junior high schools are substantially larger (by several orders of magnitude) than elementary schools and that instruction is also more likely to be organized departmentally. As a result, junior high school teachers typically teach several different groups of students, making it very difficult for students to form a close relationship with any school-affiliated adult precisely at the point in development when there is a great need for guidance and support from nonfamilial adults. Such changes in student-teacher relationships are also likely to undermine the sense of community and trust between students and teachers, leading to a lowered sense of efficacy among the teachers, their increased reliance on authoritarian control practices, and an increased sense of alienation among the students. Finally, such changes decrease the probability that any particular student's difficulties will be noticed early enough for the student to receive the necessary help, thus increasing the likelihood that students on the edge will slip onto the negative motivational and performance trajectories that lead to increased school failure and dropout.

In earlier sections, we presented examples of how such school- and classroom-level characteristics may affect both teacher beliefs and practices, which affect children's development. But until quite recently, the relation of school transitions to these characteristics has rarely been considered. The extant work on these characteristics is reviewed next.

AUTHORITY RELATIONSHIPS   Despite the increasing maturity of students, junior high school classrooms, compared to those in elementary school, often are characterized by a greater emphasis on teacher control and discipline and by fewer opportunities for student decisionmaking, choice, and self-management (see, for example, Midgley and Feldlaufer 1987; Moos 1979). For example, junior high school teachers spend more time maintaining order and less time teaching than elementary school teachers (Brophy and Everston 1976). Similarly, sixth-grade elementary school math teachers reported less concern with control and discipline than seventh-grade junior high school math teachers reported one year later for the same students (Midgley, Feldlaufer, and Eccles 1988). Midgley and Feldlaufer (1987) reported that both seventh-graders and their teachers in the first year of junior high indicated that students had fewer opportunities to participate in classroom decisionmaking than did these same students and their sixth-grade elementary school teachers one year earlier.

Stage-environment fit theory suggests that the mismatch between young adolescents' desires for autonomy and control and their perceptions of the opportunities in their learning environments should result in a decline in their intrinsic motivation and interest in school. Mac Iver and Reuman (1988) compared changes in intrinsic interest in mathematics for adolescents reporting different patterns of change in their opportunities for participation in classroom decisionmaking across the junior high school transition. Those adolescents who perceived their seventh-grade math classrooms as providing fewer opportunities than had been available in sixth-grade math reported the largest declines in intrinsic interest in math between sixth and seventh grades.

AFFECTIVE RELATIONSHIPS   Junior high school classrooms are characterized by a less personal and positive teacher-student relationship than is found in elementary classrooms. Given the association between classroom climate and student motivation, the move into a less supportive classroom leads to a decline in interest in the subject matter being taught in that classroom, particularly among the low-achieving students (Midgley, Feldlaufer, and Eccles 1988).

TEACHER EFFICACY   Junior high school teachers also feel less efficacious than elementary school teachers, especially with low-ability students (Midgley, Feldlaufer, and Eccles 1988). Differences in teachers' sense of efficacy before and after the transition to junior high school contribute to the decline in the confidence of early adolescents, particularly low-achieving adolescents, in their academic abilities and potential (Midgley, Feldlaufer, and Eccles 1989).

ORGANIZATION OF INSTRUCTION   The shift to junior high school is also associated with an increase in practices such as whole-class task organization and between-classroom ability grouping (see Eccles and Midgley 1989; Oakes 1981). As noted earlier, such changes increase social comparison, concerns about evaluation, and competitiveness (see Eccles, Midgley, and Adler 1984; Rosenholtz and Simpson 1984), as well as teachers' use of normative grading criteria and more public forms of evaluation, both of which have been shown to have a negative effect on adolescents' self-perceptions and motivation.

GRADING PRACTICES   There is no stronger predictor of students' self-confidence and efficacy than their grades. Grades drop for many early adolescents as they make the junior high school transition (Eccles and Midgley 1989; Simmons and Blyth 1987). This decline in grades is not matched by a decline in the adolescents' scores on standardized achievement tests, suggesting that the decline reflects a change in grading practices rather than a change in the rate of the students' learning (Kavrell and Petersen 1984). Simmons and Blyth (1987) documented the impact of this grade drop on subsequent school performance and likelihood of dropping out. Even controlling for a youth's performance prior to the school transition, the magnitude of the grade drop following the transition into either junior high school or middle school was a major predictor of early school leaving.

MOTIVATIONAL GOALS   Classroom practices related to grading practices, support for autonomy, and instructional organization affect the relative salience of the mastery versus performance goals that students adopt as they engage in learning tasks. The types of changes associated with the school transition in the middle grades should precipitate a greater focus on performance goals. Teachers and students in middle school indicated that performance-focused goals were more prevalent and task-focused goals were less prevalent in the middle school classrooms than did teachers and students in elementary school classrooms (Midgley, Anderman, and Hicks 1995). In addition, elementary school teachers reported using task-focused instructional strategies more frequently than did middle school teachers. Finally, at both grade levels the extent to which teachers were task-focused predicted the students' and the teachers' sense of personal efficacy; personal efficacy was lower among the middle school participants than among the elementary school participants.

Transition to Middle School: Policy Implications

The research reviewed in this section suggests that the transition to middle school is a difficult one for many children, that the school and classroom environments of middle school often do not match well with developmental needs, and that the typical kinds of instruction enhance extrinsic motivation and performance goals and decrease children's competence beliefs and intrinsic motivation. The resulting "poor fit" between the early adolescent and the classroom environment increases the risk of negative motivational and achievement outcomes, especially for those having academic difficulty. These and other difficulties that students experience in traditional junior high schools led many school districts to create middle schools, which would better meet the developmental needs of early adolescents (for discussion of the middle school movement, see Irvin 1992; Lipsitz et al. 1997).

Some attempts to deal with these issues start in elementary school, where elementary school teachers work with students to help them prepare for the transition. Many middle schools now have orientations for parents and students to begin to accustom students to what the new school will be like. To ease students' transitions into the middle school environment, many schools have created "schools within a school," especially for the youngest students in the school. They are housed in one part of the building, have lunch with students their own age, and generally are sheltered from the older students. These practices help establish a sense of community among the younger students, allowing them to be more comfortable in the new environment.

A related practice is teaming, in which teachers teaching various subjects work together with a group of 100 to 150 students. The teaming approach replaces the departmental structure, under which teachers teaching a given subject meet together. The advantages of the teaming approach include coordination of material across subject areas and a chance for teachers to work with a smaller group of students and therefore get to know them better. The teams meet to discuss students' progress in the different subjects, so teachers become concerned with the "whole child" rather than just one specific subject. Teaming can be done at all grade levels in middle school.

Another important change is providing students with the opportunity to meet with teachers in settings outside the classroom. Some teachers enjoy being mentors for students, and many early adolescents need guidance from supportive adults. These kinds of teacher-student relationships involve students more fully in the school and can help early adolescents deal with many issues. Systematic evaluations of the effects of these kinds of changes in early adolescents' motivation and achievement are needed.

SCHOOL-COMMUNITY LINKAGES

James Comer (1980) has stressed the importance of school-community links (see also Nettles 1991; and Sampson, this volume). He argues that schools are a part of the larger community and that they are successful only to the extent that they are well integrated into that community. For example, schools need to be well connected to social services and to play a cooperative role in furthering the well-being of children and their families. Conversely, communities need to be actively engaged in their schools. For example, connecting the business community to the school can increase opportunities for students to make a smooth transition from school into the world of work. Such opportunities can range from field trips to employment settings, apprenticeships, and the direct involvement of employees in the instructional program of the school. Researchers have found that school-community linkages can lead to improvement in adolescents' achievement (Jordan and Nettles, forthcoming; Sanders 1996a,1996b).

Closer ties between schools and communities may be especially important in high-risk neighborhoods that lack structured opportunities for youth after school (see, for example, Carnegie Council on Adolescent Development 1989). In most communities, adolescents finish school by 2:00 or 3:00 P.M. Typically, their parents are working until early evening, leaving the adolescents largely unsupervised. Communities miss an opportunity to foster positive development through meaningful activities in this un-supervised period, which is also the time when adolescents are most likely to engage in problem behaviors. A closer collaboration between communities and schools could help solve this dilemma. School buildings could be used as activity centers, or school and community personnel could work together to design a variety of programs to meet the multiple needs of their youth (for further discussion of community programs, see Sampson, this volume). One promising program that attempts to facilitate school, family, and community connections is the National Network of Partnership-2000 schools. This program, based at Johns Hopkins's Center for Research on the Education of Students Placed at Risk, functions in several states across the country (see Sanders 1996a). Each year the program focuses on specific goals, such as improving student attendance or improving student achievement.

CONCLUSION

We began by summarizing what is known about motivation to learn, focusing on developmental changes in students' motivation through the elementary and middle school years. We described how the characteristics and practices of schools influence motivation and achievement. Thinking of schools as complex organizations, we stressed the interface of schools with the developmental trajectories of individuals.

We discussed the kinds of programs that have been developed to deal with the declines in students' motivation. These include programs designed to serve individual children, classroom-based programs, and programs involving change in entire schools. We also discussed efforts to ease children's transition from elementary school to middle school, such as creating teams of teachers working with the same group of children, creating "schools within schools," reducing the use of tracking, and establishing teacher-student mentoring programs. These changes in school structure and organization are designed to facilitate children's optimal development during the early adolescent years by providing a better fit between the qualities of the school environment and the developmental needs of early adolescents. These efforts need to be evaluated systematically in the next few years.

The writing of this chapter was supported in part by Grant HD17553 from the National Institute of Child Health and Human Development to Jacquelynne S. Eccles, Allan Wigfield, and Phyllis Blumenfeld.

REFERENCES

Alexander, Karl L., Susan L. Dauber, and Doris R. Entwisle. 1993. "First-Grade Classroom Behavior: Its Short- and Long-term Consequences for School Performance." *Child Development* 64(2): 801–3.

Alexander, Karl L., and Doris Entwisle. 1988. "Achievement in the First Two Years of School: Patterns and Processes." *Monographs of the Society for Research in Child Development* 53 (2, serial no. 218).

Ames, Carole. 1992a. "Achievement Goals and the Classroom Motivational Climate." In *Student Perceptions in the Classroom,* edited by Dale H. Schunk and Judith Meece. Hillsdale, N.J.: Lawrence Erlbaum.

———. 1992b. "Classrooms: Goals, Structures, and Student Motivation." *Journal of Educational Psychology* 84(3): 261–71.

Anderman, Eric M., and Martin L. Maehr. 1994. "Motivation and Schooling in the Middle Grades." *Review of Educational Research* 64(2): 287–309.

Anderman, Eric M., Martin L. Maehr, and Carol Midgley. Forthcoming. "Declining Motivation After the Transition to Middle School: Schools Can Make a Difference." *Journal of Research and Development in Education.*

Arbreton, Amy J., and Jacquelynne S. Eccles. 1994. "Mothers' Perceptions of Their Children During the Transition from Kindergarten to Formal Schooling: The Effect of Teacher Evaluations on Parents' Expectations for Their Early Elementary School Children." Paper presented at the American Educational Research Association conference, New Orleans (April 1994).

Ashton, Patricia. 1985. "Motivation and the Teacher's Sense of Efficacy." In *Research on Motivation in Education,* vol. 2, *The Classroom Milieu,* edited by Carole Ames and Russell Ames. Orlando, Fla.: Academic Press.

Au, Kathryn H. 1997. "Ownership, Literacy Achievement, and Students of Diverse Cultural Backgrounds." In *Reading Engagement: Motivating Readers Through Integrated Instruction,* edited by John T. Guthrie and Allan Wigfield. Newark, Del.: International Reading Association.

Au, Kathryn, Judith A. Scheu, Alice J. Kawakami, and Patricia A. Herman. 1990. "Assessment and Accountability in a Whole Literacy Curriculum." *The Reading Teacher* 43(8): 574–78.

Blumenfeld, Phyllis, V. Lee Hamilton, Steven Bossert, Kathleen Wessels, and Judith Meece. 1983. "Teacher Talk and Student Thought: Socialization into the Student Role." In *Teacher and Student Perceptions: Implications for Learning,* edited by John Levine and Margaret Wang. Hillsdale, N.J.: Lawrence Erlbaum.

Blumenfeld, Phyllis C., Elliott Soloway, Ronald W. Marx, Joseph S. Krajcik, M. Gzidal, and Annemarie Palincsar. 1991. "Motivating Project-Based Learning: Sustaining the Doing, Supporting the Learning." *Educational Psychologist* 26(3/4): 369–98.

Boggiano, Ann K., Ann Shields, Marty Barrett, Teddy Kellam, Erik Thompson, Jeffrey Simons, and Phyllis Katz. 1992. "Helplessness Deficits in Students: The Role of Motivational Orientation." *Motivation and Emotion* 16(3): 271–96.

Borkowski, John G., and Nithi Muthukrisna. 1995. "Learning Environments and Skill Generalization: How Contexts Facilitate Regulatory Processes and Efficacy Beliefs." In *Recent Perspectives on Memory Development*, edited by F. Weinert and W. Schneider. Hillsdale, N.J.: Lawrence Erlbaum.

Brophy, Jere E. 1985. "Teachers' Expectations, Motives, and Goals for Working with Problem Students." In *Research on Motivation in Education*, vol. 2, *The Classroom Milieu*, edited by Carole Ames and Russell Ames. New York: Academic Press.

———. 1998. *Motivating Students to Learn*. Boston: McGraw-Hill.

Brophy, Jere E., and Carol Evertson. 1976. *Learning for Teaching: A Developmental Perspective.* Boston: Allyn and Bacon.

Brophy, Jere E., and Thomas L. Good. 1974. *Teacher-Student Relationships.* New York: Holt, Rinehart and Winston.

Carnegie Council on Adolescent Development. 1989. *Turning Points: Preparing American Youth for the Twenty-first Century.* New York: Carnegie Corp.

Casserly, Pamela. 1980. "An Assessment of Factors Affecting Female Participation in Advanced Placement Programs in Mathematics, Chemistry, and Physics." In *Women and the Mathematical Mystique*, edited by Lynn Fox, Linda I. Brody, and Dianne Tobin. Baltimore: Johns Hopkins University Press.

Coie, John D., and Kenneth A. Dodge. 1998. "Aggression and Antisocial Behavior." In *Handbook of Child Psychology*, 5th ed., vol. 3, edited by William Damon and Nancy Eisenberg. New York: John Wiley.

Coie, John D., and Gary Krechbiel. 1984. "Effects of Academic Tutoring on the Social Status of Low-Achieving, Socially Rejected Children." *Child Development* 55: 1465–78.

Cole, David A. 1991. "Preliminary Support for a Competency-Based Model of Depression in Children." *Journal of Abnormal Psychology* 100(2): 181–90.

Comer, James. 1980. *School Power.* New York: Free Press.

Cooper, Paul, and Graham Upton. 1990. "An Ecosystemic Approach to Emotional and Behavioral Difficulties in Schools." *Educational Psychologist* 10: 301–21.

Covington, Martin. 1992. *Making the Grade: A Self-worth Perspective on Motivation and School Reform.* New York: Cambridge University Press.

Covington, Martin V., and Carol L. Omelich. 1979. "Effort: The Double-edged Sword in School Achievement." *Journal of Educational Psychology* 71: 169–82.

Deci, Elwood L., and Richard M. Ryan. 1985. *Intrinsic Motivation and Self-determination in Human Behavior.* New York: Plenum Press.

Dornbusch, Sanford. 1994. "Off the Track." Presidential address at the biennial meeting of the Society for Research on Adolescence, San Diego (February 1994).

Dreeben, Robert, and Rebecca Barr. 1988. "Classroom Composition and the Design of Instruction." *Sociology of Education* 61(3): 129–42.

Dryfoos, Joy G. 1990. *Adolescents at Risk: Prevalence and Prevention.* New York: Oxford University Press.

Dweck, Carol S. 1975. "The Role of Expectations and Attributions in the Alleviation of Learned Helplessness." *Journal of Personality and Social Psychology* 31: 674–85.

Dweck, Carol S., William Davidson, Sharon Nelson, and Bradley Enna. 1978. "Sex Differences in Learned Helplessness: 2. The Contingencies of Evaluative Feedback in the Classroom, and 3. An Experimental Analysis." *Developmental Psychology* 14(3): 268–76.

Dweck, Carol S., and Elaine S. Elliott. 1983. "Achievement Motivation." In *Handbook of Child Psychology,* vol. 4, edited by P. H. Mussen. New York: Wiley.

Dweck, Carol S., and Therese E. Goetz. 1978. "Attributions and Learned Helplessness." In *New Directions in Attribution Research,* vol. 2, edited by J. H. Harvey, William Ickes, and R. F. Kidd. Hillsdale, N.J.: Lawrence Erlbaum.

Eccles, Jacquelynne S. 1984. "Sex Differences in Achievement Patterns." In *Nebraska Symposium on Motivation 1984: Psychology and Gender,* vol. 32, edited by Theo Sonderegger. Lincoln: University of Nebraska Press.

———. 1989. "Bringing Young Women to Math and Science." In *Gender and Thought: Psychological Perspectives,* edited by Mary Crawford and Margaret Gentry. New York: Springer-Verlag.

———. 1993. "School and Family Effects on the Ontogeny of Children's Interests, Self-perceptions, and Activity Choice." In *Nebraska Symposium on Motivation, 1992: Developmental Perspectives on Motivation,* edited by Janis E. Jacobs. Lincoln: University of Nebraska Press.

Eccles (Parsons), Jacquelynne, Terri F. Adler, Robert Futterman, Susan B. Goff, Carol M. Kaczala, Judith L. Meece, and Carol Midgley. 1983. "Expectancies, Values, and Academic Behaviors." In *Achievement and Achievement Motivation,* edited by J. T. Spence. San Francisco: Freeman.

Eccles, Jacquelynne S., and Rena D. Harold. 1991. "Gender Differences in Sport Involvement: Applying the Eccles Expectancy-Value Model." *Journal of Applied Sport Psychology* 3(1): 7–35.

Eccles, Jacquelynne S., and Carol Midgley. 1989. "Stage-Environment Fit: Developmentally Appropriate Classrooms for Early Adolescents." In *Research on Motivation in Education,* vol. 3, edited by R. Ames and C. Ames. New York: Academic Press.

Eccles, Jacquelynne, Carol Midgley, and Terri Adler. 1984. "Grade-Related Changes in the School Environment: Effects on Achievement Motivation." In *The Development of Achievement Motivation,* edited by John G. Nicholls. Greenwich, Conn.: JAI Press.

Eccles, Jacquelynne S., Carol Midgley, Allan Wigfield, Christy M. Buchanan, David Reuman, Constance Flanagan, and Douglas Mac Iver. 1993. "Development During Adolescence: The Impact of Stage-Environment Fit on Adolescents' Experiences in Schools and Families." *American Psychologist* 48(2): 90–101.

Eccles, Jacquelynne, and Allan Wigfield. 1985. "Teacher Expectations and Student Motivation." In *Teacher Expectancies,* edited by J. B. Dusek. Hillsdale, N.J.: Lawrence Erlbaum.

———. 1995. "In the Mind of the Actor: The Structure of Adolescents' Achievement Task Values and Expectancy-Related Beliefs." *Personality and Social Psychology Bulletin* 21: 215–25.

Eccles, Jacquelynne S., Allan Wigfield, and Phyllis Blumenfeld. 1984. *Psychological Predictors of Competence Development.* Grant 2 R01 HD17553-01. Bethesda, Md.: National Institute of Child Health and Human Development.

Eccles, Jacquelynne S., Allan Wigfield, C. Flanagan, C. Miller, D. Reuman, and D. Yee. 1989. "Self-concepts, Domain Values, and Self-esteem: Relations and Changes at Early Adolescence." *Journal of Personality* 57(2): 283–310.

Eccles, Jacquelynne S., Allan Wigfield, and Ulrich Schiefele. 1998. "Motivation to Succeed." In *Handbook of Child Psychology,* 5th ed., vol. 3, edited by Wamon Damon (series ed.) and Nancy Eisenberg (volume ed.). New York: Wiley.

Eccles-Parsons, Jacquelynne, Carol M. Kaczala, and Judith L. Meece. 1982. "Socialization of Achievement Attitudes and Beliefs: Classroom Influences." *Child Development* 53: 322–39.

Entwisle, Doris R., and Karl L. Alexander. 1993. "Entry into School: The Beginning School Transition and Educational Stratification in the United States." *Annual Review of Sociology* 19: 401–23.

Epstein, Joyce L., and James M. McPartland. 1976. "The Concept and Measurement of the Quality of School Life." *American Educational Research Journal* 13(2): 15–30.

Finn, Jeremy D. 1989. "Withdrawing from School." *Review of Educational Research* 59: 117–42.

Fink, Cheryl, Ann K. Boggiano, and Marty Barrett. 1990. "Controlling Teaching Strategies: Undermining Children's Self-determination and Performance." *Journal of Personality and Social Psychology* 59(5): 916–24.

Fuligni, Andrew J., Jacquelynne S. Eccles, and Bonnie L. Barber. 1995. "The Long-term Effects of Seventh-Grade Ability Grouping in Mathematics." *Journal of Early Adolescence* 15(1): 58–89.

Gambrell, Linda, and Barbara Marniak. 1997. "Incentives and Intrinsic Motivation to Read." In *Reading Engagement: Motivating Readers Through Integrated Instruction,* edited by John T. Guthrie and Allan Wigfield. Newark, Del.: International Reading Association.

Gamoran, Adam, and Robert D. Mare. 1989. "Secondary School Tracking and Educational Inequality: Compensation, Reinforcement, or Neutrality?" *American Journal of Sociology* 94(5): 1146–83.

Goodenow, Carol. 1993. "Classroom Belonging Among Early Adolescent Students: Relationships to Motivation and Achievement." *Journal of Early Adolescence* 13(1): 21–43.

Graham, Sandra. 1991. "A Review of Attribution Theory in Achievement Contexts." *Educational Psychology Review* 3(1): 5–39.

Graham, Sandra, and George Barker. 1990. "The Downside of Help: An Attributional-Developmental Analysis of Helping Behavior as a Low-Ability Cue." *Journal of Educational Psychology* 82(1): 7–14.

Guthrie, John T., and Solomon Alao. 1997. "Designing Contexts to Increase Motivations for Reading." *Educational Psychologist* 32(2): 95–105.

Guthrie, John T., Peggy Van Meter, Ann D. McCann, Allan Wigfield, Lois Bennett, Carol C. Poundstone, Mary Ellen Rice, Frances M. Gaibisch, Brian Hunt, and Ann Mitchell. 1996. "Growth of Literacy Engagement: Changes in Motivation and Strategies During Concept-Oriented Reading Instruction." *Reading Research Quarterly* 31(3): 306–25.

Harter, Susan. 1981. "A New Self Report Scale of Intrinsic Versus Extrinsic Motivation in the Classroom: Motivational and Informational Components." *Developmental Psychology* 17: 300–12.

———. 1990. "Causes, Correlates, and the Functional Role of Global Self-worth: A Life-Span Perspective." In *Perceptions of Competence and Incompetence Across the Life Span,* edited by John Kolligian and Robert Sternberg. New Haven, Conn.: Yale University Press.

Higgins, E. Tory, and Jacquelynne Eccles-Parsons. 1983. "Social Cognition and the Social Life of the Child: Stages as Subcultures." In *Social Cognition and Social Development,* edited by E. Tory Higgins, Diane N. Ruble, and Willard W. Hartup. Cambridge: Cambridge University Press.

Hill, Kennedy T., and Seymour B. Sarason. 1966. "The Relation of Test Anxiety and Defensiveness to Test and School Performance over the Elementary School Years: A Further Longitudinal Study." *Monographs for the Society for Research in Child Development* 31 (2, serial no. 104).

Hill, Kennedy T., and Allan Wigfield. 1984. "Test Anxiety: A Major Educational Problem and What to Do About It." *Elementary School Journal* 85: 105–26.

Hoffmann, Lois, and H. W. Haeussler. 1995. "Modification of Interests by Instruction." Paper presented at the annual meeting of the American Educational Research Asssociation, San Francisco (April 1995).

Hokoda, Audrey, and Frank D. Fincham. 1995. "Origins of Children's Helpless and Mastery Achievement Patterns in the Family." *Journal of Educational Psychology* 87(3): 375–85.

Irvin, Judith L., ed. 1992. *Transforming Middle-Level Education: Perspectives and Possibilities.* Boston: Allyn and Bacon.

Jordan, Will, and Saundra Nettles. Forthcoming. "How Students Invest Their Time Outside of School: Effects on School-Related Outcomes." *Social Psychology of Education.*

Jussim, Lee, Jacquelynne S. Eccles, and S. Madon. 1996. "Social Perception, Social Stereotypes, and Teacher Expectations: Accuracy and the Quest for the Powerful Self-fulfilling Prophecy." In *Advances in Experimental Social Psychology,* edited by Leonard Berkowitz. New York: Academic Press.

Kavrell, S. M., and Anne C. Peterson. 1984. "Patterns of Achievement in Early Adolescence." In *Advances in Motivation and Achievement,* vol. 5, edited by Martin L. Maehr. Greenwich, Conn.: JAI Press.

Kellam, Sheppard G., G. W. Rebok, R. Wilson, and L. S. Mayer. 1994. "The Social Field of the Classroom: Context for the Developmental Epidemiological Study of Aggressive Behavior." In *Adolescence in Context: The Interplay of Family, School, Peers, and Work in Adjustment,* edited by Rainier K. Silbereisen and Eberhard Todt. New York: Springer-Verlag.

Lipsitz, Joan, M. Hayes Mizell, Anthony W. Jackson, and Lean M. Austin. 1997. "Speaking with One Voice: A Manifesto for Middle-Grades Reform." *Phi Delta Kappan* 78(7): 533–40.

Mac Iver, Douglas. 1988. "Classroom Environments and the Stratification of Students' Ability Perceptions." *Journal of Educational Psychology* 80(4): 1–40.

Mac Iver, Douglas, and David A. Reuman. 1988. "Decisionmaking in the Classroom and Early Adolescents' Valuing of Mathematics." Paper presented at the annual meeting of the American Educational Research Association, New Orleans (April 1988).

Maehr, Martin L., and Carol Midgley. 1996. *Transforming School Cultures to Enhance Student Motivation and Learning.* Boulder, Colo.: Westview Press.

Midgley, Carol, Eric Anderman, and Lynley Hicks. 1995. "Differences Between Elementary and Middle School Teachers and Students: A Goal Theory Approach." *Journal of Early Adolescence* 15(1): 90–113.

Midgley, Carol, and Harriet Feldlaufer. 1987. "Students' and Teachers' Decisionmaking Fit Before and After the Transition to Junior High School." *Journal of Early Adolescence* 7(2): 225–41.

Midgley, Carol, Harriet Feldlaufer, and Jacquelynne S. Eccles. 1988. "The Transition to Junior High School: Beliefs of Pre- and Post-Transition Teachers." *Journal of Youth and Adolescence* 17(1): 543–62.

Midgley, Carol M., Harriet Feldlaufer, and Jacquelynne S. Eccles. 1989. "Changes in Teacher Efficacy and Student Self- and Task-Related Beliefs During the Transition to Junior High School." *Journal of Educational Psychology* 81(2): 247–58.

Moos, Rudolf H. 1979. *Evaluating Educational Environments.* San Francisco: Jossey-Bass.

Nettles, Saundra. 1991. "Community Involvement and Disadvantaged Students: A Review." *Review of Educational Research* 61(3): 379–406.

Nicholls, John G. 1979. "Development of Perception of Own Attainment and Causal Attributions for Success and Failure in Reading." *Journal of Educational Psychology* 71: 94–99.

———. 1984. "Achievement Motivation: Conceptions of Ability, Subjective Experience, Task Choice, and Performance." *Psychological Review* 91: 328–46.

———. 1989. *The Competitive Ethos and Democratic Education.* Cambridge, Mass.: Harvard University Press.

———. 1990. "What Is Ability and Why Are We Mindful of It? A Developmental Perspective." In *Competence Considered,* edited by Robert J. Sternberg and John Kolligian. New Haven, Conn.: Yale University Press.

Oakes, Jeannie. 1981. "Tracking Policies and Practices: School by School Summaries." A Study of Schooling: Technical report 25. Los Angeles: University of California Graduate School of Education.

Oakes, Jeannie, A. Gamoran, and R. N. Page. 1992. "Curriculum Differentiation: Opportunities, Outcomes, and Meanings." In *Handbook of Research on Curriculum,* edited by Phillip Jackson. New York: Macmillan.

Pallas, A. M., Doris R. Entwisle, Karl L. Alexander, and M. F. Stluka. 1994. "Ability-Group Effects: Instructional, Social, or Institutional?" *Sociology of Education* 67(1): 27–46.

Parsons, Jacquelynne E., and Diane N. Ruble. 1977. "The Development of Achievement-Related Expectancies." *Child Development* 48: 1075–79.

Parsons, Jacquelynne S., Carol M. Kaczala, and Judith L. Meece. 1982. "Socialization of Achievement Attitudes and Beliefs: Classroom Influences." *Child Development* 53: 322–39.

Rholes, William S., Janette Blackwell, Carol Jordan, and Connie Walters. 1980. "A Developmental Study of Learned Helplessness." *Developmental Psychology* 16: 616–24.

Roeser, Robert. W., Jacquelynne S. Eccles, and Arnold J. Sameroff. 1998. "Academic and Emotional Functioning in Early Adolescents: Longitudinal Relations, Patterns, and Predictions by Experience in Middle School." *Developmental Psychopathology* 10(2): 321–52.

Rosenbaum, James E. 1976. *Making Inequality: The Hidden Curriculum of High School Tracking.* New York: Wiley.

Rosenholtz, Susan J., and Steven H. Rosenholtz. 1981. "Classroom Organization and the Perception of Ability." *Sociology of Education* 54: 132–40.

Rosenholtz, Susan J., and Carol Simpson. 1984. "The Formation of Ability Conceptions: Developmental Trend or Social Construction?" *Review of Educational Research* 54: 31–63.

Rutter, Michael. 1983. "School Effects on Pupil Progress: Research Findings and Policy Implications." *Child Development* 54(1): 1–29.

Sanders, Mavis G. 1996a. "School-Community Partnerships and the Academic Achievement of African American, Urban Adolescents." Report 7. Baltimore, Md.: Johns Hopkins University Center for Research on the Education of Students Placed at Risk.

———. 1996b. "Volunteers Help at School and at Home." Baltimore, Md.: National Network of Partnership-2000 Schools.

Schunk, Dale H. 1991. "Self-efficacy and Academic Motivation." *Educational Psychologist* 26(3/4): 207–31.

Simmons, Roberta G., and Dale A. Blyth. 1987. *Moving into Adolescence: The Impact of Pubertal Change and School Context.* Hawthorn, N.Y.: Aldine de Gruyter.

Skinner, Ellen A., and Michael J. Belmont. 1993. "Motivation in the Classroom: Reciprocal Effects of Teacher Behavior and Student Engagement Across the School Year." *Journal of Educational Psychology* 85(4): 571–81.

Slavin, Robert E. 1990. "Achievement Effects of Ability Grouping in Secondary Schools: A Best-Evidence Synthesis." *Review of Educational Research* 60(3): 471–99.

Steele, Claude M. 1992. "Race and the Schooling of Black Americans." *Atlantic* 269(4): 67–78.

Stipek, Deborah J. 1996. "Motivation and Instruction." In *Handbook of Educational Psychology,* edited by David Berlina and Robert C. Calfee. New York: MacMillan.

Stipek, Deborah J., and Douglas Mac Iver. 1989. "Developmental Change in Children's Assessment of Intellectual Competence." *Child Development* 60: 521–38.

Thorkildsen, Theresa A., and John G. Nicholls. 1998. "Fifth-Graders' Achievement Orientations and Beliefs: Individual and Classroom Differences." *Journal of Educational Psychology* 90(2): 179–201.

Weiner, Bernard. 1986. *An Attributional Theory of Motivation and Emotion.* New York: Springer-Verlag.

Weinstein, Rhona. 1989. "Perceptions of Classroom Processes and Student Motivation: Children's Views of Self-fulfilling Prophecies." In *Research on Motivation in Education,* vol. 3, *Goals and Cognitions,* edited by Carole Ames and Russell Ames. New York: Academic Press.

Wentzel, Kathryn R. 1999. "Social-Motivational Processes and Interpersonal Relationships: Implications for Understanding Motivation at School." *Journal of Educational Psychology* 91(1): 76–97.

Wigfield, Allan, and Jacquelynne S. Eccles. 1989. "Test Anxiety in Elementary and Secondary School Students." *Educational Psychologist* 24(2): 159–83.

———. 1992. "The Development of Achievement Task Values: A Theoretical Analysis." *Developmental Review* 12(3): 265–310.

Wigfield, Allan, Jacquelynne S. Eccles, and Paul R. Pintrich. 1996. "Development Between the Ages of Eleven and Twenty-five." In *Handbook of Educational Psychology,* edited by D. C. Berliner and R. C. Calfee. New York: Macmillan.

Wigfield, Allan, Jacquelynne Eccles, Douglas Mac Iver, David Reuman, and Carol Midgley. 1991. "Transitions at Early Adolescence: Changes in Children's Domain-Specific Self-perceptions and General Self-esteem Across the Transition to Junior High School." *Developmental Psychology* 27(4): 552–65.

Wigfield, Allan, Jacquelynne S. Eccles, Kwang S. Yoon, Rena D. Harold, Amy J. Arbreton, Carol R. Freedman-Doan, and Phyllis C. Blumenfeld. 1997. "Changes in Children's Competence Beliefs and Subjective Task Values Across the Elementary School Years: A Three-Year Study." *Journal of Educational Psychology* 89(3): 451–69.

Chapter 6

Promoting Positive Outcomes for Youth: Resourceful Families and Communities

Margaret Beale Spencer and Dena Phillips Swanson

This chapter focuses on the ways in which families manage to raise successful adolescents in resource-poor environments. It provides a framework for identifying buffers to offset the negative effects of growing up in poor families and neighborhoods. Too frequently, intervention programs are designed with central assumptions about the homogeneity of the experience of participants (that is, the common context-linked experiences and similarities of their lives), about program quality (as a source of human capital enrichment), and about the levels of resource allocation required for human capital enhancement. As posited by Carol Weiss's (1995, 1997) perspective on the role of theories of change for intervention, our view represents a particular theory of change that emphasizes the need to consider and integrate the contribution of several factors generally ignored: gender, race, context character, immigration status, and ethnicity.

An introduction and brief overview of relevant adolescent and family themes is presented first. The primary focus of the chapter is a review of literature about diverse families' efforts to raise successful youths in impoverished environments and about programs designed to support these families. We also describe effective buffers for offsetting the negative stressors and adverse impacts with which these youth must deal.

THE FAMILY AS A UNIT OF HUMAN CAPITAL INVESTMENT

Independent of ethnicity, social class, and race, parenting remains one of the most important tasks of child-rearing adults (Erikson 1963; Tamir and Antonucci 1981). For visible minorities, immigrants, and low-resource families, these developmental tasks are particularly complex and difficult (see Spencer 1983, 1990). Economic problems can have a negative impact on the ability to parent effectively. In addition, immigrant families and minority parents are frequently subjected to uncommonly high levels of risk that are rarely acknowledged.

Families and neighborhoods play a protective role in the lives of children and adolescents. However, their efforts require supportive social policies and programs. For example, offering apprenticeship options, particularly for males, can foster youths' search for instrumentality in the world of work. Low-resource neighborhoods require external sources of support for maximizing investments in human capital. A nurturing context for individual development along with parental provisions of psychosocial assistance and support are both nested in the community.

Awareness that development occurs within a context of environmental influence has a long history (see, for example, Bronfenbrenner 1979; Garbarino 1982). The ways in which parents and families affect developmental processes during adolescence have not, however, received serious, policy-relevant consideration. Although the disadvantaged status of minority Americans and immigrants has long been recognized, the effects of living in a race-divided society on individual developmental processes, family tensions, parenting strategies, and subsequent opportunities have received minimal attention.

The American Context of Risk: The Case of Racial and Ethnic Minorities

Leon Chestang (1972) suggested that American culture and social policies are fraught with discrepancies between what is wanted and what is expected from minority group members. On the one hand, while independence, social responsibility, and competence are desired as life-course outcomes, the built-in obstacles to achieving those outcomes are many. Tedd Kochman (1992) suggested that African American communities are characterized by crowding problems, hazardous waste facilities, and other high-risk environmental conditions that increase stress, decrease ability to cope, diminish the sense of community and psychological mutuality, and result in heightened behavior problems. However, research and policy tend to focus on adolescent behavior *problems* (for example, the traditional "violence initiatives") instead of on strategies that explore more interactive and transactional influences on untoward outcomes. Family and neighborhood supports can buffer the stress associated with the inadequacy of youths' individual and context matches. Particularly for males, the adult instrumentality expectation—the acquisition and maintenance of stable work and the formation of healthy families—exacerbates the difficulty of their parenting efforts and their transition from the teen years into adulthood. Accordingly, adolescence is associated with youthful vulnerability to unproductive coping patterns (for example, early school leaving), highly challenging parental requirements as developmental tasks, and social policy responses that exacerbate unsupportive social contexts (for example, minimally supportive educational settings and lack of apprenticeship opportunities).

Across the life course, encounters in diverse cultural settings (home, school, peer group, community) influence how individuals perceive and experience the self. How the individual processes these diverse experiences has an impact on both self-appraisal (for example, how much he feels valued or valuable) and the attributional aspects of the self (for example, abilities and physical attributes). The individual's phenomenological processes involve making inferences about other individuals' thoughts, feelings, perceptions, and attitudes. These processes are critical for directing behavior, conceptualizing possibilities, determining emotional responses, and maximizing school adjustment and expressed effort.

Cultural themes affect the inference-making processes. The intensity of the adolescent peer culture affords a vivid illustration. Underlying the identity-focused cultural ecological (ICE) perspective is the phenomenological variant of ecological systems theory (PVEST), an inclusive theoretical approach. Together they help to interpret adolescent coping patterns in high-risk environments (Spencer 1995) and provide a comprehensive heuristic device as a theory of change for designing and evaluating interventions. They can also assist parents and neighborhoods in facilitating developmental outcomes for youth. An ICE perspective and PVES theorizing emphasize that both the individual's *experience* and her *perception* of experience in culturally diverse contexts influence how she forms an identity and experiences a sense of self (for example, as a learner, a girl, an efficacious parent). Similarly, assessing parental socialization efforts requires an understanding of the motivations that undergird normative parental responses.

CULTURE AND CONTEXT   Minority group membership and immigration status represent extra sources of risk, but this is rarely acknowledged by social policy initiatives. For example, nonpaid parental leave legislation assists parents with middle-income jobs but may be of little benefit to low-income families (see Spencer, Blumenthal, and Richards 1995).

Sociologists emphasize three elements in the definition of a minority group (Jaret 1995): it is visible to others and distinct from others (especially the dominant groups) because of certain physical and cultural characteristics; it appears relatively powerless, subordinate, and unequally treated; and it has developed a sense of identity or group consciousness, including an awareness of social isolation, stigmatization, persecution, and discrimination by the larger society.

Inequality of position compromises school adjustment, limits economic opportunities, and undermines productive life-course outcomes for those who are socially isolated and stigmatized. Given a lack of opportunities for minority group members, the status inequities they experience can encourage "reactive" or negative identity because of stress-producing situations that require maladaptive coping. That is, as adolescents develop, their lives are progressively exposed to diverse expressions of social stereotypes (for example, assumptions about manhood and respect) and institutional biases (such as adverse educational practices and negative teacher perceptions). Crucial to adolescent development is the availability of parental and neighborhood supports to counter the effects of societal stereotypes and biases. For example, extramural athletic activities support sportsmanship and relationship development but require local resources such as gyms, other athletic facilities, and parks. Similarly, neighborhood-based apprenticeships make a critical contribution to youth development and function as safe introductions to the world of work. The adolescent experiences work as much for the valued "instrumental" lessons learned as for the economic consequences. The apprentice work experience provides youth with myriad lessons in how to work without the significant economic and (negative) self-esteem correlates generally associated with adult work failure. However, safe extramural activities are not available in many disadvantaged neighborhoods. Thus, without organized recreational and work options, immigrant and minority adolescents are perceived as threatening adults or gang members in need of control rather than as young people who need support.

CONTEXT AND NORMATIVE DEVELOPMENTAL PROCESSES Adolescents simultaneously experience a desire for acceptance, self-consciousness, cognitive awareness, and the anticipation of assuming adult roles. Given systematic societal biases and diminished achievement expectations, poor minority parents have greater and more complex socializing responsibilities toward their young. And disadvantaged youths themselves have life experiences that are dramatically different from those of their advantaged counterparts; expected earnings, job opportunities, educational attainment, health, and life expectancy are all compromised by the family's economic status. Social conditions influence youths' perceptions of their opportunities and role in society and also affect how parents try to provide opportunities for their children's transition into adulthood (Spencer 1983, 1990).

Parents can also facilitate youths' meaning-making processes. Consider, for example, the emerging resilience of many African American youth in high-risk environments. For these youth, resiliency is associated with particular parental psychosocial characteristics (Spencer 1983). Parental cultural identity features (for example, the ability to transmit cultural information about the group's history, strengths, and societal situation) foster the rearing of children who have Afrocentric cultural values that emphasize appreciation for the group (Spencer 1983, 1990). When parents help their children develop a positive racial and cultural identity—for example, by providing activities that validate the group's cultural heritage—they are encouraging the development of resilience. Kwanza celebrations and rite-of-passage traditions, particularly for African American males, have become fairly common.

Puerto Rican celebrations, for instance, have become a virtual tradition in many large urban settings. The "two-context" lifestyle of many Puerto Ricans has implications for youthful identity processes. Puerto Rican dual identity is influenced by regular travel between the island and the mainland. As noted by Carmen Rodriquez-Cortes (1990), the development of ethnic identity differs for island and mainland youth because of the greater exposure of the latter to multicultural groupings. This exposure makes the acculturation and identity formation responsibilities of parents more challenging (and expensive). This additional parental task is exacerbated by a priori economic challenges.

African American adolescents are exposed to the same level of violence, aggression, and gratuitous sex in the media to which all American youth are exposed. They are unique, however, in several respects. They are objects of stereotyped *expectations* of violence, psychopathology, and aggression. They generally attend resource-weak schools and are often taught by teachers who do not wish to teach in minority communities. Few role models are available to them for guidance, mentoring relationships, and support. As suggested by Chestang (1972), they share with their parents the experience of societal inconsistency in that they are the object of personal injustices from which there is no legal protection. Often chronically impoverished, they have little evidence that academic motivation and performance translate into productive experiences in the workforce (and thus, they are assumed, too often, to equate an academic orientation with "acting white"). Little is known about these context-linked experiences. At the relational level, little is known about basic parent-youth relationships for minority Americans (Spencer 1990). In contrast, much has been written about Euro-Americans' child-parent relationships (see, for example, Steinberg 1999).

Ian Canino and Luis Zayas (1997) noted that Puerto Rican adolescents are influenced by competing value systems. On the one hand are values concerning family closeness and filial obligations to parental demands. On the other hand, American values emphasize physical and psychological independence from the family. Vijay Ranganath and Veena Ranganath (1997) reported the difficulties experienced by Asian Indian parents and children at adolescence. One important value of Asian Indian families is strong disapproval of dating and premarital sex. The interdependence of the family unit is emphasized even in areas of career choice and marriage. Consequently, parents are perceived as intrusive. Parents, on the other hand, maintain their right to exercise authority. Given such diverse values, parent-child relations are often significantly strained.

As a normative psychosocial developmental task, establishing an identity during adolescence requires understanding oneself as a member of a society within a particular ethnic, cultural, religious, or political tradition. Parenting and other socializing adults in the neighborhood and school play important supportive roles. In addition, an "orientation to habitual right action," as described by James Youniss (1998), is fundamental to identity insofar as defining oneself entails becoming part of a normative cultural tradition. Youths who are members of devalued subcultural groups may infer a need to react against broader societal traditions (that is, to deploy maladaptive, reactive coping methods). If that reaction suggests to some a lack of moral fiber, it may also represent an unconscious reaction to lack of access to mainstream opportunities. From an adult perspective, assertive parental responses to institutions, such as local schools, may represent their reactions to systemic inequities, or they may be perceived as anger and outrage, thus contributing to further stigmatization.

African American boys are generally viewed with dissonance and trepidation in many situations, including educational settings (see Cunningham 1994; Spencer and Cunningham, forthcoming). It may be daunting for them to manage an ego-supporting identity while coping with generalized, negative racial imagery. Especially in school settings, the extra burden of racial stereotyping, and reactive responses to it, compromise school adjustment and affect learning opportunities (see Spencer 1999).

The tasks associated with establishing a moral identity are particularly salient; attendant stresses and coping behaviors may enhance school adjustment, on the one hand, or provide fodder for further misinterpretation, on the other. Negative coping methods may be emotionally comfortable in the short run but exacerbate the situation in the long run. For some low-resource males, the reactive responses are often linked to gender identity themes. Single-gender schools are one response to this problem. To ascertain which context best meets their children's needs, parents need to be knowledgeable about their children's development, gender-linked issues and achievement, and available "best-practice" methods. Gender themes require particularly careful attention given the poorer performance outcomes for many low-resource male minority youth. Minority parents may thus invest more human capital without obtaining better results.

CONTEXT, NORMATIVE DEVELOPMENTAL PROCESSES, AND GENDER   Adolescents in devalued subgroups of a minority group (such as African American males) experience heightened self-consciousness and a less appropriate fit with school performance expectations, and they are more likely to develop a disrupted self-image than are nonminority youth. Given stigmatization, racism, and socioeconomic inequities, youth often infer that they are not viewed with the respect accorded to others, even as they pursue an orientation of "habitual right action," or attempt to behave in socially appropriate ways. Unfortunately, their efforts infrequently are equated with principled and moral values. They frequently behave this way in hostile contexts or minimally supportive environments. This behavior challenges parents to increase their own monitoring behaviors (Swanson, Spencer, and Petersen 1998) and underscores the importance of after-school programs during middle childhood and safe, supervised, afternoon programs for adolescents not engaged in apprenticeship programming.

What is valued and expected for American youth is that they will develop autonomy as they move into positions that demand responsible and independent behavior. One aspect of independence is "value autonomy": "having a set of principles about what is right and what is wrong, about what is important and what is not" (Steinberg 1999, 278). For African American male adolescents, three salient aspects of autonomy are linked to normative cognitive shifts. First, adolescents become increasingly abstract in their thinking; accordingly, youths may decide that they are not interested in adhering to mainstream dress codes, academic expectations, or language styles. Second, their beliefs are increasingly connected to ideological positions. Thus, when the group's behavior—such as academic effort—is neither accorded respect by their school and peers nor assumed to be deserving of it, they may develop a reactive coping response that "demands" respect. For example, the exaggerated sex role orientation often feigned by urban youth is assumed to be both "okay" and the only method for obtaining "earned" or "owed" respect (see Cunningham 1994). Accordingly, *successful* parental efforts to communicate the duality of youths' experiences result in efficacious youth (see Spencer 1990). Parents who provide proactive representations of cultural traditions (for example, cultural programming through community, church, and school) can deflect problematic adolescent coping responses. This is often more difficult for immigrant parents because the parent-youth relationship is also under stress owing to frequent clashes between youths' attempts to acculturate rapidly and their parents' allegiance to cultural traditions (see Raganath and Raganath 1997).

The third component of autonomy suggests that beliefs become nested in youths' own values, as opposed to being a system of values adopted from parents, teachers, and other adults (Steinberg 1999, 297–98). These changes are especially important for African American male youths. They must form an understanding of the world as they struggle with inequitable conditions. We expect competence and resiliency from students, although we do not appreciate how they conceptualize their challenges. To illustrate, we hypothesize that for African American males, a special value of concern is the acquisition of respect. If respect from the broader society, and particularly in school settings, is not forthcoming, they may adopt a reactive or less constructive coping response. For example, engaging in "habitual right actions," such as hypermasculinity, that are the opposite of those valued by society may be seen by youths as effective in generating "respect" even though they add to group stigma, reinforce personal risk from juvenile justice representatives, and undermine school adjustment and academic achievement. Youth respond forcefully to perceptions of "being dissed" (disrespected) (see Stevenson 1997). However, their level of hypersensitivity and hyperawareness is consistent with normative adolescent cognitive transformations. The difference is the level of hostility of the environment for particular urban youth.

Familial Efforts to Raise Successful Youths in Resource-Poor Environments

African American and other stigmatized youth (such as Hispanics and Native Americans) may equate "acting white" with a particular psychological response. Although they consistently report putting a high value on education (see Spencer 1983, 1999), the psychological orientation of these youth is often to reject academic contexts that ignore them. This rejection and turning away from learning opportunities by "fragile" adolescents may aid their psychological adjustment in the short run, but it diminishes their future opportunities.

NORMATIVE ADOLESCENT PROCESSES AND THE IMPACT OF RACIAL-ETHNIC GROUP MEMBERSHIP

Special supports that recognize and provide a voice for parents of poor and minority children have been neglected. One method of preventing harm to adolescent development is to build self-esteem and social competence by teaching traditional academic and vocational (work-linked) skills and honing contextually sensitive parenting skills. From a PVES perspective, such efforts develop buffers to alleviate stress responses. Social support networks and psychological intervention can prevent transmission problems by promoting *adaptive coping* to reduce future risks.

As an illustration, summer school programs provide recreation and activities for youths who are not working during the summer months. They also serve many other purposes, including remediation and prevention of learning deficits, prevention of juvenile delinquency, and promotion of positive self-esteem and positive attitudes toward learning. Remedial programs offer students opportunities to meet minimum competency standards and to retake courses they have failed.

These programs can also target vulnerable areas for disadvantaged youth and offer accelerated programs for those with academic talent.

We believe that school systems need to implement intensive and integrated "wrap-around" services to maximize students' productive outcomes, competence, and school adjustment. To illustrate, the empowerment of families involves three factors: resources, competence, and self-efficacy. Adequate resources can alleviate risk factors, while competence and self-efficacy can promote adaptive coping. Efforts to empower disadvantaged families have focused on two of these factors—resources and competence—through the enhancement of parental advocacy. Enhancing resources and competence has increased parental knowledge about services and rights and promoted communication and problem-solving skills. However, parents have also tended to respond to these efforts with an antiprofessional stance, that is, to view their relationship with the professional as adversarial (*maladaptive coping*). Our approach does not focus solely on parental involvement; rather, it promotes the parental choice to be involved, as well as the development of partnerships between parents and professionals.

Intervention programs designed to promote family involvement must enhance parental knowledge of mental health services and resources, promote communication and assertiveness skills, and motivate parents to become involved by giving them a sense of self-efficacy with regard to their children's mental health. Self-efficacy yields a sense of competence that consistently predicts success in health-related areas. Such an example was found in the Creating Lasting Connections (CLC) program, which sought to increase the resiliency assets of the community, the family, and the youths. The program chose as a primary target alcohol and drug use among high-risk youths aged twelve to fourteen. The primary purpose was to delay the onset of alcohol and drug use in this population and to reduce the frequency of use in this population by strengthening family resilience. The program was implemented in five church communities in rural, suburban, and inner-city settings with 143 parents and 183 youths. Program components included parent or guardian and youth training, early intervention services, and follow-up case management services. Evaluation data were collected through interviews and questionnaires before program initiation, after six to seven months of parent and youth training, and at the one-year follow-up. Results by Knowlton Johnson and his colleagues (1996) showed that the program produced positive direct effects on family resilience. The evaluation also found positive moderating effects: the onset of alcohol and other drug use was somewhat delayed, and the frequency of alcohol and other drug use among youths was somewhat decreased. The youth participants adapted conditionally, the report concluded, to changes in the family resilience factors targeted by the program.

In an effort to foster and promote resiliency on a national level, annual congressional appropriations are provided by the National Children, Youth, and Families at Risk (CYFAR) Initiative and the Cooperative State Research, Education, and Extension Service (CSREES). The funds are allocated to forty-four land grant university extension services for community-based programs for at-risk children and their families. The CYFAR Initiative, begun in 1991, is based on research on effective programs for at-risk youth and families and on the human ecological principle of working across the life span in the context of the family and community. To ensure that the critical needs of children and families are met, the CYFAR Initiative supports comprehensive, intensive, community-based programs developed with active citizen participation in all phases. The initiative promotes the building of resiliency and other protective factors in youth, families, and communities through collaborative partnerships to achieve sustaining outcomes (see Myrek, Mancini, and Brock 1999). State Strengthening (STST) projects serve as the CSREES mechanism for funding community-based projects and expanding statewide capacity for supporting and sustaining programs for at-risk youth and families. The STST projects target children aged prekindergarten to nineteen, with some projects incorporating parental components.

The STST projects frequently focus on a specific age group and domain of intervention, such as reading and computer literacy for third- to fifth-graders. Many of the programs that target adolescents work to prevent behavioral problems, often without proactive parental inclusion. The initiatives of the Pennsylvania State Strengthening (PaSTST) Project, however, are aimed at providing a more stable community ecology for youth and include behavioral interventions that encourage parental involvement. These initiatives are based on collaborative efforts that link various college campuses with local community, private, and state agencies. The PaSTST Project comprises several programs for rural and urban youth. The rural program focuses on expansion of educational after-school and summer activities and adult-family programs (family fun nights and "Focus on the Family" workshops). This program to meet the needs of youth and their families has met with such overwhelming acceptance and community investment that expansion to other regions is anticipated.

Operationalizing Cultural Diversity

Cultural diversity—racial and ethnic group designations—matter and have important implications for school adjustment. As noted by Robin Jaret (1995), "peoplehood" and "ethnocentrism" are key terms for understanding ethnicity.

PEOPLEHOOD A sense of peoplehood is a basic feature of ethnicity and ethnic groups (Jaret 1995, 50). The term suggests a special sense of attachment or connectedness that people in the group feel for each other, along with an attendant and shared sociopsychological identification. This shared identification represents a spiritual bond and a special "we-feeling" that suggests a belief in a common origin, ancestry, or descent across generations (Jaret 1995, 50). A sense of peoplehood may be found in diverse forms and settings, both locally and across national boundaries. It may be evident, for example, as ingroup solidarity and mutual trust among members of the same American Indian tribe, or as a concern shared by American Jews for Jews in Russia and Israel. Similarly, American blacks may demonstrate a strong attachment to blacks in Africa. Accordingly, students may not adjust well to in-school curricular themes whose narrow historical accounts fail to present history from the group perspective of their people or distort historical fact (for example, accounts that assume African American history began with American slavery). Accordingly, when adolescents are prohibited from wearing T-shirts that bear peoplehood themes, their aggressive responses (based in their perception of being "dissed") (see Stevenson 1997), although inappropriate, may be due to the difference between the meanings they give to this clothing and the evaluative inferences and judgments articulated as dress codes by adults. Parents who include these cultural understandings in their socialization efforts raise teens who have less cultural dissonance and more psychic energy for intellectual pursuit (see Spencer 1983, 1990).

A presentation of history that fails to acknowledge the contributions of diverse cultural groups undermines school adjustment for ethnic and racial minorities. Specifically, the attribution of all positive societal accomplishments to Euro-Americans places a burden on white youth: their identity formation becomes more stressful since only positive outcomes are deemed permissible. Jaret (1995, 52) suggested that a youth's ethnic identification may function as a link to other persons or objects, manifested in part by the rewards or penalties attached to the various ethnic identities. Too often left underanalyzed in the effort to understand youths' unavoidable consciousness of race, ethnicity, and self is the role of their developmental stage and the underlying contribution of cognitive processes. These cognition-dependent mechanisms are linked to psychological processes such as identity formation (see Spencer and Markstrom-Adams 1990) and achievement (see, for example, Spencer and Dornbusch 1990; Matute-Bianchi 1986).

ETHNOCENTRISM Ethnocentrism may be defined as the belief that one's group is dominant and represents the standard against which all others are judged. It suggests the supremacy of one's own people and their ways of doing things. The phrase suggests an inflated preference for one's own group and a concomitant undervaluing of or aversion to other groups (see Cornell and Hartmann 1998; Brislin 1990; LeVine and Campbell 1972). For example, assimilation is a common social orientation expected of minority group members; it requires conformity to majority-group norms and disregards the minority group's culture, language, and ethnic institutions. Assimilation requirements affect a student's ability to adjust to classroom settings. Accordingly, ethnocentrism spawns a particular ethnic identity or orientation to the student's reference group and makes assumptions about the quality of his self-esteem. However, students' orientation to their reference group varies significantly as a function of their developmental status (being a young child, an adolescent, or an adult) and of the quality of the stigma associated for them with reference-group membership.

Ethnocentrism suggests that negative attitudes toward others originate from a need to preserve positive self-judgments or self-esteem by projecting one's own negative traits onto others. It is unclear whether fervent liking for one's own group is consistently associated with a firm disdain of other groups. In contrast, cultural pluralists appreciate their own group and simultaneously value other cultures. Theories of ethnic-racial identity development generally support pluralistic or multicultural perspectives as the highest stage of development. They view ethnocentrism, a common aspect of ethnic identity, as less virulent than the view that inherent biological factors account for racial inferiority and superiority.

Eurocentric attitudes and beliefs are present in children as young as three years of age (see Spencer 1983; Spencer and Markstrom-Adams 1990). It is not surprising, then, that between-group tensions are common among American schoolchildren. Teachers' negative expectations for particular ethnic, racial, or immigrant children may lead them to evaluate behavior more negatively. For example, teacher assessments of the typically active or rough-and-tumble behavior of young boys as aggressive behavior in minority boys may explain the generally higher rate of minority boys in behavior-disordered (BD) classrooms.

A major problem with the early literature was its deficit orientation in explaining minority youths' achievement and behavioral patterns. Yet the ethnocentric patterns of white children may compromise school adjustment for nonmajority-group children.

A related issue is the impact of ethnocentrism on the psychological well-being and identity processes of whites. The literature has always assumed the coexistence of minority psychopathology and problem outcomes, on the one hand, and white Americans' presumably healthy psychological well-being as the standard, on the other. There has been minimal discussion of the potential psychological vulnerability and problematic school adjustment for all students when the formerly dominant reference group is treated as an emergent subgroup as a consequence of immigration and birth-rate differentials. Accordingly, communicating culturally diverse values in the classroom requires different methods and conveys different meanings in the second grade than it does in the twelfth grade. Parents and school administrators are generally unprepared for these sensitive tasks. Teaching in teams of more culturally competent teachers, administrators, and staff matched with less experienced teachers, administrators, and staff offers hope as one strategy. Bringing in parents as informal cultural interpreters creates opportunities to build mutual respect; parents, irrespective of their economic resources and English-language skills, can be perceived as a resource and partner in the education of their youngsters. Such practices communicate to parents that their involvement in the educational process will not undermine their own adult ego processes. Like parents, teachers and administrators should be trained in the normative developmental experiences, particularly as they relate to the lack of continuity between contexts (home, school, neighborhood, peer group) for youth of color. Teacher training should increase teachers' exposure to theories of normal child development (including the experiences of youth of color); raise their awareness of cultural similarities and differences in attitudes toward education and learning styles; and enhance their ability to interact with children and parents from culturally different backgrounds.

As an ecologically based program, the School Transitional Environment Project (STEP) provides support for students who are making the transition from smaller schools to larger feeder schools (for example, from elementary school to middle school, or from middle school to high school). The program is designed to address the concerns associated with youths' simultaneous experiences of developmental and contextual transitions. The purpose is to minimize the anxiety and behavior problems associated with transitions by creating a supportive environment (see

Felner et al. 1993). To accomplish this goal, the role of the homeroom teacher was redefined to allow the teacher to serve as an adviser to a cohort of students and as a liaison between the students, their families, and the school. Teachers' advising activities include assisting students in course selections, addressing truancy concerns with families, and meeting with students' core teachers to assist in early identification of those who need additional counseling or support. Although STEP exemplifies a proactive, context-sensitive response to the developmental experiences of youth, this program and others like it still need explicitly to integrate teacher training in cultural competence.

A clinical component (still only an exploratory idea) would allow teachers to use particular theoretical frameworks to understand and differentiate the individual needs of their students. Like the moral development curriculum designed by Lawrence Kohlberg (1975), this approach would assume that teachers can provide differentiated feedback to students that would aid their higher-level functioning. Such a method would provide opportunities for teachers to explore their own feelings, reference-group orientation, and thinking about diversity independent of their ethnicity, race, and national origin.

An example of such a program is the Start-on-Success (SOS) Scholars Program. Designed for special needs students (Spencer, Ashford, and Youngblood 1998), SOS represents a partnership between the National Office on Disability, the city school system, a private university, and the families of student participants. Instead of taking their classes in their school building, students participate in the program on a neighboring university campus. They spend each afternoon in classes with two reassigned public school teachers and two assistant teachers; mornings are spent at an on-campus job. Teachers and job supervisors participate in a theoretically driven (PVEST) training program that is framed in quasiclinical and developmental terms (Weiss 1995). The goal is to ensure that students are understood, treated fairly, and taught using developmentally sensitive methods and culturally sensitive values. The students become familiar with the intervention's theory of change by frequently reprimanding each other concerning the need to produce less maladaptive and more adaptive or productive coping skills(!). They are able to transfer their training and experiences from the classroom to the work site and back home to their respective neighborhoods.

Thirteen of the fifteen graduates had full-time jobs within three weeks following graduation. The specialized programming had a success rate of 87 percent, as compared with the national statistic of 37 percent. Even as it is undergoing an in-depth evaluation, the SOS Scholars Program has already earned national recognition as an effective model for special needs students.

Diverse Family Types and the Acquisition of Good Youth Outcomes

We need frameworks that explain the variations in the character of adolescent transitions in the contexts of families, peers, and social structures. Anne-Marie Ambert (1997, 41) allowed that "a percentage of adolescents do cause a great deal of problems for parents, society and themselves. They consequently receive media coverage and attention from professionals." But the many young people who make their way through adolescence without much disruption "do not receive much publicity."

Parents and adolescents frequently enter this developmental period with feelings of trepidation and fright. The major responsibilities associated with the parenting and teaching of an adolescent may generate feelings of dread and anxiety in the adults charged with these socializing processes because they are exposed to the same media coverage of poor adolescent adjustment.

The contexts of both schooling and family are undergoing major changes. With increasing numbers of immigrant children in the classroom, teachers are teaching students from diverse cultures. Students share classrooms and compete for educational resources and supportive attention and understanding with classmates who are from distinct cultural traditions and have developed unique identities.

Traditionally the family met both the instrumental and expressive needs of its young. Child-rearing in large urban settings, irrespective of ethnicity, race, or social class, now presents significant challenges. Neighbors may be strangers. It is more difficult to identify and gain access to social supports. Such an impersonal society underscores the need to find intimacy, a sense of belonging, and emotional security in the family itself (Rice 1999). In impersonal social contexts, many of them characterized by emotional isolation, the capacity of teens and parents to develop close relationships with others is vital to identity and represents a source of emotional security (Rice 1996).

Our theoretical framework (PVEST) uses the ICE perspective to seek a better understanding of how parental inputs affect youth outcomes as adolescents make the transition between childhood and adulthood (see figure 6.1). As a heuristic device for organizing a life-course approach to family influences on productive youth outcomes, the ICE perspective has special relevance for the adolescent years (see Spencer 1995; Swanson, Spencer, and Petersen 1998). The theoretical synthesis (PVEST) links risk to stress, coping strategies, stable identity processes, and specific life-stage outcomes.

A Phenomenological Variant of PVES Theory

As opposed to focusing narrowly on pathology and problem behaviors, the PVES theory acknowledges the importance of the normative factors, such as family influences (Allen 1985) and physiological processes (Anderson, McNeilly, and Myers 1991), that produce context- and culture-linked developmental discontinuities as well as continuities across the life course. Thus, life-course perspectives on *normative* developmental processes (Brim 1976; Elder 1985) have been incorporated with our own empirical and conceptual research efforts. Finally, competence theorizing (White 1959; Smith 1968) and important classroom practices, pedagogy, and schooling themes (Clark 1983; Tharp and Gallimore 1988; LeGall 1990; Nettles 1991; Winfield 1991) are also incorporated.

FIGURE 6.1 / Phenomenological Variant of Ecological Systems (PVES) Theory

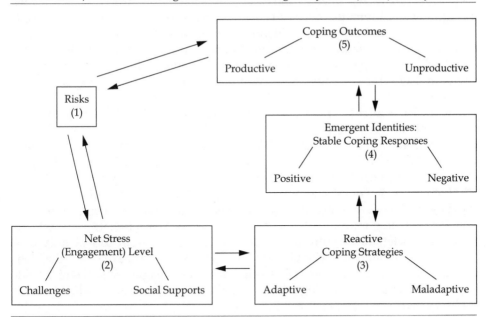

Source: Authors' compilation.

One cannot assume that children and adolescents think as adults do; it is critical to learn about young people's subjective perspectives of their experiences. We must explore their phenomenal world—as it appears to them (see Crain 1992, 94).

As illustrated in figure 6.1, ongoing, dynamic, cognition-associated recursive processes serve a self-evaluative function. They appear to be linked to the experience of stress engagement (2). Stress engagement is the net level of stress experienced when considering both challenges and social supports. For example, an adolescent makes inferences about parental intrusiveness or negative teacher perceptions and perceives himself to be unpopular with peers. However, parental monitoring efforts may result in either good stress engagement (for example, the adolescent perceives his parents as attentive) or bad stress engagement (the adolescent perceives the parents' involvement as uninvited and intrusive). Stress engagement requires the deployment of reactive coping methods (3) and indicates the use of responsive problem-solving strategies; the coping methods deployed represent either maladaptive or adaptive solutions.

The fourth component of PVES theory notes the use of emergent identities as a stable coping response. Emergent identities evolve from the patterned coping methods that were previously deployed. For example, for middle childhood through adulthood, the choice of an aggressive attitude and sex role orientation by males is a maladaptive problem-solving strategy that may result in a stable hyper-masculine identity. Component five cites adverse and productive coping outcomes.

An example of an adverse outcome for a six-year-old might be kindergarten retention related to a teacher's perception that he lacks internal controls (that is, engages in aggressive or immature behavior). Another adverse outcome is an adolescent with a hypermasculine emergent identity leaving school early because of authority conflicts with teachers and administrators. A productive life-stage outcome might be academic persistence for a youngster in middle school who has a culturally pluralistic ethnic identity, or successful navigation of an ESL program for an immigrant child.

The HIPP (Health Information Providers and Promoters) Scholars Program is one component of a large evaluative project on youth of diverse backgrounds living in urban environments (Spencer 1997). HIPP is a health-focused intervention program only for students with passing or average grades (Cs and Ds). The goal of the program is to transform students by facilitating the development of a new identity as a HIPP scholar in lieu of the alternative identity as a low achiever. Participants learn about the health issues facing urban low-resource communities and become responsible for providing information about these issues to their families, peers, schoolmates, and neighbors. Youth are expected to generalize from this identity as a provider and promoter of health information to the school context, where the identity can promote a view of themselves as learners. The engaging activities of providing information and supporting others generally support productive identities and resiliency in these students.

PVES theory suggests that an inclusive and culturally sensitive approach can generate more effective pedagogy, make it easier to implement need-specific and culturally sensitive parental support programs, promote responsive and supportive family policy, and aid in the identification of the best practices required for effective child-rearing environments. In sum, such frameworks provide methods for formulating prediction models that are age- and gender-sensitive and culturally relevant, and they give parents more information about supportive socialization strategies, thus enhancing the possibility of productive youth outcomes.

INTERPRETING PATTERNS OF PARENTAL INFLUENCES AND GOOD YOUTH OUTCOMES

Parenting is challenging at best and a source of stress at worst. About one-third of adolescents have difficult times; however, many of them experience problems that have been present since childhood. Issues of ethnicity, race, gender, socioeconomic disparity, and societal inequity make adolescence more challenging for some. Chronic adverse neighborhood conditions only exacerbate the situation. The familiar African axiom cited in Hillary Rodham Clinton's book is generally accepted as fact: "It takes a village to raise a child." The rules and structures of parenting practices are the cornerstone for interpreting the parent-adolescent relationship, and they are not implemented across families on the same "playing fields."

Punishment by parents (usually labeled "parental restrictiveness") is often tied to the assumption that control is the major purpose of parenting. Parents who over-control may believe it is their responsibility to impose their will on the child; some may even assume that a child's will must be broken. Restrictive parenting styles are linked with diverse problematic outcomes, including lower self-esteem (Loeb, Horst, and Horton 1980), lower levels of empathy, and weaker social problem-solving skills (Jones, Rickel, and Smith 1980). On the other hand, in their effective interventions, parents attempt to include their own phenomenological view of the world. Parenting is a foundational aspect of adult identity for many. Supportive programs that fail to link their methods to the parents' perspective are clearly less effective.

PVES theory analyzes behavioral patterns as linked to the parents' own meaning-making processes. Low-resource, immigrant, and minority parents living in high-risk contexts may continue socialization traditions that were appropriate for earlier periods or different cultural niches. Recent studies examining the predictors of neighborliness provide insights into parental use of less effective rules of socialization (see, for example, Unger and Wandersman 1982).

Authoritarian rather than authoritative parenting is viewed as controlling, although some parents with this style may also be construed as quite warm (Ambert 1997, 44). However, for some immigrant and American minority families, rule structures are linked with cultural traditions and filial respect. For many of these families, it is important to maintain cultural traditions, mitigate peer group influences, head off the potentially reactive role of group identity, and prevent the frequent devaluing of minority status and cultural traditions in public schools.

Recent research (Spencer, Kim, and Marshall 1987; Swanson, Spencer, and Petersen 1998) suggests that the experiences of African American and Hispanic youths (see Matute-Bianchi 1986) occur within a context of risk that challenges their cultural identity. The issue is important and parallel to the experiences of the Buraka, a minority group in Japan. The Burakumin are labeled and treated as an outcaste community; the academic performance of Burakumin youths is below average, like that of many African Americans and Hispanics in this country. However, because the Buraka are perceived by Americans as Japanese, they are treated as a favored minority in this country. Thus, no mediating parental socialization efforts are required for Burakumin youth in American schools because they are treated with respect (see Spencer, Kim, and Marshall 1987). In other words, the quality of schooling matters (Irvine 1988), the affective climate is important, and the partnering between home and school is critical (Clark 1983). Like mainstream families, minority and immigrant families value education and view school achievement and completion as the conduit for success. When asked directly, minority adolescents also value education and understand the linkages between academic effort and long-term success. From a PVEST framework, less stigmatizing feedback and treatment would aid minority youths' use of productive coping strategies. Better learning environments and home-school partnerships would aid their acquisition of identities and outcomes that demonstrate their identification with schooling.

For any student, adjustment to novel or unfamiliar learning contexts requires adaptive responses. Contemporary educational settings differ significantly from those experienced by teachers, school administrators, and parents in their own adolescence. Schools often mirror societal attitudes more generally, thus increasing the probability of negative teacher perceptions, cultural misinterpretations, and stressed intergenerational relations. For example, minority boys are often treated and perceived by their teachers as frightening "short" adults and as sources of risk, threat, and violence when they grow to be adolescents. It is difficult to teach young people who are feared and not valued as learners.

School adjustment may be defined as the degree of school acculturation or adaptations required to maximize the educational fit between the student's qualities and the multidimensional character and requirements of the learning environment. Jewell Gibbs (1988) chronicled the multiple sources of cultural discontinuities between school and community for African American males; Maria Matute-Bianchi (1986) described similar experiences for American youth of Mexican and Japanese descent. Wade Boykin (1986) characterized the cultural disconnect between home and school for black youth as a triple quandary—competition between mainstream experience, the minority experience, and the black cultural experience. Informed and sensitive policies and programs should diminish the need for a double consciousness (Du Bois 1902) or a triple quandary (Boykin 1986).

The Aspiring Youth After-School Program in Texas provides educational instruction, mentoring, and enrichment activities at local schools. It is designed to increase the aspirations of middle school students and to encourage them to remain in school. Like their counterparts in many other in-house after-school programs, these students receive additional instruction to enhance their reading, mathematics, computer, art, and other school-based skills. The program also provides consistent interaction with positive role models to bolster youths' self-esteem, and it facilitates the development of mentoring relationships with community and business leaders. Following academic enrichment, students participate in group sports to develop a sense of belonging and to learn about competition and sportsmanship. They compete in academic and art contests at the end of each session (fall, spring, summer) and in an athletic tournament. Each session climaxes with an awards ceremony that includes a talk about school and life goals by a role model.

EFFECTIVE SOCIAL POLICY AND VULNERABILITY

All youth are psychologically vulnerable (Anthony 1974). However, low-risk environments may offset the expression of vulnerability, whereas high-risk environments may guarantee it. Structural conditions linked to poverty, race, and ethnicity can make it necessary for character training to take place in a "hostile environment" (Chestang 1972). Resilient youth may live under conditions of risk but not demonstrate vulnerability. For disadvantaged adolescents, developmental crises and stresses often are compounded by unstable factors in their sociocultural milieu (Spencer and Markstrom-Adams 1990). Effective social policies for poor, immigrant, and minority youth support greater resilience and reduce the likelihood of adverse outcomes by implementing changes relevant to the group's structural condition. Thus, supportive youth policies can mitigate the impact of a low-resource environment and reduce tensions for parents concerned about their children's experiences and expectations. This can be accomplished when schools work with parents to facilitate good youth outcomes. An adolescent's interaction with supportive adults provides him with emotional sustenance, informational guidance, and tangible assistance. Safe, positive role models are also helpful to youth in proposing and identifying life choices.

Policy proposals seldom consider their impact on youth *and their families*. In recent years, Congress has considered two programs to support families. The first focuses on "dead-beat" parents to ensure that child support is paid by nonresident parents; the second, known as Policies to Strengthen Families, seeks to support families, particularly those with young children, that are negatively affected by social and economic pressures. Like many "family-focused" policies, however, neither program considers adolescents and their parents as sources for good outcomes, and both neglect the multiple sources of support (neighborhoods, schools) required to achieve this goal.

Youth employment opportunities are in short supply, especially jobs that can enhance psychological functioning, such as apprenticeship programs (Erikson 1968). Even magnet school programs, which use the parental choice concept, do not address instructional improvements for all public school children. In many public and private agencies that serve economically and socially disadvantaged individuals, the least powerful people receive the fewest services. Combined with educational failure and few employment opportunities, factors such as adolescent crime and teenage childbearing create long-term social devastation (see Schorr 1997).

Many sociocultural deficits stem from inequities in the educational and economic systems. In contrast to the popular impression, African American low-income students and their parents place a high value on education and express high educational aspirations. Despite these aspirations, many perform poorly academically. Policymakers should endorse programmatic strategies to enhance academic skills without undermining self-esteem and peer relations. Policymakers must understand child and adolescent development and how institutions (schools) and conditions (limited training opportunities) outside the child and family either promote or prevent poverty (Comer 1988). James Comer sought to address the developmental and educational needs of inner-city youth by bridging home and school; the School Development Program was the result. Comer incorporated a plan to improve educators' understanding of child development and to foster healthier relations between school and home. Within schools, the program mobilizes an entire community of adult caretakers—teachers, administrators, counselors, nonteaching staff, parents, and community members—to facilitate and support students' development and have an impact on their academic success.

The education of most poor youth will not be improved by reforms that primarily address personnel and curriculum standards. School reorganizations focus more on school size and staff control than on improving staff-family-student relationships. Most poor children fail in school because of the lack of continuity between their experiences and relationships at home compared to those expected by their school. Low-income and racially and ethnically diverse children are more likely to be academically successful when schools decrease the alienation between schools and families and their social networks (Comer 1988). Schools need to make it possible for children to experience the positive attachment and bonding, imitation, identification, and internalization of attitudes and values that lead to optimal development and learning. Most school interventions pay too little attention to the relationship between sociocultural and emotional development and the school climate.

Low-income parents may be less able to help their children with homework because their own education is generally poor (Spencer 1983). Economically impoverished parents share with middle-income white parents the same hopes and expectations for their children's educational attainment and subsequent employment (Spencer 1990, 1999). Many poor children attain more education than their parents, but it may not be sufficient to help them obtain the jobs they want or the ones they will need to sustain themselves and a family.

There remains a problem that is related to the discrepancy between the promises of a high school diploma and the realities of the workforce (Gibbs 1988). Feeling barred from lucrative work and unable to obtain further education (even when desired), some high school graduates perceive themselves as effectively cut off from the American dream.

Some adolescents who leave school early and become young parents ultimately become self-supporting, responsible, and productive adults; more, however, are trapped by joblessness, single parenthood, poor work skills, and limited opportunities. Youth need opportunities to develop and demonstrate the marketable and personal competencies required to build their leadership skills and a sense of empowerment. For example, youth who are given responsibilities at home, at school, and in related activities (sports teams, clubs, youth programs) and who are expected to succeed have high levels of life satisfaction, high self-esteem, and a positive attitude. Many youth, however, lack the effective supports and services needed to become self-sufficient. These young people—unemployed or unemployable—take on early parenting responsibilities but are unable to form stable families. Disconnected from the mainstream and unable to make the transition to productive adulthood, they risk becoming trapped at the bottom of American society.

In identifying policy reforms, it is necessary to understand the coping problems of the racial-ethnic minority poor as issues of relationship, development, and reactive behavior. Confrontational behaviors, such as aggressiveness and hypermasculinity, are often rigorously addressed as problematic for not only the individual adolescent but also for others affected by these behaviors. Inhibited and depressed behaviors are less problematic for others, but they are just as disturbing to youths' development. Interventions that focus on multiple areas, such as academic support and interpersonal skill development, should be given high priority.

Because it is a time of exploration and cognitive transformations, adolescence provides opportunities for growth and positive development that can be facilitated through parenting strategies and integrated services and programs. Among minority youth, positive racial-ethnic identity, positive gender identity, and the development of skills and interpersonal competencies in conjunction with available supports are vital for resilience. Supports for increasing parenting skills and resources and creating institutional partnerships can and should be made available through schools, community organizations, and churches.

Support for the preparation of this chapter was made possible through funding to the first author from the Ford Foundation, the Commonwealth Fund, the Office of Educational Research Improvement (OERI), the National Institute of Mental Health (NIMH), and the Kellogg Foundation.

REFERENCES

Allen, Walter R. 1985. "Race, Income, and Family Dynamics: A Study of Adolescent Male Socialization Processes and Outcomes." In *Beginnings: The Social and Affective Development of Black Children,* edited by Margaret Beale Spencer, Geraldine K. Brookins, and Walter R. Allen. Hillsdale, N.J.: Lawrence Erlbaum.

Ambert, Anne-Marie. 1997. "The Parent-Adolescent Relationship." In *Parents, Children, and Adolescents: Interactive Relationships and Development in Context.* New York: Haworth Press.

Anderson, Norman B., Maya McNeilly, and Hector Myers. 1991. "Autonomic Reactivity in Hypertension in Blacks: A Review and Proposed Model." *Ethnicity and Disease* 1: 154–70.

Anthony, E. J. 1974. "Introduction: The Syndrome of the Psychologically Vulnerable Child." In *The Child in His Family: Children at Psychiatric Risk,* edited by E. J. Anthony and Cyrille Koupernik. New York: Wiley.

Boykin, A. Wade. 1986. "The Triple Quandary and the Schooling of Afro-American Children." In *The School Achievement of Minority Children,* edited by Ulric Neisser. Hillsdale, N.J.: Lawrence Erlbaum.

Brim, O. Gilbert. 1976. "Life-Span Development of the Theory of Oneself: Implications for Child Development." In *Advances in Child Development and Behavior,* vol. 11, edited by H. Ruse New York: Academic Press.

Brislin, Richard W., ed. 1990. *Applied Cross-cultural Psychology.* Newbury Park, Calif.: Sage.

Bronfenbrenner, Urie. 1979. *The Ecology of Human Development: Experiments by Nature and Design.* Cambridge, Mass.: Harvard University Press.

Canino, Ian, and Luis H. Zayas. 1997. "Puerto Rican Children." In *Transcultural Child Development: Psychological Assessment and Treatment,* edited by Gloria Johnson-Powell and Joe Yamamoto. New York: Wiley.

Chestang, Leon W. 1972. "The Dilemma of Biracial Environments." *Social Work* 17(3): 100–105.

Clark, Reginald M. 1983. *Family Life and School Achievement: Why Poor Black Children Succeed and Fail.* Chicago: University of Chicago Press.

Comer, James P. 1988. "Educating Poor Minority Children." *Scientific American* 259(5): 42–48.

Cornell, Stephen, and Douglass Hartmann. 1998. *Ethnicity and Race.* Thousand Oaks, Calif.: Pine Forge Press.

Crain, William. 1992. *Theories of Development: Concept and Applications.* Englewood Cliffs, N.J.: Prentice-Hall.

Cunningham, M. 1994. "Expressions of Manhood: Predictors of Educational Achievement and African-American Adolescent Males." Ph.D. diss., Emory University.

Du Bois, W. E. B. 1902. *The Philadelphia Negro.*

Elder, Glen H., Jr. 1985. *Life-Course Dynamics: Trajectories and Transitions, 1968–1980.* Ithaca, N.Y.: Cornell University Press.

Erikson, Erik. 1963. *Childhood and Society,* 2nd ed. New York: Norton.

———. 1968. *Identity: Youth and Crisis.* New York: Norton.

Felner, Robert D., Steven Brand, A. M. Adan, and Peter F. Mulhall. 1993. "Restructuring the Ecology of the School as an Approach to Prevention During School Transitions: Longitudinal Follow-ups and Extensions of the School Transitional Environment Project (STEP)." *Prevention in Human Services* 10(2): 103–36.

Garbarino, James. 1982. *Children and Families in the Social Environment.* New York: Aldine de Gruyter.

Gibbs, Jewell T. 1988. *Young, Black, and Male in America: An Endangered Species.* Dover, Mass.: Auburn House.

Irvine, J. J. 1988. "An Analysis of the Problem of Disappearing Black Educators." *Elementary School Journal* 88(5): 503–13.

Jaret, Robin. 1995. *Contemporary Racial and Ethnic Relations.* New York: HarperCollins.

Jones, D. C., A. U. Rickel, and R. L. Smith. 1980. "Maternal Child-Rearing Practices and Social Problem-Solving Strategies Among Preschoolers." *Developmental Psychology* 16(3): 241–42.

Johnson, Knowlton, T. Strader, M. Berbaum, D. Bryant, G. Bucholtz, D. Collins, and T. Noe. 1996. "Reducing Alcohol and Other Drug Use by Strengthening Community, Family, and Youth Resiliency: An Evaluation of the Creating Lasting Connections Program." *Journal of Adolescent Research* 11(1): 36–67.

Kochman, Tedd J. 1992. "The Relationship Between Environment Characteristics and the Psychological Functioning of African American Youth." Honors thesis (psychology), Emory University.

Kohlberg, Lawrence. 1975. "The Cognitive-Developmental Approach to Moral Development." *Phi Delta Kappa* 56(10): 671.

LeGall, S. 1990. "Academic Achievement Orientation and Help-Seeking in Early Adolescent Girls." *Journal of Early Adolescence* 10: 176–90.

LeVine, Robert Allen, and D. Campbell. 1972. *Ethnocentrism: Theory of Conflict, Ethnic Attitudes, and Group Behavior.* New York: Wiley.

Loeb, R. C., L. Horst, and P. J. Horton. 1980. "Family Interaction Patterns Associated with Self-esteem in Preadolescent Girls and Boys." *Merrill-Palmer Quarterly* 26: 205–17.

Matute-Bianchi, Maria E. 1986. "Ethnic Identity and Patterns of School Success and Failures Among Mexican-Descendants and Japanese-American Students in a California High School: An Ethnocentric Analysis." *American Journal of Education* 95: 233–55.

Myrek, L. I., J. A. Mancini, and D. J. Brock. 1999. "Continuity, Success, and Survival of Community-Based Projects: The National Youth at Risk Program Sustainability Study." Publication 350–801. Washington, D.C.: U.S. Department of Agriculture.

Nettles, S. M. 1991. "Community Contributions to School Outcomes of African American Students." *Education and Urban Society* 24(1): 132–47.

Ranganath, Vijay M., and Veena K. Ranganath. 1997. "Asian Indian Children." In *Transcultural Child Development: Psychological Assessment and Treatment,* edited by Gloria Johnson-Powell and Joe Yamamoto. New York: Wiley.

Rice, F. Philip. 1996. *Intimate Relationships, Marriages, and Family.* Mountain View, Calif.: Mayfield.

———. 1999. *The Adolescent: Development, Relationships, and Culture,* 9th ed. Boston: Allyn and Bacon.

Rodriquez-Cortes, Carmen. 1990. "Social Practices of Ethnic Identity: A Puerto Rican Psycho-Cultural Event." *Hispanic Journal of Behavioral Sciences* 12: 380–96.

Schorr, Lisbeth B. 1997. *Common Purpose: Strengthening Families and Neighborhoods to Rebuild America.* New York: Anchor Books/Doubleday.

Smith, M. B. 1968. "Competence and Socialization." In *Socialization and Society,* edited by J. A. Clausen. Boston: Little, Brown.

Spencer, Margaret Beale. 1983. "Children's Cultural Values and Parental Child-Rearing Strategies." *Developmental Review* 3: 351–70.

———. 1990. "Parental Values Transmission: Implications for Black Child Development." In *Interdisciplinary Perspectives on Black Families,* edited by James B. Stewart and Harold Cheatham. New Brunswick, N.J.: Transaction.

———. 1995. "Old Issues and New Theorizing About African American Youth: A Phenomenological Variant of Ecological Systems Theory." In *Black Youth: Perspectives on Their Status in the United States,* edited by Ronald L. Taylor. Westport, Conn.: Praeger.

———. 1997. "(Funded) Resiliency-Enhancement: Programmatic Support for Ethnically Diverse Urban Youth." Proposal submitted to the Office of Educational Research Improvement (OERI), Washington, D.C.

———. 1999. "Social and Cultural Influences on Social Adjustment: The Application of an Identity-Focused Cultural Ecological Perspective." *Educational Psychologist* 34(1): 43–47.

Spencer, Margaret Beale, C. Ashford, and J. Youngblood. 1998. "The Use of a Model Demonstration/Outreach Program for the Preparation of Leadership Personnel for Secondary School Disabled Youth." Proposal submitted to the U.S. Department of Education.

Spencer, Margaret Beale, J. Blumenthal, and E. Richards. 1995. "Child Care and Children of Color." In *Escape from Poverty: What Makes a Difference for Children,* edited by Jeanne Brooks-Gunn and P. Lindsay Chase-Lansdale. New York: Cambridge University Press.

Spencer, Margaret Beale, and M. Cunningham. Forthcoming. "Patterns of Resilience and Vulnerability: Examining Diversity Within African-American Youth." In *Ethnicity and Diversity: Minorities No More,* edited by Geraldine K. Brookins and Margaret Beale Spencer. Hillsdale, N.J.: Lawrence Erlbaum.

Spencer, Margaret Beale, and Sanford Dornbusch. 1990. "Challenges in Studying Minority Youth." In *At the Threshold: The Developing Adolescent,* edited by S. Shirley Feldman and Glen R. Elliott. Cambridge, Mass.: Harvard University Press.

Spencer, Margaret Beale, S. Kim, and S. Marshall. 1987. "Double Stratification and Psychological Risk: Adaptational Processes and School Experiences of Black Children." *Journal of Negro Education* 56(1): 77–86.

Spencer, Margaret Beale, and C. Markstrom-Adams. 1990. "Identity Processes Among Racial and Ethnic Minority Children in America." *Child Development* 61(2): 290–310.

Steinberg, Laurence. 1999. *Adolescence.* New York: McGraw-Hill.

Stevenson, H. C. 1997. "'Missed, Dissed, and Pissed': Making Meaning of Neighborhood Risk, Fear, and Anger Management in Urban Black Youth." *Cultural Diversity and Mental Health* 3(1): 37–52.

Swanson, Dena Phillips, Margaret Beale Spencer, and Anne Petersen. 1998. "Identity Formation in Adolescence." In *The Adolescent Years: Social Influences and Educational Challenges,* edited by Kathryn Borman and Barbara Schneider. In *Ninety-seventh Yearbook of the National Society for the Study of Education,* part 1. Chicago: University of Chicago Press.

Tamir, L. M., and T. C. Antonucci. 1981. "Self-perception, Motivation, and Social Support Through the Family Life Course." *Journal of Marriage and the Family* 43: 151–60.

Tharp, Ronald G., and Ronald Gallimore. 1988. *Rousing Minds of Life: Teaching, Learning, and Schooling in Social Context.* Cambridge: Cambridge University Press.

Unger, D. G., and Abraham Wandersman. 1982. "Neighboring in an Urban Environment." *American Journal of Community Psychology* 10(5): 493–509.

Weiss, Carol H. 1995. "Nothing as Practical as Good Theory: Exploring Theory-Based Evaluation for Comprehensive Community Initiatives for Children and Families." In *New Approaches to Evaluating Community Initiatives: Concepts, Methods, and Contexts,* edited by James P. Connell, Ann C. Kubish, Lisbeth B. Schorr, and Carol H. Weiss. Washington, D.C.: Aspen Institute.

———. 1997. "How Can Theory-Based Evaluation Make Greater Headway?" *Evaluation Review* 21(4): 501–24.

White, Robert. 1959. "Motivation Reconsidered: The Concept of Competence." *Psychology Review* 66(5): 297–333.

Winfield, Linda F. 1991. "Resilience, Schooling, and Development in African-American Youth." *Education and Urban Society* 24(1): 5–14.

Youniss, James. 1998. "Symposium Submission Summary Statement." Unpublished submission statement for the Identity and the Moral Life of Adolescents Symposium panel, Society for Research on Adolescence Conference, San Diego (February 27, 1998).

Chapter 7

The Neighborhood Context of Investing in Children: Facilitating Mechanisms and Undermining Risks

Robert J. Sampson

In this chapter, I examine four issues regarding the neighborhood context of investing in children. I begin by reviewing some of the defining themes of community and neighborhood, placing present concerns within a larger intellectual history. Second, I highlight the dimensions along which local communities in the United States are stratified ecologically, showing that they vary greatly in terms of racial isolation and the concentration of socioeconomic resources, and that social problems such as predatory crime, public disorder, poor health, and other detriments to children's well-being tend to come bundled in geographical space.

I then examine what neighborhoods supply for children and how structural forces in the larger environment shape the internal dynamics of local communities. I consider a general theory of community social organization that specifies how the social mechanisms that are relevant for children—such as informal social control and intergenerational closure—vary across neighborhoods. I also discuss what research tells us about the ways in which structural characteristics (for example, economic segregation, residential stability) and spatial externalities promote or inhibit neighborhood social organization.

The final section describes promising neighborhood strategies for advancing new knowledge and building assets for children. I highlight the steps that policy might take to improve the collective capacity of low-income neighborhoods.

Some caveats are in order. First, my discussion pertains largely to local geographical communities or residential settlements, typically known as neighborhoods or local community areas. Second, I underscore how disadvantaged and low-income neighborhoods, especially the concentrated poverty areas of our large cities, fare with respect to community social organization. Third, I touch on, but do not elaborate, the substantial literature on operational definitions of neighborhoods. Fourth, I do not dwell on the methodological limitations to neighborhood research (for recent overviews, see Tienda 1991; Cook, Shagle, and Degirmencioglu 1997; and Duncan and Raudenbush 1999). Finally, I do not review the vast literature evaluating community interventions (see, for example, Rossi 1999; and Connell et al. 1995).

Interventions at the neighborhood level have rarely been targeted at the theoretical issues discussed here. Those that have, however, such as citizen involvement in community policing (Skogan and Hartnett 1998), are highlighted wherever relevant.

LOCAL COMMUNITY IN MODERN SOCIETY

Barry Wellman (1979) summarized a classical tradition in urban sociology under the label "Community Lost," invoking the idea that the social ties of modern urbanites have become impersonal, transitory, and segmented, hastening the eclipse of local community and feeding processes of social disorganization. "Community Lost" is a salient theme that has a venerable history in twentieth-century sociology and popular wisdom.

Research suggests, however, that the "lost" thesis is naive and that the perceived loss of community is premature. Ethnographic research from the 1940s to the 1960s discovered thriving urban communities and ethnic enclaves where kinship and friendship solidarities flourished (Gans 1962). William F. Whyte (1943) criticized the notion that slum communities were "disorganized" after discovering the intricate social ties embedded within the social structure of a low-income Italian area of Boston. Especially in poor urban neighborhoods, extensive evidence of dense social networks and strong local identification ("Community Saved") has been found (Wellman 1979).

There is a compromise that can be made between the "Community Lost" and "Community Saved" arguments. Social-network theorists have shown that, contrary to assumptions of a decline in primary relations, and contrary to the "saved" image of dense parochial ties, most urbanites create nonspatial communities with viable sets of social relations dispersed in space (Tilly 1973, 211). Urban dwellers, especially in the upper-income brackets, might not know (or want to know) their neighbors, but they have interpersonal networks spread throughout the city, the state, and even the country. Wellman referred to this thesis as "Community Liberated," or what might be called community *beyond* propinquity. This does not mean that local relations are unimportant, only that they are no longer controlling for many areas of social life. Such contingency of commitment to locality has also been defined as the "community of limited liability" (Janowitz 1975), where attachment to neighborhood is contingent, voluntary, and based on instrumental values tied to rational investment rather than the constrained interpersonal ties that characterized the "urban villages" of our past (see also Chaskin 1995).

In short, I argue that the local community has been transformed rather than lost, helping us to distinguish what communities do and do not supply for children in mass society (Sampson 1999). Namely, urbanites rely less on local neighborhoods for psychological support, cultural and religious nourishment, and economic needs or transactions (for example, shopping and work) than in the past. Given modern technology, we shop, work, go to church, and make friends throughout geographical space and, increasingly, in cyberspace. This suggests that interventions at the local level are unlikely to succeed if they penetrate only the private world of personal relations or child-rearing. We do not need communities as much as we did in the past to satisfy our private and personal needs, which are now best met elsewhere, nor even to meet our sustenance needs, which appear to be dispersed in space.

On the other hand, the local community remains important as a site for the realization of common values in support of safe and mutually supportive child-rearing. As shown later in the chapter, childhood risk and protective factors are concentrated geographically. The local community remains important for another reason—economic resources and social-structural differentiation in general are very much a spatial affair in the United States. The bedrock of physical and human capital (for example, income, education, housing stock) is distributed unevenly across ecological space—often in conjunction with ascribed characteristics, such as racial composition. The continuing, and in some cases increasing, significance of such ecological differentiation bears on our understanding of the well-being of children and adolescents.

Defining Local Community

Before addressing ecological differentiation, however, I briefly consider operational definitions of community and neighborhood. A traditional definition of "neighborhood," as proposed by Robert Park (1916, 147–54) long ago, refers to an ecological subsection of a larger community—a collection of both people and institutions occupying a spatially defined area that is conditioned by a set of *ecological, cultural,* and *political* forces. Park claimed that the neighborhood was the basis of social and political organization, although not in a formal sense. He may have overstated the cultural and political distinctiveness of residential enclaves, but it is important to recognize that neighborhoods are ecological units nested within successively larger communities (114). There is no one neighborhood but many neighborhoods that vary in size and complexity depending on the social phenomenon of interest and the ecological structure of the larger community. Most cities comprise *local community* or *city planning* areas that have reasonable ecological integrity. Although large, these areas often have well-known names and borders, such as freeways, parks, and major streets. For example, Chicago has seventy-seven local community areas, averaging about forty thousand persons, that were designed to correspond to socially meaningful and natural geographic boundaries. Some boundaries have changed over time, but these areas are widely recognized by administrative agencies and local institutions. *Census tracts* refer to smaller and more socially homogeneous areas of roughly three thousand to five thousand residents; their boundaries are usually drawn to take into account major streets, parks, and other geographical features. A third and even smaller area approximating the layperson's concept of "neighborhood" is the *block group*—a set of blocks averaging approximately one thousand residents.

It remains the case, however, that ecological units such as community or planning areas, census tracts, and block groups offer imperfect operational definitions for research and policy. One implication of the "Community Liberated" argument is that social networks may also be boundless in physical space (Wellman 1979). Yet operationally, geographical units are reasonably consonant with the notion of over-lapping and nested ecological structures, and generally they possess more integrity with respect to geographical boundaries, land use patterns, and social homogeneity than cities or metropolitan areas.

ECOLOGICAL DIFFERENTIATION AND COMMUNITY STRATIFICATION

Research traditions rooted in "social area analysis" and "factorial ecology" have es-tablished key structural characteristics that vary between neighborhoods, chiefly along dimensions of socioeconomic stratification (for example, poverty or occupa-tional attainment), family and life-cycle status, residential stability (home ownership and tenure), race-ethnicity, and urbanization (density). The best-known explanation for the clustering of multiple forms of social and economic disadvantage is William Julius Wilson's (1987) theory of the *concentration effects* arising from living in an im-poverished neighborhood. Wilson argued that the social transformation of inner-city areas in recent decades has increased the concentration of the most disadvantaged segments of the black population—especially poor, female-headed families with chil-dren. At the national level in 1990, 25 percent of poor blacks lived in concentrated-poverty neighborhoods, compared to only 3 percent of poor whites (see Jargowsky 1997, 41). These differential ecological distributions systematically confound rela-tionships between race and individual outcomes with racial differences in commu-nity contexts.

The concentration of poverty and joblessness (Wilson 1996) has been fueled by macrostructural economic changes, including a shift from goods-producing to service-producing industries, the increasing polarization of the labor market into low-wage and high-wage sectors, and the relocation of manufacturing out of the inner city. The related exodus of middle- and upper-income black families from the inner city has also, according to Wilson (1987, 56), removed a social buffer that was able to deflect the negative influences of prolonged joblessness and industrial trans-formation. The social milieu of increasing stratification among blacks differs signif-icantly from the environment in inner-city neighborhoods in previous decades. In other words, income mixing within communities was once more characteristic of ghetto neighborhoods, whereas inequality among communities today has become more pronounced as a result of the increasing spatial separation of middle- and upper-income blacks from lower-income blacks (see also Jargowsky 1997).

Douglas Massey and Nancy Denton (1993) have described how the increasing so-cial differentiation caused by economic dislocation interacting with racial residential segregation creates a set of structural circumstances that reinforce the effects of social and economic deprivation. In a segregated environment, exogenous economic shocks cause a downward shift in the distribution of minority income, increasing the poverty rate for the group as a whole but also increasing the geographic concentration of poverty. This geographic intensification occurs because the additional poverty cre-ated by macroeconomic conditions is spread unevenly over the metropolitan area

(Massey 1990, 337). At the other end of the income distribution, Massey (1996) noted the growing geographic concentration of predominantly white *affluence,* suggesting a society increasingly bifurcated by wealth. Thus, Wilson and Massey have both conceptualized, though for different reasons, race-linked social change as a structural characteristic reflected in local environments.

Consequences for Children and Adolescents

Indicators of economic disadvantage and racial isolation not only are concentrated ecologically but tend to be clustered with a set of troublesome behaviors, some of which are likewise increasing in concentration. In a case study of Cleveland, Julian Chow and Claudia Coulton (1992) operationalized Wilson's theory of social transformation by searching for evidence of structural change in the ecological distribution and interrelationship of adverse conditions such as violent crime, drug addiction, teenage pregnancy, and welfare dependency. Comparing 1980 and 1989, they showed that the earlier period was characterized by an evenly distributed three-factor structure defined by unruliness (for example, weakened social control of adolescents), family vulnerability (for example, single-parent households and poor maternal and child health), and dangerousness (crime and drug arrests). By 1989, however, these social conditions had become more interrelated, and one factor, which they called impoverishment, had emerged as the dominant construct.

The neighborhood concentration of child-linked social problems has a long history. Discovered by Clifford Shaw and Henry McKay (1969) in the 1920s, Chicago neighborhoods characterized by poverty, residential instability, and high rates of crime and delinquency were also plagued by high rates of infant mortality, low birthweight, tuberculosis, physical abuse, and other factors detrimental to child development. The close association of delinquency rates with a host of social problems that directly influence children has emerged repeatedly over time. The range of child and adolescent outcomes correlated with multiple forms of concentrated disadvantage includes infant mortality, low birthweight, teenage childbearing, low academic achievement and educational failure, child maltreatment, and delinquency (Brooks-Gunn et al. 1993; Duncan, Brooks-Gunn, and Klebanov 1994; Coulton et al. 1995; Elliott et al. 1996; Furstenberg et al. 1999; for a recent overview, see Brooks-Gunn, Duncan, and Aber 1997a, 1997b). There is clearly a connection between healthy child development and neighborhood characteristics.

Summary

Empirical research on ecological differentiation has established a reasonably consistent set of facts relevant to an understanding of the neighborhood context of investing in children. First, there is considerable race-linked economic inequality between neighborhoods and local communities, evidenced by the clustering of indicators of socioeconomic status (both advantage and disadvantage) with racial isolation. Even in areas of racial or ethnic homogeneity, however, economic segregation reigns supreme (Jargowsky 1996, 1997). Second, myriad problems are bundled together in neighborhoods, including crime, adolescent delinquency, social and physical disorder, public incivilities, and poor child health. Third, these two sets of clusters are themselves related—neighborhood predictors common to child and adolescent "outcomes" include concentrated resource disadvantage, residential instability, and family disruption. Fourth, ecological stratification of local communities by social class, poverty, race, family status, and crime is a robust phenomenon that emerges at multiple levels of geographical structure, whether measured by local community areas, census tracts, or other "neighborhood" units. Fifth, the ecological concentration of poverty, racial isolation, and social disadvantage has increased significantly during the 1980s and 1990s, as has the concentration of affluence (Massey 1996; Jargowsky 1996, 1997).

Despite globalization and urbanization, and despite a complex overlapping structure, neighborhood differentiation thus remains persistent in American society. As any real estate agent or home owner will attest, location does matter. But why does neighborhood matter, and for what? Taken together, the findings on neighborhood differentiation yield a potentially important insight in thinking about this question. If numerous child outcomes are linked across neighborhoods and are also predicted by similar structural characteristics, then there may be a common underlying cause. Thus, the next section asks the general question: What are the *social mechanisms* by which neighborhood structures—especially the concentration of poverty, racial segregation, and residential stability—matter for children?

FACILITATING MECHANISMS AND UNDERMINING RISKS

Community social organization may be conceptualized as the ability of a community structure to realize the common values of its residents and maintain effective social controls (Kornhauser 1978; Bursik 1988; Sampson and Groves 1989). Social control refers to the capacity of a social unit to regulate itself according to desired principles—to realize *collective,* as opposed to forced, goals (Janowitz 1975, 82, 87). This conception is similar to Charles Tilly's (1973) definition of collective action— the application of a community's pooled resources to common ends. Common ends include the desire of community residents to live in a safe and orderly environment free of predatory crime, and in neighborhoods characterized by economic sufficiency, efficacious schools, adequate housing, and a healthy environment for children. The capacity to achieve such goals is linked to both informal role relationships established for other purposes and more formal, purposive efforts to achieve social regulation through institutional means (Kornhauser 1978).

A social control framework does not require homogeneity. Diverse populations do agree on common goals, such as safety for children. And social conflicts do rend communities along the lines of economic resources, race, political empowerment, and the role of criminal justice agents in defining and controlling crime, particularly drug use and gangs (Meares and Kahan 1998). It is around the distribution of resources and power that conflict usually emerges, not the content of core values (Kornhauser 1978). According to Philip Selznick (1992, 369), the goal of community is the reconciliation of partial with general perspectives on the common good.

This conception of social control leads me to problematize the internal homogeneity of a community and focus on the variable forms of social organization—both formal and informal. I also focus on neighborhoods and local community areas rather than elevating solidarity or identity to the major definitional criteria. Following Tilly (1973, 212), I "choose to make territoriality define communities and to leave the extent of solidarity problematic." Thus, dimensions of local social organization are analytically separable not only from sources of variation (for example, racial segregation, concentrated poverty, instability) but from the social mechanisms that may result.

Networks, Social Capital, and Collective Efficacy

The social control approach to community is related to what John Kasarda and Morris Janowitz (1974, 329) called the "systemic" model: the local community is viewed as a complex system of friendship and kinship networks and formal and informal associational ties rooted in family life, ongoing socialization processes, and local institutions (see also Sampson 1988). Key systemic dimensions of community social organization are the prevalence, interdependence, and overlapping nature of social networks (for example, the density of acquaintanceship, intergenerational ties, and network overlap), local participation in formal and voluntary organizations, and the span of collective attention that the community directs toward local problems.

This approach to social control is compatible with recent formulations of "social capital." James Coleman (1988, 98) defined social capital by its functions: it is created when the structure of relations between persons facilitates action, "making possible the achievements of certain ends that in its absence would not be possible." By contrast, physical capital is embodied in observable material form, and human capital is embodied in the skills and knowledge acquired by individuals. Social capital is less tangible, for it is a social good embodied in the relations between persons and positions (Coleman 1990, 304). Robert Putnam (1993, 36) defined social capital as "features of social organization, such as networks, norms, and trust, that facilitate coordination and cooperation for mutual benefit." Unlike physical capital, social capital becomes depleted if not used on a regular basis.

Social capital is thus not an attribute of individuals but rather inheres in the structure of social organization (Coleman 1990). It follows that local communities high in social capital can better realize common values and maintain effective social controls. Neighborhoods characterized by an extensive set of obligations, expectations, and interlocking social networks that connect adults are best able to facilitate the informal social control and support of children (Sampson 1992). For example, when parents know the parents of their children's friends, they can observe their children's actions in different circumstances, talk to each other about the children, compare notes, and establish norms (Coleman 1988). Such intergenerational closure of local networks provides the children with social capital of a collective nature. One can extend this model to closure among networks involving parents and teachers, religious and recreational leaders, businesses that serve youth, and perhaps even agents of criminal justice (Sampson 1992).

Social networks and closure are not sufficient, however, to understand local communities. Networks are differentially invoked, and dense, tight-knit networks may actually impede social organization if they are isolated or weakly linked to collective expectations for action. Relatedly, the term "social capital" is perhaps misleading in that it alludes to a commodity or thing rather than a dynamic process (Sampson, Morenoff, and Earls 1999). At the neighborhood level, the willingness of local residents to intervene for the common good depends, in large part, on conditions of mutual trust and shared values among neighbors. One is unlikely to intervene in a neighborhood context where the rules are unclear and people mistrust or fear one another.

Private ties notwithstanding, then, it is the linkage of mutual trust and the shared willingness to intervene for the common good that defines the neighborhood context of what my colleagues and I (Sampson, Raudenbush, and Earls 1997) have termed *collective efficacy*. Just as individuals vary in their capacity for efficacious action, so too do neighborhoods vary in their capacity to achieve common goals. And just as individual self-efficacy is situated rather than global (one has self-efficacy relative to a particular task or type of task), neighborhood efficacy exists relative to the tasks of supervising children and maintaining public order. I thus view social capital as referring more to the resources or potential inherent in social networks, whereas collective efficacy for children is a task-specific construct that refers to shared expectations and mutual engagement by parents in the support and social control of children (Sampson, Raudenbush, and Earls 1997; Sampson, Morenoff, and Earls 1999).

Institutions and Public Control

The systemic model of informal social control and collective efficacy does not ignore institutions, nor does it fail to take into account the wider political environment in which local communities are embedded. The institutional component of the systemic model is the resource stock of neighborhood organizations and their linkages with other organizations, both within and outside the community. Neighborhood organizations reflect the structural embodiment of community solidarity, and thus the instability and isolation of local institutions are key factors underlying the structural dimension of social organization. Ruth Kornhauser (1978, 79) argued that when the horizontal links between institutions within a community are weak, the capacity to defend local interests is weakened. Many communities exhibit intense private ties (for example, among friends and kin) yet still lack the institutional capacity to achieve social control (Hunter 1985).

Vertical integration is potentially more important. Robert Bursik and Harold Grasmick (1993) highlighted the importance of *public* control, defined as the capacity of local community organizations to obtain extra-local resources (such as police and fire services or block grants) that help sustain neighborhood social stability and local controls. Albert Hunter (1985, 216) argued that parochial social control—within-community social order based on interpersonal networks and the interlocking of local institutions—"leaves unresolved the problems of public order in a civil society." The problem is that public order is provided mainly by institutions of the state, and we have seen a secular decline in public (citizenship) obligations in society accompanied by an increase in civil (individual) rights. This imbalance of collective obligations and individual rights undermines social control. According to Hunter (1985), local communities must work together with the forces of public control to achieve social order, principally through an interdependence between private (family), parochial (neighborhood), and public (state) institutions such as the police and the schools.

Routine Activities

A concern with human ecology leads us to consider another frequently overlooked dimension in discussions of neighborhoods—how land use patterns and the ecological distribution of daily routine activities bear on children's well-being. The location of schools, the mix of residential with commercial land use (such as strip malls), public transportation nodes, and large flows of nonresident population, for example, are relevant to organizing how and when children come into contact with other peers, adults, and commercial activity. The "routine activities" perspective in criminology (Cohen and Felson 1979) builds on the insight that predatory crime involves the intersection in time and space of motivated offenders, suitable targets, and the absence of capable guardians. Because illegal activities feed on the spatial and temporal structures of routine legal activities (for example, transportation, work, and shopping), the differential land use of cities affects neighborhood crime and disorder patterns. In particular, the placement of bars, liquor stores, strip-mall shopping, subway stops, and unsupervised play spaces determines the distribution of high-risk situations for children. Routine activity theory also posits that neighborhood effects are likely to be context-specific rather than enduring. Correlating characteristics of the neighborhood of one's residence with individual "outcomes" such as crime and school achievement implicitly assumes, however, enduring effects, because in many cases the behaviors themselves unfold in different neighborhood contexts (schools, parks, inner-city areas). Consider the nature of routine activity patterns in modern cities, where residents traverse the boundaries of several neighborhoods in any one day (Felson 1987). Children occupy many different contexts and in fact may experience numerous residential environments as well. It thus pays to take seriously how neighborhoods fare as units of control, guardianship, and socialization over their own public spaces. Here the unit of analysis becomes the neighborhood, and the phenomenon of interest the child behavior within its purview.

STRUCTURAL DIFFERENTIATION
AND NEIGHBORHOOD MECHANISMS

Neighborhood-level social mechanisms such as those just explicated are embedded in structural contexts, spatial dynamics, and a wider political economy of place. For example, social ties and the density of acquaintanceship vary widely across communities, and these variations are positively related to community residential stability (Sampson 1988). At the individual level, length of residence has a positive relationship with local friendships, attachment to the community, and participation in local social activities. At the community level, residential stability has significant contextual effects on an individual's local social ties and participation in local social activities (for example, visitation and leisure-time entertainment), even after accounting for compositional factors such as age, social class, and life cycle. These findings suggest that residential stability promotes a variety of social networks and local associations, thereby enhancing the social capital and collective efficacy of local communities.

Neighborhood variations in informal social control and institutional vitality are also linked to patterns of resource deprivation and racial segregation. Wilson (1996) has posited the corroding effects on neighborhood social organization of concentrated joblessness and the social isolation of the urban poor. In such areas of economic distress, the incentives for active participation in the social aspects of community life are reduced. He has also proposed that the number of employed adults who mentor and guide youth through troubled circumstances in low-income communities has declined over the years along with the employment and manufacturing base of inner-city areas. Wilson and I have argued (Sampson and Wilson 1995) similarly that the loss of stable employment and the outmigration of middle-class families in distressed urban areas have undermined the collective socialization of youth as reflected in neighborhood monitoring, institutional resources, and adult role models.

The importance of economic stratification at the upper end of the distribution is also apparent. Jeanne Brooks-Gunn and her colleagues (1993, 383) reported that for numerous child and adolescent outcomes (such as high school dropout, problem behaviors, and out-of-wedlock births), the *absence* of affluent neighbors was more important than the *presence* of low-income neighbors. High economic status proved to be more important than the poverty status, racial composition, or family structure of neighborhoods, supporting theories that focus on "collective socialization," where neighborhood adult role models and monitoring are seen as important ingredients to a child's socialization.

An emerging body of research has attempted to link neighborhood mechanisms to both structural differentiation and adolescent-related outcomes. Byron Groves and I (Sampson and Groves 1989, 789) found that the prevalence of unsupervised peer groups in a community had the largest overall relationship with rates of street robbery and violence victimization in England. Local friendship networks (the percentage of friends in the neighborhood) and organizational participation by residents had smaller but significant negative associations with robbery. Moreover, the largest overall effect on offender-based rates of personal violence was unsupervised peer groups (793). Variations in the structural dimensions of community were also shown to mediate in large part the effects of community socioeconomic status, residential mobility, ethnic heterogeneity, and family disruption in a manner consistent with social disorganization theory. Namely, mobility had significant inverse effects on friendship networks, family disruption was the largest predictor of unsupervised peer groups, and socioeconomic status had the largest (positive) effect on organizational participation.

Delbert Elliott and his colleagues (1996) examined survey data collected in 1990 from neighborhoods in Chicago and Denver. A multilevel analysis revealed that a measure of "informal control" was significantly and negatively related to adolescent problem behavior in both sites. Control also mediated the prior effects of neighborhood structural disadvantage—declining poor neighborhoods displayed less ability to maintain social control and in turn suffered higher delinquency rates. More recent research in Chicago has examined shared expectations among neighbors for intervening in public acts of deviance by children (such as skipping school or spray-painting graffiti). Variations in the informal social control of children across neighborhoods were positively related to residential stability and negatively related to concentrated poverty. Moreover, informal social control emerged as a significant inhibitor of adolescent misbehavior (Sampson 1997).

Although limited, the cumulative results of recent research support the notion that neighborhoods characterized by mistrust and perceived lack of shared expectations, sparse acquaintanceship and exchange networks among residents, attenuated social control of public spaces, a weak organizational and institutional base, and low participation in local voluntary associations face an increased risk of crime, public disorder, and a wide range of troublesome child and adolescent behaviors (school dropout, teenage childbearing, reduced achievement). Perhaps more important, core dimensions of community social organization and collective action are systematically structured (although not determined) by neighborhood differentiation in terms of wealth, jobs, family status, race-ethnicity, residential stability, and land use.

Metropolitan Inequality

To understand neighborhood-level variations, and ultimately to design community interventions, we must also take into account extra-local forms of metropolitan inequality, because structural differentiation is shaped, both directly and indirectly, by the decisions of public officials and businesses. For example, the destabilization of many inner-city neighborhoods has been facilitated not only by individual preferences, such as voluntary migration patterns, but by government decisions on public housing, incentives for suburban growth in the form of tax breaks for developers and private mortgage assistance, highway construction and urban "renewal," economic disinvestment in inner cities, and zoning restrictions on land use (Logan and Molotch 1987).

Population abandonment is also driven as much by spatial diffusion processes (such as changes in proximity to violent crime) as by the internal characteristics of neighborhoods (Morenoff and Sampson 1997). In particular, housing decisions are often made by assessing the quality of neighborhoods relative to what is happening in surrounding areas. Parents with young children are sensitive to the relative location of neighborhoods and schools in addition to their internal characteristics. Jeffrey Morenoff, Felton Earls, and I (Sampson, Morenoff, and Earls 1999) have thus argued that the benefits for children that might accrue from neighborhood collective efficacy and social capital are conditioned by the characteristics of spatially proximate neighborhoods, which in turn are themselves linked to adjoining neighborhoods. Our argument implies that a major source of variation in social support and investment for children stems from the spatially linked inequalities that characterize the wider metropolitan system.

Crime, Disorder, and Exposure to Violence

Neighborhoods can also be sources of risk for children, especially with respect to disorder and crime. Research shows significant long-term negative effects of exposure to violence on child and adolescent development (Earls and Barnes 1997). Ambient levels of victimization and exposure to violence thus represent a threat to children. Wesley Skogan (1986) has also discussed the indirect "feedback" processes linked to crime and disorder, including physical and psychological withdrawal from community life; a weakening of the informal social control processes that inhibit crime; a decline in the organizational life and mobilization capacity of the neighborhood; deteriorating business conditions; the importation and domestic production of delinquency and deviance; and further dramatic changes in the composition of the population. For example, if people shun their neighbors and local facilities out of fear of crime, local networks and organizations have fewer opportunities to take hold. Relatedly, street crime may be accompanied by residential outmigration and business relocation from inner-city areas (Morenoff and Sampson 1997). Social disorder also reinforces stereotypes of urban inhabitability. As a result, disorder can lead to demographic "collapse" and a weakening of the informal control structures and mobilization capacity of communities (Skogan 1990, 21). Recent research supports the proposition that disorder increases robbery, which in turn is caught up in a negative reciprocal relationship with collective efficacy (Sampson and Raudenbush 1999).

TOWARD THEORETICALLY GROUNDED POLICY

The most important implication of this chapter is that policy should bring together resident-based, informal social control, local institutions, and extra-local (public) control, while at the same time ameliorating the constraints imposed by structural differentiation in the form of resource inequality, racial segregation, concentrated poverty, and residential instability. In particular, community interventions are notably hard to implement and have achieved only limited success in the areas that need them the most—poor, unstable neighborhoods with high crime rates (Hope 1995; Skogan and Hartnett 1998). "One-shot" or short-run interventions that try to change isolated or specific behaviors without confronting their common antecedents are also highly susceptible to failure.

Moreover, community-level interventions to increase neighborhood "self-help" and local voluntarism have succumbed to the lack of organization they seek to supplant. The paradox is that self-help strategies for "community" give priority to the very activities made impossible by the social isolation of residents in unstable and economically vulnerable neighborhoods (see Hope 1995, 24, 51). Thus, neglecting the vertical connections (or lack thereof) that residents have to extra-communal resources and sources of power obscures the structural backdrop to community social organization.

Even if we fully account for the wider structural context within which local communities are embedded, neighborhood interventions will fail unless they pull the appropriate internal levers of change. Seeking to penetrate the private world of personal relations and re-create a mythical past where everyone knew their neighbors is a recipe for failure (Sampson 1999). In fact, community interventions seem to fall down the hardest when the major thrust is to change individual behaviors by promoting friendships among neighbors (Hope 1995). A focus on resurrecting local friendships reflects a nostalgia for a village life that is long gone from most cities (Skogan 1990, 156). For better or worse, in many neighborhoods, neighbors are acquaintances or strangers rather than friends. Where local friendship ties *are* strong, they result not from government intervention but from natural processes induced over time by structural factors, such as residential stability and the density of families with children (Sampson, Morenoff, and Earls 1999).

Returning to the notion of the "community of limited liability," I thus argue that neighborhood policy should focus less on the private or personal realm and more on the realization of public goods and the shoring up of a community's structural base. We should, in other words, intervene where communities need it the most—in restoring safety, resources, and stability. This requires the self-help of communities, to be sure, but self-help must be balanced by investment from the outside, strong linkages to extra-local sources of support, and policies that are sensitive to the potentially disruptive forces of neighborhood instability and unchecked development (such as urban sprawl). The following is a sketch of the contours of what effective neighborhood policies might look like from the perspective of increasing the capacity of local communities to support healthy child development (see also Sampson 1999).

Community Policing and Reducing Social Disorder

Establishing social order and reducing crime are the first and most important items of business undergirding an investment in children's assets. It is very difficult to sustain successful child development in a neighborhood context of rampant fear, mistrust, social disorder, and exposure to violence. Predatory crime and "incivilities," such as garbage in the streets, public drinking, and prostitution, also increase fear of crime and promote a downward spiral of decay and population depletion (Skogan 1990). Reclaiming safe and orderly streets is thus a basic need upon which other interventions depend.

To foster a climate of safety, public order, and social organization, neighborhood policy might consider collective strategies to clean up physical incivilities such as litter, vandalized cars, broken windows, and drug needles; remove or rehabilitate abandoned housing; stagger bar closing times to control unruly crowds; "picket" or protest unwanted public drinking, drug use, and prostitution; organize walking groups for adults in public areas; promote neighborhood-generated referendums on bar licensing and other zoning issues; and create "graffiti patrols" and "phone trees" that would enable residents to keep track of new incidents of disorder and promptly report them to the police (see Carr 1998). There is limited evidence on the effectiveness of these strategies, although neighborhood-based interventions that target physical signs of decay (abandoned buildings, graffiti) have been found to increase perceptions of safety and public order (Hope 1995, 59). I would argue that informal social control as conceptualized here is not the same thing as "neighborhood watch" interventions as commonly implemented. Such interventions may or may not foster social control; the evidence suggests that neighborhood watch programs targeted specifically to crime are largely ineffective.

Linking informal with formal social control, however, depends ultimately on governmental support strategies. The most promising strategy is the integration of *problem-solving* with *community policing*. Problem-solving policing focuses police attention on the problems that lie behind crime incidents (such as disorder) rather than on the crime alone. Community policing emphasizes the establishment of working partnerships between police and communities to reduce crime and enhance security (Moore 1992, 99). There is encouraging news that police efforts to help residents solve local disorder and crime problems are working in many large U.S. cities (Skogan 1994, 1996).

Community policing is perhaps more relevant because it explicitly attempts to foster greater civic involvement by residents in the general life of their neighborhoods. Indeed, one of the major goals of community policing is for the police to spark a sense of local ownership over public space and thus greater activation of informal control. Persuading the public to view the police as partners in the effort to establish safe communities is crucial—citizen calls to the police, after all, are a form of social control "from the bottom up." Thus, informal social controls need not exclude the police, and in fact most acts of informal control involve some form of collaboration between the police and the public.

There is recent evidence that community policing has led to increases in police-citizen collaboration to foster safer neighborhoods. For example, Wesley Skogan and Susan Hartnett (1998) reported large declines in social disorder and crime in a quasi-experimental evaluation of police districts where community policing was initiated in Chicago. Although residents must take partial responsibility for stemming the threat of neighborhood decay, the optimal strategy seems to be one that involves both police and residents in the co-planning and execution of measures to control crime, restore order, and enhance the safety of children in public places (see Meares and Kahan 1998).

Another recent example of community partnerships with the police is found in Boston. Although not developed under the rubric of community policing, the "Ten Point Coalition" was formed by a group of inner-city Boston ministers in the early 1990s to deal with the sharply increasing problem of youth violence. As Jenny Berrien and Christopher Winship (1999) have observed, a long-standing problem in the minority communities of Boston (and elsewhere) was a lack of trust and working relationship between the police and residents. When violence began to increase, residents were faced with a profound conflict—they wanted safe streets for their children, but they also objected to having their sons hauled off to jail en masse. Heavy-handed police tactics (such as aggressive search and frisk procedures targeted at black males) only made matters worse. As a result, it became difficult in Boston and in many inner-city communities to reach a consensus on what constituted legitimate and constructive police activity.

The key to Boston's Ten Point Coalition was to create what Berrien and Winship (1999) termed an "umbrella of legitimacy" under which the police could work. Rather than shut out the police, religious leaders in Boston's black community demanded change and essentially became an *intermediary* institution between the police and the community, adjudicating between conflicting goals and providing legitimacy for proper police activities. The ministers asserted that inner-city residents wanted not less police but a different kind of police (see also Meares and Kahan 1998). They thus took responsibility for insisting on both social order among local youth *and* non-abusive, nonracist methods on the part of the police. Only with the latter came the former. And only the religious leaders had the local social capital and legitimacy in the eyes of residents to lead this effort.

Evaluation of the success of the Ten Point Coalition is still ongoing, but Berrien and Winship (1999) have made a convincing case that much of the large drop in the youth violence rate in Boston in the mid-1990s was attributable to the working partnership between the police and the public that was brokered by ministers. Such a connection between the police and the church is surely controversial (Meares and Kahan 1998), but the connection makes theoretical sense and should be considered as part of a larger portfolio of policies to ensure the safety of children.

Building Intergenerational Ties

As described earlier, a major dimension of social organization is the ability of a community to supervise adolescents' and children's peer groups. Unruly public behavior by youth is a signal that the neighborhood is losing ground to a peer-controlled system. Policies to encourage the informal social control of peer groups might include organized supervision of leisure-time youth activities; enforcement of truancy and loitering laws; staggered school closing times to reduce the threshold or flash points of peer congregation; parent surveillance and involvement in after-school and night-time youth programs (recreational and educational); and adult-youth mentoring systems.

The key to these measures is positive *intergenerational connections* between youth and adults in the community through volunteer efforts. Stricter sanctions, such as curfews for children in public areas, may also be necessary, but my focus is on the informal social controls that arise naturally and positively from ongoing social interactions. The evidence is mixed, although a recent evaluation of youth-oriented development programs concluded that intergenerational mentoring holds promise. Based on their review of the only "rigorous" evaluation of a youth mentoring program, Jodie Roth and her colleagues (1998, 436) argued that the evaluation "provided evidence for the value of caring relationships between adults and youth created and supported by programs." Mentors who did not attempt to change their mentee but rather attempted to build a trusting and supportive relationship driven by the interests of the youth were the most likely to be successful. This finding is consistent with the theoretical framework of this chapter: informal social supports through intergenerational closure.

Integrating Community with Child Development Policy

I noted earlier the substantial connection between neighborhood economic disadvantage and indicators of health and child development (for example, maltreatment, low-birthweight babies, and infant mortality). It follows that community-based interventions are needed to promote prenatal health care, infant-child health, and support programs for family management (for example, enhancing skills in child-rearing or conflict resolution). There is some evidence to support this position. An evaluation by the National Academy of Sciences (1981, 58) showed that infant mortality rates can be reduced significantly with community interventions. This same study also found that community programs "significantly reduce the incidence of premature, repeated teenage pregnancy, the number who conceive after 35, and the number of families with more than four children." Similarly, Roderick Wallace and Deborah Wallace (1990, 417–18) provided evidence that governmental community intervention helped to reduce the infant mortality rate in New York from 1966 to 1973. The reductions in infant mortality and low birthweight associated with community interventions to increase the accessibility and quality of health services undermine the notion that health care utilization is explained only by individual-level characteristics.

Investing in children's health, then, requires that we address the ability of institutional structures to link pregnant mothers with support systems (see Zuckerman and Kahn, this volume). Community-level interventions, if successful, are an investment in future generations that will be felt over the long run (Sampson 1992). Hence, health initiatives for children are naturally connected to more general issues of community social organization (see also Earls and Barnes 1997).

Promoting Housing-Based Neighborhood Stabilization

The political economy of cities reminds us that policies on zoning, child health, safety, social order, and community policing need to be coordinated with efforts to preserve residential stability and otherwise improve the social, economic, and physical infrastructure of neighborhoods. One policy option is joint public-private ventures to help stabilize and revitalize deteriorating inner-city neighborhoods. My focus is primarily on investment in the physical structure of declining, but still reachable, communities. As already noted, population instability and housing decay in poor neighborhoods are linked to crime and social problems among youth. The implication is that community-based policy interventions may help reverse the tide of social decline in concentrated poverty areas. Among others, these policies include resident management of public housing; tenant buyouts; rehabilitation of existing low-income housing; strict code enforcement by city government; and low-income housing tax credits.

The hope is that by acting to reduce population flight, residential anonymity, and housing deterioration, neighborhood stabilization and ultimately a more cohesive environment for youth socialization will emerge. This strategy is compatible with that promoted by community development corporations (CDCs). Such interventions appear viable and capable of stabilizing low-income communities. For example, several CDC efforts are revitalizing previously declining areas and increasing residential stability and may lead to safer neighborhoods in the process (Briggs and Mueller 1996).

Deconcentrating Poverty

Housing policies also need to address the virulent forms of racial and economic segregation in many cities. Although community-level interventions cannot change the macrostructural economy and depleted industrial base in urban America, the ecological concentration of poverty and racial segregation can be addressed in part by two approaches: the dispersement of concentrated public housing, and scattered-site, new, low-income housing. The evidence that dispersement policies and scattered-site housing can work is small and controversial, and general public resistance to living near the poor is no doubt a long-lasting barrier.

Still, there are encouraging signs that community development policy and evaluation research are in a position to take advantage of, and build on, numerous "natural experiments" going on around the country. For example, the Chicago Housing Authority has embarked on a plan to relocate units of the Cabrini-Green project across the city so as to break down the severe segregation and concentrated poverty presently found there. Deteriorating high-rise complexes in other cities are also being scheduled for dispersement. Moreover, there is quasi-experimental evidence that offering inner-city mothers on welfare the opportunity to relocate to more thriving neighborhoods improves social outcomes both for them and for their children (see Rosenbaum and Popkin 1991).

Perhaps the best empirical evidence relevant to housing changes and neighborhood effects is found in the Moving To Opportunity (MTO) experiment in five cities. The MTO program randomly assigns housing project residents to one of three groups: an experimental group receiving housing subsidies to move into low-poverty neighborhoods, a group receiving conventional section 8 housing assistance, and a control group receiving no special assistance. Jens Ludwig, Greg Duncan, and Paul Hirschfield (1998) used data from the Baltimore site to examine the frequency of criminal activity among adolescents. The analysis was based on 358 children aged thirteen to seventeen who lived in Maryland for one year following baseline random assignment. Overall, the findings showed a sizable and significant reduction in the percentage of boys arrested for violent and other crimes in the experimental versus control group (Ludwig, Duncan, and Hirschfield 1998; Duncan and Raudenbush 1999). These results linked to neighborhood change suggest hope for positive outcomes of housing policies that encourage (but do not require) increased neighborhood integration among classes and races.

Maintaining the Municipal Service Base

Declining city municipal services for public health and fire safety appear to have contributed to the instability of poor communities. Based on an analysis of the "planned shrinkage" of New York City fire and health services in recent decades, Wallace and Wallace (1990, 427) argued: "The consequences of withdrawing municipal services from poor neighborhoods, the resulting outbreaks of contagious urban decay and forced migration which shred essential social networks and cause social disintegration, have become a highly significant contributor to decline in public health among the poor." The loss of social integration and networks from planned shrinkage of services may increase behavioral patterns that may themselves cause further social disintegration (427). This pattern of destabilizing feedback (Skogan 1986) is central to an understanding of the role of governmental policies in fostering the downward spiral of low-income, high-crime areas. Housing and community-based policies should thus be coordinated with policies to maintain fire, sanitation, and other vital municipal services.

Increasing the Community Organizational Base

Stable interlocking organizations within a neighborhood form the institutional infrastructure for effective community social control (Sampson 1999). The ability to secure public and private goods and services that are allocated by groups and agencies located outside of the neighborhood is another hallmark of effective organization. It follows that interventions should seek to promote community organization through overlapping involvement by residents in local organizations and voluntary associations, horizontal ties between neighborhood institutions, and the vertical integration of local institutions with city hall and other extra-local resources. Although this type of mobilization is difficult and somewhat ambiguous, it seems reasonable to argue that even small successes will accumulate over time to promote a more stable and longer-lasting community social organization. As noted, one way for community organizers to start building partnerships with agencies of public order and with local residents is through community policing (Skogan 1994; Skogan and Hartnett 1998).

CONCLUSION

It is important on three grounds to emphasize caution in thinking about neighborhood policies for investing in children. First, the evidence on "neighborhood effects" is mixed and complex. Research has only recently begun to measure directly the social mechanisms hypothesized to explain neighborhood effects (see, for example, Sampson, Morenoff, and Earls 1999). Methodological issues, such as differential selection or compositional effects, measurement error and shared method variance, and simultaneity bias, seriously challenge our ability to draw definitive conclusions on the role of neighborhood context (see also Jencks and Mayer 1990; Tienda 1991; Cook, Shagle, and Degirmencioglu 1997; and Duncan and Raudenbush 1999). Neighborhoods are also more heterogeneous internally and less "monolithic" than commonly believed (Furstenberg et al. 1999). Causal effects have not been definitively established, and so policy recommendations must flow from a preponderance of evidence coupled with strong theory.

Second, I would caution against falling into the trap of local determinism (Sampson 1999). Part of the appeal of "community" is the image of local residents working collectively to solve their own problems. The American ideal of residents joining forces to build community and maintain social order is largely a positive one, but this is not the only or even the most important American ideal. What happens within neighborhoods is shaped by extra-local social forces, the wider political economy, and citywide spatial dynamics. In addition to encouraging communities to mobilize through self-help strategies of informal social control, we need to promote aggressive strategies to address the larger social-ecological changes that have battered many inner-city communities. The specific nature of such efforts is beyond the scope of this chapter, but that should not detract from the importance of policies at the political and macrosocial levels. Recognizing that community social action is possible does not absolve policymakers of the responsibility for seeking equality of opportunities at the neighborhood as well as the individual level (see also Sampson 1999).

Third, there are obvious limits to "community" and neighborhood-level interventions. Achieving common goals in a diverse society is not easy and has proven problematic for communitarian thinking in an age of individual rights (Selznick 1992; Etzioni 1996). When we pursue informal social control and collective goods, we run the risk of unnecessarily restricting freedoms; individuals may face unwanted and even unjust scrutiny. For example, surveillance of "suspicious" persons in socially controlled communities can be translated into the wholesale interrogation of racial minorities (Skogan 1990). Suppose further that a community comes together, with high social capital and cohesion, to block the residential entry of a racial outgroup. Such exclusion prompted Gerald Suttles (1972) to warn of the dark side of "defended neighborhoods."

We must therefore balance concerns for the collective with a concern for social justice. For this reason, I have focused on widely expressed and shared desires for neighborhoods, especially social order and public safety. My strategy relies on shared values for a safe and healthy environment for children, not on divisive policies that separate by race and class. Nonetheless, the pursuit of common goals must proceed cautiously and with respect for individual rights, diversity, and limits on state power. Fortunately, legal justice and "community" are not the antinomy that common wisdom suggests (Selznick 1992). The constitutional law tradition has long been concerned with balancing individual rights against the need to promote the health and safety of communities. The very notion of police power suggests the tension, long recognized by the Supreme Court, between individual rights and the pursuit of social order (Gillman 1996). Bringing back law and social justice to efforts to implement or reform neighborhood policy is a welcome and necessary move (Sampson 1999).

Portions of this chapter are drawn from Robert J. Sampson, "What 'Community' Supplies," in *Urban Problems and Community Development*, edited by Ronald Ferguson and William Dickens (Washington, D.C.: Brookings Institution Press, 1999); and from Robert J. Sampson, Jeffrey Morenoff, and Felton Earls 1999, "Beyond Social Capital: Spatial Dynamics of Collective Efficacy for Children," *American Sociological Review* 64, 633–60.

REFERENCES

Berrien, Jenny, and Christopher Winship. 1999. "Should We Have Faith in the Churches?: The Ten Point Coalition's Effect on Boston's Youth Violence." Paper presented at the Joint Center for Poverty Research, Northwestern University/University of Chicago, Evanston, Ill. (January 14, 1999).

Briggs, Xavier de Souza, and Elizabeth Mueller, with Mercer Sullivan. 1996. "From Neighborhood to Community: Evidence on the Social Effects of Community Development" (executive summary). New York: Community Development Research Center, New School for Social Research.

Brooks-Gunn, Jeanne, Greg Duncan, Pamela Kato Klebanov, and Naomi Sealand. 1993. "Do Neighborhoods Influence Child and Adolescent Behavior?" *American Journal of Sociology* 99(2): 353–95.

Brooks-Gunn, Jeanne, Greg Duncan, and Lawrence Aber, eds. 1997a. *Consequences of Growing Up Poor* (vol. 1). New York: Russell Sage Foundation.

———. 1997b. *Neighborhood Poverty: Policy Implications in Studying Neighborhoods* (vol. 2). New York: Russell Sage Foundation.

Bursik, Robert J. 1988. "Social Disorganization and Theories of Crime and Delinquency: Problems and Prospects." *Criminology* 26(4): 519–52.

Bursik, Robert J., and Harold Grasmick. 1993. *Neighborhoods and Crime: The Dimensions of Effective Community Control.* New York: Lexington.

Carr, Patrick. 1998. "Keeping Up Appearances: Informal Social Control in a White Working-Class Neighborhood in Chicago." Ph.D. diss., University of Chicago.

Chaskin, Robert. 1995. "Defining Neighborhood: History, Theory, and Practice." Chicago: Chapin Hall Center for Children, University of Chicago.

Chow, Julian, and Claudia Coulton. 1992. "Was There a Social Transformation of Urban Neighborhoods in the 1980s?: A Decade of Changing Structure in Cleveland, Ohio." Unpublished paper. Cleveland: Center for Urban Poverty and Social Change, Case Western Reserve University.

Cohen, Lawrence, and Marcus Felson. 1979. "Social Change and Crime Rate Trends: A Routine Activity Approach." *American Sociological Review* 44: 588–608.

Coleman, James S. 1988. "Social Capital in the Creation of Human Capital." *American Journal of Sociology* 94(Suppl.): S95–120.

———. 1990. *Foundations of Social Theory*. Cambridge, Mass.: Harvard University Press.

Connell, James, Anne Kubisch, Lisabeth Schorr, and Carolyn Weiss, eds. 1995. *New Approaches to Evaluating Community Initiatives*. Queenstown, Md.: Aspen Institute.

Cook, Thomas, Shoba Shagle, and Serdar Degirmencioglu. 1997. "Capturing Social Process for Testing Mediational Models of Neighborhood Effects." In *Neighborhood Poverty: Policy Implications in Studying Neighborhoods*, edited by Jeanne Brooks-Gunn, Greg J. Duncan, and Lawrence Aber (vol. 2). New York: Russell Sage Foundation.

Coulton, Claudia, Jill Korbin, Marilyn Su, and Julian Chow. 1995. "Community-Level Factors and Child Maltreatment Rates." *Child Development* 66: 1262–76.

Duncan, Greg, Jeanne Brooks-Gunn, and Paul Klebanov. 1994. "Economic Deprivation and Early Child Development." *Child Development* 65(2): 296–318.

Duncan, Greg, and Stephen Raudenbush. 1999. "Assessing the Effects of Context in Studies of Child and Youth Development." *Educational Psychologist* 34(1): 29–41.

Earls, Felton, and Jacqueline Barnes. 1997. "Understanding and Preventing Child Abuse in Urban Settings." In *Violence and Childhood in the Inner City*, edited by Joan McCord. New York: Cambridge University Press.

Elliott, Delbert, William J. Wilson, David Huizinga, Robert J. Sampson, Amanda Elliott, and Bruce Rankin. 1996. "The Effects of Neighborhood Disadvantage on Adolescent Development." *Journal of Research in Crime and Delinquency* 33(4): 389–426.

Etzioni, Amitai. 1996. *The New Golden Rule: Community and Morality in a Democratic Society*. New York: Basic Books.

Felson, Marcus. 1987. "Routine Activities and Crime Prevention in the Developing Metropolis." *Criminology* 25(November): 911–31.

Furstenberg, Frank, Thomas Cook, Jacqueline Eccles, Glen Elder, and Arnold Sameroff, eds. 1999. *Managing to Make It: Urban Families and Adolescent Success*. Chicago: University of Chicago Press.

Gans, Herbert. 1962. *The Urban Villagers*. New York: Free Press.

Gillman, Howard. 1996. "The Antinomy of Public Purposes and Private Rights in the American Constitutional Tradition; or, Why Communitarianism Is Not Necessarily Exogenous to Liberal Constitutionalism." *Law and Social Inquiry* 21(Winter): 67–77.

Hope, Tim. 1995. "Community Crime Prevention." In *Building a Safer Society*, vol. 21, *Crime and Justice*, edited by Michael Tonry and David Farrington. Chicago: University of Chicago Press.

Hunter, Albert. 1985. "Private, Parochial, and Public Social Orders: The Problem of Crime and Incivility in Urban Communities." In *The Challenge of Social Control*, edited by Gerald Suttles and Mayer Zald. Norwood, N.J.: Ablex.

Janowitz, Morris. 1975. "Sociological Theory and Social Control." *American Journal of Sociology* 81(July): 82–108.

Jargowsky, Paul. 1996. "Take the Money and Run: Economic Segregation in U.S. Metropolitan Areas." *American Sociological Review* 61(6): 984–98.

———. 1997. *Poverty and Place: Ghettos, Barrios, and the American City.* New York: Russell Sage Foundation.

Jencks, Christopher, and Susan Mayer. 1990. "The Social Consequences of Growing Up in a Poor Neighborhood." In *Inner-City Poverty in the United States,* edited by Laurence Lynn and Michael McGeary. Washington, D.C.: National Academy Press.

Kasarda, John, and Morris Janowitz. 1974. "Community Attachment in Mass Society." *American Sociological Review* 39(June): 328–39.

Kornhauser, Ruth. 1978. *Social Sources of Delinquency.* Chicago: University of Chicago Press.

Logan, John, and Harvey Molotch. 1987. *Urban Fortunes: The Political Economy of Place.* Berkeley: University of California Press.

Ludwig, Jens, Greg Duncan, and Paul Hirschfield. 1998. "Urban Poverty and Juvenile Crime: Evidence from a Randomized Housing-Mobility Experiment." Working paper. Joint Center for Poverty Research, Northwestern University and University of Chicago.

Massey, Douglas S. 1990. "American Apartheid: Segregation and the Making of the Underclass." *American Journal of Sociology* 96(2): 338–39.

———. 1996. "The Age of Extremes: Concentrated Affluence and Poverty in the Twenty-first Century." *Demography* 33(4): 395–412.

Massey, Douglas S., and Nancy Denton. 1993. *American Apartheid: Segregation and the Making of the Underclass.* Cambridge, Mass.: Harvard University Press.

Meares, Tracey, and Dan Kahan. 1998. "Law and (Norms of) Order in the Inner City." *Law and Society Review* 32: 805–38.

Moore, Mark. 1992. "Problem-Solving and Community Policing." In *Modern Policing,* vol. 15, *Crime and Justice,* edited by Michael Tonry and Norval Morris. Chicago: University of Chicago Press.

Morenoff, Jeffrey, and Robert J. Sampson. 1997. "Violent Crime and the Spatial Dynamics of Neighborhood Transition: Chicago, 1970–1990." *Social Forces* 76(1): 31–64.

National Academy of Sciences. 1981. *Toward a National Policy for Children and Families.* Washington, D.C.: U.S. Government Printing Office.

Park, Robert. 1916. "The City: Suggestions for the Investigations of Human Behavior in the Urban Environment." *American Journal of Sociology* 20: 577–612.

Putnam, Robert. 1993. "The Prosperous Community: Social Capital and Community Life." *The American Prospect* (Spring, 13): 35–42.

Rosenbaum, James, and Susan Popkin. 1991. "Employment and Earnings of Low-Income Blacks Who Move to the Suburbs." In *The Urban Underclass,* edited by Christopher Jencks and Paul Peterson. Washington, D.C.: Brookings Institution.

Rossi, Peter. 1999. "Evaluating Community Development Interventions." In *Urban Problems and Community Development,* edited by Ronald F. Ferguson and William T. Dickens. Washington, D.C.: Brookings Institution.

Roth, Jodie, Jeanne Brooks-Gunn, Lawrence Murray, and William Foster. 1998. "Promoting Healthy Adolescents: Synthesis of Youth Development Program Evaluations." *Journal of Research on Adolescence* 8(4): 423–59.

Sampson, Robert J. 1988. "Community Attachment in Mass Society: A Multilevel Systemic Model." *American Sociological Review* 53: 766–69.

———. 1992. "Family Management and Child Development: Insights from Social Disorganization Theory." In *Advances in Criminological Theory,* vol. 3, edited by Joan McCord. New Brunswick, N.J.: Transaction.

———. 1997. "Collective Regulation of Adolescent Misbehavior: Validation Results from Eighty Chicago Neighborhoods." *Journal of Adolescent Research* 12(2): 227–44.

———. 1999. "What 'Community' Supplies." In *Urban Problems and Community Development*, edited by Ronald F. Ferguson and William T. Dickens. Washington, D.C.: Brookings Institution Press.

Sampson, Robert J., and W. Byron Groves. 1989. "Community Structure and Crime: Testing Social Disorganization Theory." *American Journal of Sociology* 94(4): 774–802.

Sampson, Robert J., Jeffrey Morenoff, and Felton Earls. 1999. "Beyond Social Capital: Spatial Dynamics of Collective Efficacy for Children." *American Sociological Review* 64(5): 633–60.

Sampson, Robert, and Stephen Raudenbush. 1999. "Systematic Social Observation of Public Places: A New Look at Disorder in Urban Neighborhoods." *American Journal of Sociology* 105: 603–51.

Sampson, Robert J., Stephen Raudenbush, and Felton Earls. 1997. "Neighborhoods and Violent Crime: A Multilevel Study of Collective Efficacy." *Science* 277(5328): 918–24.

Sampson, Robert J., and William Julius Wilson. 1995. "Toward a Theory of Race, Crime, and Urban Inequality." In *Crime and Inequality,* edited by John Hagan and Ruth Petersen. Stanford, Calif.: Stanford University Press.

Selznick, Philip. 1992. *The Moral Commonwealth: Social Theory and the Promise of Community.* Berkeley: University of California Press.

Shaw, Clifford, and Henry McKay. 1969. *Juvenile Delinquency and Urban Areas.* 2nd ed. Chicago: University of Chicago Press. (Originally published in 1942)

Skogan, Wesley. 1986. "Fear of Crime and Neighborhood Change." In *Communities and Crime,* edited by Albert J. Reiss Jr. and Micael Tonry. Chicago: University of Chicago Press.

———. 1990. *Disorder and Decline: Crime and the Spiral of Decay in American Neighborhoods.* Berkeley: University of California Press.

———. 1994. "The Impact of Community Policing on Neighborhood Residents: A Cross-Site Analysis." In *The Challenge of Community Policing: Testing the Hypotheses,* edited by Dennis Rosenbaum. Newbury Park, Calif.: Sage Publications.

———. 1996. "Evaluating Problem-Solving Policing." Paper presented at the international conference "Problem-Solving Policing as Crime Prevention," Stockholm (September 10–11).

Skogan, Wesley, and Susan Hartnett. 1998. *Community Policing, Chicago Style.* New York: Oxford University Press.

Suttles, Gerald. 1972. *The Social Construction of Communities.* Chicago: University of Chicago Press.

Tienda, Marta. 1991. "Poor People and Poor Places: Deciphering Neighborhood Effects on Poverty Outcomes." In *Macro-Micro Linkages in Sociology,* edited by Joan Huber. Newbury Park, Calif.: Sage Publications.

Tilly, Charles. 1973. "Do Communities Act?" *Sociological Inquiry* 43(314): 209–40.

Wallace, Roderick, and Deborah Wallace. 1990. "Origins of Public Health Collapse in New York City: The Dynamics of Planned Shrinkage, Contagious Urban Decay, and Social Disintegration." *Bulletin of the New York Academy of Medicine* 66(5): 391–434.

Wellman, Barry. 1979. "The Community Question: The Intimate Networks of East Yorkers." *American Journal of Sociology* 84: 1201–31.

Whyte, William F. 1943. *Street Corner Society: The Social Structure of an Italian Slum.* Chicago: University of Chicago Press.

Wilson, William Julius. 1987. *The Truly Disadvantaged: The Inner City, the Underclass, and Public Policy.* Chicago: University of Chicago Press.

———. 1996. *When Work Disappears: The World of the New Urban Poor.* New York: Alfred A. Knopf.

Part IV

Transitions from School to Young Adulthood

Chapter 8

The Transition from School to Work: Is There a Crisis? What Can Be Done?

Debra Donahoe and Marta Tienda

B ecause full-time employment usually permits financial independence as well as social and emotional independence, there is great societal interest in the transition to adulthood. The ability of young adults to establish independent households, to be financially independent, and to achieve social and emotional maturity depends on how well they prepare themselves to compete for and secure well-paying jobs and to participate in social, civic, and familial activities.

The transition from school to work embraces youth sixteen to twenty-four years old, the age limits demarcating, respectively, the legal age to leave school and the age by which the majority of college-goers have graduated. This age group is very heterogeneous developmentally, and the activities pursued over this phase of the life course vary considerably among demographic groups (Marini 1984, 1987; Hogan and Astone 1986; Ahituv, Tienda, and Tsay 1998). For example, many youth combine school and work, while others withdraw and return after testing the labor market (Coleman 1984; Marini 1987). Some youth begin a family before leaving school or entering the labor market, while others prolong marriage and family until they have established a career. Despite this variation in the timing of key life-course events (Rindfuss 1991), increasing commitment to employment is a defining feature of the school-to-work transition, which is considered complete when youth devote themselves full-time to labor-market activities.

Various journalistic and academic accounts present today's adolescents and young adults as a generation in crisis—one confronting drug and alcohol abuse, teenage childbearing, increasing poverty rates, decaying family structures, declining academic performance, alarming high school dropout rates, and high rates of joblessness. Several of these problems relate specifically to the school-to-work transition. During the 1960s and 1970s, portrayals of the difficulties that youth faced in making the school-to-work transition focused on the most disadvantaged youth, mainly urban black youth. Since the mid-1980s, though, concerns have been broadened to include all noncollege-bound youth (William T. Grant Foundation 1988; Osterman 1995; Sum et al. 1997). However, it is not clear that this perception of crisis is warranted or that a substantial segment of American youth is really in danger of not making a successful transition to adulthood.

A synthesized and stylized depiction of the problematic aspects of the transition from school to work might read as follows:

Many youth leave school ill prepared for employment in a labor market that increasingly rewards and demands technical as well as cognitive skills. Owing to a lack of institutional or personal ties to jobs or training programs and skill deficits accumulated over years of substandard or inappropriate schooling, noncollege-bound youth experience high unemployment and an extended period of "thrashing" or "milling about." During this period, job turnover is high and the pattern of jobs held reveals no obvious career orientation. The jobs available to youth provide low wages and few benefits, and they offer limited chances for upward mobility. These circumstances engender low levels of attachment to major social institutions and a period of extended economic and social adolescence.

We question whether the dismal tone of this description is justified and whether the problems faced by the current generation are worse than those faced by youth in the recent past. In other words, are youth truly in crisis, or has pessimism about specific problems and specific segments of the youth population distorted perceptions about today's adolescents and their future life chances?

In this chapter, we focus on two domains that are assumed to be problematic for some adolescents and young adults—namely, education and employment—and the intersection of the two institutions that govern these arenas, schools and the labor market. First, we examine which aspects of the stylized depiction of the transition from school to work presented previously are valid in light of relevant research findings. We ask several specific questions: Is this a new problem, or has the character of the transition changed in recent decades? If so, what aspects of the transition pose new problems? Are youth themselves to blame for their problems, or have market opportunities undermined their economic footing? Finally, do all youth experience difficulties making the transition from student to independent worker, or are some groups at greater risk of failure?

In the second section, we answer these questions by examining trends in educational attainment and academic achievement, seeking to understand whether youth today are less prepared to enter the labor market than their counterparts were in the past. We utilize data on the cohort of young adults who entered the labor market in the early 1980s to better document the within-cohort heterogeneity of experience. Next, we document trends in labor supply and unemployment, analyzing the timing of arrival to stable employment and documenting the diversity of transition experiences. Our reading of the evidence leads us to redefine the nature and extent of the problems involved in making the transition from full-time student to independent adult.

In the third section, we examine different options for human asset accumulation—investing in schooling or investing in early work experience—and how each pays off. Clearly, though, the school-to-work transition can be shaped by forces beyond the control of individuals, such as labor-market conditions and public institutions. In fact, recent policy initiatives, such as the 1994 School to Work Opportunities Act (STWOA), reveal an increasing governmental desire to alter the transition process. Thus, in the fourth section, we evaluate two types of school-to-work programs: those focused on in-school youth (first-chance programs) and those focused on out-of-school youth (second-chance programs). In the final section, we bring together lessons from the previous sections and make broad policy recommendations for improving the labor-market prospects of adolescents and young adults.

THE SCHOOL-TO-WORK TRANSITION—PAST AND PRESENT

In this section, we examine trends in educational attainment, labor-force participation, and unemployment, paying explicit attention to racial-ethnic and sex differences in these outcomes. We also present evidence on the timing of arrival to stable employment and trends in labor-market opportunities for youth.

Education and Skills Trends

Whether young adults are ill prepared to enter the labor market rests at the core of the school-to-work debate. If a lack of appropriate skills causes young people to have labor-market difficulties, policies that focus on increasing academic rigor, providing appropriate vocational education, and opening up opportunities for training are warranted. If, on the other hand, youths' difficulties finding jobs are due to a lack of institutional linkages between schools and employers and to changes in the structure of employment opportunities and wages, policy remedies would differ. In addressing these questions, we emphasize two issues: whether young workers today are more poorly trained than their counterparts in the past, and whether the skills obtained by students have changed relative to the skills demanded by employers.

There is no strong evidence that the young are less prepared academically to work now than in the past. As shown in figure 8.1, the high school graduation rates of twenty- to twenty-four-year-olds rose between 1976 and 1995, but differentially among blacks, whites, and Hispanics. (Trends were nearly identical for both sexes.) The graduation rates of whites remained stable at 86 percent, but black rates converged with those of whites, rising from 72 to 82 percent. Hispanic graduation rates showed no improvement, remaining low at 59 to 60 percent. These rates are due in part to the influx of poorly educated immigrants. Andrew Sum, Neal Fogg, and Robert Taggart (1996) estimated that the number of immigrants aged eighteen to twenty-four with less than a high school education nearly doubled between 1980 and 1995, compared to an 18 percent decline in high school dropouts for the population as a whole. Similar trends by race-ethnicity obtain for college graduation rates. Average educational attainment has increased with age, both because of the secular increase in college attendance and completion rates and because of the greater number of young adults pursuing postgraduate degrees (Mare 1995). However, race and ethnic differentials in college graduation are even more pronounced than for high school completion, especially since the immigration of unskilled workers increased after 1970 (Smith and Edmonston 1997; Tienda and Liang 1994).

FIGURE 8.1 / High School Completion of Adolescents and Young Adults, by Race-Ethnicity, 1976 to 1995

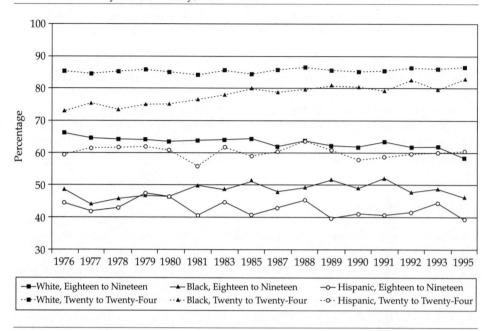

Source: U.S. Bureau of the Census, Current Population Reports, P20–459, P20–462, P20–475.

Data from the National Longitudinal Survey of Youth (NLSY) provide a more dramatic picture of educational differentials. Figures 8.2 and 8.3 chart the number of grades completed by white, black, and Hispanic men (figure 8.2) and women (figure 8.3) by age. Race and ethnic differences emerge in secondary school, widen at the transition into college, and widen again at the transition to college completion (Tienda and Ahituv 1996; Ahituv, Tienda, and Tsay 1998). By ages twenty-four to twenty-five, white males have completed almost one and a half more grades of school than Hispanics, and almost one year more than blacks. For women, race and ethnic differentials are smaller, mainly because women average slightly higher education at every age than males. Thus, large shares of Hispanics—more so than blacks and whites—are at high risk of experiencing labor-market difficulties as young adults.

Despite largely optimistic trends in education attainment, concern about a decline in achievement is widespread, fueled mainly by news coverage of a decline in test scores. Although test scores did fall during the 1960s and 1970s, this decline was driven largely by the fact that later test takers included broader segments of the student population. Since the 1980s, test scores have rebounded, though recent gains appear not to have totally offset earlier declines. On a positive note, minority students have made significant gains in achievement relative to non-Hispanic whites (Koretz 1992). The National Assessment of Educational Progress Survey (NAEPS) is the best

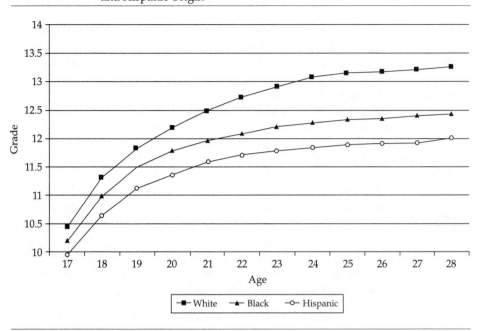

Source: Tienda, Hotz, and Ahituv (1998).

FIGURE 8.3 / Age-Specific Grades Completed: Young Women by Race
and Hispanic Origin

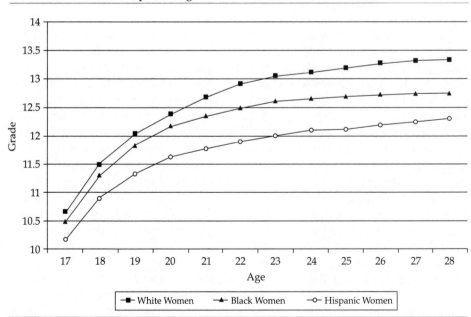

Source: Authors' calculations from NLSY.

measure of achievement over time (Stedman 1998). NAEPS trends in the math, science, reading, and writing scores of seventeen-year-olds reveal little difference in achievement between the earliest points of evaluation—depending on the subject in question, from 1969 to 1984—and 1996 (Campbell, Voelkl, and Donahue 1997). In short, trends in test scores also provide no evidence of a skills crisis.

Stability in both educational attainment and academic achievement does not mean that youth are adequately prepared for the labor market. The general consensus is that both the basic and vocational skills of noncollege-bound youth are inadequate (Bailey 1991; Levitan and Gallo 1991; Lynch 1994; Stedman 1998). This problem is especially severe among minorities and youth who reside in risky urban environments (Lerman 1996). International comparisons that show that U.S. students fare poorly on math and science tests have provided troubling evidence of a skills deficit (Mullis 1998). Further evidence comes from employers, who often claim that today's youth lack "soft skills," such as dedication to work and discipline (Kantor 1994; Olson 1994). Moreover, as Lisa Lynch details in the first chapter of this volume, profound changes in the technological demands of the workplace have *increased* the need for skilled workers. Though the skills of youth may not have deteriorated, they are not improving and thus are not keeping pace with employer demand.

Labor-Force Participation and Unemployment Trends

Are youth more or less likely to participate in the labor force now compared to the recent past? Do youth today experience higher unemployment than previous generations? Increasing youth unemployment would provide at least partial evidence of a more problematic school-to-work transition.

Figures 8.4 and 8.5 show trends in the labor force activity rates of adolescent and adult men (figure 8.4) and women (figure 8.5) by age, race, and Hispanic origin. Keeping in mind that youth labor-force activity fluctuates with the business cycle, falling slightly during recessions and rebounding somewhat during recovery and growth periods, there is limited evidence that labor-force participation has been declining since the mid-1970s. In part, this is because there were sizable declines in black male participation earlier, in the 1950s and 1960s, as agricultural employment fell (Cogan 1982). The labor-force activity rates of young women have increased gradually, while the rates for young men have fallen. The highest participation rates are for whites, the lowest for blacks, and the rates for Hispanics are between these extremes. On balance, trends in labor-force participation suggest no cause for alarm about the declining labor-market attachment of youth. However, these aggregate generalizations may not apply to specific segments of the youth population, such as inner-city minority youth (Foster 1995).

Participation rates include both the employed and the unemployed. Unemployment rates are a better barometer of the difficulties that youth experience in gaining access to the world of work. In fact, it was the sharp rise in black youth unemployment during the 1970s that first raised concern about a youth labor-market

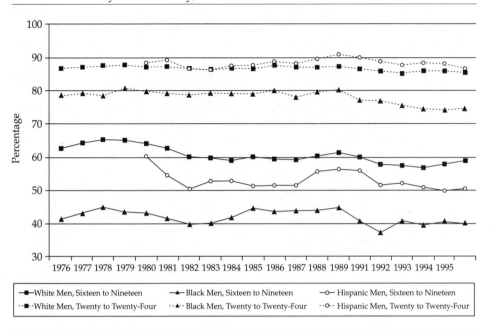

Source: U.S. Bureau of Labor Statistics, *Handbook of Labor Statistics* (1989 and 1997).

FIGURE 8.5 / Labor-Force Participation of Adolescent and Young Adult Women
by Race-Ethnicity, 1976 to 1995

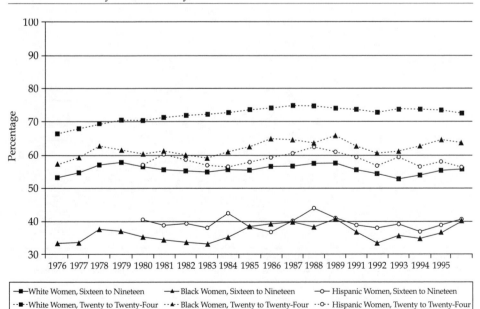

Source: U.S. Bureau of Labor Statistics, *Handbook of Labor Statistics* (1989 and 1997).

crisis (Freeman and Holzer 1986; Rees 1986). Figures 8.6 and 8.7 provide evidence that unemployment rates of minority youth are both appreciably higher than those for nonminority youth and are more sensitive to cyclical variation (Rees 1986; Hirschman 1988).

Unemployment rates for adolescent males (aged sixteen to nineteen) were higher than those for older youth (aged twenty to twenty-four) throughout the period of observation. Figures 8.6 and 8.7 show not only that adolescent unemployment rates are higher than those for young adults, but also that the rates for the younger men and women are more sensitive to economic trends. Just as minorities, especially blacks, tend to be buffeted more violently by economic cycles, so the labor-force experiences of adolescents vary more than those of young adults. The severity of the black male youth unemployment problem, however, is evidenced by the fact that the *older* cohort of black youth has higher unemployment rates than the *younger* cohort of white youth at every year of observation. Furthermore, the *older* cohort of black youth has virtually the same unemployment rate as the *younger* cohort of Hispanic youth prior to 1985, and only slightly lower rates thereafter. In fact, adolescent black males aged sixteen to nineteen have the highest unemployment rates of any group throughout the 1976 to 1996 period.

FIGURE 8.6 / Unemployment Rates for Adolescent and Young Adult Men by Race-Ethnicity, 1970 to 1995

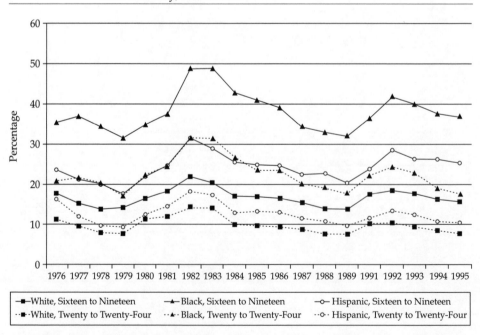

Source: U.S. Bureau of Labor Statistics, *Employment and Earnings* (January issues, annually).

FIGURE 8.7 / Unemployment Rates for Adolescent and Young Adult Women
by Race-Ethnicity, 1970 to 1995

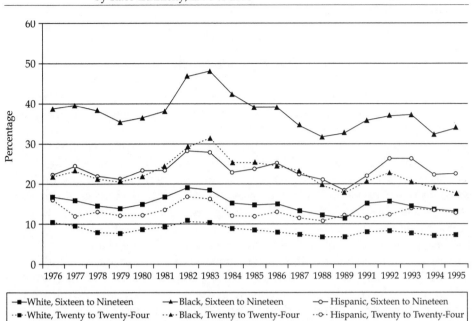

Source: U.S. Bureau of Labor Statistics, *Employment and Earnings* (January issues, annually).

Figure 8.6 shows that black adolescent unemployment peaked at nearly 50 percent during the recession of 1981 to 1982 and fell gradually thereafter to a low of 31 percent in 1989, rising again during the recession of 1991 to 1992. The strong economic performance of the 1990s had lowered unemployment for this younger cohort of blacks to under 30 percent by 1996. During this period, unemployment rates for white young adults of the same age fluctuated over a narrower range and were well below the lowest levels for black youth. Hispanic unemployment rates peaked at 31 percent during the 1982 recession but have not declined with improvement in general economic conditions. Trends in adolescent female unemployment rates were similar to those for adolescent men, but often a couple of percentage points lower.

Overall, these data do not support the conclusion that the transition from school to work has become more difficult in the recent past: the unemployment of both male and female black adolescents and young adults is currently at or very near its lowest level in the 1976 to 1996 period. Unemployment for whites and Hispanics is also not far removed from its lowest levels during this period. Thus, consistent with our investigation of educational attainment and academic achievement, our inquiry into youth labor-force participation and unemployment trends suggests that labor-market circumstances have not deteriorated in ways that render the school-to-work transition more problematic. However, these aggregate trends do not address the issue of "thrashing" or "milling about" that is said to characterize the school-to-work transition and may determine whether youth settle into stable employment in young adulthood. We turn to this topic next.

The Timing of Arrival to Stable Employment

Youth employment instability—whether termed "churning" (Osterman and Iannozzi 1993), "shopping and thrashing" (Topel and Ward 1992), or, more technically, employment turnover—refers to the extent to which early labor-market activity is characterized by a shifting from job to job and from periods of work to periods of nonwork. Jacob Klerman and Lynn Karoly (1994) noted that labor-force instability increases the probability of unemployment, leading to decreases in accumulated labor-force experience and potential decay in skills and human assets. If firms perceive unstable youth to be poor prospects for investment, instability may also decrease the likelihood of accumulating firm-specific tenure and training. For these reasons, labor-force instability may reduce wage growth and future labor-market success and prolong the transition from economic adolescence to adulthood.

Whether these potential negative outcomes obtain depends on the extent to which youth have difficulty establishing themselves in stable employment. However, there is no agreed-on definition of stable employment or accepted age by which a transition to stable employment should have occurred. Joseph Hotz and Marta Tienda (1998) offered two benchmarks for first stable employment: employment that lasts for at least six months and involves fifteen or more hours of work per week, and employment that lasts for at least a year and is undertaken on a full-time basis. Accordingly, for young men the median age of arrival at first job is approximately eighteen using the less restrictive definition, and twenty-three using the restrictive one. For young women the respective medians are nineteen and twenty-three years of age. Race and ethnic variation in the timing of arrival at first job follows a predictable pattern: black men lag behind whites and Hispanics regardless of definition, and white men arrive at stable employment slightly earlier than Hispanic men using the less restrictive definition and slightly later using the restrictive definition. For women, regardless of definition, whites arrive at stable employment first, followed by Hispanics and then blacks. Research based on other definitions has reached similar conclusions (Klerman and Karoly 1994; Osterman 1995).

Thus, available evidence does not support a pessimistic interpretation of the statistically average age at which youth achieve stable employment, since that figure is somewhere in the early twenties for most cohorts. However, delayed entry into stable employment is currently a problem for youth who do not finish high school and for black youth regardless of high school graduation. Given our emphasis on trends, it is important to note that since the early 1970s labor-market prospects do seem to have worsened for all young workers without a high school degree.

Current Labor-Market Opportunities for Youth

That the average young adult does not have particular difficulty finding a job or sticking with a job for some amount of time does not mean that the available jobs pay enough to support families or build careers. Recent trends in wages and wage differentials suggest that job quality has been an issue for youth making the transition from school to work in the 1980s and 1990s. First, real wages for male workers have fallen substantially over the past two decades. Second, though workers of all ages have seen their real wages fall, the earnings of young workers have declined at rates substantially greater than those experienced by older workers (Rasell, Bluestone, and Mishel 1997). Third, educational attainment now exerts a stronger influence on wages than in the past. Because employers are willing to pay a premium for skills, a college education is increasingly rewarded. As a result, the wage gap between high school- and college-educated youth has increased appreciably.

Wage trends suggest that to an increasing extent, jobs that pay living wages, offer reasonable security, and provide benefits now require more than a high school education. For youth who do not pursue postsecondary training, income prospects, if not employment prospects, are bleak. To the extent that skill requirements continue to increase, the skill deficit of noncollege-educated youth will present a growing human asset problem in negotiating the school-to-work transition (Bailey 1991; Osterman 1995). Youth with the greatest skills deficits, particularly high school dropouts—among whom minorities are overrepresented—will be especially disadvantaged in making the transition to full-time employment and warrant special policy attention.

Recapitulation of the School-to-Work Transition Problem

The evidence reviewed earlier suggests that the difficulties encountered in the transition from school to work depend largely on adolescents' educational attainment and race and ethnic background. The problem for youth whose education ends with high school is not a lack of jobs, but a lack of good jobs for which they are qualified. Though there is evidence that skill demands are rising and will probably continue to do so for the foreseeable future, this increase has not been precipitous. What is most troubling for the majority of youth is not a lack of skills, but rather the decline in wages for those who lack college degrees.

Future demographic trends do not bode well. During the period of falling wages, youth were to some extent protected by their small cohort size. However, the baby boomlet generation is now entering young adulthood. In addition, if the prevailing minority disadvantage continues, demographic trends will exacerbate labor-market problems. Not only will the youth cohort grow in size, but the minorities will increase their share of the total. For example, 11 percent of those aged fourteen to twenty-four in 1990 were Hispanic. The U.S. Census Bureau has projected that Hispanics will exceed 15 percent by 2005, and over 20 percent by 2025. If current trends in Hispanic educational underachievement persist, and if the demand for high skills continues to rise, Hispanic youth will confront even greater labor-market disadvantages in the future than they face now.

DEBATES ON HUMAN ASSET ACCUMULATION VIA THE SCHOOL-TO-WORK TRANSITION

The presumption that adolescent employment can strengthen the transition from school to work has been implicit in the design of youth training programs since the 1960s. For example, the 1974 President's Science Advisory Committee Report recommended that high school students acquire work experience that would socialize them into adult roles and enhance their labor-market prospects (President's Science Advisory Committee 1974). Less than a decade later, the National Commission on Educational Excellence (1983) challenged this recommendation, questioning whether adolescent jobs actually provide opportunities for youth to practice responsibility, to interact with adult role models, and to acquire work-related skills. That report emphasized the deleterious consequences, claiming that work could undermine investment in academic pursuits and possibly even accelerate early school withdrawal (see also Greenberger and Steinberg 1989).

In a literature laden with controversy and methodological difficulties, there is consensus that the vast majority of students acquire some work experience before leaving school; that students who work differ from those who do not (Keithly and Deseran 1995; Hotz and Tienda 1998); that the consequences of summer employment differ from those of academic-year work; and that the consequences of adolescent employment hinge crucially on the amount of time spent on the job (Tienda and Ahituv 1996; Schoenhals, Tienda, and Schneider 1998). There is less agreement about whether, how much, and in what ways youth employment influences scholastic performance and educational attainment or subsequent labor-market outcomes. Neither is there consensus about the relationship between youth employment and various dimensions of psychological and emotional well-being.

The idea that adolescent work experience is a valuable human asset that yields returns over the entire work life course is reasonable. But if working while in school curtails the acquisition of basic academic skills by truncating educational careers, the long-term net benefits may be small or even negative, particularly in a climate of rising returns to skill. Thus, the potential benefits of early labor-market entry depend on the relative allocation of time between school and work; on how early work activities influence decisions about school continuation; and on whether youth actually acquire work skills on the job (Hotz et al. 1997; Carr, Wright, and Brody 1996; Ruhm 1997b).

There are several theoretical reasons to expect adolescent employment to influence both school continuation decisions and subsequent employment prospects. Socialization theory postulates that early work experiences impart a realistic grasp of adult alternatives and shape economic and social aspirations. From a socio-psychological perspective, "socialization through work" implies that success in a job as an adolescent can facilitate the development of self-esteem, foster independence, broaden the base of appropriate role models, and provide feedback to youth who are in the process of forging their adult roles (President's Science Advisory Committee 1974; Steinberg, Greenberger, and Garduque 1981; Mortimer and Finch 1986).

Human capital theory applauds early work experience for enhancing subsequent labor-market success through wage gains and higher employment. The theoretical models of Jacob Mincer (1962, 1974) and Gary Becker (1993) stress the value of work experience and on-the-job training in generating marketable skills that increase work-ers' productivity in later years. However, empirical analyses have been less success-ful at predicting *what types of skills* gained from early work have payoffs in later life. This makes it very difficult to draw lessons about what types of experiences are most beneficial for program design or youth employment policy initiatives. Nevertheless, human capital theory recognizes that investments in education are important for wage gains, and that to the extent that early work interferes with educational attain-ment its ultimate benefits diminish.

Disagreement about the costs and benefits of youth employment is striking given that vast resources have been invested in youth employment and training programs since the 1960s. Thus, we review evidence about the developmental, educational, and labor-market consequences of youth employment to assess what is known about these aspects of the transition from student to adult work roles. (For a more compre-hensive discussion of these topics, see Donahoe and Tienda 1998). Next we describe the varying pathways from school to work of black, white, and Hispanic men and women during the 1980s and early 1990s. Coupled with evidence of the varying re-turns to different forms of human capital investment, this description of the demo-graphic diversity of investment illustrates the early origins of unequal labor-market outcomes.

Psychological and Emotional Consequences of Adolescent Employment

An active area of research continues to be the question of whether and how the work experiences of enrolled adolescents influence a range of attitudinal, cognitive, and behavioral outcomes, including mastery of developmental tasks, mental health, con-trol orientation, self-esteem, and deviant activity. These studies align in roughly two camps, emphasizing either positive or negative consequences.

Developmental psychologists argue that even entry-level, dead-end jobs in the highly formative adolescent period socialize youth in ways that are beneficial to their later career (Mortimer and Finch 1992, 1996). Another claim is that frequent job chang-ing among youth is less a sign of problematic instability than of a normal develop-mental process representing a progression from less complex jobs to those requiring more intensive work activity (Mortimer et al. 1990). Work may also contribute to social and psychological development by requiring youth to shift between diverse roles and to interact frequently with strangers (Steinberg et al. 1981); by providing opportunities to learn useful skills that shape occupational value formation (Mortimer et al. 1992); and by providing opportunities for autonomy that are crucial for self-esteem (Mortimer and Finch 1986). Jeylan Mortimer and Michael Finch (1992) claimed that even if researchers cannot show positive outcomes of employment on measures of psychological well-being, youth's self-perceptions of the benefits of working are consistently high. If perceptions drive behavior, employment may engender positive effects indirectly.

Much of the conventional wisdom about positive socialization relies on a dated understanding of the adolescent workplace. In a direct challenge to the President's Science Advisory Committee Panel (1974), Laurence Steinberg and his various associates have claimed that there is no evidence of a link between high school work experience and socialization of youth into an adult world, partly because the context and content of the typical youth job have changed (Greenberger and Steinberg 1989). In their view, age-segregated workplaces limit the amount of interaction between youth and adults and may actually strengthen peer culture and increase deviance (but not serious criminality) through negative socialization processes. These negative socialization experiences are manifested in more frequent absences from school as well as increased use of alcohol, nicotine, and other drugs. Similarly, among youth who work long hours, Michael Shanahan and his colleagues (1991) alleged that employment heightens depressed mood, and Wendy Manning (1990) showed that youth employment diminishes parental surveillance. In a recent overview paper, even Mortimer and Finch (1996) conceded that the consequences of part-time work depend on the quality of the work experience and the context in which it occurs (see also Markward 1991).

In sum, there is little consensus about whether and how youth employment influences sociopsychological well-being. Unfortunately, most studies that evaluate the sociopsychological effects of adolescent employment suffer from serious methodological difficulties, most notably being subject to selection biases, failing to control for unobserved heterogeneity, and attributing to work the differences among youth arising from unobserved characteristics (Caspi et al. 1998). Although more recent papers have attempted to address criticisms about selection biases (see, for example, Steinberg, Fegley, and Dornbusch 1993), few analysts of psychological outcomes have satisfactorily resolved this problem. Highlighting the potential importance of methodological rigor for this area of research is the finding of Mark Schoenhals and his colleagues (1998) that many of the differences between workers and nonworkers exist *prior* to employment and have little bearing on how employment experiences influence sociopsychological well-being.

Educational Consequences of Adolescent Employment

Those who would encourage youth enrolled in school to work presume that employment does not undermine scholastic achievement or educational attainment.

Even though the majority of enrolled workers graduate, there remains considerable uncertainty about the educational consequences of adolescent employment. One point of consensus is that deleterious educational consequences are more likely when teenagers work more than twenty hours per week.

Several mechanisms link intermediate educational outcomes with ultimate educational attainment. For example, early employment affects scholastic performance by reducing time spent on homework (D'Amico 1984; Marsh 1991; Lewin-Epstein 1981). In addition, teachers report that students who work seem more fatigued in class (Bills, Helms, and Ozcan 1995), are more likely to be absent from school (Marsh 1991), and are less likely to maintain their time commitment to school-related activities that increase satisfaction with the schooling experience (Greenberger and Steinberg 1986).

Schoenhals and his colleagues (1998) examined the consequences of youth employment and distinguished between time allocation effects, through which employment cuts into leisure and homework time, and socialization effects, which foster attachment to work. Finding no evidence that work during high school undermines the scholastic performance of student workers, they argued that the adverse effects found in previous research were attributable to preexisting differences among youth who elect to work a low, moderate, or high number of hours per week. The authors showed that the main effect of youth employment was on leisure activities: the more youth work, the more they decrease the time they spend watching television.

Marta Tienda and Avner Ahituv (1996) evaluated the influence of average weekly hours worked on the odds of remaining in school and found that excessive commitment to work not only increased the likelihood of premature withdrawal but also lowered the odds of continued education beyond secondary school among those who do graduate. They identified eleventh grade as a particularly vulnerable point in adolescents' school careers because it represents the first real choice between school and work for students who are not age-grade delayed. (For an argument that the period of greatest vulnerability is earlier, see Greenberger and Steinberg 1986.) Also, the school continuation decisions of disadvantaged youth, especially Hispanics, are more sensitive to variation in hours worked than are the decisions of nondisadvantaged youth. Lauri Steel (1994) found race and ethnic differences in the influence of early work experience on subsequent school enrollment probabilities, with the magnitude of these effects depending on the intensity of work activity. Tienda and Ahituv (1996) showed that youth who do not work at all are at extremely high risk of dropping out of school. Thus, both excessive work and total labor-market detachment are associated with premature school withdrawal, suggesting that a one-size-fits-all strategy to connect youth to jobs may be misguided.

The effects of early work on young women are similar to those on young men. Ahituv, Tienda, and Tsay (1998) showed that young women who have some attachment to the labor market are less likely to withdraw from either secondary school or college. This finding supports initiatives that recommend employment to strengthen the connection between school and work. However, the strong negative effect of average weekly hours on school continuation decisions tempers this inference: young women working excessive hours when they are enrolled in school are at great risk of premature school withdrawal and unlikely to continue beyond secondary school if they do graduate.

Labor-Market Consequences of Adolescent Employment

The labor-market consequences of work experience acquired at early ages have been the subject of extensive investigations. There is a diversity of opinion about the consequences of early work experience on later unemployment, hours worked, and wage rates, ranging from strong optimism (Carr, Wright, and Brody 1996; Ruhm 1997a), to caution about the endurance of positive effects (Hotz et al. 1997; Mare 1995), to doubt about whether there are any significant effects at all (Hotz et al. 1997). At one extreme, Christopher Ruhm (1997a, 770) asserted that "student employment raises future productivity through skills, knowledge, work habits, and experience provided on-the-job by far more than it detracts from educational human capital investments," and he concluded that light to moderate work commitments should be encouraged. Joseph Hotz and his colleagues (1997) claimed, however, that working while in school does not generate a return over and above that accruing to the additional schooling that working students acquire. Thus, they argued, young men would achieve much higher wages by attending school full-time rather than combining school with work. One important difference between Ruhm (1997b) and Hotz and his colleagues (1997) is their implementation of controls for unobserved characteristics that sort youth into varied pathways from school to work. The many ways in which workers differ from nonworkers are important because they signal preexisting differences among youth that are likely to influence both human capital investment and employment choices.

Another point to consider is whether the effects of early employment differ by demographic group. Michael Foster (1995), for example, claimed that disadvantaged teens benefit less from working than do other teenagers partly because of the greater number of hours they work. Although research on young women is less common, Ahituv and his colleagues (1998) speculated that excessive commitment to work during school probably inhibits long-run wage growth through lower investments in formal schooling.

In sum, the educational consequences of adolescent employment are more important than the acquisition of work experience per se. Of course, this conclusion depends on whether youth are bound for college and how much they work while enrolled in school. Many educational effects of early employment operate through short-term outcomes, such as absence from school, less time spent on homework, and lower grades. These short-term consequences have long-term ramifications because students who continue in school longer and eventually earn higher wages quickly surpass students with less education and more work experience. Moreover, returns to employment during high school and college are neither large nor long-lasting. Rising returns to education at the turn of the century, compared to the 1970s, indicate that the most prudent strategy of human asset investment emphasizes educational attainment, especially postsecondary schooling.

Labor-Market Entry and Pathways from School to Work

The "usual" conception of the school-to-work transition as a move from full-time school to full-time work applies to only a small fraction of young men and women. Most youth experience a range of part-time work activities, often while still in school, before they attain their first full-time employment. James Coleman (1984) in particular underscored the extensive overlap between school and work, particularly for white men, who experienced both longer educational careers and earlier work activity than blacks. In fact, the complexity of the transition to adulthood has increased as the period of "economic adolescence" has become more protracted (Marini 1987). As discussed earlier, different investment strategies can have important consequences for future economic well-being.

FIGURE 8.8 / Distribution of Young Men's Activity States by Age and Race-Ethnicity

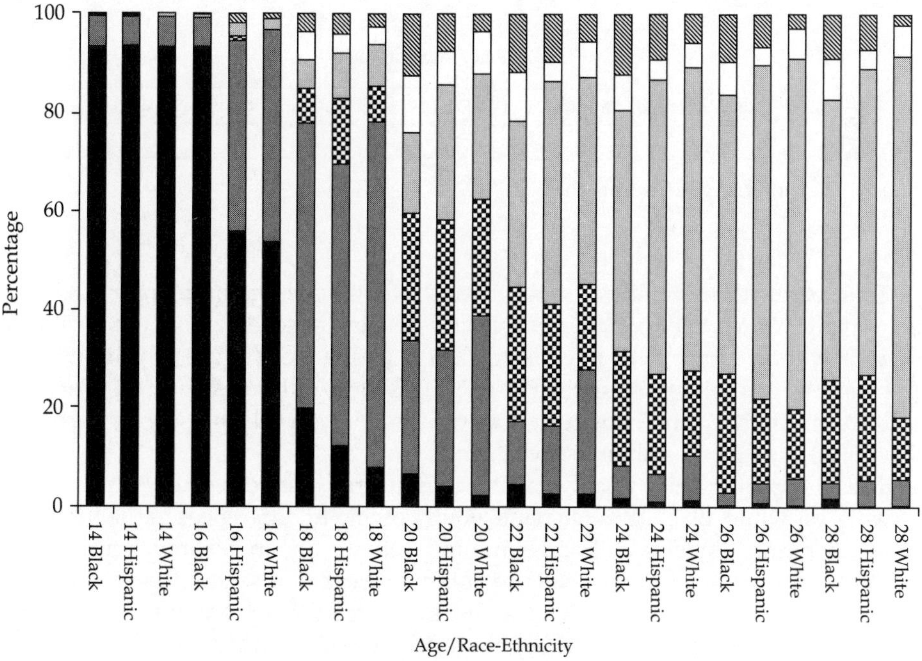

Source: NLSY data; Ahituv, Tienda, and Hotz (1997).

FIGURE 8.9 / Distribution of Young Women's Activity States by Age and Race-Ethnicity

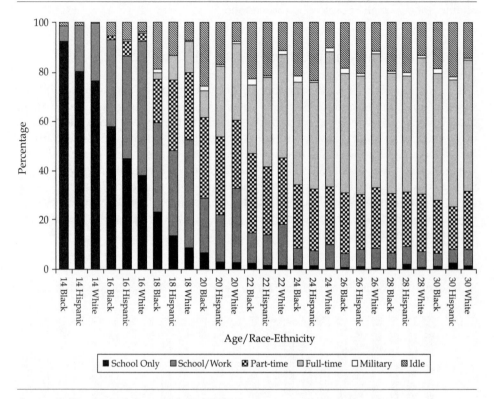

Source: Authors' calculations from the NLSY.

To illustrate the diversity of investment strategies among youth, figures 8.8 and 8.9 use NLSY data to depict the complex sequencing of school, work, and military service over the early life course for a cohort of young men (figure 8.8) and women (figure 8.9) aged thirteen to sixteen in 1979. This figure allocates youth at every age into six mutually exclusive activity states: school only; work and school; part-time work; full-time work; military service; and idleness.

The age-specific activity state distributions portray distinct *pathways* from school to work for white, black, and Hispanic youth, owing to differences in the timing of school departure, in the likelihood of military activity, and in the prevalence of idleness. Whites are much more likely to combine work and school than minorities. Hispanics are much more likely to withdraw from school prematurely and work part- or full-time. Blacks, on the other hand, prolong schooling while delaying labor-market entry and enlist in the military at higher rates than either white or Hispanic males. Finally, there are large differentials in idleness rates, with young black men reaching double digits after age twenty. Hispanic men experience less idleness than blacks, but more than whites (Ahituv, Tienda, and Tsay 1998).

For women, race and ethnic differences in school departure and labor-market entry are governed only partly by the timing of births (Ahituv, Tienda, and Tsay 1998). In general, women's pathways parallel those of men, except that Hispanic women are more likely both to exit school prematurely and to delay labor-market entry compared to whites, a prospect that puts them at a double disadvantage in the accumulation of human capital. Another difference is that higher shares of adolescent women enrolled in school work at young ages, probably because they are more likely than young men to have informal domestic jobs. Equally striking is the delayed labor-market entry of young black women, who, like their male counterparts, prolong school attendance. Finally, minority women have a high level of idleness relative to whites after age eighteen.

These pathways from school to work imply unequal levels of education and accumulated work experience. Obviously, youth who enter the labor force at younger ages can accumulate more work experience than those who delay employment. Though acquiring work experience at the expense of educational investment can ultimately have deleterious consequences for labor-force standing, the acquisition of work experience in tandem with increasing education may result in compounded human capital assets.

Using NLSY data again, figures 8.10 and 8.11 summarize race and ethnic differences in accumulated work experience for young men (figure 8.10) and women (figure 8.11) as they make the transition from student to full-time worker. In contrast to the trends in graded schooling (figures 8.2 and 8.3), which revealed large schooling deficits between Hispanic versus black and white youth, during the 1980s and early 1990s Hispanics acquired more work experience than their black counterparts, but less than whites. This is because Hispanic youth enter the labor market at younger ages on average, often at the expense of schooling (Ahituv, Tienda, and Tsay 1998; Hotz and Tienda 1998). In both panels of figures 8.10 and 8.11, the black experience curve is well below the white and Hispanic curves. Moreover, the racial-ethnic experience gaps increased over time for both men and women. For example, at age eighteen, white men had accumulated six months more work experience than black men, and four months more than Hispanic men. By age twenty-two, the experience gap between black and white young men had risen to 1.2 years, but the Hispanic-white experience gap was only one-third as great at that age (0.4 years). At the last age we observed these youth, the experience gap between black and white men had approached 2.0 years, compared to only 0.7 years for Hispanic and white men.

For women, a roughly similar pattern obtains except that the experience differentials are roughly twice as large at most ages. For instance, at age eighteen, white women averaged 0.7 years more work experience than their black age counterparts, and 0.4 years more than Hispanics. By age twenty-two, the comparable differentials were 1.6 and 0.9 years for blacks and Hispanics, respectively. By the end of the observation period, white women averaged 2.3 years more experience than blacks and 1.5 years more than Hispanics. The lower levels of experience accumulated by women can be traced to the assumption of family responsibilities that limit the amount of time spent in the labor market (Forste and Tienda 1992; Ahituv, Tienda,

FIGURE 8.10 /   Age-Specific Cumulative Years of Work Experience: Young Men
by Race-Ethnicity

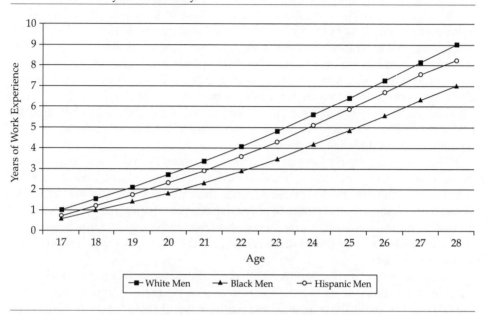

Source: NLSY data; Tienda, Hotz, and Ahituv (1998).

and Tsay 1998). However, widened experience differentials *within* sex groups suggest that other factors are involved, notably group differences in educational
investment decisions (Hispanics) and in labor-market opportunities (blacks) and
differential selection into the three modal pathways from school to work (Ahituv,
Tienda, and Tsay 1998).

Thus, there are notable differences in early labor-market experience by race and
ethnicity owing to differences in the timing of labor-force entry and the stability
of employment. Coupled with the differences in educational attainment detailed
earlier, these early labor-market profiles help explain the differential success of
demographic groups in adult employment and earnings growth.

PRIVATE AND GOVERNMENT PROGRAMS FOR YOUTH

Given the prevailing perception that significant proportions of American youth
experience a rocky transition from school to work, the number of advocates for
structured school-to-work programs has been growing. Two significant pieces of
legislation—the 1990 Carl Perkins Act and the 1994 School to Work Opportunities
Act—undergird efforts to revitalize the school-to-work movement. The former
provides funding for programs that integrate vocational and academic education,

FIGURE 8.11   /   Age-Specific Cumulative Years of Work Experience: Young Women
                    by Race-Ethnicity

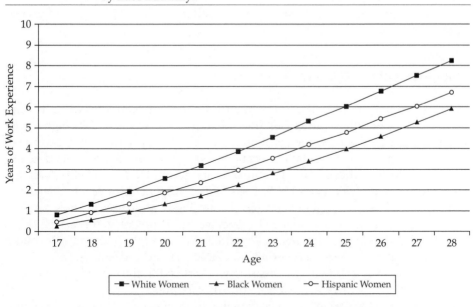

Source: NLSY data; Tienda, Hotz, and Ahituv (1998).

including the efforts of vocational schools to enhance their academic content and
of magnet schools to increase the amount of contextual learning in their curricula
(Bodilly et al. 1993).

   The more expansive STWOA broadens the policy focus from the labor-market
problems of minority youth only to the transition process for all noncollege-bound
youth (Osterman 1995). This legislation is a five-year effort to create a school-to-
work transition system that includes school-based, work-based, and connecting activity components. The goal is to construct a school-to-work *system* involving collaboration between employers, organized labor, educators, public agencies and
community groups, and students, rather than a disparate collection of unrelated
programs (Hershey et al. 1997). Ideally, such a system would include academic instruction, including new pedagogies, such as more applied teaching methods; career development activities to increase student awareness of their interests, options,
and goals; vocational skills training integrated with academic or remedial instruction
as appropriate; work-based education coordinated with school-based instruction;
and "connecting activities," which link employers, students, and schools, including
postsecondary institutions, to form an explicit hierarchy of education and training
opportunities (Grubb 1996; Hershey et al. 1997).

   The STWOA provides states with seed money to distribute to local communities
to finance the design and implementation of innovative plans. States and localities
have broad latitude to design their systems, including freedom to choose from

among the many possible program types. In the most common types of school-to-work programs, we discuss their possible benefits and disadvantages and review available program evaluations.

School-to-Work Programs

The most common approach to preparing the noncollege-bound for work has and continues to be vocational education (Rosenbaum 1996). Nearly all U.S. high school students completed at least one vocational course in the early 1990s, but fewer than 10 percent majored in a particular vocational education area such as allied health services, agriculture, business and commerce, or trade and technical fields (National Center for Education Statistics 1997). The original proponents of vocational education contended that occupational training more closely addresses the needs of students not planning to attend college by teaching necessary job and practical skills; that the programs serve students better suited to applied than academic learning; that vocational tracks serve as conduits to employers and prevent aimless drifting in the labor market; and that by increasing workers' skills, the United States would become more competitive in the international economy.

Evidence about the benefits of vocational education is mixed. Some studies find positive effects on wages and the likelihood of subsequent employment (Rosenbaum 1996), but these outcomes depend on the population segment under consideration and the specific focus of the vocational program. Young women benefit more than men from enrollment in vocational tracks (Arum and Shavit 1995; Rumberger and Daymont 1984; Kang and Bishop 1989); gains in employment and wages are larger for minority than for nonminority youth (Lerman and Pouncy 1990; Foster 1995); and positive benefits accrue only from participation in business and commerce programs for women, and in trade and technical programs for men (Arum and Hout 1998). Not surprisingly, the benefits of vocational education also depend on securing a job in the field within which training was received, but less than one-third of vocational students work in their field after graduation. This mismatch between training and employment remains a serious failure of vocational education (Lerman and Pouncy 1990).

Cooperative education, or "co-op," is a specialized form of vocational education that serves only a small number of high school students. Less than 4 percent of high school students were enrolled in co-op in the 1989–1990 school year (Bailey and Merritt 1993). Co-op typically fills half of the school day with part-time, paid employment for which students also receive high school credit. Though half of the day is spent in academic classes that are approved by a co-op coordinator, coordination between these classes and the work experience is usually weak, and students earn no recognized workplace credentials through their employment (Olson 1997). The putative benefits of cooperative education include work experience in better-quality jobs than students could obtain on their own, an opportunity to earn wages while still in school, and the high school diploma itself (Bailey and Merritt 1993). Although evaluations suggest that cooperative education clarifies career goals and increases student self-confidence, motivation, and school satisfaction (Kerka 1989), there is no evidence that it yields postgraduation employment gains (Stern et al. 1990, as cited in Bailey and Merritt 1993).

Career academies are a more recent school-to-work innovation. First established in 1970 in Philadelphia, there are now more than three hundred such programs nationwide (Olson 1997). A career academy is organized as a "school within a school" for a relatively small number of students and teachers who focus on vocational, occupational, or industrial themes, such as electronics, health careers, finance, or tourism. Academic coursework is tailored to the particular occupational focus of the academy and generally includes more applied learning opportunities than a general or college preparatory curriculum. Another feature of the career academy is the involvement, to varying degrees, of local employers who serve as advisers or mentors to students, help with curricula, and provide job shadows and in-school or summer internships or work experience. Presumably, career academy students benefit from the more intimate nature of the academy, the exposure to careers and concrete workplaces, and the increased relevance of their academic coursework. A related but less intensive and restrictive program initiative is the career major or occupational-academic cluster. Schools that take the career major approach provide all students with the opportunity to explore career options by exposing them to several careers and then requiring them to focus on one or more career pathways by participating in a series of courses related to their interests (Bailey 1991).

Evaluations of career academies find positive effects on intermediate outcomes, such as student motivation and aspirations, but it is unclear whether academies have longer-term effects on schooling and employment outcomes. Evaluation of California's academies found evidence of lower dropout rates among academy students compared to similar nonacademy students, but no significant differences in employment and postsecondary school attendance patterns (Dayton, Weisberg, and Stern 1989, as cited in Bailey and Merritt 1993). Because the students under study were not involved in academies long enough to determine graduation and employment effects, the Manpower Demonstration Research Corporation's recent evaluation focuses instead on whether career academies provide an atmosphere more conducive to student motivation and learning than normal high schools. Although students reported increased motivation and engagement in school, their behaviors did not actually indicate increased engagement (Kemple 1997). Anecdotal and qualitative studies of career academies find student satisfaction with their programs to be high (Olson 1997).

What distinguishes technical preparation, or "tech-prep," programs is the link between the last two years of high school and community college programs in specific occupational areas, such as health care, industrial engineering, or automotive technology (Olson 1997). By 1990 there were over 120 tech-prep programs in 33 states (Delaware Consortium on Technical Preparation Programs 1991, as cited in Bailey and Merritt 1993), and the Carl Perkins Act included funds to encourage the further implementation of this school-to-work model. During high school, students enrolled in tech-prep demonstrate proficiency in core subjects, such as mathematics and science, so that they are prepared for the technical coursework they will encounter at the postsecondary level. There may or may not be a work-based learning component to tech-prep programs, but local employers are expected to play at least coordination and consultation roles (Bailey and Merritt 1993).

Tech-prep is intended to forge formal links between secondary and postsecondary education and thereby encourage students' continued education. Because students take high school classes tailored to the community college program of their choice, they do not arrive unprepared and need not take remedial or repetitive classwork. As with many emerging school-to-work program designs, the impact of tech-prep programs on education and work outcomes has not been systemically evaluated. However, available evidence suggests that this approach can lead to higher academic achievement, decrease premature high school withdrawal, and increase postsecondary school enrollment (Bailey and Merritt 1993).

Although traditional vocational education, cooperative education, career academies, career clusters, and tech-prep programs all contribute to the recent upswing in the school-to-work movement, youth apprenticeships have attracted the most attention in the popular press and, to some extent, in policy dialogues. Involving much more extensive employer involvement and work-based learning components than other school-to-work programs, the youth apprenticeship model is the most ambitious program under discussion because it involves a radical restructuring of the educational system. Youth apprenticeships are at one end of the spectrum of school-to-work programs; basic educational improvement and reform are found at the other end, and all other programs discussed previously occupy the middle ground (Lerman 1996).

To a large extent, support for youth apprenticeships derives from the perceived success of the German apprenticeship system (Bailey and Merritt 1993). However, proponents recognize the differences between the American and German contexts; the apprenticeship model would have to be adapted to the realities of U.S. economic, political, and educational systems and social sensibilities (Lynch 1994). Youth apprenticeships feature a "contractual agreement between employers, workers, and schools whereby a seventeen- to eighteen-year-old (high school junior or senior) combines work-based and school-based learning over a two- to three-year period to achieve a certified competency in a career field along with a high school degree" (Lerman 1996, 144). This description, of course, belies the complexity of the arguments for and against the youth apprenticeship model and the complexity of any actual large-scale implementation.

Proponents see many advantages. Overall, the high school experience of apprenticeship students is expected to be more rewarding. Contextual learning approaches would integrate the academic and work-based elements of the apprenticeship program and increase the relevance of classwork to the world of work, thus tightening the fit between general education and the nonacademically oriented student. Presumably, motivation would increase as students visualized links between academic subjects and the skills required for specific occupations. Assignments of more coveted apprenticeships—and hence of better postgraduation jobs—to higher-achieving students also should increase incentives to perform scholastically and to appreciate the value of academic subjects. And as school satisfaction and achievement increase, school retention should also improve. The work-based learning element of apprenticeships is considered particularly valuable. Students would have increased contact with mentoring adults concerned with their skill development. Because real employers would provide vocational training to apprentices, the relevance of the skills learned to current labor-force needs would be ensured. The quality of employment—the apprenticeship—would also be higher than that of jobs students found on their own, and higher than the quality of those provided through traditional co-op programs. Finally, by providing explicit links between students, schools, and employers, the apprenticeship model should reduce the drifting or thrashing period and hasten the onset of both social and economic adulthood.

Apprenticeships are particularly appealing for disadvantaged and minority youth, whose school-to-work transitions are the most problematic. Apprenticeships offer disadvantaged students the constructive adult ties they often lack, discourage participation in illicit or harmful behaviors, and provide the formal links to employers on which more advantaged youth depend (Lerman 1996; Osterman 1995; Lerman and Pouncy 1990; Olson 1997).

The apprenticeship model has its critics as well. One issue is whether employer interest is sufficient to expand apprenticeships. Lynn Olson (1997, 240) suggested that apprenticeships are most likely to succeed "in industries with a deep concern for quality, a desperate need for qualified workers, and enough prosperity to invest in the future." Economists who criticize the youth apprenticeship model have contended that it creates barriers to employment and encourages discrimination against women and minorities (Lerman 1996). The experiences of Turks in Germany, who participate in the apprenticeship system less extensively and in less desirable jobs than native Germans (Bailey and Merritt 1993), qualifies the assertion that apprenticeships would offer particular benefits to minority youth. Lisa Lynch (1994) cited two more potential weaknesses of the apprenticeship model: the increased attachment to a specific occupation that may become obsolete in the future, and the tendency to model apprenticeship training on manufacturing jobs, which are declining as a share of all jobs.

Harvey Kantor (1994) questioned the true severity of the youth labor-market problem and the focus on training—rather than broader policies designed to discourage discrimination and ensure full employment—as the best way to improve young adult employment prospects. He cautioned that the purported benefits of a youth apprenticeship system are similar to those originally attached to vocational education (benefits that, he argued, have not in fact accrued) and warned that apprenticeships could become yet another form of prejudicial tracking. Paul Osterman (1995) has joined Kantor in also questioning the premise that a skills crisis underlies youths' labor-market problems and that apprenticeships would address this deficit, thus raising productivity and wages and increasing the number of high-quality jobs available.

The programs reviewed thus far are intended to improve the school-to-work transition for noncollege-bound youth. Targeted or "second-chance" job training programs are designed to address the training needs of a narrower segment of the population, namely, the disadvantaged and minority youth whose labor-market problems are most severe. The major economic rationale for these types of programs is that they correct market or institutional failures, such as the inability of the disadvantaged to pay for training, and that they compensate for poor public school performance by giving dropouts another opportunity to achieve (Friedlander, Greenberg, and Robins 1997). Examples of federally funded job training programs for youth have included Job Corps, the longest-running youth employment program, JOBSTART, JTPA, CETA, and STEP (see also Pouncy, this volume).

With some caveats, however, the evidence suggests that job training programs for youth have not provided significant employment or earnings gains, or that they have provided such limited benefits that they fail to move youth out of poverty (see Heckman, this volume). Why do job training programs not work? According to Norton Grubb (1996), the reasons include their limited scope and time frame; a misguided emphasis on job placement, which assumes that the problem is unemployment rather than lack of skills; the low quality of the job-related training provided and its lack of relevance to jobs accessible to youth; the use of ineffective and inappropriate pedagogy; and the special problems of socially disadvantaged youth and the youth labor market, including a negative youth culture, the compounding of multiple social problems experienced by inner-city youth, and the reluctance of employers to hire young workers.

This is not to say that no youth programs have produced positive effects. However, the positive effects of second-chance programs tend to be associated with smaller demonstration programs and are often based on less rigorous evaluations than the random assignment experiments conducted on the major federal programs. Smaller, more intensive demonstration programs may indeed offer significant benefits, but their relevance to national policy is questionable since it is doubtful that they could be replicated on a scale large enough to recommend them as a viable policy alternative.

POLICY IMPLICATIONS

We began our investigation of the school-to-work transition by seeking to reevaluate the extent of the problem faced by youth as they move from the student to the worker role. We found that early labor-market difficulties remain concentrated among the most disadvantaged youth and ethnic minorities. Academic skills are lower among urban and ethnic minorities, and Hispanics continue to exhibit troubling high school dropout rates. Although minorities of both sexes show higher unemployment rates than whites, joblessness is most serious for black males. Among the groups experiencing a delayed transition to stable employment are black youth and high school dropouts.

Trends in wages, however, do present more generalized labor-market problems for youth. Wages have fallen more for young workers than for experienced workers, though they have just recently begun to rebound. In addition, the gap between the wages of high school- and college-educated workers, although beginning to stabilize, has increased appreciably. Therefore, earning a living wage has become difficult for high school dropouts and, increasingly, for those who do not pursue higher education. The greatest impact of these wage trends, once again, is on minorities, because they disproportionately make up the lower educational groups.

School-to-work transition problems may not be endemic, but youth still need to make careful human capital investment decisions. Wage trends, in fact, highlight the necessity of prudent early strategies. Given the opportunity either to invest in schooling or to acquire early work experience, the empirical evidence demonstrates the clear advantage of maximizing educational attainment. Youth who underinvest in education face grim labor-market prospects. Each additional year of schooling, whether at a junior college or a four-year institution, is associated with significant wage gains (Kane and Rouse 1995). Although there is debate about the consequences of early work on sociopsychological health, educational achievement, and later labor-market outcomes, one thing is clear: extensive involvement in the labor market is detrimental to youth well-being. Negative outcomes across several domains are associated with long work hours while in school.

Thus, the amount of time devoted to the labor market while enrolled in school should be kept to levels that do not undermine educational pursuits. Although some research suggests that students are more vulnerable to the effects of employment early in their school careers, there is no clear consensus about the period of greatest vulnerability. The available evidence does not provide a sufficient basis for eliminating youth employment from the design of school-to-work programs, provided that the time commitment to work activities is reasonable and that the work activity reinforces the goal of maximizing educational attainment.

Our review suggests that the growing interest and investment in school-to-work programs like vocational education, co-op, career academies, tech-prep, and apprenticeships cannot be justified on the basis of a widespread and increasing crisis in young adult labor-market outcomes. Furthermore, it is not clear that the problem of low wages, which is of more general concern for noncollege-bound youth, can be addressed by school-to-work programs or other forms of educational reform. In other words, demand factors are part of the problem, and work preparation programs focus on supply-side solutions (Kantor 1994; Osterman 1995).

However, there *are* compelling reasons to recommend the STOWA approach and some of its programs as sound public policy. As highlighted earlier, the key to a successful transition entails ensuring that educational investments are maximized. This suggests that school-to-work programs, at least for the general youth population, should be evaluated more on the basis of their effects on educational attainment than on the basis of their job-specific training. The value of school-to-work programs for most youth is in improving educational attainment both directly, through formal linkages between educational institutions (such as tech-prep programs), and indirectly, through improvement in educational quality and satisfaction. Most school-to-work advocates acknowledge as much. Programs are touted more for their value as educational reform than as workforce preparation. Moreover, their value as workforce preparation is basic rather than specific. School-to-work advocates argue that integrating vocational and academic education will aid students in an economy that increasingly requires continual learning (Urquiola et al. 1997), not that programs will turn out legions of high school graduates with specialized job skills.

To succeed, school-to-work programs must be designed within the context of general educational reform. This includes continuing efforts to improve basic skills and further the adoption of integrated curricula by increasing the applied learning component of academic courses. We do not believe that the extent of the school-to-work transition problem warrants large-scale investment in youth apprenticeship programs. Rather, we would recommend pursuing those programs that require less intensive employer involvement. Reviews of career academies suggest that these programs are very promising as a form of basic educational reform that highlights career awareness. Tech-prep, because it smooths the transition to community college and higher education, is particularly laudable. Linking activities of all types, including those with employers, should be pursued for the benefit of the general youth population.

For those segments of the youth population who have real difficulties establishing themselves in the labor market, school-to-work programs hold promises that targeted or "second-chance" programs cannot offer. Job training on a large scale does not work for youth. Years of programs and evaluations attest so well to this fact that it is difficult to justify their existence. Nevertheless, it is also clear that certain youth need more help making the transition to work and achieving economic independence than can reasonably be expected from efforts aimed mainly at improving educational quality. Although the needs of the so-called forgotten half can probably be met within the broader rubric of school reform, including school-to-work programs, disadvantaged youth and minorities—those youth who are both more likely not to work at all and to drop out of school prematurely—*should* be targeted for special assistance.

Programs that explicitly connect students with high-quality jobs are more appropriate for this segment of the youth population, who often experience difficulty securing employment on their own. Quality co-op jobs that teach real skills would be beneficial, as would apprenticeships developed at the local level. The movement to develop skills certifications would give the noncollege-bound something to show for their work-based learning. It is vital, however, that the importance of academic skills be heightened rather than diminished and that pathways to higher education be emphasized rather than blocked. The noncollege-bound should not lose the ability to attend college if they so choose.

Of course, disadvantaged students will also benefit from reforms designed to help the majority. In fact, one of the most promising reform strategies involves melding the needs of both groups as much as possible while retaining special components for youth who need more attention—targeting within universalism. For example, career academies could include extra time spent at internships and tech-prep programs could feature stronger work-based learning components for students identified as at risk. This approach would avoid total separation of student groups—tracking—while giving targeted youth additional opportunities to acquire work skills.

This approach is not without its dangers. School-to-work advocates emphasize that in order to succeed, school-to-work programs must draw from a broad base of students and not simply become dumping grounds for poor achievers. Failure to attract a broad base of student participation will result in stigmatization, as has occurred with vocational education curricula and co-op programs in the past (Kantor 1994). However, it is unrealistic to expect one program to serve all youth. Negotiating a balance between school-to-work programs as educational reform for the majority and extra help for the minority will probably be one of the movement's most difficult challenges in the future.

The research for this chapter was supported by grants from the William T. Grant Foundation and the National Science Foundation (SBER 9601995). We gratefully acknowledge the institutional support of the Office of Population Research and superb technical assistance from Pamela Bye-Erts.

REFERENCES

Ahituv, Avner, Marta Tienda, and V. Joseph Hotz. 1997. "Pathways from School to Work Among Black, Hispanic and White Young Men in the 1980s." Unpublished paper. Princeton University.

Ahituv, Avner, Marta Tienda, and Angela Tsay. 1998. "Early Employment Activity and School Continuation Decisions of Young White, Black, and Hispanic Women." Revision of paper presented at the 1996 annual meetings of the Population Association of America.

Arum, Richard, and Michael Hout. 1998. "The Early Returns: The Transition from School to Work in the United States." In *From School to Work: A Comparative Study of Educational Qualifications and Occupational Destinations*, edited by Yossi Shavit and Walter Muller. New York: Clarendon Press.

Arum, Richard, and Yossi Shavit. 1995. "Secondary Vocational Education and the Transition from School to Work." *Sociology of Education* 68(3): 187–204.

Bailey, Thomas. 1991. "Jobs of the Future and the Education They Will Require: Evidence from Occupational Forecasts." *Educational Researcher* 20(2): 11–20.

Bailey, Thomas, and Donna Merritt. 1993. "School-to-Work Transition Project: The School-to-Work Transition and Youth Apprenticeship: Lessons from the U.S. Experience." New York: Manpower Demonstration Research Corporation.

Becker, Gary S. 1993. *Human Capital: A Theoretical and Empirical Analysis with Special Reference to Education*, 3rd ed. Chicago: University of Chicago Press.

Bills, David, Leila Helms, and Mustafa Ozcan. 1995. "The Impact of Student Employment on Teachers' Attitudes and Behaviors Toward Working Students." *Youth and Society* 27: 169–93.

Bodilly, Susan, Kimberly Ramsey, Cathleen Stasz, and Rick Eden. 1993. "Integrating Academic and Vocational Education: Lessons from Eight Early Innovators." Berkeley: National Center for Research in Vocational Education, University of California.

Campbell, Jay R., Kristin E. Voelkl, and Patricia L. Donahue. 1997. "NAEP Trends in Academic Progress: Report in Brief." Washington, D.C.: National Center for Education Statistics.

Carr, Rhoda Viellion, James D. Wright, and Charles J. Brody. 1996. "Effects of High School Work Experience a Decade Later: Evidence from the National Longitudinal Survey." *Sociology of Education* 69(1): 66–81.

Caspi, Avshalom, Bradley R. Wright, Terrie E. Moffitt, and Phil A. Silva. 1998. "Early Failure in the Labor Market: Childhood and Adolescent Predictors of Unemployment in the Transition to Adulthood." *American Sociological Review* 63(3): 424–51.

Cogan, John. 1982. "The Decline in Black Teenage Employment: 1950–1970." *American Economic Review* 72(4): 621–38.

Coleman, James. 1984. "The Transition from School to Work." *Research in Stratification and Mobility* 3: 27–59.

D'Amico, Ronald. 1984. "Does Employment During High School Impair Academic Progress?" *Sociology of Education* 57(July): 152–64.

Dayton, Charles, Alan Weisberg, and David Stern. 1989. "California Partnership Academies: 1987–1988 Evaluation Report." Berkeley: Policy Analysis for California Education, University of California.

Delaware Consortium on Technical Preparation Programs. 1991. *Technical Preparation Quarterly* newsletters.

Donahoe, Debra, and Marta Tienda. 1998. "Human Asset Development and the Transition from School to Work: Policy Lessons in the Twenty-first Century." Working paper 98–4. Princeton, N.J.: Office of Population Research, Princeton University.

Forste, Renata, and Marta Tienda. 1992. "Race and Ethnic Variation in the Schooling Consequences of Female Adolescent Sexual Activity." *Social Science Quarterly* 73(1): 12–30.

Foster, Michael E. 1995. "Why Teens Do Not Benefit from Work Experience Programs: Evidence from Brother Comparisons." *Journal of Policy Analysis and Management* 14(3): 393–414.

Freeman, Richard B., and Harry J. Holzer. 1986. "The Black Youth Employment Crisis." In *The Black Youth Employment Crisis*, edited by Richard B. Freeman and Harry J. Holzer. Chicago: University of Chicago Press.

Friedlander, Daniel, David H. Greenberg, and Philip K. Robins. 1997. "Evaluating Government Training Programs for the Economically Disadvantaged." *Journal of Economic Literature* 35(December): 1809–55.

Greenberger, Ellen, and Laurence Steinberg. 1986. *When Teenagers Work: The Psychological and Social Costs of Adolescent Employment.* New York: Basic Books.

———. 1989. *When Teenagers Work: The Psychological and Social Costs of Adolescent Employment.* New York: Basic Books.

Grubb, Norton W. 1996. *Learning to Work: The Case for Reintegrating Job Training and Education.* New York: Russell Sage Foundation.

Hershey, Alan M., Paula Hudis, Marsha Silverberg, and Joshua Haimson. 1997. "Partner in Progress: Early Steps in Creating School-to-Work Systems." Washington, D.C.: U.S. Department of Education.

Hirschman, Charles. 1988. "Minorities in the Labor Market." In *Divided Opportunities: Minorities, Poverty, and Social Policy,* edited by Gary D. Sandefur and Marta Tienda. New York: Plenum.

Hogan, Dennis P., and Nan Marie Astone. 1986. "The Transition to Adulthood." *Annual Review of Sociology* 12: 109–30.

Hotz, V. Joseph, Linxin Xiu, Marta Tienda, and Avner Ahituv. 1997. "Are There Returns to the Wages of Young Men from Working While in School?" Paper presented at the annual meeting of the American Economic Association, Chicago (January 1998).

Hotz, V. Joseph, and Marta Tienda. 1998. "Education and Employment in a Diverse Society: Generating Inequality Through the School-to-Work." In *American Diversity: A Demographic Challenge for the Twenty-first Century,* edited by Nancy Denton and Stuart Tolnay. Albany: State University of New York Press.

Kane, Thomas J., and Cecilia E. Rouse. 1995. "Labor Market Returns to Two- and Four-Year Colleges: Is a Credit a Credit, or Do Degrees Matter?" *American Economic Review* 85(3): 600–614.

Kang, Suk, and John Bishop. 1989. "Vocational and Academic Education in High School: Complements or Substitutes?" *Economics of Education* 8(2): 133–48.

Kantor, Harvey. 1994. "Managing the Transition from School to Work: The False Promise of Youth Apprenticeship." *Teachers College Record* 95(4): 442–61.

Keithly, Diane, and Forrest Deseran. 1995. "Households, Local Labor Markets, and Youth Labor Force Participation." *Youth and Society* 26: 463–92.

Kemple, James J. 1997. "Career Academies: Communities of Support for Students and Teachers: Emerging Findings from a Ten-Site Evaluation." New York: Manpower Demonstration Research Corporation.

Kerka, Sandra. 1989. "Cooperative Education: Characteristics and Effectiveness." Washington, D.C.: Office of Education, Research, and Improvement.

Klerman, Jacob Alex, and Lynn A. Karoly. 1994. "Young Men and the Transition to Stable Employment." *Monthly Labor Review* 117(8): 31–48.

Koretz, Daniel. 1992. "What Happened to Test Scores, and Why?" *Educational-Measurement: Issues and Practices* 11(4): 7–11.

Lerman, Robert I. 1996. "Building Hope, Skills, and Careers: Creating a Youth Apprenticeship System." In *Social Policies for Children,* edited by Irwin Garfinkel, Jennifer C. Hochschild, and Sara S. McLanahan. Washington, D.C.: Brookings Institution.

Lerman, Robert I., and Hillard Pouncy. 1990. "The Compelling Case for Youth Apprenticeships." *Public Interest* 101(June): 62–77.

Levitan, Sar, and Frank Gallo. 1991. "Preparing Americans for Work." *Looking Ahead* 13(1/2): 18–25.

Lewin-Epstein, Noah. 1981. "Youth Employment During High School." Washington, D.C.: U.S. Department of Education.

Lynch, Lisa M. 1994. "Payoffs to Alternative Training Strategies at Work." In *Working Under Different Rules,* edited by Richard B. Freeman. New York: Russell Sage Foundation.

Manning, Wendy. 1990. "Parenting Employed Teenagers." *Youth and Society* 22: 184–200.

Mare, Robert D. 1995. "Changes in Educational Attainment and the Timing of Entry into Parenthood." In *State of the Union: America in the 1990s,* edited by Reynolds Farley. New York: Russell Sage Foundation.

Marini, Margaret Mooney. 1984. "The Order of Events in the Transition to Adulthood." *Sociology of Education* 57(2): 63–84.

———. 1987. "Measuring the Process of Role Change During the Transition to Adulthood." *Social Science Research* 16(1): 1–38.

Markward, Martha. 1991. "The Socialization of Youths in the Workplace: Implications for School Social Work." *Social Work in Education* 13(4): 236–44.

Marsh, Herbert W. 1991. "Employment During High School: Character Building or a Subversion of Academic Goals?" *Sociology of Education* 64(July): 172–89.

Mincer, Jacob. 1962. "On-the-Job Training: Costs, Returns, and Some Implications." *Journal of Political Economy* 70(1): 281–302.

———. 1974. *Schooling, Experience, and Earnings.* New York: National Bureau of Economic Research/Columbia University Press.

Mortimer, Jeylan T., and Michael D. Finch. 1986. "The Development of Self-esteem in the Early Work Career." *Work and Occupations* 13: 217–39.

———. 1992. "Work Experience in Adolescence." Paper commissioned for Public/Private Ventures, Philadelphia.

————, eds. 1996. *Adolescents, Work, and Family: An Intergenerational Developmental Analysis.* Thousand Oaks, Calif.: Sage Publications.

Mortimer, Jeylan T., Michael D. Finch, Timothy J. Owens, and Michael Shanahan. 1990. "Gender and Work in Adolescence." *Youth and Society* 22(2): 201–24.

Mortimer, Jeylan T., Seongryeol Ryu, Katherine Dennehy, and Chaimun Lee. 1992. "Part-time Work and Occupational Value Formation in Adolescence." *Social Forces* 74(4): 1405–18.

Mullis, Ina. 1998. "Comment." In *Brookings Papers on Education Policy*, edited by Diane Ravitch. Washington, D.C.: Brookings Institution.

National Center for Education Statistics. 1997. "Findings from Vocational Education in the United States: The Early 1990s." Washington: U.S. Department of Education, Office of Education, Research, and Improvement.

National Commission on Educational Excellence. 1983. "A Nation at Risk: The Imperative for Educational Reform." Washington: U.S. Government Printing Office.

Olson, Lynn. 1994. "Bridging the Gap." *Education Week on the Web* (January 26). Available on the world wide web at: http://www.edweek.org/ew/1994/18work.h13.

————. 1997. *The School to Work Revolution.* Reading, Mass.: Addison-Wesley.

Osterman, Paul. 1995. "Is There a Problem with the Youth Labor Market, and If So, How Should We Fix It?: Lessons for the United States from U.S. and European Experience." In *Poverty, Inequality, and the Future of Social Policy: Western States in the New World Order*, edited by Katherine McFate, Roger Lawson, and William Julius Wilson. New York: Russell Sage Foundation.

Osterman, Paul, and Maria Iannozzi. 1993. "Youth Apprenticeships and School-to-Work Transitions: Current Knowledge and Legislative Strategy." Working paper 14. Philadelphia: National Center on the Educational Quality of the Workforce.

President's Science Advisory Committee. 1974. *Youth: Transition to Adulthood: A Report of the Panel on Youth.* Washington: Executive Office of the President.

Rasell, Edith, Barry Bluestone, and Lawrence Mishel. 1997. *The Prosperity Gap: A Chartbook of American Living Standards.* Washington, D.C.: Economic Policy Institute.

Rees, Albert. 1986. "An Essay on Youth Joblessness." *Journal of Economic Literature* 24(June): 613–28.

Rindfuss, Ronald R., C. Gray Swicegood, and Rachel A. Rosenfeld. 1987. "Disorder in the Life Course: How Common and Does It Matter?" *American Sociological Review* 52(December): 785–801.

Rindfuss, Ronald R. 1991. "The Young Adult Years: Diversity, Structural Change, and Fertility." *Demography* 4 (November 28): 493–512.

Rosenbaum, James E. 1996. "Policy Uses of Research on the High School-to-Work Transition." *Sociology of Education* (extra issue): 102–22.

Ruhm, Christopher J. 1997a. "The Effects of High School Work Experience on Future Economic Attainment." Washington, D.C.: Employment Policies Institute.

————. 1997b. "Is High School Employment Consumption or Investment?" *Journal of Labor Economics* 15(4): 735–76.

Rumberger, Russell W., and Thomas N. Daymont. 1984. "The Economic Value of Academic and Vocational Training Acquired in High School." In *Youth and the Labor Market: Analyses of the National Longitudinal Survey*, edited by Michael Morus. Kalamazoo, Mich.: W. E. Upjohn Institute for Employment Research.

Schoenhals, Mark, Marta Tienda, and Barbara Schneider. 1998. "The Educational and Personal Consequences of Adolescent Employment." *Social Forces* 77(2): 725–64.

Shanahan, Michael, Michael D. Finch, Jeylan T. Mortimer, and Seongryeol Ryu. 1991. "Adolescent Work Experience and Depressive Affect." *Social Psychological Quarterly* 54(4): 299–317.

Smith, James P., and Barry Edmonston, eds. 1997. *The New Americans: Economic, Demographic, and Fiscal Effects of Immigration.* Washington, D.C.: National Academy Press.

Stedman, Lawrence C. 1998. "An Assortment of the Contemporary Debate over U.S. Achievement." In *Brookings Papers on Education Policy,* edited by Diane Ravitch. Washington, D.C.: Brookings Institution.

Steel, Lauri. 1994. "Early Work Experience among White and Non-White Youths: Implications for Subsequent Enrollment and Employment." *Youth and Society* 22(4): 419–47.

Steinberg, Laurence, Suzanne Fegley, and Sanford M. Dornbusch. 1993. "Negative Impact of Part-time Work on Adolescent Adjustment: Evidence from a Longitudinal Study." *Developmental Psychology* 29(2): 171–80.

Steinberg, Laurence, Ellen Greenberger, Maryann Jacobi, and Lauri Garduque. 1981. "Early Work Experience: A Partial Antidote for Adolescent Egocentrism." *Journal of Youth and Adolescence* 10: 141–57.

Stern, David, Martin McMillion, Charles Hopkins, and James Stone. 1990. "Work Experience for Students in High School and College." *Youth and Society* 21(3): 355–89.

Sum, Andrew, W., Neal Fogg, and Robert Taggart. 1996. "From Dreams to Dust: The Deteriorating Labor Market Fortunes of Young Adults." Report 96–02. Baltimore, Md.: Sar Levitan Center for Social Policy Studies, Institute for Social Policy Studies, Johns Hopkins University.

Sum, Andrew, Stephen Mangum, Edward deJesus, Gary Walker, David Gruber, Marion Pines, and William Spring. 1997. "A Generation of Challenge: Pathways to Success for Urban Youth." Monograph 97–03. Baltimore, Md.: Sar Levitan Center for Social Policy Studies, Institute for Social Policy Studies, Johns Hopkins University.

Tienda, Marta, and Avner Ahituv. 1996. "Ethnic Differences in School Departure: Does Youth Employment Promote or Undermine Educational Attainment?" In *Of Heart and Mind: Social Policy Essays in Honor of Sar A. Levitan,* edited by Garth Mangum and Stephen Mangum. Kalamazoo, Mich.: W. E. Upjohn Institute for Employment Research.

Tienda, Marta, V. Joseph Hotz, and Avner Ahituv. 1998. "Local Labor Markets and Employment Experiences of Black, White, and Hispanic Young Men During the 1980s and Early 1990s." Paper presented at the 93rd American Sociological Association annual meeting, San Francisco(August 1998).

Tienda, Marta, and Zai Liang. 1994. "Poverty and Immigration in Policy Perspective." In *Poverty and Public Policy,* edited by Sheldon H. Danziger, Gary D. Sandefur, and Daniel H. Weinberg. Cambridge, Mass.: Harvard University Press.

Topel, Robert H., and Michael P. Ward. 1992. "Job Mobility and the Careers of Young Men." *Quarterly Journal of Economics* 107(May): 439–79.

Urquiola, Miguel, David Stern, I. Horn, C. Dornsife, B. Chi, L. Williams, D. Merritt, Karen Hughes, and Thomas Bailey. 1997. *School to Work, College, and Career: A Review of Policy, Practice, and Results 1993–1997.* Berkeley, Calif.: National Center for Research in Vocational Education.

William T. Grant Foundation, Commission on Work, Family, and Citizenship. 1988. *The Forgotten Half: Pathways to Success for America's Youth and Young Families.* New York: William T. Grant Foundation.

Chapter 9

New Directions in Job Training Strategies for the Disadvantaged

Hillard Pouncy

In its 1988 report *The Forgotten Half,* the William T. Grant Foundation cited 1980 census data showing that half of American adults age twenty-five and older had no formal education beyond high school and were at increased risk of poverty. This report influenced social policy, including that of the Clinton administration. A decade later, when the American Youth Policy Forum (Halperin 1998) revisited the subject,[1] half of all adults still had no formal education beyond high school, but the situation among youth had changed dramatically—only one-third of youth between the ages of eighteen and twenty-four now formally end their education with high school. This "forgotten third" remain at risk of becoming the working or, worse, nonworking poor. Another third take postsecondary courses but earn no degree. The remaining third finish college.

Despite an economic boom in the 1990s that makes the American job market "the envy of the world" (Freeman and Rodgers 1999), the median real weekly earnings of young adults (ages sixteen to twenty-four) who work full-time have declined significantly since the 1970s, and those declines vary by educational attainment. In a 1997 survey (Sum and Fogg 1999), about three-fifths of high school dropouts experienced at least one of four major labor-market problems: unemployment, underemployment, discouragement, or working poverty.[2] About half of high school graduates who have ended their education and about half of youth with three years or less of postsecondary education had labor-market problems. Only one-fifth of youth with a college education or more had similar problems. Sum and Fogg (1999, 30) concluded: "The members of the nation's Forgotten Half failed to achieve any progress in obtaining access to full-time jobs with wages equal to our earnings adequacy standard between 1989 and 1997."

Since the 1960s, job training programs have targeted the disadvantaged and dislocated, seeking to increase their skills and help them find work. I propose that we expand the scope of job training policies to include programs such as the one, for example, that helps people who are severely disconnected from the labor market become involved in "meaningful activities" that at least help their children.

This chapter focuses on programs to help the disadvantaged increase their skills enough to gain access to full-time, well-paid employment. However, given the nature of today's economy, reliance on traditional job training efforts may not meet the needs of local employers. In addition, a job training approach that is too narrowly defined may be defeated by limitations of the individual's social and physical capital (Sampson 1999; Ferguson and Stoutland 1999), as well as by larger structural issues related to employer location and demands. The actions and attitudes of peers, neighborhoods, entire communities, and labor markets may negate individual gains in skills or discourage individuals from making investments in mainstream society.

To date, attempts to overcome the limitations of overly narrow human capital approaches have taken two forms. One recommends abandoning the strategy in favor of making preventive investments elsewhere (see Heckman and Lochner, this volume). A second encourages continued investments in job training policy, coupled with a search for ways to make its programs more effective at scale (Hollister 1989; Friedlander, Greenberg, and Robins 1997; LaLonde 1995).

This chapter first defines job training, then discusses the history of public job training programs and their legacy. It then considers the limits of traditional job training programs and how they could be expanded to account for structural, social, and physical barriers to employment and training. I also discuss recent programs that may help graduates of job training programs increase their wages enough to leave poverty. An example of this is the Center for Employment Training (CET). The next two sections review evaluation and replication issues, and the last summarizes the discussion and makes recommendations.

THE AMERICAN JOB TRAINING EXPERIENCE: A BRIEF BACKGROUND

What is job training? Where is the boundary separating job training from work and education? Does job training work? Who pays for job training, and does it serve the individual's interests? Does job training help the disadvantaged?

Job training has been formally defined as "coursework, either full- or part-time, in an occupational or technical field for the purpose of obtaining a vocational credential, such as a vocational certificate, occupational license, or other vocational diploma or degree" (Barnow and Aron 1989, 469). Between the two poles of informal training and formal coursework are myriad activities that can be characterized as "time away from work for purposes of training."

In 1996, private employers spent an estimated $300 billion on job training (Bassi and Van Buren 1999), including nearly $55 billion on formal efforts that sent workers to in-house programs and classrooms, nearby community colleges, or outside consultants and vendors (Bassi and Van Buren 1999). The average firm spent about $500 per person for formal courses, which were viewed as investments in those who showed promise, ability, commitment, or other desired qualities (Veum 1995). The remaining $240 billion was spent on informal, on-the-job training for new recruits (Bassi and Van Buren 1999). Employees also invest their own funds in training.

What happens when a third party, the government, pays for training and the trainees are disadvantaged? The federal government spent an estimated $130 billion on employment and training programs between 1967 and 1989 (Tom McInery, personal communication 1999). Daniel Friedlander, David Greenberg, and Philip Robins's (1997) estimate for annual spending in the 1990s ranged from $3.8 billion for direct spending on job training for the disadvantaged to $14 billion for training services more broadly defined.

John Bishop (1990) suggested that government training increased the productivity of some trainees. The standard assessment, however, is based on a question asked by Robinson Hollister, Peter Kemper, and Rebecca Maynard (1984): "What is the difference between participants' post-program earnings and the earnings they would have received had they not participated in training?" A recent evaluation of national training efforts concluded that job training programs for the disadvantaged have raised the earnings for adult men and women to some degree, but not for youth (Friedlander, Greenberg, and Robins 1997). However, it has been noted that training "makes economically disadvantaged persons less poor, but the gains are not sufficiently large to lift many out of poverty" (LaLonde 1995, 165).

Job Training: An Accidental Policy

Job training policy does not adequately serve the disadvantaged, in part because it was originally designed for a different population. Programs were first developed to resolve various crises, ranging from the reentry problems of returning World War I veterans to the difficulties encountered by workers made obsolete by automation.

Although some trace the policy's origin to the Merrill Land Grant College Act of 1862 (Stacey and Alsalam 1990), the first modern job training program was funded under the Vocation Rehabilitation Act of 1918. It provided training for returning World War I veterans as a onetime response to their employment crisis. Later, the Civilian Conservation Corps (CCC), funded in 1933 under Roosevelt's New Deal, included some on-the-job training for young men living in residential camps and working on public conservation projects.

The more sustained impulse to provide job training was a response to recessions and the presumed problem of automation. The first program to link job training policy to a recession was the 1961 Area Development Act. Under the assumption that the recession was an early sign of the consequences of automation, it funded loans to businesses in depressed areas and provided training for unemployed workers (LaLonde 1995).

The Kennedy administration responded to the fears and problems associated with the 1961 recession, which sent unemployment levels to 7 percent, by formulating the 1962 Manpower Development and Training Act (MDTA). Although economists debated whether high unemployment resulted from softness in demand or from the impact of automation, the strategy of equipping skilled workers—heads of families and "the backbone of the labor force"—with skills for new jobs carried the day.

By 1964, most of the skilled workers targeted by the program were back at work, many at their old jobs. One observer noted that in the process, "the MDTA discovered the hard-to-employ—a considerable number of poorly educated, low-skilled individuals with an erratic or no employment history" (Wahman 1999, 51). The program was then reorganized as an antipoverty tool. It created the Job Corps (serving 40,000 individuals in 1966), classroom training (140,000), on-the-job training (125,000), referrals to vocational and technical schools, and other services. From this period to the present, "hard-to-employ," economically disadvantaged workers have been the main target of public job training efforts.

During another recession, Congress added the 1971 Emergency Employment Act (EEA), funded with $2.2 billion to provide public service employment for the unemployed, including Vietnam War veterans. The Nixon administration replaced the EEA and the MDTA with the Comprehensive Employment and Training Act of 1973 (CETA), permanently changing job training policy. In keeping with the administration's interest in revenue sharing, it decentralized the programs by providing block grants to the states to operate CETA programs.

The Reagan administration abolished CETA and implemented the 1982 Job Training Partnership Act (JTPA). The president and Congress were not motivated by a recession but were responding to political pressures to end CETA job creation and the irregularities attributed to the program. The JTPA retained CETA's decentralized structure but abolished public employment, cut back funding for job training, and added services for the dislocated.

The JTPA included Title IIA (adults) and Title IIC (youth) (training services for the economically disadvantaged), Title IIB (summer employment and training for youth ages sixteen to twenty-one), Title III (training for dislocated workers), Title IVA (training for Native Americans and migrant and seasonal farm workers), Title IVB (the Job Corps), and Title IVC (veterans' training programs).

The major JTPA innovation was to make job training an employer-led partnership between government (federal, state, and local) and the private sector. Federal funding was based on each state's population of unemployed and disadvantaged. In turn, each state funded impoverished local areas, or service delivery areas, using the same formula. Employers were then given at least 51 percent of the seats on each service delivery area's grant-making body, called the private industry council (PIC). In theory, this arrangement ensured that programs would produce graduates who had skills that local employers wanted.

The JTPA funding formulas also tried to control program quality by setting performance standards for PICs. Those that exceeded standards received incentive funds, whereas a governor could reorganize a PIC that failed to perform adequately two years in a row.

In 1998, Congress reorganized job training programs and replaced JTPA with the Workforce Investment Act (WIA), which consolidates JTPA with the Perkins Vocational Training Act and more than sixty other programs. The WIA's main innovation is training vouchers, an idea developed by former Secretary of Labor Robert Reich. Workers receive vouchers and information about training providers in their area, and then shop for a job training program. The WIA, like all programs since the MDTA, assumes that job training is useful in fighting poverty.

Does a program originally developed to serve experienced workers displaced by automation provide enough resources to help the economically disadvantaged—who may or may not be ready to work—overcome many barriers to employment?

The Job Training Effort in Retrospect

Since the 1960s, there have been three constants in job training programs: their definitions of disadvantaged youth and adults; severe underfunding, given the size of the population that needs job training; and skills training that leaves most clients in poverty.

Those eligible for job training include welfare recipients or youth living in a welfare household; youth and adults who live in households in which family income has been below the poverty level for six months; individuals who receive food stamps; dislocated workers; foster children who are state wards; and adults with severe disabilities. JTPA programs for disadvantaged adults and youth (Titles IIA and IIC) served fewer than 1 percent of those who were eligible (see table 9.1). In 1996, the two programs provided services to (terminated) about 228,000 of the 41 million people who were eligible.[3] Among youth under twenty-one, the program mainly served high school dropouts.

Like its predecessors, the JTPA was severely underfunded, but it is unclear whether under funding was the sole reason the program was underutilized. It also may not have been attractive enough to secure a larger clientele. Sum and Fogg (1997) showed that funding for all employment and training programs in 1997 was about 25 percent of the amount (in constant dollars) provided in 1979. (They selected 1979 because it was a high point in employment and training funding.) The number of out-of-school youth has declined by 25 percent in the last seventeen years, but there were more economically disadvantaged, out-of-school young adults in 1995 and 1996 than there were in 1980. Moreover, black, Hispanic, and Asian youth make up a growing proportion of disadvantaged youth. The net effect of these two trends—decreasing

TABLE 9.1 / Title IIA (Disadvantaged Adults) and Title IIC (Youth): Program Eligibles and Program Participants (Terminees) Compared

Selected Characteristics	1993 JTPA Population	1996 JTPA Population
All eligibles	39,249,796	40,531,948
Sixteen to twenty-one	5,315,214	5,282,771
Twenty-two to fifty-four	23,469,083	24,449,805
Fifty-five and older	10,465,499	10,799,372
All terminees (IIA and IIC)	347,622	227,855
Adults (IIA)	180,178	151,155
Youth (IIC)	167,444	76,700

Sources: Bennici (1998); U.S. Department of Labor (1998).

funding and a growing population of disadvantaged—is that underinvestment in disadvantaged youth is increasing.

Approximately 30 percent of young adults who have left school are jobless. In 1995, Title II-C and Job Corps programs served fewer than 3 percent of jobless out-of-school youth (Sum and Fogg 1997).

The JTPA program had positive effects on the earnings of adult men and women, but the opposite impact on youth (Bloom et al. 1994; Bloom et al. 1997; Friedlander, Greenberg, and Robins 1997). The earnings of men increased by 10 percent and the earnings of women increased by 15 percent. Youth lost earnings ($171) (Council of Economic Advisers 2000; Friedlander, Greenberg, and Robins 1997). Where there were gains, they were too small to lift many participants out of poverty.

The Limits of Traditional Approaches to Job Training

A pure job training strategy should be ideal, not only for disadvantaged out-of-school youth and adults but for all noncollege youth and adults. Whether the problem is lack of financing, lack of interest or ability, or barriers to higher education, the one attribute shared by all noncollege youth is that they have ended their formal schooling. To secure skills for good jobs, job training would seem to be the correct approach.

Why does the effort not work better? The answer is that participants have more trouble in their lives than the programs could correct. Douglas Besharov (1999) found that perhaps 15 percent of young adults between eighteen and twenty-four were severely disconnected from mainstream society. They were so disconnected that during the six years after high school—the crucial period for investing in skills—they spent three years or more idle and unconnected to any mainstream institutions.

A recent study of the labor-market activities of a sample of welfare recipients demonstrates that they face multiple barriers to entry into the labor force, including: lack of a high school education: lack of work experience or relevant skills; perceptions of employer discrimination; lack of access to transportation; mental health problems; poor health (theirs or their children's); and severe domestic abuse (Danziger et al. 1999). Half of the sample reported transportation problems, one-third had low educational levels, one-quarter had mental health issues, one-fifth had physical problems, and about one in ten had perceived prior workforce discrimination. Almost all recipients (85 percent) had experienced at least one barrier to employment. Multiple barriers were common—37 percent experienced two or three barriers, 24 percent four to six barriers, and 18 percent seven or more barriers.

The chances that a woman would work twenty hours a week decreased significantly as the number of barriers increased. Women with no barriers had an 80 percent chance of working this much. With one barrier, this rate fell to 71 percent; with two to three, the rate dropped to 62 percent; with four to six barriers, the rate fell to 41 percent; and with seven or more barriers, it was only 6 percent.

This multiple barrier perspective suggests how job training practitioners might interpret the diversity in the disadvantaged and noncollege populations. When job training practitioners describe a client as "hardest to serve," or "not ready to work," we might imagine an individual who faces so many barriers that her employment prospects are low. When practitioners describe a client as "hard to serve," or "job-ready," we might imagine an individual who faces only a few barriers to work. When practitioners describe clients as "the working poor," we might imagine individuals who have already graduated from a job training program and are seeking to increase their wages, presumably without going to college. We might also want practitioners who serve clients along this spectrum of barriers to hand off clients to one another as their trainees increase their skills and reduce the number of barriers they face.

In reality, practitioners do use the language of "hardest to serve," but they also believe that counting barriers cannot account for intangible factors that give one client the resilience to overcome significant barriers and leave another unable to take advantage of significant opportunities. How practitioners take note of barriers and provide comprehensive frameworks that help their clients, and how they provide appropriate services, is discussed in the next section.

PROMISING JOB TRAINING ALTERNATIVES

This section focuses on a particularly comprehensive program, the Center for Employment Training (CET), which primarily works with hard-to-serve populations and addresses structural, social, and skills barriers to employment. No single job training program is so comprehensive that it can adequately address the needs of the hardest to serve while also helping the hard to serve and the working poor. Even the most comprehensive program provides some mechanism to screen for the subpopulation that can benefit most from its services.

Drawing on work by Edwin Melendez and Bennett Harrison (1998), the discussion is broken into three parts: the training program from the client's perspective, from a community perspective, and from an employer's perspective.

CET is a living archive of the major social movements, antipoverty efforts, job training innovations, and community development efforts of the last three decades. It has links to César Chávez and the grape-worker struggles of the 1960s and 1970s, Martin Luther King and the civil rights movement, the "liberation theology" of Catholic social reformers, the participatory community action approaches of the Community Action Program and the Model Cities program, the Peace Corps, and the community development corporations envisioned by Robert Kennedy.

Initially, the Center for Employment Training was the Santa Clara County arm of the Opportunities Industrial Center (OIC), a national program with roots in the civil rights movement. The OIC program was originally located in East Palo Alto, where it served a Mexican immigrant population unable to find full-time permanent jobs in Santa Clara County. In 1972, CET, or Centro de Entrenamiento para Trabajo, separated itself from its OIC parent and adopted a different training philosophy and program model. Recently it has expanded from San Jose, California, to the rest of the nation.

Training from the Client's Perspective

Job training programs offer services from a menu that includes various types of class-room training, subsidized on-the-job training and other work experience options, job search assistance, and other personal services, including financial support, child care, and counseling (see table 9.2). They differ in how they mix these services and the order in which they send trainees through them. Some structure program segments in linear blocks, while others operate more flexibly. They also differ in how long they extend program services and the populations in which they specialize.

TABLE 9.2   /   JTPA Services for Adult Trainees, 1993 to 1996

	1993	1994	1995	1996
Total terminees	180,178	175,647	162,120	151,155
Percentage who received and completed				
Any below	62	71	74	76
Basic skills training	14	17	18	17
Occupational skills training (not on-the-job)	40	45	49	52
On-the-job training	10	10	9	8
Work experience	3	4	5	5
Other skills training	7	9	10	11
Any two or more	10	13	15	15
Percentage receiving various support services				
Any below	51	55	52	48
Transportation	21	24	23	20
Health care	4	4	4	3
Housing or rental assistance	3	3	2	2
Personal counseling	29	31	27	24
Needs-based payments	14	15	14	11
Other	13	17	15	13
Areas of occupational training				
Managerial and administrative			1	1
Professional and technical			18	18
Clerical and administrative support			30	30
Service			21	21
Production and related			28	27

Sources: Bennici (1998); U.S. Department of Labor (1998).

The CET model combines these program elements with certain innovations:

1. The *integrated classroom* blends vocational training with counseling functions. The training is based on workplace simulations, with counseling delivered through workplace metaphors. The report card is a paycheck. Full pay is an "A." Absences and discipline problems reduce the grade and the pay. The job supervisor serves as a trainer, disciplinarian, counselor, and mentor who deals with work-related problems. Other more serious and personal problems are farmed out to other resource counselors.

2. CET also blends its simulated workplace and classroom through *contextual learning*. Basic skills, including English as a second language, are integrated into vocational training. Traditional programs teach math, reading, and other basic skills separately, away from the shop floor and with a separate staff.

3. CET fuses the classroom with the real workplace through the OIC innovation of primarily developing *job-relevant skills* that are valued by local employers.

4. Many traditional programs test applicants and select those likely to succeed in their program, then graduate enrollees within a standard, fixed period (Melendez 1996). CET admits applicants without testing—*open entry*—but its regimen quickly eliminates those who are not ready to work. The time to graduation is open-ended. Students move through the program at their own pace and graduate when both trainer and student believe the latter is prepared to accept a job offer. CET also offers continuing services to program graduates, who may return for additional training.

5. CET staffers form *quality circles*. Each staffer—the technical instructor, the counselor, the basic skills instructor, the support counselor, and the job developer—contributes to a learning plan tailored to each student. Such plans detail the resources each student will need and outline how the staff will inculcate workplace norms and soft skills such as correct dress and self-presentation.

CET is thus an innovator in its blending of job training components. Other nontraditional programs now incorporate similar efforts and add their own innovations tailored to the populations they serve. For example, America Works—a private, for-profit job placement and support agency in New York, Connecticut, and Indiana—specializes in "work first" training for welfare recipients. After a six-week job readiness course that stresses soft skills, trainees are handed over to placement counselors who find them full-time jobs while continuing to offer support services. The program pays wages and provides benefits to its graduates for four months, after which time employers have the option to hire them. In testimony to Congress in 1995, Ray Marshall reported that America Works places about 60 percent of its enrollees, of whom 68 percent are hired permanently by employers at an average earnings of $15,000 per year, including benefits.

Another New York City program, STRIVE, works with a ready-to-work clientele similar to that served by CET. They differ in that CET's first-generation immigrant clients are less likely to feel a deep opposition to mainstream society, since most of them left Mexico to find work and secure mainstream benefits. Many attributes of STRIVE's clients were captured in a monograph by Phillip Bourgois (1995), who noted that the language, demeanor, dress codes, and patterns of interpersonal relations that inner-city youth use for survival on the street constitute a barrier to employment. STRIVE operates a three-week attitudinal training course that uses "reality-testing" techniques pioneered in drug rehabilitation programs to help trainees overcome attitudinal and other barriers to the workplace. STRIVE's director, Rob Carmona, told a congressional committee that by 1995, New York City STRIVE had placed roughly eleven thousand individuals in jobs and had retained 76 percent of them in those jobs for at least two years.

A Chicago program, Project Match, began as a comprehensive Head Start program operating in the Cabrini-Green housing project (Herr and Halpern 1991, 1993; Herr, Wagner, and Halpern 1996). Like CET, it is an open-entry program, but its clients are the very hardest to serve. Its innovation is that it helps clients who are not ready to work find "meaningful activities," like volunteering for brief sessions at their child's day-care center. On the basis of these meaningful activities, the program helps its clients negotiate a complex, multistep ladder to jobs and attachment to mainstream society at their own pace. Many never progress far enough along the ladder to find steady employment. In a sample study of program outcomes, after three years about one-quarter had no employment, over one-third worked steadily, and the rest were at various levels of unsteady employment (see figure 9.1). The program's

FIGURE 9.1 / Project Match Sample Study: Longitudinal Outcomes

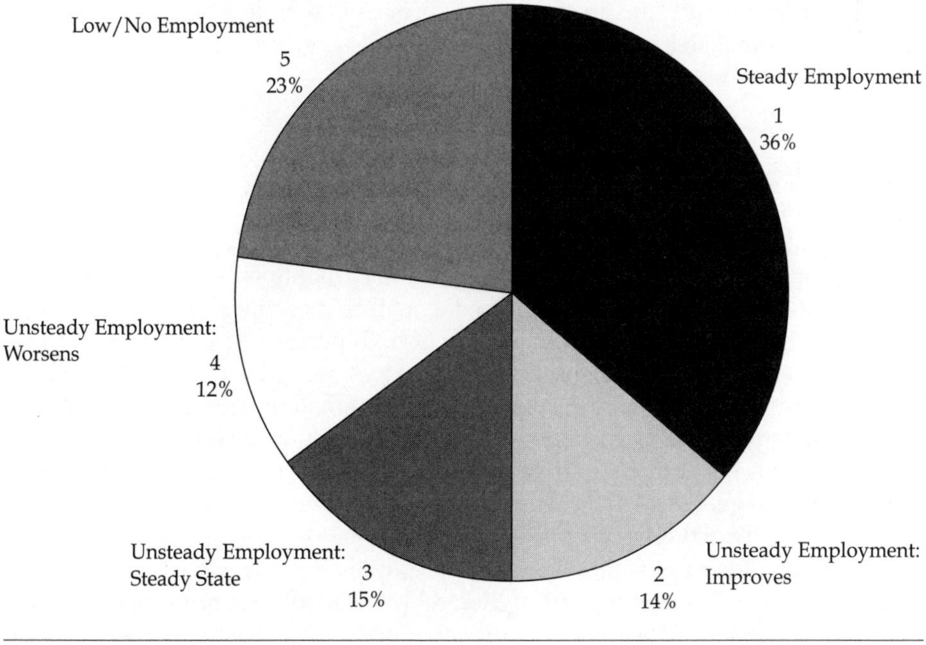

Low/No Employment
5
23%

Steady Employment
1
36%

Unsteady Employment:
Worsens
4
12%

Unsteady Employment:
Steady State
3
15%

Unsteady Employment:
2 Improves
14%

Source: Wagner et al. (1998).

director, Toby Herr, suggests that its "meaningful activities" strategy may prove useful as an alternative to welfare reform dilemmas over what to do for those who cannot work (Wagner et al. 1998). Giving credit for part-time or volunteer work would allow the hardest-to-serve to remain on welfare in an exempt category presently allowed by Congress; this option would not be available if the government chose instead either to do nothing or to provide public-sector jobs of last resort.

Training from the Community's Perspective

Melendez and Harrison (1998) observed that CET's long roots within social movements allowed it to become a trusted institution in its community; its effective community ties thus made the agency an able recruiter of labor.

Carol Stack (1974) suggested that poor people in communities like the one served by CET have to rely on extended families and a few strong friendships for resources that supplement their low incomes. According to Stack, the habits and mindsets that maintain "strong tie" fictive kinships between members of a community (the term is from Granovetter 1974) are, paradoxically, poor at helping those members find jobs and secure services from outside agencies. The main reason is that networks based on kin and a few close relationships are attenuated. It helps to have an uncle at the office. It helps even more to have an effective résumé that can be disseminated in a national job market.

CET is able to open up and extend the job search network of families that otherwise avoid "nonfamily" institutions. Other groups like Project Match and STRIVE also work to establish trust and then "open up" closed groups, gangs, families, and neighborhoods.

Training from the Employer's Perspective

In a study of Wisconsin's metalworking industry, Robert Howard (1991) found four training patterns. One group in the industry trained a highly skilled, high-wage labor force. Because they were large firms, they did not fear "poaching" from smaller firms that might have let them bear the expense of high-performance training, then recruited those workers at a slightly higher salary. A second group pursued a low-skilled, low-wage strategy. A third group was too small to have a choice about its training strategy but wanted a high-wage labor force and would have supported that industry practice. A fourth group of firms too small to operate autonomously preferred a low-wage, low-skilled workforce and would not support other industries investing heavily in workers.

This study illustrates some aspects of the employer perspective on the benefits and problems of job training. At higher skill levels, job training improves productivity and performance, but the costs are higher. Unless one firm is large relative to others, or a group of firms can share costs and manage their training investments, firms may be able to secure higher-skilled workers only by hiring college graduates.

Federally funded training programs could play a mediating role, solving these training dilemmas by taking on the costs of training in ways that solve the "poaching problem." In fact, the JTPA program included the employer-dominated private industry councils, which could at least provide a low-end version of such a training system. However, employers serving on the councils were usually a diverse group who saw themselves as trustees of public funds, not as organizers of a training cooperative. The Boston PIC was a well-known exception (Kopp, Goldberger, and Morales 1994).

CET and OIC are also exceptions. It was OIC philosophy to work with employers, survey their training needs, and provide trainees with skills that matched those needs. CET refines this structure and philosophy and carries it out more aggressively than its predecessor. It surveys employers and determines which skills are in high demand. It follows up its surveys with interviews of personnel managers and agencies within the regional market. With this information, it decides which employers will make good training partners. It then adds the new skills to its curriculum and trains workers in the skills that local employers are seeking. Its job developers maintain relations with firms and monitor their changing needs. This embeds CET within local employer culture, creating what Mark Granovetter (1974) termed the weak ties that give a job applicant who uses them the best chance of securing a job.

Recently, Marc Elliot (1998) at Public/Private Ventures and Jack Litzenberg at the Mott Foundation have elaborated on this idea of community-based training organizations in partnership with local employers. They termed the strategy "sectoral development": community-based partnerships that target an occupational niche within a local economy and provide high-grade trainees for those employers. Such programs closely calibrate their training practices to an employer's standards and needs. The benefit to trainees is that their long-term needs are also addressed by the duration of the partnership.

Job training programs that seek to operate sectoral programs must have the following capacities:

- They should be mission-driven—even low-level staff members should be able to tell outside interviewers about the program's mission and how they fit into it.
- They should see both the employer and the workers as their clients.
- They must be ready to change as the local labor market changes.
- They should train clients to meet industry-level performance standards and expectations.
- They should place clients in "good jobs" that lead to lower-middle- or middle-income wage levels.

When job training programs provide high-skills training for local employers, they may be able to help working poor youth and adults secure wage growth sufficient to move them out of poverty. One demonstration program, the Access, Supported Advancement, and Placement Program (ASAP) operated by STRIVE, has been able to do this. Initially the average participant earned approximately $12,000 per year. After two years, program graduates earned an average of $22,308 at a Boston site and $20,301 at a New York City site.

EVALUATIONS

When job training strategies are placed within frameworks that address structural, social, physical, and other noneducational barriers to work, the results can be an improvement over JTPA outcomes. CET, for example, has demonstrated a statistically significant, long-term impact on participant earnings and employability. The Office of the Chief Economist of the U.S. Department of Labor concluded that CET netted an increase in the early 1990s of about 33 percent beyond expectation in the annual earnings of out-of-school youth, whereas the comparable rate of return for Job Corps was about 15 percent (Melendez and Harrison 1998, 5). Job Corps costs more— $20,000 at that point per successful enrollee versus $7,000—and takes longer—one versus thirty weeks, but Job Corps is also a residential program with other attributes. It is rated strongly for its socialization effects, for example, temporarily removing youth from hig-crime areas (Melendez 1996).

Over two decades, evaluators have consistently found highly positive results. In his assessment of the Minority Female Single Parent Demonstration, Robinson Hollister (1990) reported that CET was the only site, out of four examined, that had positive results, increasing annual incomes of participants by $2,000. The MDRC's random assignment study of JOBSTART found that CET outperformed thirteen other programs for training criminal offenders and high school dropouts, giving them a $6,700 earnings increase within four years of placement (Melendez 1996).

A Department of Labor evaluation comparing the performances of all 105 OIC centers in the early 1970s found that CET scored highest in national ratings of retention and placement rates (Friedlander, Greenberg, and Robins 1997). Other evaluations in the 1980s found CET to be effective when working with hard-core unemployed, farmworker youth, and people with limited English skills.

Other community-based programs that place human capital strategies within frameworks that address attitudinal, social, and structural barriers—for example, STRIVE, Project Match, and ASAP—seem to have been as effective but have not yet been rigorously evaluated. As discussed later, a major requirement for moving the field to scale is useful evidence of what augmented job training programs can do.

REPLICATION

A major challenge for policymakers has been how to expand programs like CET, STRIVE, Project Match, and America Works and implement them on a national scale. So far, the evidence suggests that they cannot be replicated at scale.

Several factors are at work here. These model programs have all been developed by charismatic, highly motivated, even "visionary" leaders. Their home sites are well suited to their local communities. OIC addressed the needs of an African American inner-city community; CET met the needs of a Hispanic community; Project Match worked well in a Chicago housing project; STRIVE and America Works were neatly tailored to the situation in New York City. All had strongly motivated staffs.

Partly in response to the recommendations of the Commission on Workforce Quality and Labor Market Efficiency (1989), in 1992 the Department of Labor funded a replication of CET in fifteen sites to determine whether the program retained its effectiveness while working with different populations. Early process evaluations by Mathematica Policy Research (Hershey and Rosenberg 1994) and Melendez (1996) concluded that, at least initially, all program sites failed to replicate the original CET model.

Melendez (1996) traced the problem to two factors: new clients and new hosts. The program is not as effective when it serves a different, heavily welfare-based population. As Melendez noted:

> Previously, despite the mix of hard-to-serve trainees, former farm workers constituted the dominant group in many classrooms at any given time. Whether on some type of public assistance or not, most participants decided on their own to enroll in the training. Many of them had some prior work experience. The present replication context is very different. More than before, participants with little work experience, and many who are mandated by law to enroll in training, share classrooms with others who also have had little work experience. This is the case in most East Coast CET sites.

The program is also not as effective when PICs start and operate new sites. As noted earlier, Melendez and Harrison (1998) believe that the program's links to indigenous community groups is an important factor in its effectiveness. The program's early expansion in the 1970s was accomplished in a "bottom-up" fashion, whereas the replication sponsored by the Department of Labor in the 1990s was mostly a "top-down" affair. The result was that more poorly structured versions of the program served a more difficult clientele.

Most replicated sites did not have established relationships with community-based organizations that were capable of establishing the community trust discussed earlier. Most sites had weak links to employers and did not use their skills surveys to recruit employers. Most sites did not implement all of the training model—open access, contextual learning, and so on. Most sites run by independent operators were not confident that a CET model would work in their locales and reduced the model to "a mere collection of techniques for providing training 'services'" (Melendez 1996, 59). Most sites did not offer a menu of skills large enough to allow trainees to make adjustments if they became unhappy with their initial choices.

Despite these concerns, Melendez (1996) found evidence that the sites that were more faithful to the CET model included key personnel who were directly accountable to the central office in San Jose. This early evaluation of the CET replication reinforces the idea that job training is an "art" dependent on unique personalities and local community attributes. Another interpretation, however, is that the replication resembled the JTPA experience because the effort used the JTPA replication model.

JTPA, like most block grant programs, achieves its goals through funding formulas, contracts, and rules. This is a loose control model, useful when programming goals are simple and broad and faithful compliance is not a priority. When the program or demonstration seeks adherence to a well-specified model, this replication strategy gives local sites so much autonomy that there is little chance that the program model will be tested (Pouncy and Hollister 1997). CET's experiences demonstrate this point. In 1995 CET received 60 percent of its funding from categorical JTPA grants, but its program model violated most JTPA norms (for example, by including open-ended training periods and open entry). CET defeated categorical restrictions (funds for targeted populations) by securing agreements with JTPA to report program spending as contributions toward student "tuition."

Programs like CET may also replicate themselves by establishing branch programs under the direct supervision of a home office or by licensed agreements with independent sites that give the home office the power to review such sites and determine whether they are complying with the model. CET did replicate itself in just this fashion throughout the 1970s and 1980s. The program was able to achieve significant compliance in part because new sites usually hired personnel from the central office, creating administrative networks of friendship and trust.

The lesson to be drawn from these replication efforts is that, to be successful, programs like CET, Project Match, and STRIVE primarily need to replicate the trust they have established among staff, clients, communities, and employers. Recent work (Bryk et al. 1998; Ferguson et al. 1996) points to tools that may help programs evaluate their success in doing so.

Future replication efforts might test for variations in the leadership and composition of local workforce development boards (the PIC equivalents in the Workforce Investment Act). What might happen, for example, if such boards operated under the leadership of sectoral development programs?

TOWARD MORE FRUITFUL INVESTMENTS IN THE DISADVANTAGED

Over the last thirty-five years, the traditional job training approach, originally developed for an active but temporarily unemployed workforce, has become the tool of choice for the low-skilled, economically disadvantaged population that is the main target of today's workforce development activities.

Paradoxically, despite a tight economy, the need for these programs has increased at the same time that their funding and support have eroded. In the last twenty years, the number of out-of-school, disadvantaged youth has grown, as have the ranks of the working poor. Moreover, the 1996 welfare reform has increased the demand for mandatory job training programs.

Most evaluations concur that standard, federally funded job training programs have had modest success for adult women. The recent experimental evaluation of

JTPA suggests that the programs also work well for adult men. With the exception of Job Corps, however, there is little evidence that the programs work well for youth (ages sixteen to twenty-one).

Taken together, these evaluations also suggest that the primary question about traditional job training strategies should not be whether the approach works or does not work. Rather, we should be asking: When does job training work best? For whom does it work best, and in what context? What goals should it serve?

Evaluations of mandatory welfare-to-work programs suggest that "work first" works better. Classroom skills can be added after program participants have attained some work experience. As the CET effort suggests, however, when the target population consists of disadvantaged people who are not yet ready to work, it is better to offer classroom skills and vocational training up front. The CET experience suggests that job training works best when structural, social, physical, and other barriers to training and employment have been addressed.

A broad range of job training options should be made available to all noncollege youth (ages eighteen to twenty-four) who want to pursue them. Access for the disconnected and hardest-to-serve through programs like Project Match should be increased. Efforts to provide wage growth for the working poor should be a priority through strategies like sectoral development and ASAP.

The U.S. postsecondary educational system is sometimes rated as one of the best in the world. In contrast, the U.S. primary and secondary educational systems routinely score low in national comparative tests. If American youth secure a college degree or higher, they are likely to be well trained even by global standards, but if they end their formal schooling with high school, they run a high risk of being poorly trained.

In considering the problem of noncollege youth, an increasing number of researchers and practitioners now believe that a concatenated job training system may offer the best choice. Such a system would provide access for those facing many barriers to work and mainstream society, leading them all the way through to the high skills training with which they can obtain the high wages needed to move them out of poverty.

NOTES

1. See especially the chapter by Jack Jennings and Diane Stark Rentner, "Youth and School Reform: From the Forgotten Half to the Forgotten Third."

2. Andrew Sum and Neal Fogg (1999) redefine "discouragement" to apply to youth who did not work during the week of the survey but wanted to work. Their definition yields a "discouraged" population ten times larger than the Bureau of Labor Statistics count. They define "working poverty" as the poverty line for a four-person family. In 1996 that would have been $16,036, or $309 per week.

3. "Terminees" refers to program participants. "Terminated" refers to program participants who completed the program.

REFERENCES

Bane, Mary Jo, and David Ellwood. 1994. *Welfare Realities: From Rhetoric to Reform*. Cambridge, Mass.: Harvard University Press.

Barnow, Buer S., and Laurence Y. Aron. 1989. "Survey of Government-Provided Training Programs." In *Investing in People: A Strategy to Address America's Workforce Crisis*, vol. 1. Washington, D.C.: U.S. Department of Labor, Commission on Workforce Quality and Labor Market Efficiency.

Barron, John M., Mark C. Berger, and Dan A. Black. 1997. "How Well Do We Measure Training?" *Journal of Labor Economics* 15(3): 507–28.

Barron, John Mark, and Dan A. Black. 1997. *On the Job Training*. Kalamazoo, Mich.: W. E. Upjohn Foundation.

Bassi, Laurie J., and Mark E. Van Buren. 1999. "Sharpening the Leading Edge." *Training and Development* 53(1): 23–33.

Bennici, Frank. 1998. "Estimation of JTPA Title IIA and IIC Eligible Populations." Memorandum prepared by the Westat Research Corporation for the U.S. Department of Labor.

Besharov, Douglas J. 1999. *America's Disconnected Youth: Toward a Preventive Strategy*. Washington, D.C.: Child Welfare League of America.

Bishop, John H. 1990. "Job Performance, Turnover, and Wage Growth." *Journal of Labor Economics* 8(3): 363–86.

Bloom, Howard, Larry L. Orr, Steve H. Bell, George Cave, Fred Doolittle, Winston Lin, and Johannas M. Bos. 1997. "The Benefits and Costs of JTPA Title II-A Programs: Key Findings from the National Job Training Partnership Act Study." *Journal of Human Resources* 32(3): 549–76.

Bloom, Howard, Larry L. Orr, George Cave, Steve H. Bell, Fred Doolittle, and Winston Lin. 1994. "The National JTPA Study—Overview: Impacts, Benefits, and Costs of Title II-A." Report to the U.S. Department of Labor.

Bourgois, Phillip. 1995. *In Search of Respect: Selling Crack in El Barrio*. New York: Cambridge University Press.

Bryk, Anthony, Penny B. Sebring, David Kerbow, Sharon Rollow, and John Q. Easton. 1998. *Charting Chicago School Reform: Democratic Localism as a Lever for Change*. Boulder, Colo.: Westview Press.

Commission on Workforce Quality and Labor Market Efficiency. 1989. *Investing in People: A Strategy to Address America's Workforce Crisis*. Background papers. 2 vols. Washington: U.S. Department of Labor, Commission on Workforce Quality and Labor Market Efficiency.

Council of Economic Advisers. 2000. *Economic Report of the President*. Washington: U.S. Government Printing Office.

Danziger, Sandra, Mary Corcoran, Sheldon Danziger, Coleen Heflin, Ariel Kalil, Judith Levine, Daniel Rosen, Kristin Seefeldt, Kristine Siefert, and Richard Tolman. 1999. "Barriers to the Employment of Welfare Recipients." Paper prepared for the Poverty Research and Training Center, University of Michigan. Retrieved from the world wide web: http://www.ssw.umich.edu.

Elliot, Marc. 1998. "Working Ventures: An Initiative to Improve the Workforce Development Field." Working paper. Philadelphia: Public/Private Ventures.

Ferguson, Ronald F., Phillip L. Clay, Jason C. Snipes, and Phoebe Roaf. 1996. *YouthBuild in Developmental Perspective: A Formative Evaluation of the YouthBuild Demonstration Project*. Cambridge, Mass.: Department of Urban Studies and Planning, Massachusetts Institute of Technology.

Ferguson, Ronald F., and William T. Dickens. 1999. *Urban Problems and Community Development*. Washington, D.C.: Brookings Institution.

Ferguson, Ronald F., and Sara E. Stoutland. 1999. "Reconceiving the Community Development Field." In *Urban Problems and Community Development*, edited by Ronald F. Ferguson and William T. Dickens. Washington, D.C.: Brookings Institution.

Freeman, Richard B., and William M. Rodgers III. 1999. "Area Economic Conditions and the Labor Market Outcomes of Young Men in the 1990s Expansion." Unpublished paper cited with permission of the authors.

Friedlander, Daniel, David H. Greenberg, and Philip K. Robins. 1997. "Evaluating Government Training Programs for the Economically Disadvantaged." *Journal of Economic Literature* 35(4): 1809–55.

Granovetter, Mark. 1974. *Getting a Job: A Study of Contacts and Careers.* Chicago: University of Chicago Press.

Halperin, Samuel. 1998. *The Forgotten Half Revisited: American Youth and Young Families, 1988–2008.* Washington, D.C.: American Youth Policy Forum.

Herr, Toby, and Robert Halpern, with A. Conrad. 1991. "Changing What Counts: Rethinking the Journey Out of Welfare." Working paper. Chicago: Project Match.

Herr, Toby, and Robert Halpern, with Ria Majeske. 1993. "Bridging the Worlds of Head Start and Welfare-to-Work." Working paper. Chicago: Project Match.

Herr, Toby, Suzanne L. Wagner, and Robert Halpern. 1996. "Making the Shoe Fit: Creating a Work-Prep System for a Large and Diverse Welfare Population." Working paper. Chicago: Project Match.

Hershey, Alan, and Linda Rosenberg. 1994. "The Study of the Replication of the CET Job Training Model." Washington, D.C.: Mathematica Policy Research.

Hollister, Robinson G. 1989. "Black Male Youth: Their Employment Problems and Training Programs." In *Investing in People: A Strategy to Address America's Workforce Crisis,* vol. 1. Philadelphia: Commission on Workforce Quality and Labor Market Efficiency.

———. 1990. *The Minority Female Single Parent Demonstration: New Evidence About Effective Training Strategies.* New York: Rockefeller Foundation.

Hollister, Robinson G., Peter Kemper, and Rebecca Maynard, eds. 1984. *The National Supported Work Demonstration.* Madison: University of Wisconsin Press.

Howard, Robert. 1991. "New Training Strategies for a High-Performance Metalworking Industry." Technical report prepared for Jobs for the Future, Cambridge, Mass.

Kopp, Hillary, Susan Goldberger, and Dionisia Morales. 1994. "The Evaluation of a Youth Apprenticeship Model: A Second Year Evaluation of Boston's ProTech." Technical report. Boston: Jobs for the Future (March).

Krueger, Alan, and Cecilia Rouse. 1998. "The Effect of Workplace Education on Earnings, Turnover, and Job Performance." *Journal of Labor Economics* 16(1): 61–94.

LaLonde, Robert J. 1995. "The Promise of Public Sector-Sponsored Training Programs." *Journal of Economic Perspectives* 9(2): 149–68.

Melendez, Edwin. 1996. "Working for Jobs: The Center for Employment Training." Boston: Mauricio Gaston Institute for Latino Community Development and Public Policy.

Melendez, Edwin, and Bennett Harrison. 1998. "Matching the Disadvantaged to Job Opportunities: Structural Explanations for the Past Successes of the Center for Employment Training." *Economic Development Quarterly* 12(1): 3–11.

Mincy, Ronald B., and Hillard Pouncy. 1997. "Paternalism, Child Support Enforcement, and Fragile Families." In *The New Paternalism*, edited by Lawrence M. Mead. Washington, D.C.: Brookings Institution.

Pouncy, Hillard, and Robinson G. Hollister. 1997. "Net Impact Evaluation of School-to-Work: Contending Expectations." In *Evaluating the Net Impact of School-to-Work: Proceedings of a Roundtable.* Washington, D.C.: Employment and Training Administration, U.S. Department of Labor.

Sampson, Robert J. 1999. "What 'Community' Supplies." In *Urban Problems and Community Development,* edited by Ronald Ferguson and William T. Dickens. Washington, D.C.: Brookings Institution.

Stacey, Nevzer, and Nabell Alsalam. 1990. "Employer Training of Work-Bound Youth: An Historical Review and New Results." In *Investing in People: A Strategy to Address America's Workforce Crisis,* vol. 2. Washington, D.C.: U.S. Department of Labor, Commission on Workforce Quality and Labor Market Efficiency.

Stack, Carol. 1974. *All Our Kin: Strategies for Survival in a Black Community.* New York: Harper and Row.

Sum, Andrew, and Neal Fogg. 1997. "Trends in Funding for Youth Employment and Training Programs: Real Dollar Obligations for U.S. Department of Labor Employment and Training Programs for Youth, 1979–1997." Paper prepared for the Sar Levitan Center on Social Policy Studies, Johns Hopkins University, Baltimore.

Sum, Andrew, and Neal Fogg, with Sheila Palma, Neem Fogg, and P. Suozzo. 1999. "Labor Market Conditions Among Out-of-School Youth in the U.S.: The Problems of At-Risk Youth in the 1990s." Paper prepared for the "Best Practices Workshop on School-to-Work Transitions in APEC-Member Economies."

U.S. Department of Labor. 1998. "Job Training Partnership Act: 1996 Program Statistics." Washington, D.C.: Office of Policy and Research, Employment and Training Administration.

Veum, Jonathan R. 1995. "Sources of Training and Their Impact on Wages." *Industrial and Labor Relations Review* 48(4): 812–26.

Wagner, Suzanne L., Toby Herr, Charles Chang, and Diana Brooks. 1998. *Five Years of Welfare: Too Long? Too Short? Lessons from Project Match's Longitudinal Tracking Data.* Monograph. Chicago: Erikson Institute.

Wahman, Thomas W. 1999. "The Current State of Poverty in the U.S." Report to the Mott Foundation Poverty Team.

William T. Grant Foundation. 1988. *The Forgotten Half: Non-College Youth in America.* Washington, D.C.: William T. Grant Commission on Work, Family, and Citizenship.

Chapter 10

Who Is Getting a College Education? Family Background and the Growing Gaps in Enrollment

David T. Ellwood and Thomas J. Kane

Although social scientists and policymakers have spent much of the last decade documenting and diagnosing the dramatic rise in the labor-market importance of education since 1980, they have devoted relatively little time to understanding its ramifications for other social phenomena, such as student financial aid policy and intergenerational mobility. Have the rising returns to education led to increased college-going by students from all backgrounds? Has the growing inequality been mirrored by a growing inequality in college enrollment, depending on family background? This chapter examines these questions, reporting on differences in college-going by family income and parental education and asking how these gaps have changed over time.

We come to three conclusions. First, although differences in academic preparation account for much of the difference by family background, very large gaps remain in college-going by students from high- and low-income parents and from high- and low-education parents. Youth who appear to be similarly prepared academically when emerging from high school enroll in college at very different rates depending on their parents' income and education.

Second, the role of family background in determining postsecondary training choices seems to have increased over time. As the payoff to education has increased, a larger share of the high-income youth have enjoyed the added advantage of having more educated parents. In other words, college enrollment rates have risen at the top income quartile not only because family income itself has become a more important predictor of who goes to college, but because differences in average parental education for those in the top and bottom income quartiles have widened as well. Both factors have contributed to the widening of income gaps.

Third, the fact that equally prepared youth go to higher education at different rates seems to make a difference of between 5 and 10 percent in additional earnings later in life for students from more advantaged backgrounds. All else equal, any increase in the payoff to educational attainment is likely to increase the gap in expected earnings for high- and low-income youth.

TRENDS IN COLLEGE RETURNS AND ENROLLMENT

The old adage "To get a good job, get a good education," is more true today than at any time in a generation. Figure 10.1 portrays the trend in earnings differences by educational attainment for men and women ages twenty-five to thirty-four, working full-time, year-round, since 1967. The figure shows, in percentage terms, how much more college graduates earned than high school graduates did. During the late 1960s and early 1970s, the college premium actually fell for both men and women—prompting our colleague Richard Freeman (1976) to lament the plight of *The Overeducated American*. However, after 1978 the earnings difference associated with a college degree rose dramatically and has remained high. Whereas male college graduates in this age range were earning roughly 15 percent more per year in the late 1970s, they earn nearly 50 percent more today. The differential for women rose from 20 percent to nearly 60 percent.

One would have expected college enrollment to move in tandem with returns to schooling if young people were responding to perceived economic rewards. And indeed, the trend in male college enrollment has closely matched the rise and fall in the payoff to college. Figure 10.2 shows that male college enrollment fell during the early 1970s, as the payoff to college was falling, and began rising again when the college wage premium rebounded in the late 1970s.[1]

FIGURE 10.1   /   Premium for College Graduates Versus High School Graduates
                      Working Full-Time, Year-Round, Ages Twenty-Five to Thirty-Four

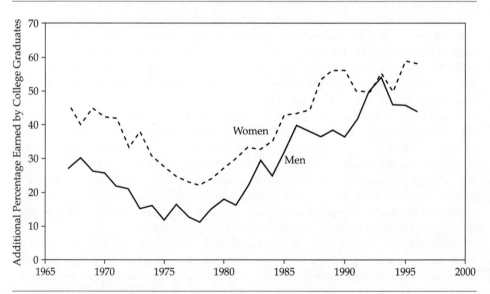

Source: Authors' tabulation of Annual March Current Population Survey data.

FIGURE 10.2 / Men and Women Ages Eighteen to Twenty-Four Enrolled in College, 1967 to 1996

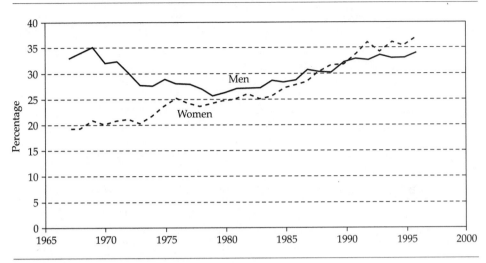

Source: Internet site of U.S. Bureau of the Census, "School Enrollment, Historical Tables," table A-5 (released August 1998)

For women, enrollments have risen throughout the period, even when the payoff to college appeared to be falling. However, the decline in the wage premium among women in the labor force simply masked a more profound change in the value of college investments for women. More opportunities for work outside the home may have offered young women who would otherwise have been at home new opportunities to reap the rewards of a college education. Therefore, despite the fact that the college earnings premium was declining for those women who were already employed, more young women could probably expect to enjoy rewarding careers. Consistent with the trends for men, the rise in college enrollment seems to have accelerated somewhat in the period after 1980, as the college wage premium rose.

Many of those on the margin, whose behavior is likely to be affected by student financial aid policy, are likely to leave school without completing a degree. However, as summarized by Thomas Kane and Cecilia Rouse (1999), the empirical literature suggests that even those who do not complete degrees earn approximately 5 to 7 percent more per year's worth of college credit, whether they attend a two- or four-year college.

In this chapter, we are primarily concerned with the pattern of college enrollment by parental income and how that pattern has been changing over time. Table 10.1, drawn from the High School and Beyond (HSB) survey of the high school classes of 1980 and 1982 and the National Education Longitudinal Study of the class graduating in 1992 (described in more detail later), shows the proportion of high school students in the early 1980s and the early 1990s who enrolled in various forms of postsecondary education in the first twenty months after the spring of their

TABLE 10.1 / Proportion of Students in the Classes of 1980/1982 and 1992 Enrolled in Postsecondary Schools Within Twenty Months of Graduation, by Type of School and Family Income

	None	Vocational Training, Other	Two-Year (Junior) College	Four-Year College
Classes of 1980 and 1982				
Lowest income quartile	43%	12%	16%	29%
Second income quartile	37	11	19	33
Third income quartile	28	10	22	39
Highest income quartile	19	6	19	55
Overall average	32	10	19	39
Class of 1992				
Lowest income quartile	40	10	22	28
Second income quartile	30	7	25	38
Third income quartile	20	6	25	48
Highest income quartile	10	5	19	66
Overall Average	25	7	23	45

Source: Based on authors' tabulation of 10,215 observations from the 1988 NELS.

senior year. (In table 10.1, sample members are categorized by the parental family income quartile.)

Among high school seniors graduating in 1992, roughly 40 percent of students from families in the lowest quartile attended no postsecondary school at all during the twenty-month period observed here, and only 28 percent attended a four-year school within the first twenty months.[2] By contrast, only 10 percent of students from families in the highest quartile failed to pursue education after high school. Moreover, two-thirds (66 percent) of youth in the top quartile went on to attend a four-year college. Among those with parental income in the top 10 percent, virtually everyone attends more school, and roughly 80 percent enter a four-year college.

Equally striking are the changes since the early 1980s. Enrollment has risen overall, with the fraction forgoing postsecondary training falling from 32 percent to 25 percent. The rise in four-year college enrollment was particularly dramatic, but the increase was distributed very unequally. The response was most sluggish for those from the lowest parental family income quartile. The fraction of students from the first parental income quartile not going on for postsecondary education fell only from 43 percent to 40 percent, and the enrollment rate in four-year schools actually fell slightly. By contrast, the proportion of youth in the top income quartile enrolling in four-year schools rose from 55 percent to 66 percent.

Although the differences in college-going by race and by gender are also intriguing, there are at least two reasons to focus on the role of family income differences. First, the government, both state and federal, heavily subsidizes the costs of postsecondary training with the stated goal of opening the doors to college to those with different resources. Our purpose in this chapter is to sort out differences in college enrollment by family income, attempting to take account of differences in academic preparation as well as other characteristics, such as parental education, as youth emerge from high school. Although such evidence is only suggestive, identifying any differences in college-going among those with similar academic preparation is the right place to start in assessing the potential importance of financial constraints.

A second reason to focus on differences in college-going by high- and low-income youth is the heightened reward provided by the labor market. The dramatic rise in the payoff to college has raised the stakes involved in the college entry decision. All else equal, a rise in the payoff to schooling would have exacerbated any gap in the earnings prospects of youth from high- and low-income families associated with differences in schooling. Therefore, differences in college entry by family income provide a leading indicator of the role of parental background in determining children's economic prospects.

We first briefly describe our empirical strategy and some of the limitations of our data. We then present the evidence on gaps in college-going by family income and parental education, decomposing such differences into the indirect effects of differences in high school grades and academic test scores and the apparently direct effects of family background. We then evaluate how college-going behavior changed between 1980/1982 and 1992. The final section weighs the importance of these differences in educational attainment for subsequent differences in income by family background.

EMPIRICAL STRATEGY

We are particularly interested in evaluating the role that family background has played in influencing enrollment decisions. Our goal is to understand both the cross-section and time-series patterns we see in table 10.1. A number of others, such as Charles Manski and David Wise (1983), Robert Haveman and Barbara Wolfe (1994), Michael McPherson and Morton Owen Schapiro (1991a), Stephen Cameron and James Heckman (1997), and Cecilia Rouse (1994), have studied the determinants of college-going for particular cohorts of youth. However, surprisingly little has been done to examine changes in the determinants of college entry over time, because there are surprisingly few surveys that collect information on college-going, parental income, achievement scores, and performance in high school over multiple time periods. Although Robert Hauser (1993) and Thomas Kane (1994, 1995) have used data from the October Current Population Survey (CPS) to track changes in college-going by family income and race over time, such data suffer from a number of limitations.[3] For instance, the October CPS does not include test scores. Moreover, the CPS fails to measure parental income for the many students who form their own households.[4]

Our strategy is to look first at the impact of various factors on the enrollment decisions of a cross-section of high school seniors from 1992, using the National Education Longitudinal Study (NELS) of a sample of eighth-grade students in 1988. Then we compare the patterns to those observed in the early 1980s using the HSB survey. Both surveys begin with a sample of students within a stratified sample of schools, collecting detailed information on the student, the student's parents (through a separate questionnaire to the parents), and the school. The surveys are longitudinal, collecting information from them while they are in school and then tracking their behavior in subsequent years.

The HSB survey began with a sample of students who were seniors and sophomores in 1980—cohorts that would have graduated in 1980 and 1982, respectively. The NELS sampled persons who were eighth-grade students in 1988 and thus became seniors in 1992. Both cohorts of students were then tracked over time. The most recent available follow-up for the NELS sample was conducted two years after high school. Therefore, to be consistent, we study the proportion of youth reporting any postsecondary education (including public and private vocational training and two- and four-year colleges) as well as enrollment in four-year colleges during the first twenty months after graduation.[5]

Key Variables

RATE OF RETURN TO SCHOOLING   In a pure cross-section regression of the sort we are doing, it is very difficult to identify the impact of differences in the financial rate of return to schooling. If students look nationally at the returns for all persons, then the perceived return does not vary in any given year. At the other extreme, if students tend to look only at the returns for people with similar demographic (racial, gender, ethnic) characteristics who live nearby, it is virtually impossible to measure the returns reliably. Thus, we have not included any direct measures of returns to schooling in our cross-section models.

ABILITY AND ACHIEVEMENT IN HIGH SCHOOL   Although labor economists often fail to find larger returns to education for those with high test scores, conventional wisdom suggests that youth who are better prepared academically gain more from postsecondary education.[6] The difficult-to-measure intellectual exertion costs required to succeed in higher education may very well be lower for those with stronger academic skills. We certainly observe that youth with higher test scores are much more likely to attend college.

The measurement of ability and achievement in high school is relatively easy in these data. In each year, a battery of tests was administered to students in their senior year. Unfortunately, the testing methodologies used in creating these tests for the HSB and the NELS were different enough that they are not comparable across years.[7] Although we use test scores to attempt to control for differences in academic preparation in a given survey, we cannot readily compare any results from the different years when test scores are included. When we compare results across years we do not include test scores.

Test scores are often used to capture achievement and ability. A second measure of achievement is high school grades. All three cohorts of students were asked to report their own high school grades. For the 1982 and 1992 cohorts, we also have actual high school transcript data. Since the transcript-reported grades and the self-reported measures were strongly correlated ($\rho = .8$) for those students for whom we had both, we used the self-reported grades for all three years.[8]

When we control for test scores and examine the remaining impact of parental resources, a couple of caveats are in order. First, much of the impact of income and parental resources may be mediated through access to better schools, more challenging teachers, and better school resources. Indeed, we would expect that low-income parents' inability to make investments in the education of their children during their development from infancy through grade twelve would be reflected in student test scores. However, since our goal is simply to identify the importance of parental financial constraints at the threshold to college, this is not a primary concern. Potentially more problematic is the fact that test scores and grades at the time of high school graduation in part reflect students' efforts in preparation for college. To the extent that children from more poorly situated families realize that they are unlikely to go to college and therefore do not work as hard in primary and secondary school to prepare for college, lower scores and grades may actually be capturing some of the effects of parental resources on later college enrollment, obscuring the true impact of parental resources. For this reason, our estimates of the impact of family income after "controlling for" test scores and grades may be thought of as a lower bound on the effects of income on college-going.

COLLEGE COSTS We supplemented the HSB and NELS data with information on the average tuition at public two-year and four-year colleges and need-based grant spending per person ages fifteen to twenty-four by state and year.[9] In 1992 the average tuition and required fees charged at public two-year state institutions ranged from less than $250 in California to more than $2,000 in Indiana, New York, Massachusetts, and Vermont. Four-year state college and university costs ranged from $1,300 in New Mexico to nearly $3,000 in Virginia and Vermont. In addition, several high-tuition states, such as Vermont, fund grant programs for low-income students. We might expect these programs to have somewhat offsetting effects.

Although we are not accounting for the full array of financial aid programs available for college students, state differences in tuition and state grant programs account for much of the variation in such costs that is independent of family background characteristics. For instance, the federal Pell Grant program provides grant aid to low-income students, but such aid is usually determined by the student's family income and assets and typically is not a function of the tuition charged.[10] Since this federal program is available to all students in the country, such variation is not helpful in evaluating the responsiveness of student decisions to differences in college costs in the cross-section.

Differences in state tuition charges represent the primary source of (hypothetically exogenous) variation in college costs. Although not everyone attends the public institutions in their state, it is presumably the cost of tuition at the public two-year or four-year college in their state that represents the relevant price for those on the margin of college attendance.[11]

PARENTAL INCOME Although to many observers the idea that parental income could have a significant effect on enrollment choices may seem obvious, economists emphasize that schooling is in part a long-term investment decision that ought to depend chiefly on the costs and benefits of the investment. The costs include both tuition and forgone earnings while in school; the benefits include the gain in earnings. With perfect capital markets, long-term investment decisions should not be much affected by the current financial circumstances of the parents.

Yet economists have long recognized that private capital markets are likely to underinvest in human capital, because students are barred from offering their future earnings as collateral to private lenders. To borrow Gary Becker's (1993, 93) phrase, "Courts have frowned on contracts that even indirectly suggest involuntary servitude." Without collateral, even those students with promising careers may have difficulty obtaining private financing. Although high-income youth may be able to secure financing from their parents, low-income youth may not enjoy such alternative sources of capital.

To remedy this problem, governments have used a variety of mechanisms—including direct subsidies to institutions, means-tested voucher programs for low-income students, and federally guaranteed loan programs—for providing the necessary financing to students and families when it comes time to invest in college. For instance, the federal government provides approximately $6 billion per year in means-tested grant aid to low-income college students through the Pell Grant program and approximately $30 billion per year in federally guaranteed educational loans.[12] State and local governments provide approximately $44 billion per annum in appropriations and unrestricted grants to public institutions to keep tuition low at public institutions, and approximately $3 billion in means-tested grant aid. In addition, Congress recently approved a number of new tax expenditures for higher education.

However, families and students could still face credit constraints for at least two reasons. First, borrowing under the federal student loan programs has always been subject to annual limits. For instance, between 1976 and 1985, the annual borrowing limit for a student was fixed in nominal dollars at $2,500, despite substantial rises in both the real and nominal tuition levels over the period. Since 1992, the most a student could borrow under the Stafford loan program has been $2,625 during the freshman year, $3,500 during the sophomore year, and $5,500 per year thereafter. Independent students (those who are married, have dependents, are veterans, or are over age twenty-four) can borrow an additional $4,000 per year during their first two years and an additional $5,000 per year thereafter. During the 1992 to 1993 school year, more than one-third of borrowers were stacked up at either $2,625 or $4,000 (Kane 1998a).

Such aid programs are designed primarily to finance the direct costs of college—namely, tuition and other educational expenses. But the real costs of college are much larger: students are also forgoing wages they would otherwise have earned if they had not enrolled in college. For instance, the average income of an eighteen- to twenty-four-year-old male high school graduate working full-time, year-round, in 1992 was $16,900. Such individuals who enroll in school full-time for nine months instead forgo earnings of $12,675—an amount that greatly exceeds the tuition costs at the average public two-year or four-year college and far exceeds the limits on state and federal aid.

Of course, many students do not choose to attend school full-time—they mix work with school. However, it is still useful to think of the earnings of full-time workers as representing the price of a "full unit" of schooling—just as we might consider the price of a full gallon of milk or a kilowatt hour of electricity even though consumers may not buy these products in full units either. In fact, mixing school and work may by itself represent evidence of imperfect capital markets: to the extent that schooling is a worthwhile investment, students who do not face cash constraints might be expected to attend school full-time and start reaping the returns of their investment as quickly as possible.[13]

A second reason why current policies are only a partial solution to the credit constraint problem is that there are large nonmonetary costs to applying for financial aid. Navigating the confusing array of financial aid forms requires a nontrivial expenditure of effort, even for those with strong literacy skills. For instance, there may be substantial costs to simply learning what types of aid are available. For those who itemize on their taxes, the financial aid form may not involve too much additional complication—but many do not itemize. The tax form and the financial aid form collect similar data on household income and household composition. However, the financial aid form also asks families to report the income not only from assets but from the value of the assets themselves. Such "hassle" costs may be particularly high for low-income, first-generation college students on the margin of attending college. Gary Orfield (1992) cites several studies suggesting that low-income families are often unaware of eligibility rules and procedures.

Of course, differences in college enrollment among similarly prepared high- and low-income students need not reflect the effect of financing difficulties. Parental income may matter for college-going for a number of reasons other than borrowing constraints. For instance, some higher-income parents are prepared to pay for all or part of a child's education but unwilling to provide the same money as a cash gift. Parental generosity that is contingent on college-going tends to increase enrollment among higher-income youth.

Moreover, the role of family income is complicated by the fact that parents' own willingness to provide support also depends on their values and expectations regarding education. Parents who themselves are educated, for example, may see the value of education more clearly and may more fully subsidize their children's college-going at any given level of income. Given all these factors, there are good reasons to suspect that parental income may indeed affect postsecondary college enrollment decisions even for equally prepared high school graduates.

In producing our estimates, we are using the family income reported by parents rather than that reported by students. As we noted earlier, few surveys include parental income for children not considered living in their parents' household, and then it is contemporaneous income, not income while in high school. Some surveys (including HSB) ask students about parental income, but we suspect that youth-reported parental income is likely to be subject to considerably greater error.[14]

However, our data on family income do have limitations. Most important, the HSB interviewed parents of only a random 15 percent of the students in the sample. Thus, our data set for the HSB sample is considerably smaller than that for NELS. A second problem with our income data is that the questions were asked in a different manner for the 1980/1982 and 1992 cohorts. Parents of the high school class of 1992 were asked to report only total family income for 1991.[15] In contrast, the parents of the 1980 sophomores and seniors were asked to report their income on nineteen different types of income separately.[16]

In general, questionnaires that ask multiple detailed questions regarding income yield higher and more reliable information on income than do single questions. When we compare the means and distributions of the family income reported in the NELS 1992 data with CPS data on the family income of families with high school seniors, the figures look surprisingly close. When we do the same comparison for the HSB 1980 data, however, we find that the HSB data show approximately 7 percent more income at most levels of the distribution. This result is surprising given that the CPS uses a method very similar to the HSB's to collect information on income.

These results imply that the family income data in the HSB and the NELS are not strictly comparable, a frustrating feature in light of our desire to understand changes over time. The primary solution we have adopted is to classify families according to family quartile in each year. Thus, even if HSB found more income than NELS did, if the rank order from rich to poor was roughly correct in each year, we can reliably compare quartiles.

Measurement error can reduce the apparent effect of family income on enrollment decisions. In many of our models, we include both parental education and family income. Since family income and parental education are correlated, and since parental education is likely to be measured with less error, it is likely that parental education captures some of the impacts of mismeasured family income.

But even if we had a highly reliable and comparable measure of annual family income for both surveys, we would still face the limitation that income in both surveys is measured for only a single year. A family's income may fluctuate up and down in any given year owing to temporary success or misfortune or because of short-term variability in the economy. Economists believe that critical investment decisions, including decisions about investing in the education of children, ought to be based on a longer-term view of the family's "permanent income" rather than on the income in any one year, especially if that income happens to be unusually high or low. As a result, economists sometimes use parental education as a proxy for permanent income. Unfortunately, parental education can also serve as a proxy for familial tastes and preferences for education. Thus, both measurement error and our inability to capture permanent income could lead to some upward bias in the estimated impact of parental education and a downward bias in the estimated effect of family income.

TASTES, ATTITUDES, AND EXPECTATIONS   Some households and some cultures seem to value education more highly than others. Young people from such homes might be expected to take high school more seriously and thus reach a higher level of achievement by high school. Yet even people with the same objective achievement as of high school, facing the same costs, might have very different perceptions about whether it makes sense to attend college. Students in some households, particularly those with parents who attended college, may have a clearer understanding of what is involved in gaining postsecondary education and be less fearful of the endeavor. Similarly, some students are more aware than others of the changing returns to college. Thus, some students may respond more quickly to the changing marketplace for college-educated labor.

Unfortunately, it is nearly impossible to measure differences in families' attitudes toward education. One approach would be to include parental education as a measure of such tastes. However, there are serious problems with using parental education in this way. For instance, we have already noted that parental education is often used as a proxy for a parent's long-term income. In other words, parental education may be measuring "ability to pay" as well as a youth's tastes for education. Moreover, parental education may actually be capturing information about financial subsidies offered by parents to induce their children to attend school. As such, parental education may be capturing part of students' response to price. Finally, to the extent that children's academic preparation at the end of high school is related to parental education, such measures may also be capturing some portion of unmeasured student achievement or ability.

Note that the same problem applies to family income. Family income may not be capturing financial effects at all; rather, it may be indicating the different tastes or values of wealthier families toward education. It is likely to be impossible to separate taste and attitude variables connected with family background from financial measures of family background.

WHO WENT ON TO COLLEGE FROM THE CLASS OF 1992?

Many of the basic patterns in our data can be illustrated with a few simple cross-tabulations. The most obvious confounding variable absent in the one-way tabulation of enrollment rates by family income in table 10.1 is ability and/or achievement in high school. It seems likely that students from higher-income families are better prepared for college and that their attendance reflects those achievements. An obvious way to examine this proposition is to compare the college-going rates by family income for people with similar test scores. Table 10.2 provides such a test for enrollment in all postsecondary education and for enrollment in a four-year college alone. This table uses math test scores—the ones that are the most powerful determinants of college enrollment in our models. We sorted the sample into thirds, using students' scores on the math portion of the test. For people in each third of measured achievement, we can then look to see how college enrollment varies by parental income quartile.

Test scores are indeed powerful predictors of who goes on to higher education. Looking at differences in the proportion of students enrolling in any postsecondary training, we find strong effects of both test scores and parental income. Within income quartiles, the odds of attending some postsecondary school rise significantly when one compares students with the lowest test scores to those with the highest. But

TABLE 10.2   /   Students in Class of 1992 Enrolling in Postsecondary Schools Within
Twenty Months, by Parental Income Quartile and Test Scores

	Math Test Tertile			Overall Average
	Bottom	Middle	Top	
Any postsecondary enrollment				
Lowest income quartile	48%	67%	82%	60%
	(1.6)	(1.8)	(2.1)	(1.1)
Second income quartile	50%	75%	90%	71%
	(1.9)	(1.6)	(1.2)	(1.0)
Third income quartile	64%	83%	95%	82%
	(2.1)	(1.3)	(0.8)	(0.8)
Highest income quartile	73%	89%	96%	90%
	(2.4)	(1.2)	(0.6)	(0.7)
Overall average	55%	79%	93%	76%
	(1.0)	(0.8)	(0.6)	(0.5)
Enrollment in a four-year college				
Lowest income quartile	15%	33%	68%	30%
	(1.1)	(1.8)	(2.5)	(1.0)
Second income quartile	14%	37%	69%	39%
	(1.3)	(1.8)	(1.8)	(1.1)
Third income quartile	21%	47%	78%	52%
	(1.8)	(1.8)	(1.5)	(1.1)
Highest income quartile	27%	59%	84%	67%
	(2.3)	(2.0)	(1.1)	(1.0)
Overall average	17%	44%	77%	47%
	(0.7)	(0.9)	(0.8)	(0.5)

Source: Based on authors' tabulation of 8,313 observations from the 1988 NELS.
Note: Standard errors in parentheses.

even within test score groups, a sizable income effect remains. If a student had an achievement test score in the lowest third, the odds of getting any postsecondary education moved from 48 to 73 percent as parents income quartile rose from lowest to highest. In the middle test score category, roughly 67 percent of high school graduates from the lowest-income families get some additional education, while 89 percent of those in the highest income group do so.

Results look even more dramatic for enrollment in a four-year school. Here, both test scores and parental income seem to play a very powerful role. Regardless of the income quartile, no more than 27 percent of students with scores in the bottom third attend a four-year college, while over two-thirds of those with scores in the top category enroll. But even within test score categories, extremely large differences remain by income. For those with test scores in the middle group, the apparent effect of family income remains sizable: 33 percent of those in the bottom quartile attend a four-year college, while 59 percent in the top quartile do so. Even in the top test category, it is striking that among young people from the poorest homes, one student in three does *not* go to a four-year school within the first twenty months after graduation, while for wealthier students in the same situation, only one in seven fails to enroll. Of course, some of the poorer students may start in a two-year school and later move to a four-year institution. (Unfortunately, the next follow-up of the NELS cohort is not to be conducted until the spring of 2000.)

In interpreting these simple results, we should recall that test score differences by income class may already reflect a feedback effect: students from poorer homes may not work as hard in school since they may believe they are unlikely to be able to afford college. Nevertheless, this simple table alone suggests that some—but not all—of the effect of family income can be traced to differences in achievement as of high school. Of course, this is but one measure of achievement. In later statistical work, we will control for other factors as well, but the table gives a sense of the impact that both achievement and parental income seem to have.

Also potentially influencing college-going are tastes, attitudes, and expectations toward education. Thus, we examine enrollment levels by parental education. Earlier we discussed the limitations of using parental education as a proxy for attitudes. Observed differences for those with different parental education almost undoubtedly reflect differences in achievement and in permanent income along with attitudes. Nevertheless, it is instructive to examine the differences within parental education and income classes. Table 10.3 offers these results. In constructing this table, we defined parental education as the maximum education received by a parent in the household. Thus, in two-parent homes, this is the highest education achieved by either the mother or father. In one-parent homes, it is the education of the custodial parent. The results are not sensitive to other ways of specifying parental education (such as the average education).

Parental education is also closely linked to postsecondary school enrollment. Looking first at the averages across all income categories, the odds that a young person who graduates from high school will soon get more education rise from 58 percent to 95 percent as the education of the parents rises. The odds of going to a four-year school jump from 21 percent to 77 percent. Even within income categories, parental education is closely linked to enrollment. If we look only at the second income quartile, we still see that attendance rates rise from 65 to 91 percent as parental education rises. One pattern of particular note suggests that at least some of the differences across education categories do indeed reflect tastes, attitudes, or information. In each income quartile, enrollment in four-year schools jumps sharply when the child comes from a home where at least one parent has a four-year degree or more. It seems quite likely that educated parents strongly encourage their children to get at least as much education as they have themselves.

As powerful as parental education is in explaining enrollment, however, parental income remains powerful as well. Among children from families in which at least one parent has some college, the odds of attending any school rise from 63 percent to 84 percent as income rises, and the odds of attending a four-year school jump from 32 percent to 52 percent. Because of measurement error and our inability to measure

TABLE 10.3 / Students in Class of 1992 Enrolling in Postsecondary Schools Within Twenty Months, by Parental Income Quartile and Education

	Highest Parental Education					
	High School Dropout	High School Graduate	Some College	College Graduate	Graduate Degree	Overall Average
Any postsecondary enrollment						
Lowest income quartile	52%	54%	63%	84%	83%	60%
	(1.9)	(1.9)	(1.5)	(3.1)	(4.8)	(1.0)
Second income quartile	65%	56%	70%	89%	91%	70%
	(3.0)	(2.0)	(1.3)	(1.8)	(2.6)	(0.9)
Third income quartile	65%	69%	80%	90%	94%	81%
	(4.7)	(2.3)	(1.2)	(1.4)	(1.3)	(0.8)
Highest income quartile	90%	71%	84%	90%	97%	89%
	(4.6)	(3.2)	(1.4)	(1.2)	(0.5)	(0.6)
Overall average	58%	60%	74%	90%	95%	75%
	(1.5)	(1.1)	(0.7)	(0.8)	(0.6)	(0.5)
Enrollment in a four-year college						
Lowest income quartile	19%	24%	32%	57%	47%	28%
	(1.5)	(1.6)	(1.4)	(4.2)	(6.4)	(0.9)
Second income quartile	19%	26%	37%	62%	60%	37%
	(2.4)	(1.7)	(1.3)	(2.8)	(4.2)	(0.9)
Third income quartile	28%	32%	46%	63%	77%	50%
	(4.4)	(2.3)	(1.5)	(2.3)	(2.2)	(1.0)
Highest income quartile	33%	32%	52%	72%	82%	66%
	(7.1)	(3.3)	(1.9)	(1.8)	(1.2)	(1.0)
Overall average	21%	27%	41%	66%	77%	45%
	(1.2)	(1.0)	(0.8)	(1.2)	(0.6)	(0.5)

Source: Based on authors' tabulation of 10,180 observations from the 1988 NELS.
Note: Standard errors in parentheses.

permanent income, it is likely that parental education is actually capturing a portion of real resource effects, not just differences in attitudes or tastes.

Of course, all of these are simple two-way tables. To fully separate out the impacts, we turn to multivariate analyses.

THE MULTIVARIATE DETERMINANTS OF COLLEGE ENROLLMENT

We described the decision to enroll in any school or to enroll in a four-year school as a function of achievement, attitudes, and current economic factors using the NELS data. Since our dependent variables are binary, we use probit models and report the impact on the probability of each variable.[17] The NELS sample is drawn from a stratified sample of eighth-grade students in public and private schools in 1988. All models also include region dummies. Since we use state-level variables as regressors, the standard errors are adjusted for clustering by state and are the robust standard errors based on the work of Peter Huber (1967) and Halbert White (1980, 1982).

We begin with a model that includes only income quartiles and gradually add other elements to see how powerful each is and to see how much of the apparent effect of income remains after their inclusion. To the extent that our measures for achievement and attitudes do not fully capture the impacts of these factors, or are measured with error, income may inappropriately capture some of these effects. On the other hand, given that family income may be measured with error, and given the likelihood that parental education is also capturing a portion of permanent income, we may be understating the impact of income.

The results can be used to answer two related questions. First, how much of the apparent difference in higher education enrollment by family income can actually be traced to other factors? Second, how powerful are various factors, such as achievement, parental education, and family income, in explaining enrollment decisions?

This basic specification—with measures of test scores, income, parental education, and college costs—is quite similar to others in the literature. Since their results are generally quite similar to ours, and to simplify discussion here, we have placed the detailed tables with their coefficient estimates in appendix tables 10A.1 through 10A.3. Instead, we illustrate the results in several summary tables.

Table 10.4 presents the results indicating the decline in the apparent differences by family income as more factors are controlled for. Each figure shows the difference between enrollment for persons from the first quartile and each of the others. Thus, we see that the difference in enrollment rates in any postsecondary school between students from the first and fourth quartiles was 26 percent when we controlled for nothing. And that difference is highly significant.

We begin by examining the results for all postsecondary enrollment. Controlling for demographics, region, and tuition levels affects the results relatively little. But when we control for achievement in high school—using test scores and high school grades—the gaps are cut sharply. The difference between the highest and lowest quartiles falls from 26 percent to 15 percent. And if we also include parental education, "only" a 9 percent high-low gap remains. That is, roughly two-thirds of the

TABLE 10.4 / Impact of Family Income on Postsecondary Education

	Differences in Enrollment Relative to the First Quartile with No Controls Included	Differences in Enrollment After Controlling for Demographics and Tuition	Differences in Enrollment After Controlling for Measured Achievement, Demographics, and Tuition	Differences in Enrollment After Controlling for Parental Education, Measured Achievement, Demographics, and Tuition
Enrollment in any postsecondary education				
Lowest income quartile	—	—	—	—
Second income quartile	8% (1.3)	10% (1.6)	4% (1.2)	2% (1.1)
Third income quartile	19% (2.8)	17% (2.2)	10% (1.8)	6% (1.4)
Highest income quartile	26% (2.1)	25% (1.6)	15% (1.5)	9% (1.3)
Enrollment in four-year college				
Lowest income quartile	—	—	—	—
Second income quartile	9% (1.5)	8% (2.0)	2% (2.2)	1% (2.2)
Third income quartile	19% (2.6)	16% (3.0)	7% (2.9)	3% (2.9)
Highest income quartile	36% (2.1)	31% (2.6)	15% (2.8)	9% (2.8)

Source: Estimated with the probits in tables 10A.2 and 10A.3 and an NELS sample of 5,463 students.
Note: Standard errors in parentheses.

apparent effect of income is associated with demographics, achievement, and parental education.

The income gaps in enrollment in a four-year institution are even larger. In this case, the original difference in enrollment rates between low- and high-income families is 36 percent. Controlling for achievement shrinks this gap to 15 percent. When we also control for parental education, we are left with only about one-fourth of our original difference resulting from parental income quartile.

A second and equally important question is: At the margin, how important are various factors other than family income in influencing enrollment decisions? In table 10.5, we summarize the probit results by using them to predict the levels in school enrollment when everything is held constant except one or two variables. We do this by predicting what enrollment would be for the entire population if they all had that one characteristic in common.[18] It is a way of using probit results to assess the impact of varying just one factor while holding all else constant. All of these results are based on the model with all of our variables included. We can thus explore the relative importance of each variable when the others are controlled for. All of the differences are statistically significant.

The table reveals an important if unsurprising pattern. It appears that high school achievement is the strongest predictor of post–high school enrollment, especially at a four-year college. This combination of grades and scores amounts roughly to going from the bottom quarter in high school achievement to the top quarter. Holding all else equal, moving from the bottom to the top in academic preparation raises the odds of getting additional schooling from 70 percent to 92 percent. Those in the bottom of high school achievement enroll in four-year schools at the rate of 29 percent, while those at the top enroll at the rate of 74 percent. These differences clearly swamp all others. A strong reading of these results would be that efforts to affect achievement through high school could have very powerful effects on later school enrollment.

Results similar to these are found throughout the literature. For instance, Stephen Cameron and James Heckman (1999) found that differences in AFQT scores represent a large share of differences in college entry by family income. Robert Hauser, Jennifer Sheridan, and John Warren (1998) also reported that family background affects schooling primarily—although not solely—through differences in test scores.

Tuition levels do show some impact here. Lowering tuition from $1,500 to $500 (1996 dollars) would increase enrollment in our data by five percentage points, from 75 percent to 80 percent. More state tuition grants also increase enrollment (see the coefficients in the appendix). We find smaller (and generally insignificant) effects of four-year tuition on enrollment in such schools. These estimates of the impact of tuition on college entry are quite consistent with the median estimate in a 1988 review of over twenty estimates of tuition impacts on college enrollment by Larry Leslie and Paul Brinkman (1988). More recently, Cameron and Heckman (1999) and Kane (1994, 1995) have reported similar results.

Parental education also plays a major role, again particularly in four-year enrollments. The odds of going to a four-year school are 40 percent if your parents only graduated from high school and 54 percent if they graduated from college. By com-

TABLE 10.5 / Estimated Marginal Effects of Various Factors on Enrollment in Any
Postsecondary School and on Enrollment in a Four-Year College

All Things Held Constant Except	Probability of Getting Any Additional Schooling	Probability of Attending a Four-Year College
Achievement		
C+ grade point average and thirty-third percentile test scores	70%	29%
B+ grade point average and sixty-seventh percentile test scores	92	74
Tuition		
Two-year tuition = $1,500	75	N/A
Two-year tuition = $500	80	N/A
Parental education		
No parent attended beyond high school	69	40
At least one parent completed four years of college	84	54
Parental income		
Parental income in the bottom quartile	73	44
Parental income in the top quartile	82	53
Family background (parental education and parental income)		
Parents with no more than high school education and income in the bottom quartile	64	37
At least one parent with four-year degree and parents' income in the top quartile	88	60

Source: Authors' calculations based on appendix tables 10A.1, 10A.2, and 10A.3.

parison, the effect of parental income, after controlling for the other factors, is more modest. For people with identical test scores, grades, and parental education, moving from the lowest to the highest quartile of family income pushes the probability of college enrollment from 45 percent to 54 percent (the nine-percentage-point gap shown in table 10.4). The rise for enrolling at any school, from 73 to 82 percent, is somewhat larger when all else is held constant.

One interesting exercise that sheds light on whether the remaining income effects are due to credit constraints is to compare the impact of tuition increases on enrollment patterns for different income levels. If parental resources are in fact influencing behavior because of credit constraints, a tuition increase of $1,000 should have a larger negative effect on low-income households than on high-income ones. A number of studies have found greater price responsiveness among low-income students.

As summarized in Leslie and Brinkman (1987), Manski and Wise (1983), Radner and Miller (1970), Bishop (1977), and Kohn, Manski, and Mundel (1976), there is greater responsiveness to tuition differences among those from the lower income quartiles. More recently, McPherson and Schapiro (1991a) and Kane (1994, 1995) also found greater impacts of tuition on the enrollment decisions of low-income youth. Although we continue to explore this issue, our findings with the NELS data are somewhat sensitive to specification. In some specifications, we find an interaction effect, but not in others. Cameron and Heckman (1999) also failed to find robust evidence of an income interaction effect: although their point estimates showed decreasing effects of tuition as parental income rises, they could not reject the hypothesis that tuition has similar effects at varying income levels. Thus, we cannot be certain whether the remaining income effects we observe are due to credit constraints or other factors.

What are we to make of these results? The fact that the apparent impact of family income is much smaller after controlling for the other factors certainly proves that current financial circumstance is not the only reason there are such large differences in college-going among low- and high-income youngsters. Combined with the modest impacts of tuition, the results clearly suggest that much of the apparent difference in enrollment cannot be attributed to pure financial factors alone.

Looking at similar results, Cameron and Heckman (1999) were led to conclude that credit constraints are unimportant and thus there is little basis for real concern about financial barriers to college. We would not go that far. First, the estimated size of family income differences is greatly diminished by the inclusion of parental education as an additional regressor. Yet including parental education almost certainly captures more than differences in parental "tastes" for education. Parental education probably artificially picks up some of the income effects due to measurement error in income and probably more closely measures a family's long-term wealth than a single year of income does. Moreover, if children from poorer families believe they are unlikely to go to school (because of financial constraints), they do not work as hard in school and achieve lower scores and grades, further obscuring the true impact of family income. Second, even after controlling for parental education, the remaining differences in college-going by family income are hardly "small." Our results imply that even when two youngsters have identical school grades and test scores and equally well-educated parents, if one is poor and one is well-to-do, their odds of attending school will differ by nearly ten percentage points.

In addition to attempting to sort out the distinct effects of income and family taste—an effort, as we described earlier, that is necessarily fraught with difficulty—an alternative approach is to identify the total effect of family background, including both parental education and income, on the enrollment decisions of equally successful high school seniors. This question is addressed by the last rows of table 10.5. Even after controlling for test scores, high school grades, the type of high school, demographics, and region, we find that the odds that two apparently equally qualified students will go to a school at all rise from 64 percent to 88 percent. The odds of four-year school enrollment move from 37 percent to 60 percent. These strike us as huge differences in enrollment for students who are so similar in their performance through high school and on standardized tests.

Although it is an uncomfortable question for economists, it is worth asking: Why should enrollment patterns for otherwise equally accomplished students be so different depending on their family background? It is extremely hard to argue that "tastes" for the experience of college properly differ between them—that the advantaged student knows she will enjoy college and the disadvantaged one knows she will not. There is no a priori reason to believe that one will do better in college or gain more than another. A pure economic model would suggest that the value of the investment would be similar—if test scores and high school grades represent adequate measures of existing human capital. Yet enrollment rates differ dramatically. Although economists are loath to judge individual actions, those high- to moderate-achieving young people from lower-status families—the "movable middle"—may be making the wrong decision for themselves and the economy.

THE IMPACT OF PARENTAL AID ON THE LIKELIHOOD THAT CHILDREN WILL ENROLL IN COLLEGE

Parents have a number of levers with which to influence the behavior of their children in the years leading up to college—advice, encouragement, information gathering, the implicit transferal of values. But direct parental subsidies may also help persuade their children to attend college. We cannot directly test the role of subsidies using the data here, but we can get a rough sense of its significance using another source. In the National Postsecondary Student Aid Survey into 1992 to 1993, students were asked to report the amount of aid they received from their parents and from other sources. They were asked to distinguish parental gifts from "loans" for which parents explicitly expected repayment (although this distinction may become ambiguous if parents implicitly expect the favor to be repaid later in life) and "in-kind" benefits such as free room and board at their parents' home. (For a subset of students, parents were also asked to report their contributions. We used parent-reported when it was available.)

The top panel of table 10.6 reports parental contributions to dependent students attending college full-time at public two-year and four-year colleges as well as at private four-year colleges relative to that provided by parents in the lowest quartile. In the first column, we see that parents in the second family income quartile whose child enrolled in a two-year school contributed $1,237 more than parents in the bottom quartile. And high-income parents of children in two-year schools contributed $2,630 more. (Note that we have adjusted for differences in tuition in two-year schools in calculating these figures. Because fixed effects are included for each school, we are essentially comparing the contributions of high- and low-income parents of students going to the same schools.) The second column in the top panel suggests that youth from the top quartile attending public four-year schools received $4,083 more from their parents annually than did youth in the bottom quartile. And high-income students received $8,420 more from their parents when attending full-time at private

TABLE 10.6 / Parental Contributions and Net College Costs for Full-Time Dependent, 1992 to 1993

	Public Two-Year	Public Four-Year	Private Four-Year
Parental contribution relative to the lowest parental income quartile (excluding loans and in-kind benefits)			
First income quartile	—	—	—
Second income quartile	$1,237	$1,341	$1,327
	(311)	(143)	(326)
Third income quartile	1,933	2,509	4,627
	(350)	(140)	(324)
Fourth income quartile	2,630	4,083	8,420
	(391)	(141)	(308)
Net cost to student relative to the lowest income quartile (tuition, total grants, and parental contribution)			
First income quartile	—	—	—
Second income quartile	−593	−38	−119
	(321)	(141)	(319)
Third income quartile	−798	−844	−1337
	(362)	(138)	(318)
Fourth income quartile	−1,732	−2210	−2876
	(405)	(140)	(302)
N =	729	7,240	4,350

Note: The figures in the table are differences in parental contributions and net costs, reported relative to those from the lowest family income quartile. When available, we used parental-contribution data available from the parent survey. When the parent survey was not available, we used the student-reported parental contribution. All above specifications include college fixed effects, that is, they compare costs for those attending the same institutions. Based on authors' analysis of the National Postsecondary Student Aid Survey, 1992 to 1993.

four-year colleges than those youth from the bottom quartile attending the same colleges.

The bottom panel of table 10.6 shows the difference in the net cost of college, including tuition, grants, and parental contributions, for students in various parental income classes—again, as compared to the bottom quartile. Owing to the means-testing of state, federal, and institutional financial aid, part of the difference in parental contributions is offset by the combination of federal, state, and institutional means-tested grant aid. However, the provision of grant aid was not large enough to offset the large differences in parental contributions to children's education. As a result, youth from low-income families still paid considerably more of the cost of attending college than higher-income youth attending the same college. For instance, a youth from the top income quartile attending a public four-year college paid $2,210 less (net of parental aid and grants) than a youth from the lowest-income quartile. The difference was even larger for those attending private four-year colleges ($2,876).

These results suggest that youth from higher-income families may attend college at higher rates simply because their parents have made the choice that is more obvious for them: paying a larger share of the costs of attending. Indeed, if we were to take the difference in parental contribution between the bottom and top income quartiles for those attending public four-year colleges—$2,210—and multiply by our estimate of the effect of a $1,000 difference in tuition (.05), we would predict a eleven-percentage-point difference in college-going for youth in the top and bottom income quartiles. This is comparable in magnitude to the difference in college-going by family income quartile reported earlier. In other words, we could explain the differences in college enrollment rates between high- and low-income youth simply by referring to the choices their parents are able to create for them by their ability or willingness to pay for college.

THE CHANGING ENROLLMENT PATTERNS BETWEEN THE EARLY 1980S AND THE EARLY 1990S

Table 10.1 also shows that enrollment differences by family income grew over time. Conceptually, the differences we observe could be the results of one of two changes. First, behavior could be unchanged for people of given characteristics, but the characteristics of high school graduates and their parents could have changed between the 1980s and 1990s. The most obvious potential change is parental education. Parents of high school seniors in the 1990s tended to have more education than parents of seniors in the 1980s. Conversely, the changes in enrollment could be the result of changed behavior by people with the same characteristics. This would be the result if children from higher-income or more educated families changed their behavior more in response to the higher returns to schooling than did children in low-income families.

Asking whether behavioral responses changed is the same as asking whether the coefficients in our models changed. Thus, we run identical models for the HSB 1980/1982 sample and the NELS 1992 sample and explore whether the coefficients change. Because the test scores are not comparable between years, we run the models with all the variables included previously, except for test scores. We still include high school grades, which alone capture a very large share of the variance in achievement in our 1992 data. Unless we have reason to believe that comparable test scores changed more for one group than for another between the early 1980s and early 1990s, this omission should not affect our comparisons between years.[19] The new coefficients are shown in appendix table 10A.4.

One way to determine whether things changed is to compare the coefficients in table 10A.4. These look surprisingly similar, though some are different statistically. An even more powerful way to examine whether changes in behavior or altered characteristics lead to the changes in enrollment is to see how we predict the enrollment patterns in the 1990s when we apply the behavioral responses we found for the 1980s to the characteristics of students and parents in the 1990s. In other words, if people in the 1990s behaved like similar folks in the 1980s, would we have expected to see the enrollment patterns we did? If we predict the 1990s well using behavioral patterns of the 1980s, then we must conclude that the changes are the result of differing characteristics, not altered behavior. If we predict poorly, then it appears that behavior changes are more important. We can also ask the question in reverse. If we use our estimated behavioral parameters for 1992 and the characteristics of people in 1980/1982, do we predict what actually happened in 1982?

The results of this simulation are shown in tables 10.7 and 10.8. The first column shows the 1980s coefficients and 1980s characteristics and thus essentially gives the actual enrollment patterns in the 1980s. The last column does the same for the 1990s, essentially showing the actual enrollment patterns in that year. The middle columns are the predicted results for each year using the behavioral estimates from one period and the characteristics from another.

Interestingly, the quality of the predictions differs slightly in tables 10.7 and 10.8. Table 10.7 shows that we would have predicted a rise in the average enrollment percentage from 68 percent to 73 percent. In fact, it rose to 76 percent. So we predict

TABLE 10.7 / Influence of Changing Characteristics and Changing Coefficients on Enrollment in Any School

	1980/1982 Characteristics		1992 Characteristics	
	1980/1982 Coefficients Actual 1980/1982	1992 Coefficients Predicted 1980/1982	1980/1982 Coefficients Predicted 1992	1992 Coefficients Actual 1992
Lowest income quartile	58%	62%	63%	62%
Second income quartile	66	73	68	72
Third income quartile	69	77	75	80
Highest income quartile	81	86	87	89
Average	68	74	73	76
High-low difference	23	26	24	27
Sum of absolute differences from actual 1982	—	24	21	29

TABLE 10.8 / Influence of Changing Characteristics and Changing Coefficients on Enrollment in Four-Year Colleges

| | 1980/1982 Characteristics | | 1992 Characteristics | |
	1980/1982 Coefficients Actual 1980/1982	1992 Coefficients Predicted 1980/1982	1980/1982 Coefficients Predicted 1992	1992 Coefficients Actual 1992
Lowest income quartile	30%	26%	35%	29%
Second income quartile	32	35	35	40
Third income quartile	36	39	46	47
Highest income quartile	55	54	67	66
Average	38	38	46	46
High-low difference	25	28	32	37
Sum of absolute differences from actual 1982	—	11	26	28

Source: Authors' calculations.
Note: Columns 1 and 4 differ slightly from table 10.7 owing to slight sample differences.

a 5 percent rise rather than an 8 percent rise. And while we would have predicted some widening in enrollment, we did not predict as much of a change as there was. Our predictions for 1980 to 1982 using the behavioral response coefficients of 1992 do considerably worse. Our predicted 1980 to 1982 numbers look more like the actual 1992 numbers than those for 1980 to 1982.

Somewhat in contrast, the predictions for four-year college enrollment prove to be surprisingly accurate. We correctly predict overall average enrollment rates for 1980/1982 using 1992 behavioral parameters, and we correctly predict 1992 rates using the 1980/1982 coefficients. Perhaps even more strikingly, we predict a widening in the differences in enrollment rates by level of family income. Simply looking visually, the predicted columns look rather close to the actual values, especially at the top end.

We are left then with several intriguing, if puzzling, results. We seem to predict patterns of four-year college enrollment pretty well, including the increasing difference in attendance by income. An obvious first question: Why would we have predicted a skewed change in enrollment? A second question: Why did we do better in our predictions for four-year schools?

Our preliminary analysis suggests that part of the key to understanding the patterns involves the changes in parental education and the correlation between parental income and parental education. Parental education rose during this period, and those rises understandably lead to a prediction that enrollment rates would rise. Rises in the fraction of parents with a college degree were particularly great.

Now the story gets slightly more complicated. Simultaneously, the returns to education also rose. As a result, education and income became more highly correlated, with the correlation rising from .3 to nearly .5 in little more than a decade. Thus, more of the differences in parental income could be traced to parental education than to other factors. By 1992, the top category of income contained an even greater share of the highly educated than before. In effect, parental education, especially college education, increased more for people in the top quartile of income. So students at the top now had a double boost: income and education were more aligned, pushing them to disproportionately higher levels of enrollment.

The fraction of parents with a college degree in the bottom quartile actually fell. Conversely, the fraction with a college degree rose most sharply in the top quartile. So the same forces that were pushing up incomes for more educated workers were also pushing up enrollments for students from the most advantaged homes. Students with highly educated parents were now getting an additional boost from the fact that the incomes of their parents had risen disproportionately. The reason the story holds less well for the enrollment overall has to do with the fact that parental education, especially having a college degree, is somewhat less important in influencing enrollment in two-year schools.

There were two factors pushing up enrollment for all groups in the 1990s: higher parental education and increasing returns to schooling. In addition, the much larger change in incomes of well-educated parents gave something of an extra boost to children in those homes. And so enrollment rose most where advantages were greatest to begin with.

DIFFERENCES IN COLLEGE ENTRY AND INTERGENERATIONAL MOBILITY

Education is arguably our most important tool for ensuring intergenerational mobility. Yet our data show that college-going differs greatly by family background, even among measurably similar students in high school. Thus, children from more advantaged homes go to college more. And in recent years, because the returns to college-going have risen sharply, the value of the additional education received by children from the advantage background has itself been multiplied. Moreover, enrollment has risen disproportionately among advantaged students. In this section, we begin to sort out what the changes in education returns and enrollment may imply for intergenerational mobility.

We begin with a straightforward conceptual model, not unlike the simple decompositions we have already done. If we compare the incomes of grown children to the incomes of their parents when the children were in high school, there is a clear correlation. Children of the well-to-do fare somewhat better on average. Some of the association between parents' income and children's is a result of the higher achievement by high school that we have already observed. Some may be traced to demographics. Some can be traced to the differences in postsecondary schooling that we have been preoccupied with here. And some is attributable to unmeasured factors such as connections, motivation, attitudes, and the like that are not captured by demographics, measured achievement as of high school, or differential post-secondary schooling patterns.

We must use the HSB survey if we are to observe children long after they complete their schooling. Unfortunately, doing so leaves us with small sample sizes, since parental income was collected only for a subset of respondents. In this case, we are able to observe these students in 1990 and 1991, between eight and eleven years after graduation. We average the earnings for 1990 and 1991 for this analysis. Those with zero incomes or who reported any school attendance during 1990 and 1991 were excluded.

After categorizing youth by parental family income quartile, we regressed their adult income on demographics, measured achievement by high school, and post-secondary schooling. Next, we determined the mean demographics, mean high school test scores and grades, and mean postsecondary schooling for each quartile of parental income. Substituting these means into the equation, it is straightforward to decompose the difference in mean incomes for students of different family income quartiles into the portion accounted for by various components.[20]

Table 10.9 shows the results of that decomposition. The overall difference in the log of adult income for students from the lowest and highest quartile homes is .19, as shown in the first column. In other words, children from higher-income homes earn on average about 19 percent more as adults roughly ten years out of high school. Of this 19 percent, 3.0 percentage points can be traced to differences in demographics, 4.2 percentage points can be traced to differences in achievement by high school (as measured by test scores and student grades), 4.4 percentage points can be traced to differences in schooling, and the remaining 7.6 percentage points are associated with other factors related to family income quartile that could not be measured. Put another way, given only the differences in educational attainment after high school of those from different family income quartiles, we would have expected children in the top income quartile to earn 4.4 percent more than youth in the bottom income quartile.

The 4 percent figure may sound small, but it is consistent with our earlier findings. In the 1980s, roughly 25 percent more children from high-income families went to four-year colleges relative to low-income families. In the twenty-five- to thirty-four-year-old age range, college graduates earned roughly 35 to 40 percent more than high school graduates by 1990 (see figure 10.1) *without controlling for high school achievement.* But when we account for the fact that part of the reason people with more education earn more is that they started with more achievements and ability, the rate of return to schooling alone would typically be only three-quarters as large—30 percent rather than 40 percent. Finally, we know that most of the other students did go beyond high school, so we would expect the difference in earnings to be less than the high school-

TABLE 10.9 / Decomposition of the Total Difference in Adult Income Associated with Parental Income While in High School

Parental Income Quartile When in High School	Total Difference in the Log of Adult Income for Students Relative to Those with Parental Income in the First Quartile	(A) Difference in Log Income Due to Differences in Demographics	(B) Difference in Log Income Due to Measured Achievement by High School	(C) Difference in Log Income Due to Final Schooling Level	(D) Difference in Log Income Due to Other Unmeasured Effects of Parental Income
Lowest income quartile	—	—	—	—	—
Second income quartile	.099	.017	.030	.011	.041
Third income quartile	.156	.030	.041	.021	.065
Highest income quartile	.192	.030	.042	.044	.076

Source: Authors' calculations.

college one—perhaps 20 percent higher rather than 30 percent. Since these regressions also condition on test scores, we might crudely multiply the 25 percent difference in postsecondary entry by the 20 percent wage premium to yield an expected gain of 5 percent. This is very close to the 4.5 percent we observe.

However, because this figure includes the full difference in educational attainment rather than the difference attributable to differences in income itself, even it overstates the effects of parental income on the outcomes for young people. We have seen that roughly half of the reason people from poorer households get less schooling has to do with achievement. Thus, perhaps a 2 to 3 percent difference in adult income in the early 1980s could be traced to the fact that measurably identical students from different family backgrounds (both parental education and income) had different rates of school attendance.

But since the early 1990s, the returns to education have grown another 50 percent, and they seem to be rising still. If all else stays the same, differences in opportunities for measurably identical high school students from different classes of home could now be yielding a 3 or 5 percent difference in later earnings. Moreover, the fact that the differential in enrollments by income also rose from 25 percent to 35 percent in the period of our data could boost the difference as high as 6 or 7 percent.

Finally, there is every reason to expect this difference to grow as these students age, because earnings for more educated persons rise more than those of less educated ones. A lifetime boost of 10 percent does not seem an unreasonable conclusion based on this data. Whether 10 percent is a large or small figure is largely in the eye of the beholder. But this source of inequality does seem particularly bothersome. Implicitly, the incomes of adults with identical high school records and identical test scores differ by as much as 10 percent simply because their family backgrounds sent some to college and not others.

These are very rough estimates indeed. They assume that other factors did not change. It may be that as education has become more important in determining future income, unmeasured parental differences become less important. But they do point to a couple of important insights.

The overall inequality in mean adult incomes of those from different family backgrounds cannot primarily be traced to differences in postsecondary education, especially when we control for high school achievement (which, of course, is itself influenced by family resources). Nonetheless, the shifting returns to college and the changing patterns of enrollment seem to be increasing this source of intergenerational transmission of advantage. And eliminating differential school enrollment for measurably identical students with different backgrounds would reduce an important and particularly difficult-to-justify source of inequality.

IMPLICATIONS FOR POLICY

As Heckman and Lochner point out in this volume, much of the difference in college-going by family income is related to differences in academic investments earlier in life—during early childhood, elementary school, and secondary school. Although these differences may themselves reflect the inaccessibility of credit for paying for worthwhile educational investments by low-income parents, they may also reflect differences in parental values and "tastes" for education. Regardless of their source, these differences in educational preparation are presumably captured by test scores and high school grades as students emerge from high school. Our results suggest that large differences in college-going remain, even among those with similar test scores and grades as they emerge from high school. A number of others, including Manski and Wise (1983) and Cameron and Heckman (1999), report similar results: differences in test scores account for part, but not all, of the total difference in college-going by family income.[21] Moreover, our results suggest that such gaps may be widening.

Although differences in college-going by family income are not sufficient on their own to establish the importance of borrowing constraints, other evidence suggests that borrowing constraints may be more important than Heckman and Lochner (this volume) assert. For instance, when put into context, most estimates of families' sensitivity to tuition increases—such as reported by Kane (1994), Cameron and

Heckman (1999), and Dynarski (1999)—are remarkably large. The estimated impact of a $1,000 rise in tuition, five to seven percentage points, is nearly as large as the rise in college enrollment following a much larger increase in the value of a college degree during the 1980s. Families appear to be much more sensitive to changes in tuition costs than they are to changes in the payoff to schooling—exhibiting behavior that would also be consistent with borrowing constraints.

Nevertheless, such aggregate evidence will never allow social scientists to resolve the debate over the importance of borrowing constraints. Too many alternative explanations are available to persuade skeptics on either side of the debate. A more fruitful line of research may be to experiment with the various ways in which government helps families pay for college.

There are two basic forms of state and federal aid for college: broad-based subsidies (such as state support for public institutions) and means-tested grant and loan subsidies, based on a family's prior income and savings. Each has advantages and disadvantages. One obvious disadvantage of broad-based subsidies is that those who would have gone to college anyway enjoy a particularly large share of such subsidies. This fact means that the cost of generating an additional college student can be quite high. For instance, our estimates suggest that an extra $1,000 across-the-board subsidy to those attending public institutions would yield a five-percentage-point increase in the proportion of high school graduates entering college within twenty months after high school. In other words, a $1,000 tuition cut for all 8 million full-time-equivalent students enrolled in public institutions of higher education would yield a five-percentage-point increase in college-going for the 2.6 million new high school graduates in a given year—implying a cost of more than $61,000 per new college entrant.

Although such aid may have other behavioral impacts, such as encouraging youth to remain in college longer, an across-the-board subsidy to keep tuition low at public institutions is a very expensive way to encourage more youth to go to college. Targeting the aid by certain types of institution or by students' financial resources, or limiting the aid to students in their first year of college, would improve the "bang for the buck." Narrowing the gap in college enrollment by family income need not require investing considerably more in higher education. It may be sufficient simply to target that aid more effectively.

On the other hand, means-testing aid, using a long list of student traits—family income, family size, family assets, number of other siblings in college, number of parents employed—makes it harder for students to anticipate the amount of available aid. Those students whose behavior we might most hope to affect—low-income, first-generation college students—are likely to be least able to navigate the complicated financial aid system. Indeed, there is very little evidence of any disproportionate increase in college enrollment for low-income youth before and after the Pell Grant program was established in the mid-1970s.[22] One reason may be that only those who had applied to college anyway became aware of the amount of aid that was available. Unfortunately, with the addition of the new federal tax credits for higher education, we have only made it more difficult for students and parents to figure out what college will actually cost them.

We would encourage further policy development in three areas. First, the Department of Education should undertake the research that would allow policy-makers to compare the relative effectiveness of different forms of aid in encouraging low-income youth to go to college. For instance, a number of policy advocates have urged an increase in grant programs (as opposed to further increases in loan programs) on the grounds that low-income students are averse to borrowing. Although it seems plausible that a dollar in grant aid would be more effective than a dollar in loan aid in affecting the choices of marginal youth (notwithstanding the pessimistic appraisal of the Pell Grant program's impacts), providing a dollar in grant aid is also much more expensive than providing an additional dollar in buying power with loan aid. A dollar in grants costs the federal government approximately six times as much as a dollar in loans, but it is not clear that an additional dollar in grants is six times more effective. Moreover, it is far from clear that an additional dollar spent to hire more high school guidance counselors would not have a larger impact than a dollar spent on either of the traditional grant or loan programs. Yet if we are ever to make any progress in shrinking differences in college-going among similarly prepared youth, such information is vital.

Second, instead of spending resources helping students and parents to understand a very complicated system, policymakers should first consider ways to lessen the complications. The binding constraint on low-income families may not be the amount they are allowed to borrow, but the informational barriers to learning just how much aid is available. As Heckman and Lochner (this volume) discuss, several programs that provided mentoring to high school students have had large impacts on college enrollment by disadvantaged youth. Government could further loosen that constraint by simplifying the formula for determining eligibility. For instance, we might consider limiting the eligibility determinants in the federal needs analysis system to family income and family size. Any loss in target efficiency should be weighed against the gains in transparency.

Third, the federal government, the states, and the schools could consider adding to the set of available policy levers by providing a larger share of the aid through income-contingent loan programs—disbursing aid using a forward-looking assessment of a student's income after college rather than a backward-looking assessment of his or her parents' income and assets before college. Such an approach has a number of advantages. First, by moving more of the means-testing from before college until after college, it clears up some of the cloud of uncertainty about how much students and parents actually have to pay out-of-pocket at the time students enter college. Second, by providing some "insurance" to both middle- and lower-income families concerned about their children's ability to pay off their college loans, income-contingent programs are likely to find a broader political constituency than programs targeted solely on the basis of the parents' past income. Third, since subsidies are based on a career's worth of a borrower's earnings rather than on a single year of the parents' and the student's income and assets before college, the tax rates can be much lower. Fourth, "forward-looking" means-testing is more appropriate for older college entrants, who do not fit the mold—a recent high school graduate living with his or her parents—that the current needs analysis system was designed to serve.

CONCLUSIONS

This chapter suggests that the rhetoric on either side of the schooling and opportunity debate is exaggerated. Although postsecondary schooling differs dramatically by family income, much of the difference can be traced to differences in achievement as of high school. Rather than reflecting income differences alone, postsecondary schooling also seems to be heavily influenced by parental education. Thus, although the gap in four-year college-going for youth from the top and bottom family income quartiles is 36 percent, the difference is only one-fourth as large if we control for achievement, demographics, tuition, and parental education. This finding, coupled with the finding that tuition rates have only a modest impact on enrollments, should raise questions about how important income differences alone are.

Conversely, we find no support for the conclusion that academic preparation accounts for all of the difference in college-going. Moreover, we think the real issue is the finding that college-going rates among young people with identical high school records and test scores differ greatly depending on the combination of parental income and education. We found that the probability of enrolling in a four-year school shot from 37 percent to 60 percent when students with similar grades and test scores came from relatively advantaged homes. We found that higher-income parents contribute far more toward their children's cost of schooling, clearly encouraging more college going. And in turn, a modest but significant share of intergenerational income inequality can be traced to these differences.

The source of the advantage clearly goes beyond income. Parents with more education must convey different expectations and information on the benefits to college. Overcoming this information and expectation gap may be the most important but difficult part of creating more similar enrollment patterns for similarly prepared children from disadvantaged families.

Perhaps the most surprising finding was that rising returns to education are making the situation worse in two respects. First, the educational advantages received by students with higher-income parents are being multiplied along with the returns to schooling. Second, because the rising returns also seem to have the effect of increasing the connection between parental education and income, students from more educationally advantaged homes are also now more advantaged in income. The joint effect of these forces is to push up enrollments most for those from the most advantaged homes.

We think it critical to end on a note of caution. Even completely equalizing educational opportunities for equally skilled students will only modestly alter inequality. Moreover, the single most powerful determinant of college-going remains high school achievement. Anything we can do to reduce the achievement gaps that are present by high school will do a great deal to equalize the enrollments of students from various backgrounds. But that effort is gargantuan indeed, and major successes remain rare. In the meantime, some financial mechanisms are available that clearly do influence enrollment. We continue to believe these are the obvious place to begin.

Beth Welty and Lauren Brown provided excellent research assistance. We are grateful for detailed comments from Francine Blau, Sheldon Danziger, Alan Krueger, Glenn Loury, Jane Waldfogel, and seminar participants in the Investing in Children conference and at the Kennedy School. Ellwood acknowledges generous support from the MacArthur Foundation. Kane acknowledges the generous support of the Andrew W. Mellon Foundation.

APPENDIX

TABLE 10A.1 / Means and Standard Deviations for Variables Used in Probit Models, Class of 1992

	Mean (Standard Deviation)
Second income quartile	0.266
	(0.442)
Third income quartile	0.259
	(0.438)
Top income quartile	0.229
	(0.420)
Female	0.510
	(0.500)
Black, non-Hispanic	0.093
	(0.291)
Hispanic	0.104
	(0.305)
Other, non-white, non-Hispanic	0.099
	(0.299)
South	0.326
	(0.469)
Midwest	0.311
	(0.463)
West	0.251
	(0.434)
Other private high school	0.057
	(0.232)
Parochial high school	0.048
	(0.213)
Two-parent family	0.692
	(0.462)
Tuition at public two-year schools	1.196
(in thousands of 1988 dollars)	(0.532)
Tuition at public four-year schools	2.363
(in thousands of 1988 dollars)	(0.732)

TABLE 10A.1 / *Continued*

	Mean (Standard Deviation)
State grants per 1,000 college-age residents	0.050 (0.046)
Standardized math test score	0.021 (0.989)
Standardized reading test score	0.003 (0.992)
Student grade point average	2.775 (0.727)
Parents high school dropouts	0.093 (0.290)
At least one parent some college	0.427 (0.495)
At least one parent college degree	0.153 (0.360)
At least one parent graduate school	0.133 (0.340)

Source: Authors' calculations.

TABLE 10A.2 / Estimated Coefficients and Standard Errors from Probit Models of All Postsecondary School Enrollment, Class of 1992

	(1)	(2)	(3)	(4)
Second income quartile	0.075 (0.013)	0.074 (0.012)	0.040 (0.012)	0.023 (0.011)
Third income quartile	0.145 (0.022)	0.138 (0.018)	0.091 (0.016)	0.060 (0.014)
Top income quartile	0.221 (0.018)	0.201 (0.013)	0.133 (0.013)	0.087 (0.013)
Female	—	0.079 (0.012)	0.052 (0.009)	0.057 (0.008)
Black, non-Hispanic	—	0.015 (0.022)	0.089 (0.015)	0.082 (0.014)
Hispanic	—	0.046 (0.019)	0.082 (0.015)	0.084 (0.013)
Other, non-white, non-Hispanic	—	0.082 (0.015)	0.057 (0.017)	0.043 (0.018)
South	—	-0.018 (0.027)	-0.009 (0.024)	-0.009 (0.023)
Midwest	—	-0.023 (0.035)	-0.001 (0.035)	-0.008 (0.034)
West	—	-0.022 (0.036)	-0.005 (0.037)	-0.012 (0.038)

TABLE 10A.2 / *Continued*

	(1)	(2)	(3)	(4)
Other private high school	—	0.132	0.086	0.060
		(0.024)	(0.022)	(0.024)
Parochial high school	—	0.109	0.067	0.056
		(0.026)	(0.026)	(0.026)
Two-parent family	—	0.035	0.025	0.028
		(0.010)	(0.010)	(0.009)
Tuition at public two-year schools	—	−0.046	−0.041	−0.045
(in thousands of 1996 dollars)		(0.021)	(0.023)	(0.023)
Tuition at public four-year schools	—	0.006	0.016	0.019
(in thousands of 1996 dollars		(0.010)	(0.011)	(0.011)
State grants (in thousands per	—	0.253	0.305	0.298
residents aged fifteen to forty-four)		(0.156)	(0.178)	(0.181)
Standardized math test score	—		0.071	0.065
			(0.012)	(0.011)
Standardized reading test score	—	—	0.023	0.017
			(0.009)	(0.009)
Student grade point average	—	—	0.124	0.115
			(0.014)	(0.014)
Parents high school dropouts	—	—	—	0.014
				(0.022)
At least one parent some college	—	—	—	0.082
				(0.012)
At least one parent college degree	—	—	—	0.121
				(0.012)
At least one parent graduate school	—	—	—	0.142
				(0.015)
Mean of dependent variable	0.768	0.770	0.770	0.770
Number of observations	5613	5463	5463	5463
Log likelihood	−2887	−2714	−2340	−2291

Source: Authors' calculations.

TABLE 10A.3 / Estimated Coefficients and Standard Errors from Probit Models of Four-Year College Enrollment, Class of 1992

	(1)	(2)	(3)	(4)
Second income quartile	0.097	0.086	0.025	0.004
	(0.015)	(0.020)	(0.024)	(0.022)
Third income quartile	0.190	0.167	0.086	0.035
	(0.026)	(0.031)	(0.035)	(0.030)
Top income quartile	0.357	0.320	0.200	0.114
	(0.021)	(0.027)	(0.037)	(0.035)

TABLE 10.A3 / *Continued*

	(1)	(2)	(3)	(4)
Female	—	0.065	0.029	0.037
		(0.014)	(0.016)	(0.016)
Black, non-Hispanic	—	0.072	0.272	0.264
		(0.027)	(0.030)	(0.031)
Hispanic	—	0.002	0.126	0.137
		(0.027)	(0.042)	(0.045)
Other, non-white, non-Hispanic	—	0.151	0.115	0.094
		(0.034)	(0.037)	(0.041)
South	—	−0.088	−0.088	−0.090
		(0.038)	(0.039)	(0.036)
Midwest	—	−0.126	−0.091	−0.100
		(0.055)	(0.064)	(0.063)
West	—	−0.201	−0.197	−0.207
		(0.056)	(0.065)	(0.064)
Other private high school	—	0.340	0.312	0.275
		(0.036)	(0.031)	(0.033)
Parochial high school	—	0.191	0.140	0.131
		(0.042)	(0.045)	(0.045)
Two-parent family	—	0.044	0.019	0.020
		(0.015)	(0.018)	(0.018)
Tuition at public two-year schools	—	0.121	0.179	0.173
(in thousands of 1996 dollars)		(0.034)	(0.044)	(0.044)
Tuition at public four-year schools	—	−0.032	−0.014	−0.012
(in thousands of 1996 dollars)		(0.017)	(0.022)	(0.021)
State grants (in thousands per	—	−0.886	−1.123	−1.143
residents aged fifteen to fourty-four)		(0.319)	(0.370)	(0.353)
Standardized math test score	—	—	0.169	0.162
			(0.016)	(0.016)
Standardized reading test score	—	—	0.032	0.025
			(0.011)	(0.010)
Student grade point average	—	—	0.257	0.247
			(0.021)	(0.021)
Parents high school dropouts	—	—	—	0.004
				(0.034)
At least one parent some college	—	—	—	0.086
				(0.025)
At least one parent college degree	—	—	—	0.193
				(0.028)
At least one parent graduate school	—	—	—	0.260
				(0.023)
Mean of dependent variable	0.468	0.473	0.473	0.473
Number of observations	5613	5463	5463	5463
Log likelihood	−3681	−3432	−2674	−2929

Source: Authors' calculations.

TABLE 10A.4 / Probit Models of Enrollment in Any School and in Four-Year Colleges, Classes of 1980/1982 and Class of 1992

	Enrolled in Any School			Enrolled in Four-Year College		
	Classes of 1980/1982	Class of 1992 (NELS)	Difference	Class of 1980/1982	Class of 1992	Difference
Second income quartile	-.0176 (.0464)	.0340 (.0154)	.0516 (.0489)	-.0704 (.0407)	.0435 (.0220)	.1139 (.0463)
Third income quartile	-.0029 (.0537)	.0728 (.0185)	.0757 (.0568)	-.0288 (.0378)	.0475 (.0333)	.0763 (.0504)
Top income quartile	.0814 (.0516)	.1117 (.0173)	.0303 (.0544)	.1178 (.0504)	.1641 (.0388)	.0463 (.0636)
Female	.0285 (.0211)	.0509 (.0094)	.0224 (.0231)	-.0252 (.0237)	.0128 (.0183)	.0380 (.0300)
Black, non-Hispanic	.1241 (.0411)	.0485 (.0179)	-.0755 (.0449)	.2812 (.0381)	.1764 (.0352)	-.1048 (.0518)
Hispanic	.0329 (.0364)	.0841 (.0172)	.0512 (.0403)	.0640 (.0639)	.1527 (.0346)	.0888 (.0727)
Other, non-white, non-Hispanic	.0748 (.0523)	.0587 (.0275)	-.0162 (.0591)	.1473 (.1023)	.0701 (.0581)	-.0772 (.1176)
South	.0132 (.0318)	.0029 (.0346)	-.0103 (.0469)	-.0227 (.0387)	-.1073 (.0421)	-.0846 (.0573)
Midwest	.0064 (.0613)	.0216 (.0466)	.0152 (.0770)	-.1065 (.0541)	-.1189 (.0699)	-.0124 (.0884)
West	-.0391 (.0587)	.0125 (.0518)	.0517 (.0783)	-.2038 (.0496)	-.1860 (.0783)	.0178 (.0927)
Other private high school	.1460 (.0412)	.1028 (.0216)	-.0432 (.0465)	.1744 (.0655)	.1941 (.0559)	.0197 (.0861)
Parochial high school	.1737 (.0705)	.0686 (.0379)	-.1051 (.0801)	.3605 (.1292)	.2311 (.0657)	-.1294 (.1449)

Two-parent family	.0654 (.0354)	.0267 (.0146)	-.0387 (.0383)	.0181 (.0347)	.0167 (.0203)	-.0013 (.0402)
Tuition at public two-year schools (in thousands of 1996 dollars)	-.0821 (.0574)	-.0333 (.0343)	.0489 (.0669)	.1572 (.0592)	.1683 (.0502)	.0110 (.0777)
Tuition at public four-year schools (in thousands of 1996 dollars)	.0410 (.0585)	.0326 (.0128)	-.0084 (.0599)	-.0416 (.0380)	.0361 (.0306)	.0777 (.0488)
State grants (in thousands per residents aged fifteen to forty-four)	.0857 (.2629)	.5745 (.2783)	.4888 (.3828)	-.8204 (.3004)	-.1128 (.3207)	-.3082 (.4394)
Student grade point average	.2366 (.0250)	.1822 (.0117)	-.0544 (.0276)	.3482 (.0280)	.3853 (.0277)	.0370 (.0394)
Student grades missing in 1980	-.0297 (.0099)	—	—	-.0463 (.0082)	—	—
Parents high school dropouts	-.0572 (.0486)	.0209 (.0231)	.0781 (.0539)	-.0144 (.0505)	-.0462 (.0317)	-.0318 (.0596)
At least one parent some college	.1190 (.0235)	.0901 (.0133)	-.0290 (.0270)	.0863 (.0332)	.1326 (.0231)	.0463 (.0405)
At least one parent college degree	.2174 (.0347)	.1450 (.0134)	-.0725 (.0372)	.2873 (.0387)	.2649 (.0300)	-.0224 (.0490)
At least one parent graduate school	.1894 (.0352)	.1725 (.0183)	-.0169 (.0396)	.3136 (.0481)	.3534 (.0210)	.0398 (.0524)
Mean of dependent variable	.6836	.7613	.0777	.3852	.4575	.0724
Number of observations	2877	5463	5463	2877	5463	5463

Source: Authors' calculations.
Note: Results are probit results indicating change in probability for change in the variable with all others evaluated at the mean.

NOTES

1. The end of college draft deferment at the end of the Vietnam War may also have contributed to the decline in male college enrollment during the early 1970s.

2. Regardless of the type of school first attended, a student who attended a four-year institution at all within the first twenty months was categorized as having attended a four-year school. Data limitations prevent our looking forward more than twenty months in later data. Some students who first attend two-year schools eventually collect a degree from a four-year school. However, the number of such eventual four-year completions is small, and it may not vary widely by socioeconomic status. In our HSB data for 1980 and 1982, we found that 16 percent of students who went to a two-year school in the first twenty months had completed a four-year degree by 1992. Interestingly, the 16 percent rate was the same for students from high- and low-income families.

3. Cameron and Heckman (1999) described the difficulties of using the October CPS in their appendix.

4. To the extent that students' decisions to move out on their own are related to their decision to attend college or not, such sample selection could be problematic.

5. The survey allows us to follow people for two years. We chose eighteen months, however, because that time frame allows us to create an absolutely consistent sample from the 1980–1982 HSB survey, which we use in a later section. To track enrollment beyond the first eighteen months in the HSB survey, it is necessary to combine data from two survey waves, and a significant number of inconsistencies arise.

6. For a discussion of the difficulties in estimating differences in the payoffs to schooling for those of varying prior academic preparation, see Card (1994) and Lang (1993).

7. In the 1980/1982 sample, a single test was administered to all seniors. Unfortunately, those administering the test found that the test inevitably did a rather poor job of distinguishing performance at the top, especially in math. A test of an acceptable length with enough basic questions to score people at the bottom could not include enough harder questions for the more advanced students. As a result, a new methodology was used in 1992. Students were given different tests depending primarily on their success on an earlier test administered when they were sophomores. There was some overlap, so that the scores could be put on a comparable scale, but the effect of the new test was to alter significantly the pattern of scores for students with stronger records. It appears that the test did precisely what was intended: the better students were more effectively scored. Unfortunately, this reduction in measurement error among the better students introduces statistical problems that make it almost impossible for us to compare scores over time. Since the 1992 test was more reliable for the high-achieving students, one would expect to see an increase in apparent test scores by level of family income or parental education, and that is precisely what we found: test scores became more correlated with income and the scores rose significantly for those from the strongest background. We know of no other data suggesting a similar trend. We think it is very likely to be a statistical artifact of the changed testing procedure.

8. See Fetters (1984) for more on the reliability of self-reported grades in the HSB.

9. These data were provided by the Higher Education Coordinating Board in the state of Washington. Tuition figures were assembled for the average four-year comprehensive

university and two-year college by state. The "comprehensive universities" represent such institutions as California State University rather than the University of California, and North Carolina A&T and Appalachian State University rather than the University of North Carolina at Chapel Hill.

10. Tuition would not matter at all for Pell Grant eligibility except that the Pell Grant cannot exceed tuition costs plus an allowance for books and living expenses. With a Pell Grant maximum of $2,400 and an average cost of attendance (including both tuition and living expenses) in 1992 of $3,705 even for students living with their parents and attending public two-year institutions part-time, Pell Grant eligibility was unrelated to tuition except at the very low income states.

11. We also assume that the supply side is completely responsive to demand changes. Given that over 85 percent of students report being accepted at their first-choice college, this seems to be a reasonable simplification. This is only fortuitous, however, given the paucity of factors affecting only demand or supply with which to estimate a system of simultaneous relationships.

12. The student aid figures are drawn from the College Board (1997). The evidence on state and local appropriations is drawn from the National Center for Education Statistics (1998, 341).

13. For more on borrowing constraints and the timing of college investment, see Wallace and Ihnen (1975), Jacoby (1991), and Kane (1996). If college is a worthwhile investment, then the present value of future earnings must exceed the up-front costs of college. Therefore, delaying college completion and pushing both the costs and the benefits of college one period back into the future must reduce the present value of the investment, since the present value of benefits delayed must exceed the present value of the costs avoided.

14. For more on the relationship between student-reported and parent-reported data, see Fetters (1984).

15. In reporting their incomes, parents were allowed to choose from among the following categories: $0; less than $1,000; $1,000 to $2,999; $3,000 to $4,999; $5,000 to $7,499; $7,500 to $9,999; $10,000 to $14,999; $15,000 to $19,999; $20,000 to $24,999; $25,000 to $34,999; $35,000 to $49,999; $50,000 to $74,999; $75,000 to $99,999; $100,000 to $199,999; and $200,000 or more.

16. In addition to being asked about wage and salary income and the business and farm income of each parent separately, parents were asked to report income from dividends, interest, trust funds, rent, Social Security and other retirement pay, unemployment benefits, gifts or inheritances, child support payments, alimony, foster child payments, AFDC, SSI, financial help from relatives, roomers and boarders, and "other income." For each source of income, parents were to choose from the following categories: $0; less than $100; $100 to $499; $500 to $999; $1,000 to $2,999; $3,000 to $4,999; $5,000 to $7,499; $7,500 to $9,999; $10,000 to $14,999; $15,000 to $19,999; $20,000 to $24,999; $25,000 to $34,999; $35,000 to $49,999; $50,000 to $74,999; $75,000 to $99,999; $100,000 to $199,999; $200,000 to $299,999; $300,000 to $499,999; and more than $500,000.

17. For binary variables, we measure the impact of moving from zero to one; for all other variables, we show the derivative at their mean.

18. Operationally this is done by setting the variable of interest to a common value in the entire sample, and then predicting the enrollment for the whole sample and repeating

this for each variable of interest. Thus, in the first row, everyone is given a C+ grade point average and test scores in the thirty-third percentile. All else about the person is unchanged, and then we use the probit model to predict the probability of going to school in the entire sample. Then the process is repeated with a B+ average and sixty-seventh percentile scores. This is equivalent in a linear regression to setting all other values to the mean and varying only one variable at a time. This method is preferable to setting everything to the mean value and varying the variable of interest since we have a nonlinear model.

19. It should be noted that in our data the reported test scores rose for students from higher-income and higher-education families and fell for students at the other end. If this trend were real, it could be very important. Unfortunately, the methodology of the tests changed in a way that would be very likely to produce this result as a statistical artifact: because more difficult questions were added to the tests taken by high-performance students, they were able to distinguish themselves more from others. We have searched for evidence from other sources that such a differential pattern might be real. For instance, Larry Hedges and Amy Nowell (1998, table 5b) did not report any increased correlation between test scores and family income during the 1980s—at least after conditioning on parental education. But we found no other suggestions that relative test scores had changed. Thus, we omitted test scores. Had we included them, essentially all of the differential change in enrollment by income class between the two periods could have been traced to the higher relative achievement of the higher-income children.

20. Mechanically, we regressed the log of mean annual earnings over the period 1984 to 1985 on a constant, three indicators for race, dummies for each of three income quartiles, math and reading test scores, self-reported high school grade point average, and dummies for educational attainment reported in 1986. The educational attainment categories used were "some college," "associate degree," "bachelor's degree," "master's degree," and "Ph.D.-professional degree." To decompose the effect of differences in each of these characteristics on the difference in mean log earnings by income quartile, we multiplied the difference in mean characteristics by the common coefficient for each characteristic.

21. As Heckman and Lochner also point out in this volume, gaps in educational attainment by family income may narrow as cohorts enter the labor market. This fact is not inconsistent with borrowing constraints. As Paul Glewwe and Hanan Jacoby (1995) and Thomas Kane (1996) pointed out, borrowing constraints may simply lead low-income families to delay educational investments. Indeed, Kane (1996) found that high school graduates, particularly low-income students, were more likely to delay college entry in high-tuition states.

22. For more on the effects of this "natural experiment," see Kane (1994) and Hansen (1983).

REFERENCES

Becker, Gary S. 1993. *Human Capital: A Theoretical and Empirical Analysis with Special Reference to Education*, 3rd ed. Chicago: University of Chicago Press.

Bishop, John. 1977. "The Effect of Public Policies on the Demand for Higher Education." *Journal of Human Resources* 12(3): 285–307.

Cameron, Stephen V., and James J. Heckman. 1997. "The Dynamics of Educational Attainment for Blacks, Whites, and Hispanics." Working paper. University of Chicago.

————. 1998. "Life-Cycle Schooling and Dynamic Selection Bias: Models and Evidence for Five Cohorts of American Males." *Journal of Political Economy* 106(2): 262.

————. 1999. "Should College Attendance Be Further Subsidized to Reduce Rising Wage Inequality?" In *Financing College Tuition: Government Policies and Social Priorities*, edited by Marvin Kosters. Washington, D.C.: American Enterprise Institute.

Card, David. 1994. "Earnings, Schooling, and Ability Revisited." Working paper 4832. Cambridge, Mass.: National Bureau of Economic Research (August).

College Board. 1997. *Trends in Student Aid: 1987 to 1997*. Washington, D.C.: College Board.

Dynarski, Susan. 1999. "Does Aid Matter? Measuring the Effect of Student Aid on College Attendance and Completion." Unpublished paper. Cambridge, Mass.: MIT.

Fetters, William B. 1984. "Quality of Responses of High School Students to Questionnaire Items." National Center for Education Statistics report NCES-84-216. Washington, D.C.: U.S. Department of Education (September).

Freeman, Richard. 1976. *The Overeducated American*. New York: Academic Press.

Glewwe, Paul, and Hanan G. Jacoby. 1995. "An Economic Analysis of Delayed Primary School Enrollment in a Low-Income Country: The Role of Early Childhood Nutrition." *Review of Economics and Statistics* 77(1): 156–69.

Hansen, W. Lee. 1983. "Impact of Student Financial Aid on Access." In *The Crisis in Higher Education*, edited by Joseph Froomkin. New York: Academy of Political Science.

Hauser, Robert. 1993. "Trends in College Attendance Among Blacks, Whites, and Hispanics." In *Studies of Supply and Demand in Higher Education*, edited by Charles Clotfelter and Michael Rothschild. Chicago: University of Chicago Press.

Hauser, Robert, Jennifer Sheridan, and John Robert Warren. 1998. "Socioeconomic Achievements of Siblings in the Life Course: New Findings from the Wisconsin Longitudinal Study." Working paper 98-02. Madison: Center for Demography and Ecology, University of Wisconsin.

Haveman, Robert, and Barbara Wolfe. 1994. *Succeeding Generations: On the Effects of Investments in Children*. New York: Russell Sage Foundation.

Hedges, Larry, and Amy Nowell. 1998. "Black-White Test Score Convergence Since 1965." In *The Black-White Test Score Gap*, edited by Christopher Jencks and Meredith Phillips. Washington, D.C.: Brookings Institution.

Huber, Peter J. 1967. "The Behavior of Maximum Likelihood Estimates Under Non-Standard Conditions." In *Proceedings of the Fifth Berkeley Symposium in Mathematical Statistics and Probability*. Berkeley: University of California Press.

Jacoby, Hanan. 1991. "Tuition, Borrowing Constraints, and the Timing of College." Unpublished paper. University of Rochester.

Kane, Thomas J. 1994. "College Attendance by Blacks Since 1970: The Role of College Cost, Family Background, and the Returns to Education." *Journal of Political Economy* 102(5): 878–911.

————. 1995. "Rising Public College Tuition and College Entry: How Well Do Public Subsidies Promote Access to College?" Working paper 5164. Cambridge, Mass.: National Bureau of Economic Research.

————. 1996. "College Cost, Borrowing Constraints, and the Timing of College Entry." *Eastern Economic Journal* 22(2): 181–94.

————. 1997. "Beyond Tax Relief: Long-term Challenges in Financing Higher Education." *National Tax Journal* 50(2): 335–49.

————. 1998a. "Are College Students Credit-Constrained?" Cambridge, Mass.: John F. Kennedy School of Government, Harvard University. Unpublished paper presented at the National Bureau of Economic Research.

———. 1998b. "Savings Incentives for Higher Education." *National Tax Journal* 51(3): 609–20.

———. 1999. "Student Aid After Tax Reform: Risks and Opportunities." In *Financing a College Degree: How It Works, How It's Changing*, edited by Jacqueline King. Phoenix: Oryx Press.

Kane, Thomas J., and Cecilia E. Rouse. 1999. "The Community College: Training Students at the Margin Between College and Work." *Journal of Economic Perspectives* 13(1): 63–84.

Kohn, Meir, Charles Manski, and David Mundel. 1976. "An Empirical Investigation of Factors Which Influence College-Going Behavior." *Annals of Economic and Social Measures* 5: 391–419.

Lang, Kevin. 1993. "Ability Bias, Discount Rate Bias, and the Return to Education." Discussion paper. Department of Economics, Boston University.

Leslie, Larry, and Paul T. Brinkman. 1987. "Student Price Response in Higher Education: The Student Demand Studies." *Journal of Higher Education* 58(2): 181–204.

———. 1988. *The Economic Value of Higher Education*. New York: Macmillan.

Manski, Charles, and David Wise. 1983. *College Choice in America*. Cambridge, Mass.: Harvard University Press.

McPherson, Michael S., and Morton Owen Schapiro. 1991a. "Does Student Aid Affect College Enrollment?: New Evidence on a Persistent Controversy." *American Economic Review* 81: 309–18.

———. 1991b. *Keeping College Affordable*. Washington, D.C.: Brookings Institution.

National Center for Education Statistics. 1998. *Digest of Education Statistics, 1997*. Washington: U.S. Government Printing Office.

Orfield, Gary. 1992. "Money, Equity, and College Access." *Harvard Educational Review* 72 (3): 337–72.

Radner, Roy, and L. S. Miller. 1970. "Demand and Supply in U.S. Higher Education: A Progress Report." *American Economic Review* 60: 326–34.

Rouse, Cecilia Elena. 1994. "What to Do After High School? The Two-Year Versus Four-Year College Enrollment Decision." In *Contemporary Policy Issues in Education*, edited by Ronald Ehrenberg. Ithaca, N.Y.: ILR Press.

Wallace, T. Dudley, and Loren A. Ihnen. 1975. "Full-Time Schooling in Life-Cycle Models of Human Capital Accumulation." *Journal of Political Economy* 83(1): 137–56.

White, Halbert. 1980. "A Heteroskedasticity-Consistent Covariance Matrix Estimator and a Direct Test for Heteroskedasticity." *Econometrica* 48(4): 817–30.

———. 1982. "Maximum Likelihood Estimation of Misspecified Models." *Econometrica* 50(1): 1–25.

Index

Boldface numbers refer to figures and tables.